STUDIES IN JUDAICA AMERICANA

by

RUDOLF GLANZ

Foreword by

JACOB R. MARCUS

KTAV PUBLISHING HOUSE, INC.
NEW YORK
1970

SBN 87068-125-7

Library of Congress Catalog Card Number: 73-116530
Manufactured in the United States of America

TABLE OF CONTENTS

FOREWORD

We are grateful to Rudolf Glanz for this collection of essays on the German Jew in the United States. Time and research will reaffirm that the Jews of Central Europe were of paramount importance in the history of American Jewry. Recently we have begun to hear the first faint croaks of revisionists questioning the significance of the German Jewish contribution to Jewish life on this continent. We are told that American Jewish history in the real sense of the term gets under way only with the East European immigrants in the 1880's. The facts, the bare facts, are otherwise.

Actually, Central Europeans dominated the American Jewish scene as early as 1720. The Sefardic synagogue rite held sway until well into the 1800's, but the ethnic culture of the Central Europeans—in a variety of forms, of course—prevailed among American Jews for some 200 years. It was only in 1920 that German Jewish hegemony was challenged—and even then not definitively—when the "Russians" established a provisional American Jewish Congress to dispute the leadership of the "German" American Jewish Committee.

Substantial numbers of Germans began coming to these shores in the 1840's. It was they who took over the synagogue-community and laid the foundations of our present Jewish megalopolitan organizational structure. They sanctioned and luxuriated in the proliferation of synagogues. "Every man to his tents, O Israel!" They created our autonomous mutual-aid and welfare societies, our clubs, our Young Mens Hebrew Associations, our shelters for the aged, our orphan homes and our hospitals. It was they who first federated our charities, who sent chaplains into the armies, established congregational unions, founded rabbinical seminaries, and created our national civic defense organizations. What we are today we owe in large part to them. "What is past is prologue" is true only in a limited sense. Without that past the future rides rudderless on the sea of history.

With one exception, all the essays in this book treat primarily of the German Jews on the American scene. But—and this is typical—Glanz concerns himself with areas which traditional, formal historians tend to ignore. Here there are no detailed descriptions of the adroit Wall Street jugglers, no in-depth studies of the accomplishments of the Seligmans and the Guggenheims, the Schiffs and the Warburgs, the department store Gimbels and Strauses. Luminaries like Brandeis, Jacques Loeb, and the Flexners are not the meat of these essays. Glanz crawls into the intestines of the common man; here is the history behind history; he deals with the lore of the people, with what the Gentile sees in the Jew and with what the Jew sees in himself.

What does Glanz write about? He starts in Europe and describes minutely the coming of the German Jews. Who they were, why they came, how they began. How did they begin? As peddlers, of course. He chronicles the annals of the nineteenth-century American Jewish community, of life in the great city of New York. The Jewish club, replete with dance hall, restaurant, library, and card rooms is described in detail; there is no attempt to gloss over the snobbery, the bitter frustrations, and the vindictive hatred of Jew for Jew, of Bavarian for Polack. All this and much more is detailed here for the sobering edification of the romantic reader. But let there be no doubt in your mind: this is history. Maybe this is the truer history.

If "no man is an iland," then the German Jew of yesterday can only be understood in relation to the American non-Jews among whom he lived. They outnumbered him more than 100 to 1. Their concept of him—and it was often a sorry one—never left him untouched. Most of Glanz's essays describe the position the German Jews occupied in the economy of Christian thinking, both German American and native American. It is instructive to see how the author compares the Jew and the California Chinese, the Yankee and the Jew and, of course, how he pays his devoirs to the Rothschild Legend. As early as ante-bellum days, burgeoning American materialism betrayed itself through its obsessive interest in this family of European bankers. Much of the Rothschild story was in the realm of myth, but this myth became flesh and profoundly influenced Christians and Jews in this land, a land where almost nothing was impossible.

Actually these essays constitute a source book. Glanz, German trained, is interested in *Stoff,* the stuff, the real stuff of which history is made. He gives the facts. In the very words of contemporaries he recites just what happened, what people said, what Jews and Gentiles believed. Here is the story of dozens of German Jewish emigrants embarking in 1839 for the distant American shore, carrying with them the sacred Scroll of the Law and ample kosher supplies for the long voyage. The murder of a Jewish peddler in Louisiana and the lynching of his three Negro assailants is copied verbatim from *Die Deborah* of 1873. The closing sentence of this unhappy record is the most significant: "Neither he [the leader of the Jewish community], nor any other Jew, however, participated in the execution of the Negroes."

In the "Fashionable Hebrew Wedding" we meet the bride, "Mrs. David Moss, a beautiful brunette, in white corded silk, Valenciennes lace, orange blossoms and wreath, diamonds." As early as 1866 a writer in the *Jewish Messenger* objected to the "exclusiveness which prompts maintenance of distinctly Jewish clubs. . . . If clubs mean anything and are better than gambling houses, we should not restrict their social advantages to personages who happen to be born Jews." We learn from Conrad Doehla's Revolutionary War diary that, unlike the Jews of eighteenth-century Germany, Rhode Island Jewish women "wear the same French finery as the women of other faiths." American Jews, we discover, deeply resented August Belmont's refusal to affiliate with them religiously. Yet for the Gentile world he was always Belmont the Jew. "When he is to be thrust upon us as a co-religionist," the Jews wrote, "we doubt the value of the accession, question the honor of the association, and therefore call for his credentials."

These essays are a quarry for the historian. They are not perfumed and rouged words to be admired one moment and discarded the next. Those who wish to know and to learn will read them with infinite profit. I end as I began: we are grateful for these studies which give us insight into the lives of a generation of immigrants who built better than they knew.

Jacob R. Marcus

American Jewish Archives
Hebrew Union College

SOURCE MATERIAL ON THE HISTORY OF JEWISH IMMIGRATION TO THE UNITED STATES, 1800-1880

INTRODUCTION

The European Reaction to Jewish Emigration

The contemporary sources, which bear on a particular phase of the history of migration, generally reveal much less than they intentionally conceal. The European society, from whose midst the emigrants poured forth, was scarcely inclined to publicize the social ills, of which emigration was one symptom. Discretion and self-esteem made that world wary of discussing social injustice and the reasons underlying the exodus, while the state and the bureaucracy had their special interests to protect. In a generation, which could not as yet understand the objective causes of emigration, it was convenient to seek special local causes in the administration of a district. No scapegoat goes willingly into the wilderness, and public functionaries stood in fear of their princes, lest their faulty administration be exposed. The princes, in turn, had to dread public opinion, which even in an age of absolutism could hinder their plans. In connection with the sale of German mercenaries to England by their princes, we find documentary proof of the fact that any sort of transfer of population ran the risk of changing the outlook of the person transferred. It is no accident that these princes made the stipulation that none of the soldiers would subsequently be permitted to settle in America, although this, to be sure, could not prevent 10,000 "Hessians" from remaining after the colonies had won their independence.

There is only one major case of an investigation of the causes of European Jewish emigration carried out by contemporaries. For the rest we are dependent on chance and on indirect sources for our knowledge of the decisive mainsprings.

Reprinted from *Yivo Annual of Jewish Social Science,* Volume VI, 1951

Historical factors are often, however, corrected by human need which are reflected in the written word. The theologians of the ol days, who were given to writing, have generally been ignored b later generations, but the literary divines have regained their im portance because of their role in the history of emigration. Firs because "spiritual care" led to an analysis of the character of th emigrants, and secondly, because even the exhortation of the emigrant was conditioned by the spirit of the time, and they thus help t reconstruct the picture which the state deliberately obscured. An finally, the most important reason, because the literary theologian turned militant, took upon himself the emigrants' struggle for exist ence and accompanied them into the New World. Thus the historian may rejoice in a literature arising out of the emigrants' life on new soil; every contemporary trying his hand as a writer may well have envied the inspiration of the minister, who was an interesting chronicler. The notes he jotted down were eagerly read, for the Old World was still full of potential immigrants to America. With the strengthening of the religious organizations in the world of the emigrés the minister's activity also became a duty to the European mother-churches, which aided their tender offshoots and later sent clergymen to guide them.

At a later period, when the picture of America had been conveyed through letters and reports from the New World and the pull exerted by America tore perceptible gaps in the communities of the lands of emigration, public discussion could no longer be avoided. The cons as well as the pros were aired. Portions of the masses ready to emigrate could still be disheartened by painting a dark picture of the new land and its social conditions. The bulk of the sources for the general history of emigration stem from this period, when in order to counteract emigration an open debate had already become necessary, one which developed on broad lines, and which offered possibilities for throwing full light from all sides on current problems. This places at the historian's disposal sources, the synthesis of which leads to a clear picture of the factors governing emigration.

The study of the Jewish sources, however, requires a much different approach. Not only the state and the Jewish society in Europe, but the emigrants themselves had to remain silent. The emigrants knew that the Jews left at home could be injured by giving wide publicity to the exodus. The exposure of one sore spot could readily produce a crop of new evils, with all sorts of accusations hurled against the Jews in the old country in response to emigré attacks. Thus their struggle for equal rights might be blocked by a campaign to drive the Jews out.

It can be accepted a rule that the more important a source is for the Jewish struggle for existence in Europe, the less valuable it is for the history of emigration. Later on, after firm communities had been built up in America, their communal interests became opposed to reporting and to indiscriminate discussion of current emigration problems. The new communities preferred to maintain a discreet silence in regard to the process of migration. There were also to be considered certain ill-disposed neighbors; antisemitism threatened to spread westward across the ocean. It may be asserted, almost as a rule, that in the articles sent from America's Jewish communities by regular correspondents (a feature inaugurated by the European Jewish journals), the essential details of emigration lost their central position.

The Character of the Sources

The study of the sources bearing on Jewish emigration cannot be expected to produce a compact body of synthesized data. Much depends on the skill of the historian in reconstructing a picture from the scattered data gleaned from the entire range of the contemporary literature. In principle, all contemporary writings have to be examined, and only the specialist's feeling for the subject can fix the boundaries of his research and keep him from wandering too far afield.

The monographic studies of emigration in general are limited to a few contributions based on the sources prior to 1880. In the Jewish field it was necessary to consult monographs of various types in order to gather the incidental references to our subject. The results proved to be quite meager, as might have been expected, because the European community studies almost invariably ignore the valuable material on emigration questions; and while the few American studies deal with immigration, they fail in most cases to organize the data or to describe the vital aspects of immigrant life.

The principal group of sources collected here are derived from the mass of periodicals and fugitive publications. In view of the relative dearth of books on American subjects published prior to 1880, one must collect the mass of data scattered throughout a vast periodical literature, which in certain important cases has been preserved in complete series. The descriptions of pioneer life, in particular, abound in references to contacts with the stream of Jewish immigrants. The accounts of travellers command a similar interest for our purpose; indeed, in many cases they relate encounters with Jewish emigrants during the crossing of the Atlantic.

The German-Jewish Period

The collection of source materials presented here covers only the period prior to 1880, the year which saw the beginning of the mass migration of Jews from eastern Europe. Until then American Jewry, with its communities in the middle and far West, had grown primarily as a result of the migration from Germany. We must, nevertheless, emphasize that the immigration of east-European Jews began long before 1880, and was in progress throughout our period. This is amply borne out by the source extracts. On the other hand, the fact that until 1880 the visible progress of American Jewry was the work of German-Jewish immigrants, is reflected in the materials bearing on this historic process, which deserve to be depicted on a broad scale.

For the sake of producing a relatively coherent picture, we have included only those sources which throw light on the cultural-historical conditions of Jewish life. This has made it necessary to exclude statistics and biographical sketches, which are devoid of general significance and which do not belong within the frame of this work.

A precondition of the decision to emigrate is the individual's ideas of the blessings of the New World, which give him in advance his image of America. This picture in the mind of the prospective emigrant becomes intertwined with his motives for emigrating and the condemnation of his inhospitable native land; the freedom, which the new world offers him, as against his slavish lot, are the motifs of an outlook often poetically expressed in the sources. Thus a pattern of ideas became the historical agent which started the Atlantic migration and produced an image of America in the broadest sense, which had tangible results, and which was transported to the New World. In the absence of a titled class, the opportunities of rising in the world seemed fantastic, in comparison with the place of man in the Old World. (See Nos. 1, 2).

In the literature designed to popularize the idea of emigration, freedom of worship is regularly represented as including Jews, while the harmony and friendship among the inhabitants are advertised as the new ideal. The basic teaching of religion found here a practical link with the needs of the day; love for one's neighbor spelled aid for the immigrant. The point that all inhabitants of America had once been strangers in the land, is forcefully stressed in the appeal to contribute funds for immigrant aid.

The Impelling Factors

Among the motives for emigrating, discrimination by officials occupies first place, but the consciousness of fixed legal disabilities served in no less a degree as a sufficient reason for leaving the homeland. The hopelessness of such a status was felt particularly by the younger generation. A last endeavor to secure an assured right of domicile and to work at a trade or practice a profession was made, and once rejected the young Jew forthwith applied for a passport. Political persecutions also brought some intellectuals who had fought for human rights in Europe. In such cases the individual had to suffer both as a revolutionary and as a Jew. It was also stressed that often enough people of means, as well as the very poor, had to emigrate. To sum up, the literature exposing the reasons for migrating to America is a storehouse of the criticism of European society. (See Nos. 3-9).

Some of our sources describe the impression made by the first visits of the emigrés, now American citizens, to their old homeland and how many of the young men were moved by this sight to prepare for the journey. In the reminiscences of such persons, particularly in retrospect from the position attained after decades of living in the New World, the motives of the emigration of 1837 are still quite prominent. (See Nos. 10-12).

Among the conditions related to emigration, apart from the familiar Jewry-taxes, the levying of taxes on emigrants was an additional motive for leaving. Such taxes clearly represented a means of exploiting a source of revenue for the last time. Where Jewish emigration was not entirely prohibited, as it was in the Danish lands, there developed detailed regulations as to the amount and collection of the tax on Jewish emigrants; for the German lands, as early as 1784 we find a summary of the regulations in an encyclopedia. The Jewish press repeatedly pointed out the difficulties that arose on account on these tax-regulations, which were by no means uniformly enforced and of which the lawyers often gave conflicting interpretations. The fact that information on emigration-taxes was included in Jewish almanacs indicates how great was the need for clarity in this matter. (See Nos. 13-15).

Disillusionment in Europe

As to the logic and advisability of emigration, there ensued, within Jewish society, an open discussion, which reveals many aspects of the situation.

At the crest of the revolutionary wave of 1848-49 any movement for organizing the emigration was on occasion branded as treason toward the fatherland, which needs all its sons as fighters. The reign of justice, for which it now behooves men to fight, was proclaimed the true fatherland of the Jews. If emigré revolutionists, it was argued, had hastened to return, only cowards would dare to plan a flight from the country.

The expectations of the enthusiasts, however, who had envisioned a new fatherland for Jews in the realization of the revolutionary idea, suffered a crushing setback in that very revolutionary war. In the most diversified localities of the Austro-Hungarian monarchy, the political struggle proved particularly disastrous for the Jews. The reports of pogroms, which filled the columns of the Jewish press, precipitated a protracted discussion as to whether this revolution could really bring them freedom. The astounding contrast between the political ideal, to which the Jews had tied all their hopes, and gruesome reality of persecutions wildly flaring up, was felt most deeply.

Wherever billboards with anti-Jewish slogans could be seen at every street-corner, the rallying cry "Up, and to America!" took the Jewish population by storm. This was no less true for Prague and Budapest than for Vienna. By the side of appeals for funds to enable poor Jews to emigrate, there was no lack of bolder projects to finance a great movement and to liquidate Jewish-owned property advantageously. Such schemes naturally followed models borrowed from the German emigration: land purchasing on a large scale through emigration-societies and the founding of colonies based on the utilization of Jewish artisans who were to be brought over. (See Nos. 16-24).

The emigration of so considerable a number of young people cut very deeply into Germany's Jewish communities, and the sources record the shrinking of numerous communities. The number of Jewish artisans, in particular, dropped rapidly, for this group had the best prospects of success in America. Many small communities, moreover, found themselves deprived of teachers and other communal functionaries, and various congregations reached the verge of dissolution.

The nature of the process, as the first stage of the transplantation of European Jewry to the New World, is made clear by the reports of the emigration of rabbis and teachers. At first these men shifted to other vocations in America, but presently the new communities began to provide opportunities for such careers. Connections were established between the American communities and those in the Old World, and were strengthened at first by requests for guidance in synagogue ritual and community organization. (See Nos. 25-30).

Across the Atlantic

No sooner had emigration become a constant process in Jewish life than it began to enjoy a place in literature. The newcomer's steps toward earning a livelihood, and his perseverance for the sake of improving his family's welfare, are repeatedly praised as the characteristic features of the immigrant's way of life. Before long his role evokes admiration; he has gathered experience that may be useful for more recent arrivals. His knowledge of the country can now protect the newcomers against blunders, spare them loss of money or waste of labor, and open up sources of credit and goods. Nor does this type of assistance escape the satirist who represents the entire procedure as a device employed by Jewish mercantile talent to profit even from the newcomers who sally forth to peddle some goods in the hinterland.

Jewish self-portrayal, too, could become satirical, namely, when the immigrant's behavior ran counter to that demanded by Jewish public opinion, and evoked disapproval. There is the parvenu, who refuses to acknowledge his duties toward the Jewish community, forgets his own humble beginnings, and ignores the needs of struggling, recent immigrants. Such selfishness can only lead to retribution. There is also the other type of snob, with a passion for posts of honor. Even when he presides over an immigrant-aid society, he would never condescend to associate with its members in private life. (See Nos. 31-32).

Organized Emigration

There was, moreover, another factor to be reckoned with: it was impossible for Jewry to permit emigration to continue in a chaotic state. Events both foreseen and unforeseen provided sufficient reasc and opportunity to bring organized assistance into play.

In Jewish circles the organized assistance began with provisio for the religious needs of the wayfarers. The transplantation of Jewish religious life to the New World also called for the shipping of ceremonial objects. The material aid furnished to emigrant groups followed the time-honored forms established among the Jews, but had to adjust itself to the special conditions of transatlantic travel. The ships carrying large groups of Jews had on board a cantor, shohet and mohel. (See Nos. 33-45).

In critical years special warnings were issued, as in 1868 one addressed to teachers, who were unable to obtain positions in America at that time.

The emigration wave from Rumania provoked widespread discussion of that government's attitude, as well as of the characteristic traits of these emigrants, whose high ratio of skilled workers was found gratifying. (See Nos. 46-53).

Echoes of the Voyage

The trip to the port of embarkation and the voyage afforded manifold opportunities for contacts between the Jewish and other emigrant groups. The departure of the Jews, as of all other emigrants, was preceded by the disposal of property, a phenomenon amply recorded in the advertising columns of the contemporary press.

Among the ports of embarkation favored by the Jewish emigrants, Le Havre was far ahead of Bremen in 1846 and 1847, while Hamburg was striving slowly to catch up with its sister port. In the contemporary literature the German emigrants' preference for Le Havre was explained by the fact that it obviated the crossing of the stormy Channel; this route was used by the Swiss exclusively and was very popular with emigrants from southern Germany. Notwithstanding these facts its use by Jewish emigrants evoked open or veiled charges that they were fleeing via France to escape military service. Occasionally, of course, there were such cases among the passengers, but these were distributed among all faiths. (See Nos. 54-58).

Early in the nineteenth century Philadelphia was superceded by New York as a port of entry. "Already in 1820 there came to New York nearly twice as many as to Philadelphia, seven times as many in 1830, fifteen times as many in 1840."

First Steps in the New World

Of the passenger lists prepared by the American authorities, only those of Pennsylvania have been preserved. The captains of the vessels calling at Philadelphia complied with the order to register their passengers more or less accurately. These records are complemented by the lists of persons who took the oath of allegiance in Pennsylvania, which not only contain Jewish names but some Hebrew signatures. In addition, Jewish immigrant groups appear in the passenger lists of the port of Mobile, Alabama, which are preserved in the National Archives at Washington, D. C. The register-books (1820-1926) of custom houses in various districts, likewise kept in the National Archives, also record other Jewish immigrant groups cleared by the officials. Other sources provide us with further typical steps involved in the journey of Jewish emigrants. (See Nos. 59-66).

The initial economic struggle of the immigrants, their first steps in the New World, exposed them to the inevitable hazards. A man could easily lose all the possessions he brought with him by trusting a stranger or by making other mistakes. In the course of time, however, there developed a ladder of progress, tested by experience, which the immigrant had to climb, rung by rung. Those who had preceded him, lent him a helping hand in the ascent toward security.

In the descriptions of life in America a favorite subject was the greenhorn, who was duped not only immediately upon landing, but in his subsequent movements through the cities as well. To be sure, even apart from bitter experiences, the newcomer had to grope his way toward an adjustment to a strange environment.

Foreign observers repeatedly emphasized the fact that immigrants, who were already economically established, rendered effective assistance to the newcomers. The characteristic form of assistance was credit; the merchandise entrusted to the immigrant enabled him to start a "business" of his own. This procedure was looked upon by the surrounding world as characteristic of the German Jews and contributed to their good repute. But observers realized also that the basis of the group's economic progress consisted of manual skills acquired in Europe, from which also derived the capacity of the German Jew for adjustment to his surroundings, which was the decisive factor.

The adoption of a trade in America for the first time was another important feature. Often the craftsman had led the life of an intellectual in Europe. The glazier's trade may serve as an illustration for the transition to handicraft; it was generally known that any man could begin with it.

The impression of prosperity, as a result of years of struggle, soon became general. It stands out as a natural result of all small beginnings. Presently the desire to get rich was ascribed to the immigrant as soon as he gained his first economic successes. The immigrants, as a whole, nevertheless, did not view themselves as a wealthy class. It was constantly, and even at a very late stage, emphasized that the small man and the man of modest standing were still predominant in the group.

An early survey of the occupations of Jewish immigrants shows that alongside a certain ratio of skilled manual workers, there was already a sprinkling in the liberal professions. At this level of economic progress a thorough mastery of English became ever more important. Accordingly, this experience was set forth as a warning to the relatively large circles of educated European Jews who as immigrants in America would lose their professional careers because of the language factor. In this connection Europe's Jewish youth was urged to learn English as the first foreign language and it was stressed that this youth would sooner or later face the question of emigration.

Projects for group colonization in America also emerged. In addition to their significance for modern Jewish history, the manner in which they were brought to the attention of the potential emigrants is in itself worthy of study. The American Mission to the Jews, too, felt impelled to work for Jewish colonization, and watched closely the impression made on Jewish emigrants by reports of 20 broad projects. This Society then proposed schemes of its own for settling Jews in America, but at the first attempt the project went to pieces. (See Nos. 67-79).

The saga of the immigrant as a peddler, a far more significant phase of American Jewish history than is generally recognized, is replete with human interest. The biographies of a number of German Jews who came with the German mercenary troops at the time of the War of Independence, as well as a study of the Jews in the rural districts of eighteenth-century Pennsylvania, leave us in no doubt that the career of the Jewish peddler antedates the great German-Jewish immigration wave of the nineteenth century, which witnessed his advancement to resident merchant with regularity. After the Civil War the Jewish peddler turned to the South, and the establishment of numerous stores in that region was the work of Jews who began their peddling during these years.

In the literary treatment of the Jewish peddler there was no lack of heavy-handed satire; the German observer had often brought along from Europe an unconscious prejudice against this figure. Yet despite this hostility, the sources in question are instructive in that they bring to light the contemporary outlook. In general, this literature yields a clear picture of the peddler exhibiting the contents of his pack before the farmer's wife in the log-cabin and of the fascination which his merchandise had for the folks in the loneliness of the wilds. Therein lies the key to the success achieved by the Jewish peddler. (See Nos. 80-87).

German Jewry Comes of Age

The beginnings of German Jewish cultural efforts were conditioned by the strict aloofness of the Sephardic aristocrats, which persisted for a long time. Only the economic success of the German Jews enabled them to overcome this exclusiveness, chiefly by marrying into the blueblooded families of Spanish-Portuguese antecedents.

The German-Jewish group in turn, would not associate with the east-European immigrants, an attitude by no means reserved for the recent arrivals. Cases are cited in the New York German-Jewish press. The Polish Jews, who opposed Reform Judaism, are placed by Max Lilienthal on a par with the more backward type of German Jews, in respect to narrow-mindedness. In Germany, Lilienthal stated, Reform gained a footing only in the large cities, whereas America's Jewish immigrants derived chiefly from the small towns of Germany, and were therefore no less antagonistic than the Polish Jews.

A Jewish traveller from Germany who observed these internal conflicts after 1840, stressed the low cultural level and disorganized state of Jewish life as a vivid impression. This chaotic state of affairs persisted longest in California, where the external organization of religious life, principally by German Jews, stood out in sharp contrast to its inner emptiness. In the new Wonderland, where the greatest changes took place in swift succession, Jewish life remained culturally barren.

The process whereby the German Jews became independent of the Sephardic religious organizations, in which they were long tolerated as poor immigrants, was accompanied by no end of backbiting.

The scions of the Portuguese families lacked, it was averred, true piety, and above all, the true spirit of charity. The German-Jewish immigrant could live fully only in institutions created by him and in which the German language would take its place. In this the German Jews followed a policy similar to that of the German churches, which attached great expectations to the fostering of the mother-tongue. Indeed, these churches pointed to the Jews as an illustration of how the retention of a sacred language could contribute to the maintenance of religious unity. In some of the institutions of the German-Jewish immigrants the use of German was made obligatory and this was proudly proclaimed. In this fashion the Jews contributed to the maintenance of the German language in America, whereas among the non-Jews the second generation usually abandoned it.

As soon as the German-Jewish communities had arrived, the east-European Jewish organizations were in turn frowned upon and their separate existence was frequently regarded as unjustified, just as the German-Jewish organizations had once been so regarded by the Portuguese Jews. Now amalgamation was demanded in the name of Americanism, and the German Jews' claim to communal leadership stood unchallenged. As the prosperous German Jews for the most part adopted Reform Judaism, they derided their Orthodox brethren from eastern Europe and cast scorn on their functionaries as ignorant *Ostjuden.*

The contribution of the German Jews to the maintenance of the German language in America was recognized by the non-Jewish immigrants. There was, nevertheless, a group of prosperous Jewish immigrants and their children, who preferred to use English exclusively, and who became the target of the cultured Germans. This campaign, indeed, took an anti-Jewish turn. Yet by the mid-nineteenth century there were in Texas and elsewhere Germans who in substantial numbers deliberately rejected the mother-tongue and tried to conceal their background.

The German-Jewish immigrants remained particularly faithful to the German theater, especially in New York. The audiences in the Bowery are described as consisting largely of Jewish clerks employed in wholesale houses.

The school system of the Jewish immigrants developed from very small beginnings. In 1844 the Bavarian Jews in Cleveland established a school for children, in which the reading and writing of Yiddish was an important subject. In the third year of its existence the school had 56, and in 1859, 86 pupils.

With the establishment of the German hegemony over American Jewry, there developed a concern for the English language as spoken by this group. The genesis of a jargon was viewed as a threat that must be averted. The seriousness of the situation was seen in the conditions prevailing in the parental home, in which the children heard only broken English and consequently spoke neither good English nor good German. In the synagogue service the German sermon was to be restricted, and the tendency toward "Germanizing the Synagogue" checked. A knowledge of English was also to be a prerequisite for functionaries recruited in Germany, and above all only trained preachers were to be encouraged to immigrate.

New Responsibilities and Problems

As Jewish immigrants gained prominent positions their participation in the activities in behalf of newcomers became quite conspicuous. Thus we find a disproportionately high ratio of Jews in the German immigrant-aid societies, which sprang up in a series of American cities.

The correspondence between the immigrants and the old country was fairly significant. The letters describing life in the new land produced the same magic effect on relatives and friends as did similar letters from America on the non-Jews. Thus the determination to emigrate was greatly promoted, and from the profusion of detail for the guidance of would-be immigrants there stand out particularly the data concerning prospects of employment and wages; the correspondents often cited illustrations of the purchasing power of the American dollar. Finally a still more convincing effect was produced by the prosperous immigrant's visit to his native place after decades of absence. Indeed, apart from such living examples, the prosperity of the emigrants was inferred from their generosity toward their kinsmen in Europe.

The biographies of numerous emigrants provide intimate reflections, which in the aggregate reveal the epoch-making process of transplanting an old community into the New World. With the aid of the sources we can follow the typical course of the successful Jewish immigrant's life from the day he decided to emigrate, through the successive stages of economic struggle in the new country, to the maturing of the new social phenomenon, which American Jewry constituted. (See Nos. 88-119).

The reports of the vicissitudes of the emigrants in European countries began to arrive when the formation of American Jewry was well advanced. The news came particularly by way of the Jewish press of France, one of the few countries which had not been a source of emigration to any extent, and which now advanced to the center of immigrant welfare activity. The general American press led the way in publishing news concerning European emigration and immigration conditions in the country, and the Jewish journals followed. Even prior to the mass migration from eastern Europe the Jewish press carried accounts of remarkable emigrant groups that were of special interest to the Jewish public. Subsequently, however, the journals adopted a policy of silence.

The collaboration of American with European Jews got into full swing only in the seventies, when Germany's industrial boom brought emigration virtually to a standstill. Now the Russian, and later the Rumanian emigrants claimed attention and this problem was at first distasteful to Jewish leadership in America. The Board of Delegates of American Israelites had given a negative reply to Adolpe Crémieux, and the only hope was California, while the desire to emigrate from eastern Europe grew apace. Friction between the American and European committees was engendered by the arrival of unsuitable immigrants, with the latter rejecting the accusation that they had sent such persons. On the New York committee's demand the emigrants assisted had to give a pledge that they would not settle in that city. The demand that only suitable emigrants be sent, is constantly reiterated, but in meeting it the German committee was concerned only with diverting the travellers away from Berlin. A review of the conflict indicates that the willingness to help was, fortunately, not impaired, and that it was undoubtedly stronger than the differences between the contending parties.

The selection and training of manual workers was immediately recognized as advantageous, and the American committees could report that there were practically no longer any immigrants in need of assistance. Such results invited further well-considered suggestions for organizing emigration. The changed conditions in Europe evoked expectations of a new exodus, and plans for the Rumanian Jews became the order of the day. In this connection the perennial projects for territorial colonization reappeared. Later the chairman of the Board of Delegates of American Israelites, during a visit to Paris, was able to give a favorable report of the results of Russian-Jewish immigration. He pointed out that many of the immigrants were already in a position to bring their families over unaided.

Now the expansion of the Alliance Israélite Universelle to America was projected, for the purpose of promoting immigrant aid. The contacts to be made at the World Exposition of 1873 were to present opportunities for this plan. The American press continued to discuss agricultural settlements. With the favorable results achieved thus far, some thought could be given to aid for less qualified immigrants, and an influx of needy Jews could be openly spoken of. By this time America was already acquainted with recently arrived beggars, for whose needs the Jewish organizations were called upon to care. This problem was, nevertheless, not permitted to disturb immigration-aid activities; unlike the situation among the German non-Jews, these immigrants were not pleading for return passage.

The Eve of Mass Migration from Eastern Europe

Emigration as a world-historical phenomenon reached its climax when the established immigrant generation undertook a self-appraisal of its achievements, and when its contemporaries summed up the results. The voices rang forth first of all from Europe, in response to the immigrants' enthusiasm over their happiness. European Jewry associated itself with the declarations of those who had become citizens of a new world.

The Jewish globe-trotter, I. I. Benjamin, who saw the new communities in full bloom, gives us an account of the typical rise of the German-Jewish immigrant. The growth of small groups into large communities, and the springing up of so many new ones had already been recorded in Jewish journals and almanacs. Over and over again religious liberty was hailed, and the eligibility of Jews for public office reiterated. The development advanced by leaps and bounds, particularly in California, where the economic position of the Jews improved steadily, and we have colorful accounts of their adjustment in the new Pacific empire. But there were setbacks in this region. Sudden economic crises, the withdrawal of capital to the stabler states on the Atlantic exposed the hollowness of a life that depended entirely on the daily tide of fortune. When things went badly, moreover, antisemitism reared its head.

The steady progress of the other states was, on the other hand, so peaceful that Europe was advised with pride that no special reports on the Jews need be expected from America, simply because everything was proceeding smoothly. A Jewish journal proudly reproduced an article from Dr. Wiesner's magazine (*The Spirit of World Literature*), which emphasized the pre-eminent position the Jews had won in America. *A Retrospect at the Year 5520* triumphantly stated that during the recent panic most Jewish houses held firm and that consequently the Jews enjoy the highest confidence in the commercial world.

The generation became conscious of the fact that the founding of new communities follows the exploitation of new territory. It realized that life in America was unique both in regard to degree of activity and, particularly, to the tempo of change.

False reports regarding the return of the immigrants to Europe could be authoritatively denied, as the Koenigsberg Committee did in 1872. The Committee stated unequivocally that, by and large, emigration had been successful and that there had been no noteworthy re-emigration.

Yet in moments of introspection one perceives a great sense of alarm as to the inner life of this immigrant generation that worships economic success above all else. A young generation was growing up without a proper education, and the parents, themselves deficient in this respect, were unable to cope with the problem. (See Nos. 120-133).

THE SOURCES

1

The Emigrant's Departure (1867)

. . . . On to freedom, on to happiness,
To the land where honey flows,
Where, braving destiny,
One enjoys world's every joy!
To the beautiful America,
By Columbus once discovered,
Where everybody deems himself happy,
Where life tastes sweeter;
Where freedom does equal rights
Distribute to all — both poor and rich —

Where the darkest light of night
Is as our daylight.
Where the hatred of the nations
Ne'er existed and never will,
Where earnings reward the deed
And also befit the reward.
Where equal rights for all
From the spring of freedom flow,
And no endless strife and feud
Between Jew and Christian rage;
Where the human right is hallowed
By word and deed alike,
And each man has his share,
Whatsoever his creed.
Where mere birth does not ennoble
As it does here among us,
Reward and blame come to all
Alike in that beautiful world!
Is it not stupid now in Europe
To stay even a single day,
Where the rulers carry on
Worse than in antiquity?
Where despotic power holds sway
As in no part of the world,
Where no deed is e'er rewarded
Even if it achieve something great.
Where only a prince of the blood
Is able to ascend a throne,
And none is chosen regent
Unless he be a royal son;
One in fine whose thought is only
How more taxes to exact
While folk languish under the burden,
One who dampens all our joy.
No, I could not bear it any longer,
Nothing's here to hold me back!
Here are a hundred and fifty *guldens,*
Already marked for voyage-costs,
And to Leipzig and to Bremen,
Goes the morning's early dawn.
And it means but "taking leave."
"Hungary, I'll see thee no more!"
On the other side of the ocean
Henceforth be my fatherland,
Where in blind delusion never
The worth of noble deeds is undervalued:
There where for the right of bondmen

Noble blood in currents flowed,
In the midst of those brave people
Take me into freedom's lap!
There afar from my own people,
Wholly strange and unbeknown,
I'll bewail thy lot distressing,
Wretched, *wretched Fatherland!*

M. Brown

College Hill, Ohio, Feb. 1, 1867.

Die Deborah, vol. xii (1866-67) p. 125.

2

[From the Yiddish]

America is a golden country.
Call that a country?
A plague take Columbus.
It's your America.
In America life is merry.
In America there is no family pride;
At home he was a cobler,
At home he was a tailor,
At home he was a thief.

3

. . . . What else should they do but seek a new fatherland, where they should exercise the profession they had learned, to show off their wares, their knowledge and their learning. A young man, capable and a professional, applied to his district court . . . in the Retzat district for a certificate of protection. It was denied to him at the first tribunal as well as repeatedly at the higher ones. He made a last attempt to obtain it, but simultaneously annexed his petition to have his passport permitting him to go abroad drawn up . . . The petitioner received the latter and emigrated.

Allgemeine Zeitung des Judentums, vol. ix (1837) p. 264.

4

Baltimore, December 9 (Private communication).

That you are surprised to open your perenniel Bavarian correspondent's letter, which bears the above place-name at its head, this surprise in reality betrays your unfamiliarity with the Bavarian literature of arrest-warrants. Yes, the Bavarian police has set, along with many others, your correspondent also on his feet, which he used in good time. But God forbid that I should on that account feel the slightest rancor against them, — what they do is well done, and just as a father chastises his son, so they chastise us democrats, lovingly and for our own good, for if you knew how I once more filled my chest with that first draught of God's free air, when I saw stretching before me like "a garden of the Lord," the majestic blessed American coast; if you knew with what a sense of relief I shook off "the pressure within the pressure" — in the general German pressure there is a special Jewish pressure — I say, if you knew all this, dear Doctor! you would have no need of any tears of compassion for me, — but you would devoutly clasp your hands and exclaim with me: What the Bavarian police does is well done.

Allgemeine Zeitung des Judentums (1850) p. 31.

5

Oldenburg, in January (*The Emigration*)

From our regional rabbi's lecture. . . .

A silk-embroiderer emigrates because his fatherland has no tolerance for his political views; the poor *Schelm Moses* must seek his salvation in America, because he is a homeless Jew . . . Among the emigrants from Germany in the past five or ten years there have been many, nay more thousands of my co-religionists, particularly from Bavaria and the adjacent Saxon lands, and it is, as a rule, the younger generation in particular that emigrates . . . . On inquiring as to the motives one usually hears the answer: We can no longer withstand the pressure and the disdainful treatment and the disgrace of isolation . . . .

Der Orient, vol. viii (1847) p. 42.

6

From Swabia (*in August*)

. . . . On the other hand, as regards the civic industrial endeavors, our youth has not lagged behind. In recent times many capable craftsmen of every kind have been trained; many of these, however, have made up their minds to emigrate, as they ran into insuperable obstacles in settling down. Most of them went to America . . . From there many have helped their poor left-behind parents with considerable sums. Among us, too, this year more have emigrated than formerly, and still more have made arrangements to settle on the other side of the ocean next year . . . Only one thing I dislike, that among those emigrating are also young people who have learned nothing substantial and who can carry on only petty commerce. As a result of emigrants' letters, many skilled workers abandon their calling to go peddling in America many hundreds of English miles inland . . . .

Israelitische Annalen, August 30, 1839, p. 278.

7

From the Pfalz. Feb. 6 (*Kölnische Zeitung*)

The emigration fever is more strongly rampant than before. Even a not inconsiderable number of Israelites are preparing to move to the free North America. Is not this impulse, which rouses and spurs on all those who desire a drastic betterment of their situation and which has become particularly powerful and self-conscious among the Jews, is not this impulse based on an actual reality? Who could dispute it? Emigration will become predominant in the region of Alzey, Worms, Osthofen, Oppenheim and Woerstadt. In Wollstein, Fuerfeld, Flonheim, Gauodernheim, and other places as well many families are making preparations for departure. Among all these families there is *not one* that one can offhand call "poor." Most of them possess a fortune of four or five thousand florins. A landed proprietor in the neighborhood of Arnsheim raised 12,000 florins through the sale of his possessions.

Allgemeine Zeitung des Judentums (1847) no. 14, p. 159.

8

Emigration

"It is no emigration — it is indeed a migration of nations," they exclaim in Bremen this year.

There is also a great movement among the German Jews from Bavaria and the Grand Duchy of Posen, from Swabia and Hesse, from Rudolstadt and the Altmark.

. . . . Emigration through which they moreover escape becoming lost in great numbers in the European proletariat.

But also from a *higher* point of view, the Jews in America must gain a broad basis; . . . the intellectuals, the scientifically trained cling to it most stubbornly. Here, too, they are seen not to be so bright as the people who let themselves be guided by their instinct. Jewish university-trained men, physicians, jurists, philologists, mathematicians, natural scientists (especially *e.g. geologists*), architects, why do you languish in Europe or barter your religion? There is the stupid delusion that there is no place in America for university-trained men. To be sure, this may be true for those who are willing to be nourished with European dry rot for their barren researches in an apartment. But learn to make your knowledge useful, to cash in on it practically — and you will have bright careers for yourselves in America . . . .

Allgemeine Zeitung des Judentums (1854) p. 192.

9

Had the writer of this article read our previous communications on these and similar emigrations of Jewish colonies from Germany, namely from Bavaria, hardly would the above inquiry have slipped him . . . As it is known, the register (*Matrikel*) makes it little short of impossible for young Israelites to set up housekeeping in Bavaria; often their head is adorned with gray hair before they receive the permission to set up house and can, therefore, think of marriage. Once having learned their profession, whereby they can hope to gain their livelihood everywhere — why should they not transfer their desires and powers to the hospitable

North America, where they can live freely alongside members of all confessions? Likewise the alien-taxes, goose-taxes, horse-taxes, etc., etc., taxes, reintroduced everywhere by the Bavarian estates and recently once more left to their sweet will, obsolete imposts that are a great burden on the Jews, and this at a time when the growing demand is confronted with the decline in industry, all this tends to cause young, strong men and even those of more advanced age, to seek their salvation in other regions of the earth, where they don't at least have to bear this!

Allgemeine Zeitung des Judentums (1839) no. 24, p. 420.

10

Munich, Sept. 3. The *Leipziger Zeitung* contains the following article sent from here concerning the recent emigration of Israelites from Bavaria . . . .

. . . "Conscription remains a thorn in the side of the Israelites. Who can blame a father if he sells out and leaves with his family? The parents are then joined by hundreds of engaged couples, candidates for degrees and physicians, commercial clerks, journeymen and every sort of people eager to work. Naturally, there is never any talk about purchases in the North American woods, of agriculture, landed estates, etc. One becomes a merchant, *i.e.* carries on trade in the ever-roaming wagons and steamboats, until one gets a house and established store, or one carries on one, two, three trades, according to what he has derived from others, in addition to what he has in passing learned here. A German is gladly accepted as a workingman in America, the German Jew is preferred to any other. Thus hoplessness at home, a secure future overseas, no pressure or persecution of one or another sort lead the Bavarian Israelite to take up the wanderer's staff."

Allgemeine Zeitung des Judentums, September 28, 1839, p. 490.

11

Bavaria

King Max, who conducts himself as the modern Maecenas of the sciences, has just declared that he is a Catholic power, and everyone knows what that is going to mean to us. There is little prospect for improvement in our circumstances, and you may rest assured that in spite of the fair condition of our Bavarian co-religionists, emigration to America and other countries will grow ever stronger . . . We have so many brothers in the Union who are getting on well and who, when they visit their old home, raise their head so proudly as free men, that as a result the young people here have become disgusted with their protected and official kind of pauperdom and have come to think more and more of packing their bundles.

Die Deborah, vol. vi (1860) p. 11.

12

How wonderfully, how very beneficially conditions have changed since 1837! In those days, when a Europe-weary Jewish journeyman used to tie up his valise and say: "I am emigrating to America," it meant that he, too, was a black sheep that was good for nothing at home and who was no loss. If a stout-hearted youth, tired of dealing in second-hand goods and snail-paced commerce, came to his parents and said: "I feel within me the power for something more substantial; let me go across the sea," the parents wept and resisted, as if their son were going to the other world, from which they could hope for neither reunion nor return. If an educated Jew, because of discriminatory laws had no prospect of either a good position or a good future, expressed his determination to go to live in the land of freedom, the father used to bewail the money he had spent in vain on his education, and the aristocracy could not comprehend at all how an educated man could so lower himself that he could prefer the distant America, the land of the uneducated, the land of the blacks and Indians, to beautiful Europe.

How conditions have changed! These unnoticed artisans, these youthful adventurers have since then become the supporters of their kinfolk in the old fatherland, the founders of unhoped-for happiness of their people, have become men of consequence and influence in the commercial Old and New World!

Many, very many of these beggarly-poor emigrants are nowadays at the head of business concerns that own enormous property, command unlimited credit and amass every single year an independent fortune in pure profit. And these gigantic fortunes have been honestly and uprightly acquired, no stain, no shadow, no blame clings to them.

These poor emigrants have become the props of their own people. How many parents who had to slave hard and bitterly, and saw facing them declining years full of cares, now live contented and carefree, through the plentiful largesses, that flow to them from their children in America. How many kindly old fathers and mothers exclaim like Jacob in the joy and gratitude of their heart: "Oh, if I were granted once more to embrace my child blessed of God, how sated with life I would then be able to die." And lo! Suddenly come the tidings: Your son is coming from America! And the youth who had departed as an ill-starred fellow, as a beggar, comes back for a visit to his paternal home; and the parents hardly recognize him again, and he tells the story of his good fortune and his abundance; and they marvel, and the whole place hearkens and exclaims: "The stone which the builders rejected hath become the foundation — the cornerstone!"

And then there are other poor emigrants, who have written to their brothers and sisters, enclosing generous sums for passage in their letters. And they have married off their sisters well and taken their brothers as partners in their businesses, so they are all faring well, superlatively well. And then one or the other of the sons went abroad and fetched the parents so that they might be able to rejoice in the good fortune of their children.

And the aged country-Jews come; the father with his silver-mounted pipe and the coat that he has been wearing for ten years, and the mother with her wig and prayerbook for women. . . .

To be sure, not all of them have reached such heights; particularly those who came over accompanied by families or those, who in the old fatherland had never learned to look out beyond the old fence in Wolfen-kukuksheim, have never succeeded as they might have dreamed during the voyage across the ocean. Yet we can count hundreds of the former group. The signs of their enterprises blaze in all the big commercial cities of the Union, such as New York, Philadelphia, Cincinnati, St. Louis, New Orleans, etc.

Die Deborah, vol. vi (1860) p. 38.

13

If a Jew emigrates from the country with his family and belongings, he is obliged to pay the emigration tax, *e.g.* in Silesia it is ten per cent, if he has lived but one year and six weeks in the country. This does not apply to Jews who have stayed in the country merely as domestic servants, even if married. In the other royal states those Jews who desire to leave the country and who must then surrender their letter of protection, are exempt from the emigration tax if they do not possess any large property of five or more thousand taler acquired in the land; also exempt is the second child, who must depart from the country, even if this person's property is of greater value. But in case they have to take an inheritance out of the country, they must pay an emigration tax on that, as well as on the sum they had previously received as a dowry.

Krünitz Enzyklopädie, s.v. "Jude," Berlin, 1784 [p. 293-618], p. 523.

14

Munich, March 10 (Private Communication). Cases of emigration to America are ever and ever increasing in number. As often, and that is almost daily, as good letters come in from the emigrants, more people make up their minds anew to take up their wanderer's staff. From tiny Hagenbach, a townlet in central Franconia, twelve young men are leaving after Passover. In Warnbach nearby there are almost no young folks to be found any longer, save those who are without means. As I have already pointed out to you, many resident families in Oettingen are about to emigrate; however, a great difficulty stands in their way. As is well known, the European governments have made a treaty with the free states of North America relative to free emigration until 1840; but the princes are entitled to demand every tenth florin of the entire property to be carried away, so that a family which is taking along some 4,000 florins must pay 400 florins to the prince. Prince von Oettingen-Wallerstein is, according to reports, going to make use of this right and many obstacles are thus set in the path of the emigrants. Besides not only artisans and merchants are emigrating but also men of the learned class, since the prospects for rabbinical or medical positions are not particularly bright owing to the vast number of candidates.

Indeed we hear that many papers are jubilant over the departure of such large groups of Jews and they express the joyous and pious wish that those remaining behind may follow those who have gone ahead; but we reply to them that to get rid of a companionship like theirs involves for us at least the exercise of self-control and self-denial, which cost the emigrants few tears, and which will some day perhaps give them some happy hours.

Allgemeine Zeitung des Judentums, April 2, 1839, p. 159.

15

The Emigration-Taxes of Jews Emigrating from Posen

Concerning these, if they have been set too high, the royal governments must make a report, in case they do not reduce them themselves. (Royal Ministers' Reports, June 18, 1840 and Sept. 8, 1840.)

Jahrbuch des Nuetzlichen und Unterhaltenden fuer Israeliten, ed. by K. Klein, vol. i (1842).

16

Whoever here believes that money grows wild on the other side of the ocean . . . for him there is no America and no freedom, for he is the slave of his God. He will do well to remain here.

But he who will not and cannot at all comprehend why a people should be branded as helots on account of their former nationality, he should leave a country that scourges him on account of his opinions. In America he can be himself.

Der Orient, vol. vi (1845) p. 366.

17

Vienna . . . June 21. Ask the despised ones, who, spurred on by the violence of our old German tyrants, had to seek refuge on the other side of the ocean, ask them how they hearkened to the echo-call of Germany's rebirth and how they hastened toward their passionately-loved fatherland, at that call. The Jewish counselors who urged the cowardly emigration to America upon the Jews, the committees which organize this cowardice and this betrayal of their fatherland, are traitors to the Jews and Judaism . . . You eternal Jews and arch-separatists, do you want still more of the special Jewish accusations? . . .

Der Orient (1848) p. 221.

18

Weekly Report

Who would find fault with the Jew, when at such a time he once more heartily longs for the Messiah, hopes for him, asks Heaven for him;

for who will reproach him who leaves his fatherland, which is not such to him, and goes on a pilgrimage to the blessed land of full liberty and equality, the United States of North America? We want to keep a sharp eye on these United States by and by, and give our readers trustworthy information on them . . .

Oesterreichisches Central Organ fuer Glaubensfreiheit, Cultur, Geschichte und Literatur der Juden, ed. by Isidor Busch (Vienna 1848) p. 57.

19

Lemberg

A great mass of the local Jewish inhabitants might gladly lend ear to the call "Up and to America", if only it had the means. Already an Emigration Society has been formed in whose name I ask for further information concerning the committee organized for the assistance of emigrants.

Ibid., p. 170.

20

Up, and to America

The harvest is past, the summer is ended,
and we are not saved.

(*Jeremiah* 8:20)

No help has come to us! The sun of freedom has risen for the Fatherland; for us it is merely a bloody northern light. The larks of salvation are caroling in the free atmosphere; for us they are merely screeching, stormy petrels. The glow of shame and quivering wrath overwhelm us when we think of the terrible hair-raising experiences that these last weeks have brought us! Because slavish hordes and shopkeeperlike scamps did not and still do not understand the spirit of freedom, *we* must pay for it. God forbid that we hold our head ready for every blow of the club, that our eye tremble before every flash of our great and small tyrants! It has gone so far that at any hour which has brought freedom into the land, there is no other desire in us save to get out of the way of *this* freedom!

They don't want it any other way and so let it be! This is not the first time that we bow to their will. For centuries our history has been nothing but mute assent to every affliction imposed, to every torture and coercion! But always to yield, always to bow our head? Once, with the permission of the "sovereign people," we want to lose our patience; for once we want to refuse — and then to get out of the way!

That is to say to America! You who do not understand the essence of history, recognize its hint in this — that four centuries ago, exactly when the Jews were persecuted most fiercely, a Genoese had to hatch out in his hot brain the creative idea of a new world, that it gave him no rest until a Spanish queen, whose general conjured up the dark form of a Torquemada and his Dominican monks bespattered with the blood of thousands of our brethren, until, we say, Isabella of Spain allowed her admiral to discover America. Our yearning now goes out to that same America, thither should you depart! "Up and to America!" We know all of your objections, but only those of little faith and the faint-hearted will listen to them. The brave, the man of resolution will not! And can you give us no other counsel, ask the others, than to take up the wanderer's staff, and with wife and child to seek the far-off, strange land? Shall we abandon the soil that has begat us, and nourished us and in which we bury our dead? Methinks I hear already something about the fleshpots of Egypt, breathe in the exhalation of golden broth and beef-a-la-mode — but I also see the people who are poking the fire and, from the flames of hatred, prejudice and narrowmindedness fetch its daily mess; by God, whoever has a palate for it, let him stay and gorge himself!

Two verses there are which at this time can serve as starting points for us. Moses spoke one: "Stand firm and still"; and Jeremiah the other: "The harvest is past, the summer is ended, and we are not saved."

To which verse do I give preference? To stand still and wait, bide patiently until all clashing interests are propitiated and expiated, until the spirit of humaneness has come out victor? Or since "no help has come to us" — to find it and leave for America?

It seems to me these two verses can well be combined! May those in our fatherland who wish "to stand firm and still" base that viewpoint in the sand of the future! We do not wish to hinder them from so doing, we wish to supply them with building stones for it ourselves, but to the other oppressed and downtrodden, the expelled and impoverished and plundered in the notorious communities, to all of whom "liberty" has brought calamity, to all those whom their heart tells: "For a long time to come we shall be unable to enjoy tranquility in the fatherland, we cannot forthwith change ourselves, nor them either, decades are necessary in order to introduce the first preparations for peace" — to all these we say: "For us no help has come. Seek it out in far-off America."

The idea is not new. We know it; but it is practical for all that. A long time ago they wanted to give Rothschild the honor of being godfather to this idea. He did not accept the honor — but wherefore Rothschild? Why not emigrate without Rothschild? Rothschild cannot further the need to emigrate, the necessity to leave; he can lend support, assist, by a means. But the *goal* you must seek without Rothschild. You shall also be assisted, you are in need — but that is a means, not a goal. Emigration, the founding of a new fatherland, the instantaneous recollection of freedom, that is the goal!

What you will do in America does not belong in the lines of this appeal. It shall only be a distress-signal, an alarm-gun or, if you will, a musical tone in this wildly-disturbed time. Become farmers, merchants or artisans, peddlers or members of Congress in Washington, exchange-brokers or vice-presidents of the Free States of North America, become cotton-planters or sugar-refiners, that concerns you not us. In your new fatherland too no one will interrogate you about it, for there an individual passes for what he is and he is what he represents. Above all become free and go to America!

Thousands have taken this step before you and still take it! Relatively few have regretted it so far. The God of your fathers shall watch over you. He will guide you safely over the tides of the ocean, over the first adversities of a new life! I do not feel uneasy about you! It is just *you* who possess the virtues and qualities — circumspection, sobriety, thriftiness, discipline and tenacity — to build up prosperity and welfare over there. Others have fallen and gone to ruin there, but you will flourish and grow; the God of liberty will be with you!

I greet your children, the children of those who have become free! *Shalom Aleichem!* A bright fervor flows through me when I think of the *free-born* children, when I think of the mothers who present them to you.

From amidst the horrors of the past weeks, therefore, through the ranks of your waylayers, persecutors and oppressors, "make way for freedom, and up and to America!"

L. KOMPERT*

Ibid., p. 77.

* Just as this article is going to press we have received news from Pesth that "as a result of the latest disturbances a Society for Emigration to the United States of North America has been formed, which counts among its members also many Christian professionals and technicians, although the great majority are adherents of the Mosaic faith.

21

Up, and to America! II

In the stress of the moment, as well as under the influence of events crashing one after the other like cudgel-blows from every side, we issued our call to all the oppressed and afflicted in Israel to leave the land of bondage and cares and to seek out the transatlantic homeland! It was perhaps an instinctive answer to the questions of so many afflicted souls in which "Get out! Get out!" thumps like an impatient creditor! But was the answer a correct one? Does our counsel to emigrate reveal an accurate appraisal of the times? The agitation and storms that have taken place this year have been so immeasurable and endless that even a far-seeing and superior understanding becomes perplexed and unclear. It is impossible to guarantee anything; even hatred, even prejudice and stupidity cannot vouch that in spite of their opposition the Jewish question may not take an unexpectedly favorable turn today or tomorrow. Yes, we who have issued the call: "To America!" live in the most firm conviction that our emancipation will take a decisive turn for the better in the immediate future. Notwithstanding, we do not hesitate for a single moment to repeat more urgently than ever before the call: "Up, and to America!" And for the simple reason that the solution to the Jewish question is so uncertain. Ten thousand people who gain freedom for themselves immediately through their departure to America are a greater gain for us than if hundreds of thousands eat their hearts out for long years to come in yearning and tribulation, helpless or gnashing their teeth. It sounds fine in books, romances and legends, when one renounces his freedom for the sake of another, allows himself to be locked up and starved for his sake and sobs and weeps with him. In reality, such an act appears as sickly sentimentalism, if not criminal. A person who can but does not become free, commits the most grave wrong; *one* person liberated is a gain that spreads over a hundred, nay, a thousand people; the pretext to wish to suffer along where others suffer, has no meaning and is an indication of cowardice. Whoever grasps the initiative of liberty is more useful and is at the same time a standard-bearer for a thousand others! And from this point of view, after mature deliberation, we repeat our call: "Up, and to America!"

This is only one, and surely not the least significant, side of emigration, namely *this*: to bolster the courage of those left behind, to lead the way for them by example, not just to emigrate, but to attain freedom. Our conditions have shaped themselves so terribly and the situation has as yet changed so little that we, who bear the loss, even here where we must let thousands of our brethren depart for strange and remote parts, for a struggle with the privations and afflictions of a new life, that even here we hope for a *stake* — the winning of our *freedom*. Or is this not the case?

This side of the emigration question, however, dwindles almost to insignificance as regards those who are really becoming free. Without any assistance, by force of its own will, our problem of emancipation thus attains solution such as it cannot hope for under the present circumstances. To become free at once, without any delay, without parliamentary pros and cons, without sympathies and antipathies, right there and then on the spot, as soon as the ship drops its anchor and the ocean strikes its partition walls. But tell it to those people, tell it to all the afflicted and the sorrowing, that straightaway on setting foot on the transatlantic soil they become free people, citizens of a free state. Uplift their souls with this sound, give warmth to our poor, inhumanly harassed, poor Jews, summon all the treasures of your speech, all the darts of your art of persuasion—for the matter is of sacred earnestness—in order to reassure them, to strengthen them and turn them to the call which you should keep repeating to them: "Up, and to America!"

Can one make a living from freedom? they will ask you. Answer them: Yes, yes, one can live. Until now you have been vegetating in bondage rather than living, and even that condition, degrading, galling and frightful that it was, fluctuating between resignation and restriction, between snatches of sunshine and darkness, was made hateful and bitter for you. Your state of vegetation was still too much to suit them. Life will come to you only in freedom. Yes, one can live from freedom, especially the Jew can do so. Oh, how you will thrive, grow and flourish! Can one live on freedom? Only on freedom — it is the real elixir of life! We have already pointed out in a previous article, how the organism of Judaism, in which we do not at all wish to deny the presence of morbid tumors and diseases, is accordingly in need of the fullest freedom for its salvation and for the advancement of all its unlimited activities. Tell it to all to whom you turn that they will find it in America in a measure which for nearly a century has been the expressed object of yearning of all Europeans. From Germany, for example, thousands of peasants go across the ocean to the New World every year; peasants who own house, homestead and land which they dispose of and convert into cash; frequently entire villages are emptied. In their urge to go overseas, these limited natures were quite conscious of their aspiration, far more conscious than any of the heroes of liberty who try it out on all instruments of the ideas of the times. *They* wanted to be free, and had they not turned their backs on their "lords" and officials, on their task-masters and tax-collectors, thousands of them would be fighting against them; and the Struve-Hecker revolt would have had a different outcome, which would have materially changed the fundamental law of the Reich from what the Committee of Seventeen has just proposed in Frankfurt.

Indeed, the example of these German peasants points the way for you! It does after all teach you what freedom is. Tell them that in America there are no restrictions on any occupation, provided it is honorable; tell them that in America Jewish industry, prudence, sobriety and thrift do not provoke any bloodthirsty and rapacious waylaying; tell them that America is big enough not to ask about one's religion, trade or definite and specific activity; explain to the "common man" that he can take with him the religion of his ancestors, and that he will find there thousands with whom he can join in practicing his religion, that Judaism over there is not without root and branches, and finally that there the *individual* comes first, then religion, state, etc.

L. Kompert.

While we commend the highly important cause discussed in these lines to all who possess a warm heart for the disconsolate situation of the Jews and who, with us, recognize that emigration in large or small groups is the most desirable and permanent means to support and prepare a better future for our brethren who are afflicted, persecuted and without means of livelihood, while we enjoin it earnestly on all who *themselves* are waiting for emigration as for a savior and are at present merely chained by circumstances to the land which is casting them out and denying them every right of a citizen; finally to all those who can and are willing to assist this cause with counsel, with word and *deed,* we address this plea; Any one in favor of it may get in touch with the committees being organized for emigration in several of the communities, and forward immediately their contribution, which will surely bring the richest fruits. The office of this paper is also ready to receive such contributions. It will deliver the same promptly to the committee being organized here and will make it generally known through several of the most widely-circulated newspapers.

The Editors.

Ibid., p. 90.

22

Up, and to America!

> What have you here and whom have you here, that you wish to dig your grave here?

With these words of the prophet we associate ourselves with the view, which is so zealously advocated by this journal, in regard to emigration to America. Yes, up, and to America! Become human beings, become free — then you can be Jews according to the word and will of God. What have you here, poor nation? Enemies and enviers who begrudge you the stale crumbs of bread, ignominy and indignity. And yet you want to prepare your grave here? Yes, yes! your grave — for here the blossoms of life do not germinate for you. It is not the clods of earth that bind the patriot; it is the memories of his youth and the ties of family that are the basis of his life, of his fatherland. You, my co-religionist, what sort of associations do you have with the soil? The memory of your humiliation, the recollection of your shame? Your family? Oh, think not of that nor of your forebears, lest you turn to hate the Christians. Now then, away from here and become free, become a human being. Still I need not repeat what has already been told to you often enough. I merely say, save the man, save the suffering, loving Jew in you, in order that you should not turn to hate the Christians; for the Christians, too, are human beings, I might say in almost the same tone of affected compassion in which their champions of emancipation used to say: "The Jews are *after all also* (!) human beings!" But let us pass from theory to practice and let us think about the means for emigration. I was just reading an appeal to America by a co-religionist in Pest who, in the name of a committee appointed for this purpose in Hungary, closes his fine article with the following important observations:

"But in order to direct the emigration to America there has been organized by the emigrating Israelites in Pest a temporary committee, which

"(a) Gathers all necessary data and information about the ways and means of overseas migration and settlement. For this purpose the committee is in touch with men at home and abroad who are in a position to provide the most necessary and most accurate information regarding this subject. At the earliest possible date it will also dispatch a commission, consisting of the most conscientious persons, equipped with all the necessary qualifications and knowledge, to North America in order there to work out the immediate measures concerning the purchase of property in that land;

"(b) The committee will conduct an accurate enrollment of all prospective emigrants possessing the necessary qualifications and resources;

"(c) It will extend its operations to the procurement of means for poor but qualified emigrants.

"(d) From time to time the committee will issue useful communications about the ways and means and progress of its activity.

In behalf of the committee,

(Signed) Adolph Dux"

So much for this appeal, which, apart from this, manifests fine sentiments and great energy. From time to time we shall publish the most appropriate news concerning the progress of this society. At this moment we wish to make the suggestion that all the societies for Jewish emigration in the Austrian monarchy and in Germany (a country so *intimately connected* with the former in regard to the Jews) unite into one Central Committee in order to combine their joint forces for this lofty mission — for truly it is as difficult as it is holy. Long live freedom!

SZ---O

Ibid., p. 111.

23

An Open Letter to All Prospective Emigrants, Particularly to Mr. Leopold Kompert

By David Mendl

With profound grief, with heavy sorrow I, too, have heard the numerous reports of Jewish persecutions; but with still more profound pain, with intense indignation, do I see the path that many of our co-religionists want to take for the preservation of their material welfare. When I first heard the call: "Up, and to America!" I considered it to be a cry of distress and for help of people sinking in a stormy sea. Still I did not believe that I should have to hear that call again after the storm had subsided, after peace had begun to come into the huts of Israel. But a poet, a poet filled with enthusiasm for Jewry, has lifted his voice: Leopold Kompert avows that his first call was, as it were, only "an instinctive reply to the inquiries of many afflicted souls."

But when the greatest peril threatens, the judicious, strong man should never silence common sense, and let sheer animal instinct hold sway. If he has once committed this error, he should not want to excuse it by sophistry.

Tell me you, who possibly know it better, what great calamity has befallen Israel that you wish to break the ties that bind you to the fatherland? Have they wanted to deprive us of our nationality, of our faith, somewhat as in the time of Antiochus? Have they stacked funeral-piles for us as for heretics? Have they consigned our suckling babes to death in the waters? Nothing of the kind (we give thanks for that). The great giant Austria that had long lain asleep in chains has awakened; it has shaken its mighty arms and flung far away the easily-broken chains; several links of these chains hit some of our co-religionists.

The press has become free, and squibs against the Jews and Jewish emancipation have issued from the rabble and come into the hands of the rabble; does that mean anything more than that street-loafers have this time begun systematically the old cry of Hep! Hep!? The bureaucracy, formerly the only legitimate power in the land, has been overthrown; its plunder-thirsty mob utilized the momentary, apparent weakness of the government to pillage Jewish residences and shops. Where it came to excesses, the narrow-minded bourgeois magistrates decreed the expulsion of the Jews from those places. However, everywhere the better elements, the intellectuals, have warmly stood up for us. Writers have disavowed those squibs. The authorities, the army and the National Guard, even Christian clergymen have made sacrifices to protect the lives and property of the Jews; indeed, among Germans, Czechs and Magyars influential voices have been heard in behalf of our rights and our freedom. Yes, while the tree of freedom showed hideous excrescences in many a place, it has borne precious fruits elsewhere; in many places the fraternization of Christian and Jewish residents was speedily and completely restored.

But even assuming that this were not the case and that an appalling calamity had actually befallen the Jews, is this the appropriate time to desert fatherland, friends and brothers and selfishly to seek one's own safety far away? No path has been prepared for the liberation of the Jews through the fact that ten thousand more Jews have become free; not all the oppressed can emigrate; and for this reason alone it is necessary to find place for freedom, one more land for freedom. "The press is free!" I cry to you once more; the press, which like a powerful lever has lifted the old tyranny from its moorings, will also do away with prejudice against you; but don't stand idle, gaping and dreaming; apply yourselves diligently and God will cause your labor to flourish.

If peril indeed does threaten the Jews, it is your sacred duty to stand beside your brethren, to battle and to wrestle, to triumph or to fall with them. Consider well before you take the step for a voyage to America; think how you would feel if a storm on the open sea were to remind you that at the same moment perhaps a still more hazardous storm is breaking over those that stayed behind, and that you have withdrawn your strongest arms from helping them. But on this point we wish to let our Leopold Kompert speak: "It sounds fine in books, romances and legends when one renounces his freedom for the sake of another, allows himself to be locked up and starved for his sake and sobs and weeps with him. In reality such an act appears as sickly sentimentalism, if not criminal." Dear *Kompert!* When Moritz Hartman, you, I and another young friend, who unfortunately has not lived to see the regeneration of Europe, strolled through the Iser valley dreaming boyishly, when at that time the idea of the grand and the sublime began to germinate in our youthfully tender souls, I never imagined that one day you would utter or even conceive such a narrow-minded (!) thought. You, the poet, separate the art of poetry from life? You forget that poetry is the spirit, the life of life? You, the poet, forget that in these momentous times it is less incumbent on us to write romances, legends, etc., for the sake of esthetics than to sow the tiny cornseed in susceptible souls? Sympathy and self-denying sacrifice, you call sentimentalism and crime? Were the deeds of Lafayette, Kosciuszko and the Philhellenes sentimentalism and crime? Is the courage of the fifty young men in Prague who cared not for their own security but who, staking their lives, defended the entrance to the Jewish quarter, to be termed sentimentalism and crime? No person with a sane head and heart would utter such a verdict.

And, to consider the subject from another point of view, I ask: "Do you really believe that you will find in America the yearned-for Jerusalem? Where *slavery* is still tolerated as a right there is no guarantee for the equality rights of the free; there rude force can turn at any moment against the weaker. Here, however, the conditions are better; old prejudices disappearing, law and justice are unfurling their banners in the land; the spirit is free of every fetter and will forcibly smash all other oppressive bonds to smithereeens. The Jew also will be given back his human dignity. And even if some time is still to elapse until our salvation is realized and even if many struggles and suffering still await us, we want to hold fast and loyally to our fatherland. There will always be time to emigrate should we again see ourselves disappointed, in spite of all human precaution, in spite of all reason.

An Open Letter on the Matter of Emigration

Most Honored Editor:

Your esteemed journal of the sixth inst. contains a glowing call to our co-religionists to emigrate to America, and never has a word been uttered at more appropriate time.

Consequently we refrain from any additional recommendation of this timely step, and we ought to await your promised further exposition of your plan*; but still we find ourselves all the more compelled to communicate to you our views on this point, since the idea of founding a Jewish colony has preoccupied us for a long time. And while we scarcely pretend to offer something perfect, one or another of our ideas should be of use in projecting or elaborating your plan.

First and foremost we lay particular stress on the word "colony"; since for the resettlement of a few well-to-do individuals there should be no need to wait for a sign of the times. We are inclined more than anybody else, however, to agree with you that it is the voice of God that is evidenced in the present events, that salvation is no longer smiling at us in Europe and that our mission is to be fulfilled in the New World.**

Duped by the princes, annoyed by the governments, and strangled by the liberated peoples, whence should we await any good? Possibly from the Reaction or from the Ochlocracy, who sneer at us each in turn and then together?

Yes, from the more lofty humanitarian point of view it might be considered desertion, for the well-to-do alone to rush toward lasting happiness and untroubled freedom, while the poor remain in their chains

* The program has been worked out and already signed by an interim committee, but the troubled situation is a great hindrance to the undertaking.—Editor.

** This we have never and nowhere said.—Editor.

of misery and bondage, cut off from the material and moral support of the emigré brethren. What else was left to them but either to pay the sovereign nation for their gradually sequestered petty trade and to receive the martyr's crown — ah, their only inheritance — for the piety of their fathers; or indeed to barter away their Jewish names at twenty-five silver rubles per soul to that irruptive Muscovitism that has the sole control over the means of grace?

But to assist the poor to emigrate through collections should be very difficult and, at best, possible only on a small scale. It is our view that the matter should be handled in a more thoroughgoing way, to wit:

A considerable capital should be raised by the sale of shares of stock. A part of this capital should be devoted to the purchase of public land in America. For this purpose about one percent of the fund subscribed should at the outset go to defray the cost of an agency to select the suitable region and to enter into negotiations with the government of the United States for the purchase of the tract. But the remainder of the fund should gradually be expended on the transportation of the colonists and the creation of homesteads for them; and in accordance with their decision, they shall be allotted houses in the city to be built or parcels of land to be cultivated each with its appurtenances, and shall assume the obligation of annual proportionate payments, so that they will in time become the owners of their property, and the shareholders will recover their money.

The amortization of the capital stock would be delayed less if the funding of the capital is of larger dimensions. That is, the greater the capital the more acreage can be purchased and the cheaper; there consequently should be left a greater surplus of land for disposal at a value many times multiplied, in the city even multiplied a thousandfold; the more — and the larger their number the more economical — colonists can be brought over; and they again, on their part, will constitute a greater point of attraction for encouraging further emigration; thus the remaining land should rise in value.

The land still available after amortizing the shares, would remain joint property to be utilized for the advancement of further emigration of poor co-religionists from Europe, whereby there might in time come into existence a state of our own and the scriptural passage דרך כוכב מיעקב might be fulfilled.

Not all the shares of stock, moreover, would have to wait for subscribers among capitalists, for the well-to-do prospective emigrants might take up a large part of them, as they would not only get a share of land at a comparatively cheaper price, but through the growth of emigration their share would acquire that much greater value, just as their own prosperity in general would become the more assured.

We do not know whether a similar *idea* lay at the basis of Sir Moses Montefiore's erstwhile project; either this is the case or, in any event the honorable Baronet should make it his own as a result of our prosopal! In reality nothing could be more serviceable to the intentions of this noble friend of humanity, inasmuch as otherwise the Russian Israelites, accustomed to bondage and darkness, would hardly make up their minds to step into entirely new surroundings, whereas a Jewish colony from Galicia might entice them as a new home! Besides, the financial part would be well-nigh taken care of, and there would remain nothing but to work out the plan in detail and to issue the necessary programs in German and Hebrew.

In that case we should like to request you to forward a number of copies for distribution in our region, as we hope to find here not only stock-holders among the capitalists and the well-to-do prospective emigrants, but — what is more important — useful colonists. Here we find among our co-religionists the so-called "rougher" trades, those that are more indispensable for a colony, such as cabinet-makers, carpenters, roofers, tinsmiths, etc.

At all events the estimable Viennese Society for the Advancement of Industry Among the Jews should be advised to concentrate its chief attention on trades of that kind. Moreover, it would meet with fewer obstacles among the Gentile instructors if it becomes known that the pupils in question intend to emigrate.

Hoping that you will not begrudge these lines space in your journal, I beg to remain,

Yours most respectfully,

THE ETERNAL JEW

Brody, May 18, 1848

(*Note to David Mendl's Letter*)

We present this article, which so warmily and eloquently handles the matter of emigration cherished by us, with a conscientiousness of utter impartiality and we refrain from any other retort save this, that we are not urging *emigration* so much as *assistance* to those who are emigrating, who already firmly resolved and, moreover, cannot help it, and we also express our conviction that through it the foundation for the happiness of thousands will be laid, as may be seen from the articles published here.

Ibid., p. 138-39.

24

Remain in the Land

. . . See here! a far-resounding call rang out: "Up, and to America!" — It was an inspiring call which made many a heart beat more quickly and strongly. "Make way for freedom, and up, and to America!" It was a call that made many an eye beam under the flash of a mighty violent agitation. But it was merely a flash "that fades at its very beginning." For more mature deliberation had forthwith cooled off and downed the enthusiasm of the moment. I do not wish to speak of the sorrow of leaving the soil of the fatherland to which our hearts are firmly bound by the finest and most intimate strings. It would be childish to succumb to such a sentiment, however powerful it might be, when one can attain freedom in its purest strain in exchange for ignominious slave chains. Nor do I want to say that the description of the sad lot of the many unprotected emigrants who embark to seek good luck and frequently find only dark misfortune has a completely depressing and disheartening effect. It may be possible to prevent this sad lot by means of a carefully-planned organiaztion of overseas colonization.

Such migrations, however, are for *individuals* only. Although 10, 20 or even 30 emigrants may depart from each district or community, — it is not possible for entire communities to do the same! There are heads of families with weakly children or with tender, sickly wives; there are men who are weak and sickly themselves; there are sons who are the sole support of their aged parents, and there are sons who have widely-ramified commercial ties. All such persons, therefore, can only gaze toward but not enter the promised land of freedom and equality.

There is another element, however. As gladly and as joyously as I and all my brethren and colleagues in Israel will proffer our hands for the realization of the call "Up, and to America," nevertheless we also hear the counter-call: "Remain in this country and find sustenance in faith and reliance."

Ibid., p. 147.

25

[From Bavaria] . . . *They are emigrating, indeed.* We have young men who have completed their apprenticeship and journeymen's years of travel just as precisely as any one of another faith, who can legally prove possession of no inconsiderable fortune, who meet all the requirements that may be made of them, and yet cannot obtain letters of protection and domicile on account of their registration number. What should such people do, who have sacrificed half their fortune in legal proceedings in order to obtain their object? . . .

Allgemeine Zeitung des Judentums, September 9, 1837, no. 66.

26

Wuerzburg, Jan. 16 (Private communication). The departures to America on the part of Jews of our district, I fear, will be very numerous. In the *Intelligenzblatt* No. 8 of this year, already *eight Jewish emigrants* have been brought to public notice. By all accounts, many Christian families, too, have made up their minds to do likewise.

Allgemeine Zeitung des Judentums, February 14, 1839, p. 77.

27

Wuerzburg, March 10 (Private communication). It was possible to foresee that emigration would not be inconsiderable this year; but unfortunately it was far greater than had been surmised! I say unfortunately because in our condition this will work perceptible disadvantages. Many a small community may easily be compelled to give up public worship and its school, because it may be unable to pay the teachers and religious functionaries, unless certain provisions are made by the state. From certain places, in which there are 30-40 Jewish families, 15-20 persons or more are leaving, and, at that, mostly young and hard-working people. At Riedenburg, a village in the province of Brueckenau, an old man of eighty-five has decided to migrate to America.

Allgemeine Zeitung des Judentums, March 30, 1839, p. 155.

28

From Swabia, February, 1840. . . . The emigration-fever has steadily increased among the Israelites of our district and seems about to reach its high point. In nearly every community there are numerous individuals who are preparing to leave the fatherland early next year and to seek their fortune on the other side of the ocean. This is particularly the case in *Ichenhausen,* the largest Israelitic community in Swabia with approximately 200 families. If I am correctly informed, there are in this place alone 60 persons contemplating the voyage. About 20 more wish to join them from *Osterburg* (a small and poor congregation of barely 25 families belonging to the Altenstadt rabbinate).

Emigration is, of course, nothing new among us, although, to be sure, it never was strong in general. For a long time we have been used to the fact that youngsters, who had gone forth into the world, with the wanderer's staff in hand, finally settled in various foreign lands because they had no prospect of establishing themselves in their birthplace (as, apart from the seven corporate restrictions, the trades become so easily overcrowded in hamlets and villages). Also since time immemorial, indigent girls (at times annually) have gone in whole groups to Italy (attracted by better wages), where they entered domestic service in Jewish communities and many stayed there.

Israelitische Annalen, 1840, p. 73.

29

The rabbinate of *Burgebrach* will shortly become vacant due to the emigration of Kunreuther, the local rabbi until now . . . The rural communities become emptier year by year; while the metropolitan cities fill up with more prosperous Jews. Whether true Judaism also follows, is another question.

Der Israelitische Volkslehrer, vol. ix (1859) p. 98.

30

America

Numerous groups of Jews, especially from Bavaria, annually migrate thither; new congregations are formed continually and already counsel is sought in European cities in regard to liturgy and the selection of rabbis (I mention here only the instance of Charleston).

Thus our wandering has finally brought us even far across the sea. May we speedily overcome all perilous obstacles which are still threatening our unity and our rights in the Old World.

Der Orient, vol. iii (1842) p. 418.

31

The Jewish Emigrant

. . . Far, far toward the West,
There is a great country,
Far across the sea it holds out
To us its brotherly hand.
  Thither shall we cross over,
  There shall be the home
  Where we can find rest
  From suffering, ignominy and agony.

DR. ROTHENHEIM

Die Déborah, vol. i (1855-56) p. 2.

32

Reformed! A Two-crayon Drawing by Louis Bill

Koenigsberg in Prussia is the first station where the emigrating Polish Jew in his flight to the Promised Land, America, begins to hold his fine curly head erect . . . Is the sudden change to be ascribed to the sight of the Pregel River which, in lively intercourse with New York Harbor, possibly emanates also some air of freedom together with the tarry smell of American ships? Or does this first metamorphosis of the emigrant have at its basis an historical element? I mean the divine commandment to our forefather Abraham, which he, in keeping with Rashi's interpretation, applies to himself: "*Emigrate!* not for my sake, but for your own good and welfare," and accordingly immediately upon getting into steerage considers himself a halfway "self-made" man. (During the voyage across he dreams of getting rich and he hears a voice which bids him begin as a glazier.) That occupation will yield you but a meager livelihood, but like hundreds of your predecessors, you will earn your living thereby, you will acquire a familiarity with places in your wanderings, learn a bit of English, and also put away some money, in order to begin a better business, such as that of old clothes.

From old clothes to new ones is but one step. Then you will wander again through Broadway and gaze at the buildings. This time, however, not in order to mend a broken window-pane, but in order to pick yourself a big house with many windows in which to manufacture new clothes to be sold in the West and South. On his arrival he changes the style of his beard, also of his clothes — at first only a little, he joins the Beth Hamdirash Hagadol . . . after five years he is, "Noah Webster, Merchant Tailor." What harm is it to you, what harm is it to the world, why should anyone care whether my name is Noah Webster or . . . King David? "I have given up my old name on the advice of an American. What anyhow, is there in a name, if only one makes money and becomes rich?" He gives up the Beth Hamidrash. "Since I have moved uptown, I belong to the Temple." He himself attends only on Rosh Hashanah, his wife also Saturday, his child — Sunday school. "Let my family derive pleasure from my thirty dollars, since I cannot have it." He grows even richer. Since he has been receiving American company in his parlor not a Yiddish word is permitted alongside the English language. Outside his home he still speaks Yiddish, still tells jokes, makes fun of Yom Kippur, fasts, suddenly goes bankrupt, loses everything, begins again to use "that old *tsores*-language." He curses his lot. A plague should have taken Columbus before he discovered America!" . . . He ends up as Missionary . . . with the name Christian Lobster. And he brings the execrations of his co-religionists upon himself.

Libanon, vol. iii (1877) no. 11, p. 162.

33

Traits of Humaneness

Letters from America bring information that last spring, during the heavy emigration of Jews, a ship whose passengers were mostly Israelites sailed to England. The majority of the passengers were in most pitiful condition, from which, it is reported, the pious sentiment and benevolent interest of the noble Mrs. von Rothschild of London saved them. As soon as she received news of the wretched state in which many of her co-religionists found themselves, she arranged for assistance to be provided for them in every possible way. The persons thus saved could not find sufficient words to describe the humane and loving attitude of Mrs. von Rothschild.

Die Synagoge, vol. i (Wuerzburg 1837) p. 104.

34

Wuerzburg, April 12 (Private Communication) . . . An interesting observation strikes the observer in looking over the names of those listed for emigration. When comparing the gentile with the Jewish emigrants one finds that the former have more family groups than single persons, the latter by far more single persons than families. From this one might also draw a conclusion as to the motives for emigration. The Jewish emigration appears to be due less to greed for gain than to the consciousness of being unable in any other way to achieve independence or to found a family.

Allgemeine Zeitung des Judentums, May 4, 1839, p. 215.

35

Wuerzburg, May 7 (Private Communication). Departures for America this year have now started on a large scale among us, and hardly a day passes without a band crossing our northern border. On May 6 the Israelites emigrating from the neighboring parts of the Bavarian and Saxon frontiers gathered in *Meiningen,* and almost 100 strong entered together upon their journey. They will betake themselves jointly to *one* ship and they intend to found a small Jewish community together in America. They are carrying a *sefer torah,* as well as a *megillah,* a shofar, etc. and have taken along likewise such persons as are qualified for the exercise of religious functions, as slaughtering, circumcision, further — religious teachers, cantors, etc. They have made the necessary arrangements in Hamburg in advance so that they may live during the voyage undisturbed in their religion. May now also God's blessing attend them and may they settle happily in the land of their new domicile!

Allgemeine Zeitung des Judentums, May 25, 1839, p. 256.

36

Ichenhausen in Wuerttemberg, June 16 (Private Communication). Today was the day of deepest sadness, of bitterest heartache for the local Israelite congregation. Six fathers of families with their wives and children, all told 44 persons of the Mosaic faith, left home to find a new fatherland in far-off America. Not an eye remained dry, not a soul unmoved, when the bitter hour of parting struck. Such departures leave a visible void in the local community, from whose midst 100 persons have left so far, and have already or will settle in the free United States of America.

Allgemeine Zeitung des Judentums, July 20, 1839, p. 347.

37

Hamburg, May 27 (Private Communication). The first transport of Jewish emigrants, 86 persons strong, is to leave in the next few days on a ship for New York. They are Bavarians from the Wuerzburg region, mostly professionals. Those who wish to eat *kosher* on the voyage, pay a trifle extra and get for this kosher meat, a separate stove and they take care of the cooking by rotation. Provision has also been made for other ritual needs on board ship.

Of what means Providence avails itself to lead the scattered fragments of Israel to the most distant lands, to take them to New Netherlands, Siberia and Ohio, and to integrate them into these lands for the higher purposes of Providence!

Besides their own religion they are also bringing to the other hemisphere the German language and German diligence. Favorable reports from their brethren who went there in recent years have hastened their decision and many more are to follow them. A young physician from Munich also departed some days ago.

Allgemeine Zeitung des Judentums, June 11, 1839, p. 282.

38

Emigration cases. A few days ago 35 Jewish emigrants from Bavaria and Bohemia bound for America passed through Leipzig. Our spokesmen, who push to the front at every opportunity, care little about *organized* emigration.

Der Orient (1844) p. 207.

39

Mainz, May 16. Two hundred *Bavarian* Jews embarked here last week, to seek a new fatherland in North America. They drew a very dismal picture of the situation of the Jews in Bavaria, where nothing else is left but to suffer or emigrate. Of these emigrants one, whom good humor did not desert even for an instant upon taking leave of his fatherland, replied to the question whether he would not come back from America: "I will not return before North America has become Bavarian."

Allgemeine Zeitung des Judentums (1845) p. 346.

40

Ellwangen, May 11. This day we saw passing through here a wholly singular company of emigrants to North America. The whole company consisted entirely of Jews from nearby *Oberdorf,* in the superior bailiwick of Neresheim. As a rule, we observe among emigrants an extreme shortage of conveyances and clothing and bad appearance in general. Here we saw affluence in everything; an elegant omnibus conveyed the group to the point of embarkation; everyone, especially the Jewish girls in the party, were smartly dressed and presented a cheerful and lively appearance. The group carries with it a *torah* written on parchment, which they solemnly consecrated in the synagogue at Oberdorf before their departure. The emigrants, twelve in number, are following their kinsmen and acquaintances, who preceded them a number of years ago, and who encouraged them to seek the yearned-for promised land in North America, where their co-religionists are not (as in most German states) deprived of their natural and civil rights because they cling to the faith of their fathers . . .

Der Orient, vol. vii (1846) p. 184.

41

Budapest, July 9, 1848. The fact that even from here ideas about emigration are strongly spreading, proves that in our country the civil status of the Jews is still very bad.

Oesterreichisches Central Organ fuer Glaubensfreiheit . . . (1848) p. 226.

42

Lemberg . . . The costs of emigration to America for one family would be sufficient to settle them here.

Ibid., p. 230.

43

Vienna . . . Moreover, if at all street-corners you read brilliant bill-boards with invectives against the Jews, if you heard Jews villified in all places; how readily you might think with us: "Up, and to America!"

Ibid., p. 237.

44

Prague. The roster of persons who have lately left Prague forever and who will leave it soon in order to seek a new, more beautiful home in North America, would fill a whole page. There are entire families, representing all vocations*, in part in good circumstances, in part barely having passage-money; some might call them cowardly, others injudicious. Whoever exercises his understanding will completely justify them, whoever knows North America will praise them as judicious and fortunate. We well realize that your committee for assistance to Jewish emigrants cannot function now, but here, too, at Budapest, where they had started so magnificently, as good as nothing at all has been accomplished. Your discussion of the question, however, has not only stimulated many to emigrate, but has enabled many to obtain greater, more eager aid from friends, and in spite of the abortive attempts elsewhere, there has been organized here in Prague also a Committee for the Assistance of Indigent Emigrants. Perhaps, in spite of the unfavorable circumstances, they will succeed in their earnest will and universal desire, felt here more than elsewhere, finally to be *free* and *happy* over *there.* I shall report shortly to you on the emigration plan of Count *Colloredo.*

Ibid., p. 281.

* Among them are two compositors, one soap-maker, several goldsmiths, doctors of medicine, but to the best of our knowledge, not a single person *of ill-repute,* as the Radicals here alleged and then retracted.

45

Havre. Recently a ship, whose passengers were all Israelites, departed from here to California. They had with them a cantor, shohet, mohel and two *sefarim,* all that pertains to the Jewish worship (*Archives israélites de France*).

Allgemeine Zeitung des Judentums (1852) no. 34, p. 402.

46

Excerpt from the minutes of the West London Synagogue of British Jews. At a general meeting of the community held on the 3rd of Adar 5606 (March 1, 1846) there was placed under consideration the call promulgated by Dr. Frankel, chief rabbi in Dresden, requesting Israelite communities to unite for the assistance of their co-religionists who have to emigrate from Russian territory, in order to escape from the ruthless persecutions to which they are exposed in that empire. Concerning this the following resolutions were passed among others: (1) that a collection should forthwith be started in order to raise a fund for the assistance of Russian-Jewish emigrants through a committee; (2) that a Board be elected to take charge of the collection and to enter into communication by letter with the honorable Dr. Frankel, etc.

Zeitschrift für die religiösen Interessen des Judentums, vol. iii (1845) p. 139.

47

An Emigration Society for Israelites. The June issue of the *Archives israélites de France* contains an article . . . (which) discusses the misery of the Jews living in Rome . . . (and) suggests . . . emigration, which it wishes to be directed primarily to America. Yes, it goes even further. All Jews who live in any lands of pressure and persecution should emigrate... For this purpose a Universal Emigration Society should be formed among the Israelites of all lands and parts of the world . . . We recall that this was recommended to the Bavarian, Hessian and Mecklenburgian Jews, that it was recommended to the Polish and Russian Jews. They did not emigrate . . . In most lands the conditions have improved and are improving daily more and more. What would have come of it if the Bavarian, Hessian and Mecklenburgian, if the Polish and the Russian, if the Tuscan Jews and the Jews of Rome had emigrated? No, the destiny of our race seems to be a different one. It should collaborate with countries and nations, so that freedom of religion and humaneness may win, and so as to present the genuine touchstone thereof! . . . We recall that in 1843 some 100 Jews in Poland addressed to us a suppliant petition with their signatures, to assist them to migrate to America or Algeria, while pointing out that 10,000 of their fellow-countrymen are ready to follow, if even the slightest prospect should open to them. At that time we moved heaven and earth, but the undertaking foundered because of the enormity of the requisite resources, if the emigrants were not to perish in still greater misery than those left here at home.

... But France should lead for once. We Jews of Germany, we, who... except for a couple of large communities, are scattered in innumerable small communities that consequently require exceptionally large sacrifices, have in recent times founded jointly many general institutions which work for the benefit of Jewry as a whole; . . . so let France lead the way this time, and we Germans will follow. . . .

Allgemeine Zeitung des Judentums (1860) p. 415.

48

Canada. Recently more than 200 Polish Jews arrived in Quebec from Hamburg and want to settle as a group in the region of Ottawa . . .

Allgemeine Zeitung des Judentums (1863) p. 809.

49

Königsberg. — On July 15 the transport (the last for the present) of Russian Jews to America was sent off from Hamburg. The embarking was personally conducted by our local rabbi Dr. Bamberger, who just happened to be there, in conjunction with Messrs. P. Simon and M. I. Michael.

Die Deborah, vol. xvi, no. 11, Sept. 9, 1870.

50

Lithuania. The departures of poor Jewish families from Lithuania are continuing. Permission to emigrate abroad is granted without restriction, but this is less favored than the trend to Russia, into which people are crowding, in spite of the fact that a guarantee of 175 rubles in cash per head is required before the passport in question, which costs 5 rubles per family, is issued. It is easy to understand why there is no prevailing trend to go abroad, for the ordinary Jew in Lithuania feels rather keenly that he is unfit to achieve something in a more highly cultured land, and that it is at all events better for him here, where he still stands to a certain degree above the general level of culture. This conviction seems also to guide the committee in their efforts for the emigrants for, while they show themselves receptive to those who are going to Russia, they are little disposed to assist an emigrant going abroad.

Die Deborah, vol. xvi, no. 6, Aug. 5, 1870.

51

Bucharest, August 19. — Yesterday's issue of *Monitorul* published the record of the debates concerning the "Emigration of Jews from Rumania." The Secretary for Foreign Affairs reported to the Cabinet Council:

"Gentlemen of the Council! In a note of August 9 Mr. Peixotto, Consul-General of America, informed me that on account of the condition of Jews in the Orient, relative to their numerical strength as well as their political status, a number of citizens of the United States of America have set about to facilitate their emigration from those countries and that for the said purpose it has been suggested to organize an Emigration Society and to promote its object with the co-operation of philanthropists in Europe and of the government. Mr. Peixotto adds that he has been ordered to ask the Rumanian government whether it would favor this proposal insofar as it concerns the Israelites of Rumania, and whether it is possible to expect any help whatever from the legislative bodies.

While awaiting the session of the chambers in order to be able to lay the proposal in question before them, I am of the opinion that the government would comply with the desire expressed to it, in that, within the limits of its power, it should facilitate the emigration of the Israelites through the issuance of passports without charge.

If you agree with my opinion, please authorize me to have the necessary orders issued to the various prefectures.

L. Kostaforu.

The Council of Ministers then decreed at its meeting of August 9 . . . to issue passports gratis to the destitute Israelites, until the legislative bodies have met . . . "

Die Deborah, vol. xviii (1872) no. 15.

52

Rumania . . . In emigrating *en masse*, the Rumanian Jews will be able to be transported in whole shiploads, as they are nearly all artisans, and namely, as the *Rumanian Post* says, shoemakers, hatmakers, weavers, glaziers, painters, machinists, stonecutters, carpenters and joiners, so they will indeed need organizational co-operation — and by no means without resources, but largely rather in a position to bear part of the cost of their transportation.

Mr. Kostaforu's passports without charge evoke a smile among them and have become the target of jest in Europe . . .

Therefore, the wealthy Israelites of the country and the friends of mankind in Europe and America should raise the material means for emigration. As can be demonstrated, the desire of the working class of the local Jews to emigrate is sincere. Two thousand fathers of families have applied for it in Bucharest, Botoshani, Braila, Galati, Bacau, Berlad, and Craiova. We ourselves have seen the register of these people giving name, age, occupation, etc. Many among them wish to undertake the journey at their own expense, others apply for partial assistance only.

Ibid., no. 23.

53

Liverpool. A number of Israelite emigrants, mostly Poles, want to embark for America. The arrangements were so made that it was possible to arrive in New York a few days before Passover. But owing to embarkation difficulties that had arisen the departure was delayed, and the emigrants were sure they would not be able to land on American soil before Passover. Thereupon the National Steamship Company provided the Israelites with *matzot* and saw to it that the religious prescriptions of the Israelite immigrants might be completely observed on board ship.

The same company had instituted steamer communication between here, Stettin and New York in 1869, and its local representative, C. Messing, had taken steps for a corresponding number of Jewish emigrants to have a complete kosher kitchen and diet established on the ship, as was made public at the time in the *Hamagid* and other publications. The outbreak of the war brought the undertaking to naught.

Israelitische Wochenschrift, vol. v (1874) p. 154.

54

From South Germany. Private Communication. The dailies and weeklies are still teeming with advertisements, in which "complete sellouts below cost at ridiculously low prices" are announced, now with one and then with another embellishment of all sorts of imaginable pretexts or subterfuges, amongst which the seller's intended emigration to America occurs quite often . . . Departures this year are truly colossal. Every person who has kinsfolk or acquaintances in America who are fairly well-to-do, gets himself ready to go there without dilly-dallying.

Der Buergerfreund, Philadelphia, June 19, 1847, p. 61.

55

The stream of German as well as of Swiss emigrants goes through the following seaports, for each of which is given the number of emigrants who embarked during the years 1844 to 1847;

	1844	1845	1846	1847
Havre de Grace	16,600	23,500	32,381	39,474
Dunkirk		2,277	1,475	
Antwerp	2,961	5,223	13,130	14,613
Rotterdam and Amsterdam	2,403	4,549	2,506	9,757
London, Liverpool *ca*	2,000	3,500	6,425	10,000
Bremen	19,863	31,849	32,256	33,682
Hamburg	1,774	2,388	4,926	8,141
Stettin		114	329	74
Total	45,601	73,400	93,428	115,741

Berghaus, Heinrich, *Die Vereinigten Staaten von Nordamerika* (Gotha 1848) p. 31.

56

The residents of South Germany turn in most cases to Havre shipping firms, perhaps for the reason that once in Havre, they no longer have to make the disagreeable voyage across the Channel . . . For this reason alone, Hamburg and Bremen will now *never* become the only seaports for those voyaging to America.

Dr. Franz Joseph Ennemaser, *Eine Reise von Mittelrhein (Mainz) über Köln, Paris und Havre nach den nord-amerikanischen Freistaaten* . . . (Kaiserslautern 1859) p. 6.

57

For many Mainz is the next rendezvous, from which the trip should be continued farther. The contracts are here distributed by the chief agent and the money still due is paid to him.

Ibid., p. 10.

58

Of this time there will also be mentioned with commendation the conduct of the Prussian, and particularly the Berlin Jews toward the Salzburg emigrants, driven out of Austria on account of their religion, and the motive for their sympathy, which, in answer to an inquiry, they gave in the following words: "They are strangers, as we, and we are citizens like you." This gives proof, not only of a noble sentiment, but also of a clear conception of their status and their task as members of the state that has admitted them as citizens.

Jahrbuch des Nuetzlichen und Unterhaltenden fuer Israeliten (Breslau 1843) p. 18.

59

The position of the poor emigrants — men, women and children, Jews, French and Germans, stowed amidships — was at the best unpleasant. As long as the weather was fine, matters went on tolerably smoothly, and we had them chirping and singing enough; but a gale set them all at loggerheads, and rumors of fights and feuds not unfrequently came aft. Three Frenchmen (Jews and sharpers if they were not maligned) seemed to be just so many stumbling-blocks to the honest Germans, and even the quality in the great cabin took a spite against them. One of their number from his oracular and star-bleached countenance was dubbed Sidrophel, and it was whispered that they conjured up bad and adverse winds. The majority of the steerage passengers were Alsatians and Bavarians, and were speeding with their little all collected around them, to settle in a new land. They were most of them musically inclined, and when the level of the sun began to glance over the bows, they usually gathered into a knot around the main mast, and sang the songs of their native land, which they and theirs had quitted for ever. Many a pleasant hour did we thus spend, as our vessel was gently heaving beneath us, and pressing toward the setting sun.

Latrobe, Charles Joseph, *The Rambler in North America 1832-1833* (New York 1835) vol. i, p. 24.

60

Old Lutherans

They learned about us immediately and the Patriarch expressed himself one day: "I am greatly surprised that your fellow-Jews from Silesia do not leave for America in greater numbers. I can show it to you black on white that already in the year 1848 they were informed and everything has turned out pretty nearly as it reads here. Here, see for yourself!" He opened a book he had been reading before; it was a periodical, *Der Rosenberg-Creutzberger Telegraph* of 1848; and in No. 81 of Nov. 28, 1848, a long article closed with the words: "Ye fellow-Jews and companions in misfortune, get used to gaze into the distant West, and become conversant with the idea. In free America the sun of freedom is shining for us, too!"

Deutsch-Amerikanische Skizzen für jüdische Auswanderer und Nichtauswanderer (Leipzig 1857) p. 10.

61

German emigration. From Nahetal, April 24. The people of Israel is roaming about every street and speculating in buying and selling.

In one case a warning has been given of a swindler firm for the transportation of emigrants which bears the Jewish-sounding name of Strauss & Co.

Deutsche Schnellpost, New York, June 7, 1843.

62

As a warning to emigrants there is pilloried at present in almost all local papers the cheating and swindler firm Strauss & Co. of Antwerp, which shipped emigrants through its agent *Anvers* (*Landstrom Quai* no. 14 in Antwerp) to New York on the steamer Iron Age, which was so wretchedly short of provisions that 16 persons died during the voyage and 4 others after the landing as a result of starvation and privations.

Weber, Dr., *Die Deutschen in Amerika* (Leipzig 1868) p. 92.

63

I had to make similar arrangements for my fellow-travelers; this incensed a dozen German drivers against me. "Now this confounded Jew has to know English and take the morsel of bread out of our mouths," cried one of them threateningly, and the chorus joined in with all possible objurgations against the Jews. . . . Aha, thought I, you have left home and kindred in order to get away from the disgusting Judeophobia, and here the first German greeting that sounds in your ears is Hep! Hep!

Wise, Isaac Mayer, *Reminiscences* (Cincinnati 1901) p. 16.

64

New York . . . The *Archives Israélites* quotes an item from a newspaper: a reimbursement of from 10 to 20 dollars per person has been voluntarily granted by the owner of the boat *Mr. Charles H. Marshall* to the Russian Jews who had been so inhumanly treated during their voyage across. The procedure of the ship-owner is a silent confession of guilt. (Hence, what circumspection must be exercised before shipping!)

Allgemeine Zeitung des Judentums (1872) p. 974.

65

Direct regular service of mail-steamers between Stettin and New York, calling at Copenhagen and Christiansund, using the new iron first-class screw steamships: *Humbold,* Captain B. Branden, June 1871; *Franklin,* Captain P. Dreier, July 1871. Fare, from Stettin:

1st class . . . . \$72.00 }
Steerage . . . . \$40.00 } in gold

To Stettin: 1 state-room, $80.00; Steerage $25.00, in gold.
Further information given in New York!

German advertisement of the Baltic Lloyd, transliterated into Yiddish, in *Hebrew News,* Jacob Cohen, Proprietor and Publisher, vol. i, no. 13, New York, July 14, 1871, p. 12.

66

New York, Apr. 27. The *Hebrew Leader* writes:

Over 80 of our co-religionists arrived among the passengers of the steamships *Baltic* and *City of Berlin* which came on the 20th and 27th inst. The head-clerk in Castle Garden informs us that of late a considerable number of *Israelites* have arrived in the United States with each steamer and from every country.

Allgemeine Zeitung des Judentums (1877) p. 349.

67

Thus they journey from one saloon to another until the greenhorn is already in need of his friends' support to set him on his feet; and they, too, are grateful enough not to leave him lying. They know well why. In the Bowery they pass by a jewelry store: Moses is standing at the door, and is examining some precious stones. "Sir," says the chap, "here we can do some business. I myself am a good hand at jewelry, these damned Jews buy the stuff cheaply and are delighted if they can get rid of it again at a small profit." "So? Then we better go inside," replies the greenhorn, whose tongue is getting to be somewhat heavy. "What is the price of this pin?" "Thirty dollars, sir!" "You're crazy, I'll be damned if I give you more than half that much." "Not a cent less, gentleman, a diamond of the first water." Here the chap turns to the greenhorn and whispers into his ear: "Don't excite the Jew, offer him 25 dollars, he will let you have it, and the thing is worth 50 dollars between brothers!"

"All right then, five dollars more!" The Jew smiles. "Five dollars still more, or don't annoy me." At a sign from the chap, the Jew hesitantly gives in and the sale is closed. Thereupon the greenhorn opens his pocketbook, in which there is unfortunately nothing but Illinois banknotes. The Jew won't accept them and the buyer is just about ready to start another dispute when the man in the blue coat pushes in between them, saying: "Hand me that 50-dollar bill. I'll give you good bills for it and still ask only 2 percent discount. Here are the 25 dollars for the pin, and 24 dollars for you, with the 2 percent discount make it 50 dollars." The greenhorn gets the pin, and with a "damn those Jews" lets himself be dragged out of the store.

(The next day)

Further, it turns out that the banknotes he had received are all counterfeit, that the pin is hardly worth 50 cents. In indignation he runs to see the

Jew, but the latter cooly denies ever having seen him, and threatens to call the police if he does not clear out immediately . . .

Teckla, Georg, *Drei Jahre in New York* (Zwickau 1862) p. 61, 64.

68

If you want to get them cheaper, you have to go to Chatham Street, but first examine the thing scrupulously before you agree to the transaction, as the clothing stores there are in Jewish hands exclusively, and it happens not infrequently that the coat-tail comes off the coat at the first brushing. I don't have to warn against certain stores, as you will not go in there anyhow, if you hear the screaming voice of the dirty auctioneer who stands on a tall stool in front of the store, holds a coat in one hand, in the other a bamboo-cane with which he beats the dirty piece of apparel and yells all the time as loudly as possible: "Who will give me, who will give me three dollars, as a first bid, it is worth ten dollars—three dollars, once, twice, three times." Hereupon he gives the coat a mighty blow with the cane and hangs it back within, only to begin right away with another item. This reminds one of the barkers in front of menageries and panoramas. But still the noise attracts some onlookers, and some sad dog from the country or sailor who would gladly once again exchange his tarred jacket for a blue coat, allows himself to be enticed, to pay the price asked for a worn-out article of clothing. Some of our German manufacturers formerly held the view that where labor was so high, good business could be done with ready-made clothing. But to speak of the last ten years, this view was erroneous. For in the first place, the duty on ready-made clothing is enormously high, then again, in the wholesale manufacture of cheaper and chiefly more practical things, more suitable to the country, the Americans have advanced further than any other industrial nation. The Berlin clothing-factories are nothing in comparison with those immense plants in New York, which can clothe the entire West and South from head to foot and, moreover, actually have traveling salesmen in every state. As for the fact that labor is higher, machines make up for that, and down there at the corner you will immediately observe a store from which thousands of working tools, namely sewing machines, come out annually.

Ibid., p. 72.

69

The wealthy younger generation set the first new immigrants in a position to begin independent business and to assist the later arrivals with their own credit. The name "German Jew" was soon in good repute among the American importers, manufacturers and wholesale merchants, — credit and profit multiplied fast, and in a few years those who had immigrated as poor manual laborers, stood out as respected and well-to-do merchants in the new fatherland . . .

Benjamin, J. J., *Drei Jahre in Amerika* . . . (Hanover 1862) vol. i, p. 46.

70

From the circumstances of a discourse being delivered in German, it will be inferred that most of the congregation who intend worshipping in Attorney Street are Germans; such is the fact — the emigration of Israelites to this country is great — the severe oppression which they are yet subject to in Poland, Bavaria and other parts of Germany, drives them to this land of religious freedom, where every man may worship his Maker . . . and if they do not bring money with them, they bring substantial wealth in their habits of industry and temperance.

Mechanics and artisans, in almost every branch, may now be found among the Jews of this city. It is estimated that the entire number of Israelites at present in New York cannot be short of ten thousand.

The Occident (1843) p. 56.

71

Many Jews have gone from Bohemia to America in recent times. It speaks volumes for these emigrants, who in great part are people of education, that over there they devote themselves to handicraft and agriculture but not at all to commerce, which here has become their aversion and not a habit. People who here become bookkeepers and counting-house clerks are now plough-boys there, and I have seen letters from them which are still full of joy and contentment. One even emigrated with his bride.

Allgemeine Zeitung des Judentums (1845) p. 628.

72

Anyone who buys himself a diamond and knows how to cut with it is a glazier, then he roams about with the glass in a frame-box (under his arm or on his back) and is called into houses; of late the Jews have taken to it, as it is a good opportunity to do business.

Albert Glass, *Das Leben in den Vereinigten Staaten* (Leipzig 1864) vol. ii, p. 565.

73

During this year very many of these gentlemen (functionaries of communities from Germany) have come over here, who could not obtain any position and had to grasp at other trades, such as peddling or handicraft . . . Thus one of these gentlemen had to open a shoemaker's shop; another is learning cigar-making, a third bookbinding; others became clerks in offices, etc.

Positions that become vacant, become so only owing to the fact that the Jewish congregations soon get tired of their cantors, are looking for a change and discharge them after the first year of their appointment. So that the cantors and teachers in Germany may pay earnest heed to the fact that here all positions are given as a rule for one year only and the appointee must submit to a new election each year. As it is so easy to acquire enemies the positions are extremely precarious. Of permanent appointments they know nothing. So it happened with the Cantor Putzel in Easton. He was inducted in Easton, Pennsylvania, two years ago, enjoyed general approval, married, and now with a wife and child, has been discharged from his position and must open a dry-goods business. He is a very decent, fine and accomplished man and nevertheless could not get along with the congregation.

Accordingly, I entreat the cantors and teachers to give heed to the contents of these lines in order that, on the one hand, they might not be quick with their decisions to emigrate, and on the other hand, if they read of a position in America sent out as an advertisement, they might well bethink themselves that they have to exchange a permanent position in their fatherland for a precarious, annual appointment here. It is extremely painful to me to hear accomplished men complain in my house that they have nothing more left but to take the pack onto the back.

DR. (MAX) LILIENTHAL.

Allgemeine Zeitung des Judentums (1848) p. 495.

74

Prosperity is growing day by day; those who had immigrated as beggars are rich after 6-10 years; and the name German Jew has become here a name of honor and a guarantee of integrity and honesty. The congregation in Baltimore, which consists mostly of Germans, and particularly of Bavarians, dedicated a new, magnificent synagogue on October 26.

Wiener Jahrbuch fuer Israeliten, vol. v (1846) p. 52-53.

75

The clothing, shoe, dry goods, and liquor, together with jewelry and rarely the grocery trade, are nearly everywhere their sole pursuit; only a few are actually engaged in shoemaking, tailoring, watchmaking, cabinet-work, upholstery, and similar branches and still wherever they seriously apply themselves for labor, they meet with average success. We do not mean, however, to assert that the above-enumerated are the only means of support of the Jews in America; for we know well enough that we have lawyers, medical doctors, bankers, some politicians and place-men, a few teachers, authors and ministers, some shipping-merchants and auctioneers, and a very few farmers, and here and there a butcher, a baker, a distiller, a brewer, a tavern-keeper, a manufacturer, a miner, a billiard-table-maker, an apothecary, a smith, a produce and cattle-dealer, a painter and glazier, and perhaps other craftsmen. But in the main we may assert that commerce is the chief means of support for Israelites, all over the country.

The Occident, vol. xv (1857-58) p. 277.

76

A Warning

Recently very many young people have been coming over again who have aspirations for positions as teachers, cantors, bookkeepers, counting-house clerks, etc., and whose education, indeed, fully entitles them thereto; but they are not familiar with the English language, and on that account they remain quite alien and without prospects here. In such cases they naturally grasp at the first best occupation, for which they have neither inclination nor aptitude. Thus it is not rare here to find a teacher as a farm-hand, a cantor as a peddler, a bookkeeper as a day-laborer, etc. The worst of it all is that if these people do not possess considerable energy they become countrified and soured before they recover from this condition. Here and everywhere one has an opportunity to see hundreds of such young, qualified men go to wrack and ruin spiritually and bodily under the burden of the peddler or by unwanted hard work, this despite the great achievement of charitable societies. But this can be helped only through this, that no educated man should let it get into his head to come to the United States without having acquired an accurate knowledge of the English language. Everyone who has friends and relatives in Europe ought to send this journal over there and try to have it circulated through European organs of the press. Every educated man, ignorant of the English language, is out of luck in America, unless he happens to have friends here to give him strong support.

It is quite unthinkable that a man should feel at ease in a land whose customs and language are strange to him. The only exception to this rule is in the case of persons who come here out of pure love of freedom and are naturally received with open arms and find their heart's yearnings satisfied. But those whom material necessity as well brings here are miserable unless they are either accustomed to physical labor or are masters of the English language. Particularly all the Jewish parents of Germany, Poland, Hungary and Italy should be made to understand this, that their children should first learn English before they study any foreign language whatever. Thereby they open to them an opportunity to migrate to the United States and to adjust themselves easily. The excess of population on the one hand and the political disturbances which continue to recur often, on the other hand, will always be favorable to emigration. Jew-baiting and racial riots are not yet over in Europe. Here they are over and freedom is assured to every upright man; those bowed down will, therefore, flee hither for a long time to come. For this reason the English language should be pursued as a study before all other languages in Europe. Moreover, the commerce between us and Germany is growing from year to year, and with commerce grows the intercourse and the necessity to understand English.

Everyone ought to take pains to transmit this warning and to spread it among his fellow-countrymen.

Die Deborah, vol. xii (1866-67) p. 102.

77

Their motto ran: To make money, etc. Those Israelites, mostly young people, who had left their homeland thirty and more years ago in order to seek their fortune in America gave proof of such a degree of courage and endurance as can hardly be conceived by the present generation. They had to tear themselves from their parents and friends perhaps never to see them again, to steal away from the fatherland which had a claim on them for military service, to undergo a wearisome, burdensome sea-voyage, and then to reach a land whose language, customs and habits they did not know. They underwent these hardships, because their homeland held only exceptional laws and disabilities for them and America was the only land where they could move freely. Arriving here, they found many a disappointment. They stood more isolated than they expected, and the struggle for existence was troublesome. Their motto was then first of all (to use an American expression) "to make a living."

After they had successfully fought for this and won and become accustomed to work, there awakened also in them the desire "to make money," all the more so since America offered manifold opportunities for that. The sudden shift from social and spiritual bondage to the most unrestricted freedom, made them sidetrack the demands of religion in the struggle for the most indispensable needs of life, in order to bestow upon it its full rights once again, if they should be in a better position to observe all religious duties. But with many, very many, habit gained the upper hand, and they deferred ever farther the day to make good their promise . . .

Israelitische Wochenschrift, vol. v (1874) p. 403.

78

The first German Israelite family came to Cincinnati in 1817 and met with so hospitable a reception, that it wrote to its co-religionists in Germany letters which were full of praise and in which it was declared that the Lord of Heavenly Hosts had prepared for its people scattered throughout the world a land of freedom and happiness in the far-off West of America. These letters powerfully stimulated the Jews of Germany to migrate to our states and as early as 1822 the followers of the Mosaic doctrine had gathered here in such numbers that they could found a Jewish congregation which held its divine services in a wooden edifice on Main Street, between 3rd and 4th Streets. This was the first synagogue in the entire West.

Tenner, Armin, *Cincinnati sonst und jetzt* (Cincinnati 1878) p. 47.

79

The success of this institution was not, however, commensurate with the expectations of its founders, and it continued in a languishing condition until the year 1819, when a new and powerful impulse was given to the sympathies of the friends of Israel in this city in consequence of the receipt of intelligence from Germany, announcing the desire of a number of Christian Jews to emigrate to the United States for the purpose of forming a Christian Jewish settlement. The expediency of such a settlement was also urgently advocated in a letter addressed by an intelligent German Jew to the Rev. I.S.C.F. Frey, who had then recently arrived in this country, and by whom these communications were laid before the public.

Until the year 1827, when a farm of five hundred acres was purchased at New Paltz, Ulster County, in this state, and prepared for the reception of converted Jewish emigrants from Europe. Several of these had in the interval arrived in this country, and been provided for in various temporary places of reception.

By this time the farm at New Paltz had become useless for the purpose for which it was originally purchased. The few remaining proselytes under the care of the society were induced to leave the establishment, and no others were found to apply for admission . . . In the year 1835 the New Paltz farm was disposed of at auction.

From a Report of the American Society for Meliorating the Condition of the Jews, and its Organ, The Jewish Chronicle.

The Occident (1843-44) p. 43-47.

80

Jacob Seasongood . . . (Süssengut) . . . July 21, 1837 in New York . . . while working by day and traveling at night by boat on the Erie Canal he arrived, in September 1837, at Chillicothe, Ohio, which at that time was the Western meeting-place of German peddlers . . . applied himself heart and soul to clothing-manufacture in which many poor and suffering families could be given employment . . . He was the first president in the Reform movement initiated by Rabbi Dr. Lilienthal . . .

Der deutsche Pionier, vol. xvi, Cincinnati, 1884-85, p. 518.

81

Marcus Fechheimer. Born July 13, 1818 at Mitwitz, in Bavaria, Marcus Fechheimer, who felt too cramped in the parental house where he was the oldest of fourteen children, came as an eighteen-year old lad in the spring of 1837 to New York; here he immediately got on his own feet by starting in his very successful career as a peddler. With a basket on his arm, the young Marcus now wandered for several years through the states of New York, Pennsylvania and Ohio; during this time (December 1839) he took up residence in Cincinnati and then, after having saved up a small sum of money, removed to the state of Alabama (whither many Germans went at that time) to try his fortune there. In a tiny town near Mobile he started a small clothing business which was very lucrative. He was, nevertheless, drawn back again to Cincinnati where several of his brothers were likewise engaged in the clothing and drygoods business.

. . . But it began to thrive especially during the war.

. . . Kehillah Kedausha Bnai Jeshurun, of which he was president for many years . . . Member of the Board of Directors of the German National Bank of Cincinnati . . .

Ibid., vol. xiii (1881-82) p. 501.

82

Itinerant Merchants

In the United States, where the farmers and planters do not live together in villages and small market-towns, as in Europe, but isolated on their own land and surrounded by it, commerce and intercourse between the various estates isolated and frequently miles away from each other, even if not hindered, is still made very difficult, and permanently established stores could contribute only to the needs and comfort of those whose settlement happened to be in the vicinity of the stores.

But since the farmer, whom his pressing labors tie him down to it, does not readily leave his land in order to purchase a small unessential article which he possibly can do without and rather gets along frequently for many days without such articles, but would actually procure them if he had them near at hand, — the merchants have found it necessary to seek him out themselves (instead of waiting for his visit), and have now criss-crossed the country either in person with their bundles of wares, or have sent out their men, while supervising the store at home themselves. This occupation was found especially to their taste by the Germans, principally by the Jews among them (for of all the itinerant *German* merchants in all America, hardly one percent are Christians) and, starting from New York and New Orleans, later from Cincinnati, they have criss-crossed every nook of the Union, with untiring perseverance.

Commerce is the vital principle of the Jews, of this America presents an incontestable proof; over there no pale is set for them within which they can move about; there they are not tied down by prejudices or laws to any occupations, to any trade, they stand on the same level with the rest of the population. But whatever they may have been engaged in in the fatherland, whatever the handicraft, whatever the profession, it is all the same: in America, where they may choose, they grasp at commerce, and with few exceptions become merchants, or, if that does not go — storekeepers and house-salesmen, "peddlers" as they are called there. Nevertheless, as has already been said, a small part of these peddlers are Christians; yet there are so few of them and they are so lost in the multitude that they hardly deserve to be mentioned, and only the genuine Yankees (the inhabitants of the northeastern states of the Union) notably compete with them, and, even in comparison with the Jews, actually occupy the first rank in this branch of business as well. But we are concerned here first of all with the Germans. Upon their arrival at one of the seaports, the cash of the itinerant merchants, at least of the poorer class, usually still consists of a few dollars with which, without any further loss of time, they do not delay to "start a business." Before all things else a narrow basket (to be slung over his neck) is acquired, into it a small stock of some ribbon and thread, a few combs and toothbrushes, suspenders and toothpicks, wonderfully sparkling shirt-buttons and needles and pins and other things of this sort, — and they are on the way to making their fortune.

The merchant starting out does not as yet understand a syllable of the language of the land, which he has now made his home, "yes" and "no" with a couple of other useful words like "very cheap" and "very good" excepted; but with an amiable boldness he seeks out preferably American homes (for the Germans themselves are bad customers) and, with the help of such barbarous words and fearful gesticulations, engages them in conversation, so that, if they don't throw him out of the door on first sight as he enters without ceremony, the people are quite usually inclined to buy some trifle, which they would naturally never in their life be able to use, — merely in order to enjoy for a short while the play of mien and mimicry, as well as the extraordinary entertainment of the "young American."

But this lasts only a few months; in an almost incredibly short time the peddler learns the country's language, at least enough to express himself intelligibly, and now his actual life begins.

Like a butterfly from a cocoon he crawls out, equipped with his huge pack and an efficient wanderer's staff, from the streets of the crowded city and flutters, if it is at all possible to flutter with a sixty-pound bale of goods on one's shoulders, out into the faraway to deliver to the distant farmers those glorious articles, which he either had bought for cash at auctions or obtained on credit from his business acquaintances.

To be sure he must pay a stated tax, the so-called "license", in the state where he does business, but beyond that he is not bound in any way and can offer for sale at any time and anywhere whatever he pleases; for this very reason they have spread out over all the eastern, southern and central states, and left chiefly to the Americans only those lying far west, and apparently they do not find at all to their liking the sight of wild beasts which continuously roam around, even if stragglingly.

Naturally the peddler picks out invariably that stretch of the country in which the majority of settlements are situated and which is still the least infested by his colleagues; thereupon he goes from one farm to another and asks whether the inhabitants are in need of his wares. Usually the answer is "No!" But as the husband is rarely at home and the women would invariably fain see what precious trinkets the seller does really carry hidden in that large, heavy pack, he easily obtains permission to open his pack and spread out his wares. Even if, after all, he does not obtain that permission, the matter remains basically the same, for he does open it withal, and he also shows off his things one after another before he leaves, — regardless of whether he sees friendly or surly onlookers around him.

But the spreading out of the wares in a lonely cabin situated far away from the cities has a double advantage; in the first place the cabin's dwellers see before their eyes many things that they could make good use of, which, indeed they might be quite in need of, and are thereby reminded of many little articles, of which they might otherwise forget, and furthermore the merchandise itself gains, too, quite a different look, when put on display in the unattractive low hut, on the rough wooden table, amid all the homely surroundings. How fascinatingly do the horn-combs painted like tortoise-shell, sparkle when held by the sly merchant against the dark head of hair of the blushing girl standing near him; how fairylike and bewitching glisten the very huge breastpins and ear-pendants on the immaculately brushed cushion of Manchester velvet and the gold rings with diamonds and rubies ranged in lines on the black roll like pretzels in the window of a bakery; what hardly surmised splendor is not revealed in the just-unpacked piece of calico, whose marvelous design with lightning-like zig-zags and countless moons and stars draw a loud "Ah!" even from the elderly farm-woman; and then at last the towels and ribbons, the mother-of-pearl buttons and hairpins with the small colored pearl glass-globes mounted on top, and the hairbows and bracelets, the chains and the fire-flashing earrings, all this must be seen in such a log-cabin surrounded by woods, in order to produce the full effect, desirable and favorable at least for the salesman.

Usually the peddler lets his merchandise out of his hands only for cash; but if he knows his people or sees from the entire surroundings that he has not much to fear, he lets it go on credit, at least in part, which affords him at the same time an excuse for a second call. It is different with the "jewelry peddlers," or those who carry only golden ornaments, certain pocket-watches and silver spoons. These never sell on credit, because they never visit one and the same place twice, for very sensible reasons: they do not place full trust in the customer's peace and they are rarely inclined to come again before the eyes of the man to whom they had sold some of their merchandise before.

The greatest fraud in this respect is practised with argental spoons, which are known in the United States under the name of German silver, and there, especially in Ohio, a dozen tablespoons are sold to the credulous farmers at eighteen and twenty dollars, under the pretext that *German* silver is merely another kind but otherwise just as good. Had the law really wanted to interfere it would not be able to prosecute, since the merchandise had been sold under the proper name of *German silver,* even if at an exhorbitant price. But the country people themselves who, as time went by, became wise even if only through loss, surely swore thereafter dire punishment to the peddler the moment he again came within their sight. But the latter was by that time at it again in another state, either farther West or South—who could tell where he had gone? It required but a few years for the poor pack-peddler to get himself a horse or even a small wagon, on which he now carried his merchandise in greater and better variety through the coutnry.

Louisiana particularly is swarming with these people, and there it happens that several of them chip in and jointly purchase a horse in order to transport their merchandise-packs; but the poor beast is then apparently to be pitied, since first, it must drag an excessive load, and usually, also, by turns, one of the hopeful young mercuries, and then it happens not infrequently that such a tormented creature collapses and can go no further.

In Louisiana the peddler's chief profit comes from trafficking with the negroes and especially the negresses, who, being unable to leave the plantations depend solely and wholly on these itinerant merchants for everything they use.

Friedrich, W. C., *Gerstacker's Gesammelte Schriften* (Jena 1872-74) vol. x, p. 196.

83

I continued my peddling until January 1835, when one evening, in deep snow and quite frozen I came to Easton, a pretty little town in Delaware, and entered an inn. A number of guests sat around the glowing stoves; and as they saw me enter, a pale and snow-covered merchant, a feeling of compassion must have come over them, for nearly every one bought something of me; and thus even in the evening, I did some good business, after I had run about the whole day in terrible winter weather, earning scarcely enough for a drink.

While preoccupied with my business, I was watched by an oldish-looking, occasionally smiling, but apparently unconcerned man behind the stove. He allowed me to finish the business in peace but then he got up, tapped me on the shoulder and bade me follow him. Out of doors his first question was whether I had a trade-license for peddling? I still felt so strange in America, and he spoke in so low a voice that I did not understand him and, therefore, looked at him in astonishment. My long, ten-days-old beard struck him, and he asked me further whether I was a Jew. He did not want to believe me when I denied it. Fortunately, I had with me the passport of my homeland, which I presented to him. Now he grew somewhat better disposed, looked at me sympathetically and said: "Since I see that you are an honest Protestant Christian I shall let you go, although I am losing twenty-five dollars through it. I have no kind feelings for the Jews, and were you one of them, I would not treat you so gently. If I wanted to arrest you, you would have to pay 50 dollars fine or, until you were able to raise it, you would have to go to jail, and half the fine would be mine. Still I shall forego that; but you better give up your trade and look for another one. Sooner or later you will be caught and then you'll be out of luck."

After having said this he shook my hand and went away . . .

When I stepped again into the room, the friendly innkeeper was able to observe my embarrassment and guess what had taken place. He praised the humane constable, laughed at his Jew-hatred, but he, too, advised me to quit my trade.

Streckfuss, G. F., *Der Auswanderer nach Amerika* (Zeitz 1836) p. 23.

84

Boston, Nov. 15 (Private communication) . . . There are men here also who would exploit the Jew-hatred which echoes so abundantly here from Europe. There are starving journalists, who cannot get a job. The drawback is indeed the enormously increased and ever-swelling immigration from Europe. There is on the one hand, a large number of such Europeans who, for lack of profitable activity, turn their eyes toward the tranquility of their industrious neighbors and do not shrink from attempts to sow the seeds of suspicion of natives among the multitude. On the other hand, there come over also many Jewish individuals who are not in the least familiar with the spirit of American life and qualified for it, a circumstance to be deplored but which cannot be of the least consequence as soon as one weighs the enormous number of Christians who immigrate and know and comprehend just as little about what they find here and what they are here to do . . . Recently several journals have busied themselves extensively with the Jews, that is with those who have immigrated and are immigrating. One newspaper, the *Volksfreund,* published in Lancaster, in the state of Ohio, is seeking to stir up the most hateful things. It charges that Jews do not engage in working in the fields, that when they come to America, they peddle or pose as scholars, preachers and poets (!); that they had had an inclination towards perpetrating fraud on the Christians, that marriages between Jews and Christians are not tolerated (!), that they cannot become good Republicans, and that they should be dispatched to Palestine (!), for which a society should be formed . . . Another newspaper, *Die alte und die neue Welt,* attacked these calumnies of the democratic *Volksfreund.*

The number of Jews in the United States has always been estimated at 15,000 souls. But this is surely not accurate, since the increase from abroad is very considerable. Very many live scattered over the wide expanse of our territory, and not a few of the German Jews deny that they are such, except when they are in need. There is no use at all to think of organization, nor even of any among the communities . . .

Here in this country, when they meet with Jews, many Christians love to talk about Old Testament matters . . .

Allgemeine Zeitung des Judentums, January 9, 1841, p. 14.

85

Many may perhaps be assisted as hitherto, by making up for them a small pack of any sort of valuable goods and sending them into the country to try their luck at peddling among the farmers, and in the small towns; and of these, we acknowledge, up to the present time many have done well and become at length merchants of higher pretensions. Nevertheless this system must come to an end; it is nearly overdone now; besides which, it is illegal in several states; for even could a license for peddling be secured, it will be at such a high rate, and clogged with so many restrictions, as either to be unattainable by the poor, or worthless for all practical purposes if they would strictly comply with the terms of law, often arbitrary and vexatious in the restrictions they contain. The very nature, moreover, of seeking a livelihood by means of small trading of this sort, has a debasing influence on the mind.

The Occident, vol. xv (1857-58) p. 297.

86

A Peddler Murdered

The *Deutsche Zeitung* of Baton Rouge, Louisiana reports:

"*Three negroes lynched.* Last week we reported that a German peddler had been murdered and robbed by some negroes at the ferry dock in West Baton Rouge. The slain man was a Jew and was given a decent burial by the Jewish Charity Organization in Baton Rouge. The culprits were unable to enjoy their booty for long; already the next morning four negroes were seized on suspicion; after a brief examination one of them was set at liberty; but the other three, still in possession of their booty, were hanged on the nearest tree without loss of time, by the outraged citizens. Such a procedure, to be sure, goes far beyond the limits of the law; but if one ponders that convicted murderers get off with one day in the penitentiary, a bit of lynch procedure like this is always to be preferred in the interest of personal security."

To this we add that the murdered man's name was Jacob Kriss and that he was supposed to have emigrated from Germany to New Orleans three months ago. Through the efforts of Mr. A. Kowalski it was possible to give the murdered man a decent burial in the local Jewish cemetery, but no further particulars about the unfortunate man could be learned. Mr. Kowalski is the elder of the local Jewish congregation and was very active in the matter; but in the execution of the negroes neither he nor any other Jew took part.

Die Deborah, vol. xx (1873) No. 21.

87

Eleven times out of ten the peddler is a Jew.

But after all the peddler is not a beggar but a house-to-house merchant, who runs about with his store on his back in order to dispose of it for good money. He has arrived today directly from Bremen or Havre, the honest Samuel or Aaron or Moses. During the long journey he was parsimonious; not only did he lose nothing, nay, he even made a little profit on the boat with his Palatinate cigars at 6 florins a thousand, which he sold at 3 cents, *i.e.* 9 kreuzer a piece, to his fellow-passengers on the ship who had run out of tobacco. Now here he is in glorious New York, in the Promised Land. What now? Honest Samuel knows perfectly.

From his boarding-house he goes forthwith to a co-religionist. He does not have far to go for "there are quite a lot" of his co-religionists in New York. The co-religionist is "well-off, that he has a nice store and in it a wife with a full, open neck and a graceful little niece, the sweet little Rebeksche with gazelle-eyes and delicate fingers which are so flexible that they nearly always produce 4 out of 3 yards;—and in addition, there is in the store a multitude of other things, such as neckties, underbodices, suspenders, ribbons, gloves, pocket-handkerchiefs, socks—a whole wardrobe.

"Regards from Aetti in Wankheim." "Ah, Sam! Sam! As I live! Sam Ferkelche from Wankheim in person." . . .

Well, well, what jollification there is! Sam was still pretty small when his uncle "Gut-ab"* left home; but the features cannot be disavowed. Sam takes after the family. Well, it is a great joy. Sam sits down.

"Well, what can we do for you, Sam?" says "Gut-ab." And so one word leads to another. Sam learns from "Gut-ab" how the latter had started and he puts it into his pipe and smokes it, and after two hours goes off to his lodging with a large bundle under his arm, and in the bundle there are drawers, undervests, socks, neckties, collars, suspenders, gloves and a multitude of other things, all necessary in life, indispensable for daily needs. Uncle "Gut-ab" did not give it to him as a present, but he has done something over and above that; he solemnly swore that he was not making a kreuzer profit on his relative; and, therefore, he was giving it to him at "cost price," *i.e.* he didn't add on 50 but only 25 percent. "One must after all do something for a brother's own son," he said to his "ma" as they were going to bed that night to sleep the sleep of the righteous.

The next morning Sam is up early on his feet. He rents himself an obscure little garret room for two dollars a month. He purchases a peddler's chest, in order to arrange his merchandise neatly therein and off he goes! He goes from house to house, up the stairs, down the stairs; the merchandise is offered cheaply! From one saloon he runs to another, from one street to another — the merchandise is offered cheaply!

At first things are hard. Here he is turned away, and there he is chased out. But Sam lets nothing discourage him. If he has disposed of nothing in ten places, in the eleventh a sixpense bobs up after all! To be sure it causes many a drop of perspiration, as it is quite hot in New York in the summer; to be sure the feet get wet through and through, for in winter it is devilish getting through the mud of the streets; to be sure, it often means: "You Jewish swindler, get thee gone!"; to be sure, many a door is slammed in his face so that his coat-tail is almost left sticking in it; to be sure, on occasion, he has to depend on the speed of his legs, when it means: "Get him, Sultan; sick him, he is of the brood of Moses!"; but all

* "Gut-ab" meant in New York German, to be affluent.—R. G.

this does not matter. In the evening when he comes to his little garret-room, he counts up his money and he sees that after all he had made a couple of shillings. "Let yourself be banged, let yourself be buffeted," his old father, Issachar of the tribe of Levi, had told him. "As nobody examines you to see how many pokes in the ribs and raps on the nose and dog-kicks you got, once you have become a rich man," he said.

Sam goes on so for a week, perhaps even a fortnight. His food is dry bread, his drink is water. In two weeks he has spent no more than his Christian fellow-immigrant in the first 24 hours.

And he has also learned something. He has learned which days are the best for making sales and which streets are the most favorable; he has learned to speak with people and understand already "Yes" and "No" and above all "How much?" He has found out where the wholesale commercial houses are located from which Uncle "Gut-ab" himself buys, and—Monsieur "Gut-ab" no longer makes 25 percent on it, in spite of "Ma" and "Rebeksche."

After three months Sam is an altogether different person. He is well off himself, at least for a peddler, and therefore, in addition to his dry bread, allows himself now and then a small piece of cheese, that is American, at nine kreuzer (3 cents) a pound. His ready cash allows him to make a larger purchase and he makes up his mind to go into "the country." The country is big and there are still places through which railroads do not run, and where the people are so good-natured or so simple that they still allow themselves to be duped a bit. Sam finds these places and the farmers are happy to see the peddler, for then they need not make the long journey to the city. But Sam is still happier, since he sells at 200 percent profit and gets a night's lodging and evening meal free.

His business is no longer in drawers and handkerchiefs and socks and suspenders and needles; he needs also buttons and needles and thread and yarn and lace and braids, and sponges and combs and steel-penpoints and pencils, and thimbles and silk ribbon; he needs everything and he has everything. Sam knows how to help himself.

Most preferably Sam goes to the New England States, Connecticut, Massachusetts, Rhode Island and whatever their names are. Here there are few or altogether no Germans and Sam no longer likes to deal with Germans, since the "how much'ing," *i.e.* dealing with Americans has become ever clearer to him. Sam's greatest affliction are the dogs on the farms and it is peculiar, but there is on American soil no dog that does not bite and bark, whenever a Jewish peddler comes. Sam would therefore rather *not* be taken for a Jew, and he forbids his German countrymen to greet him as such. To the American farmer he poses as a Canadian Frenchman and the American acts as if he believed it. Only the accursed dogs do not believe it; it is not the odor of a Canadian Frenchman!

Sam travels only by day. "Night is no man's friend," says Sam, "and for heroic valor there are the soldiers!" After two years Sam no longer travels on foot. He does not particularly love exertion and a little wagon and horses are frequently obtainable cheaply. And in a fortnight the little wagon and horse have paid for themselves, as Sam now carries also cigars and goldware from Paris. God knows that this tobacco was not grown in Havana, but in the Palatinate, and Sam knows it, too, but the farmers and their farmhands don't know it. God knows that Sam's Parisian goldware, his watch chains, his brooches, his lockets, his watches, his earrings, have never seen Paris, but come from the famous city of Providence, where nothing but Gmund gold is wrought, with no more than six carats and no less than 4 carats. God knows it, and Sam knows it, too, but the farmers' wives don't know it and the young fellows who are glad to leave "mementoes" to the girls, do not know it either. This ignorance brings in a lot of money to the peddler and one sees from this that ignorance, too, is good for something. Thus it goes on for several years, but not for longer; for the peddler's business has one great unpleasantness. Sam dare not show himself twice in the same place. Such Parisian gold turns gray and smudgy all too soon, and not everybody want to puff at his cigars, let alone suffer their odor. Sam is afraid of the cudgels; he knows their taste. Therefore Sam makes a quick decision. He gives up peddling, returns to New York after he has made a few hundred dollars, settles down and marries Rebeksche.

Sam is now a made man. He speaks nothing but English, because he has completely unlearned German. His sign does not read "Sam Ferkelche," God forbid; it says "Simmy Fairchild." Sam has become Americanized.

Griesinger, Theodor, *Lebende Bilder aus Amerika* (Stuttgart 1858) p. 20-25.

88

Portuguese and German Jew

Time which brings with it many changes in the condition of men, increased the nominal force of the German Jews and rapidly advanced them in education and enterprise, while the intermarriages of Portuguese with Portuguese, gradually diminished their number, and as at the present day it is generally admitted that the talent of Germany is with the Jew — certainly it must be conceded that there has been within the last century more enterprise, energy, and resolution, more ambition and more decision of character displayed by the German Jews than among the Portgusese, although we are bound to admit that the Portuguese Jews have ever been orthodox and strict in the observance of their religion . . . So fierce and vindictive were the prejudices entertained by the Portuguese toward the German Jews, that they mourned a son or daughter as dead, who intermarried with them.

The Asmonean, vol. iii (1850) p. 109.

89

Philadelphia, May 25. Representatives of all the local Israelite congregations were invited to the dedication (that took place yesterday) of the so-called Portuguese congregation with the exception of the Reform Congregation Kneseth-Israel. This is not at all due to religious fanaticism; for the Portuguese supply their quota of Sabbath-breakers and *trefa-eaters* just as well as do the full-blooded reformers. Nor is national antipathy to be considered the basis of this *Kherem,* since hardly a drop of Portuguese blood is to be found among these people. This is a case of *hatred of intelligence on the part of narrow-mindedness.*

Sinai, vol. v (1860-61) p. 155.

90

Whoever has read Jewish history attentively knows of the friendly reception which our German brethren met with in Amsterdam a few centuries ago, when they too wanted to enjoy freedom in Holland, and also the treatment of the Jews from Alsace at the hands of the native French Jews of Spanish descent. There was a repetition of this also in New York. The first arrivals from Germany and Poland were received in the most brotherly fashion; but as the stream began to flow stronger and many an unworthy individual came here, the newcomers began to be looked upon with hostile eyes and the principle "help yourself" was put into effect. The immigrants had not come to America to beg assistance of their co-religionists — (only beggars were assisted) but fought on their own hook. These peddlers and common manual laborers could hardly expect to be treated by the English-speaking aristocratic bankers and great merchants as equals even in respect to religion. When they visited their synagogue they were, if admitted, given permission to occupy the seats nearest the door, since only a small space was reserved for strangers. To satisfy their religious needs these peddlers and manual laborers founded congregations. Nothing was more natural than that they should adopt as their own the form of worship accustomed to from home. At that time, (and even now that these peddlers have become great merchants and the manual laborers own important factories) they had very little contact with their Portuguese brethren and still the editor thinks the former should adopt the latter's ritual . . .

Israelitische Wochenschrift, vol. v (1874) p. 403.

91

There are individual English Jews here, but the majority consists of Dutch and Polish Jews, who have immigrated here, after having lived a long time in England, and have completely adopted English customs and the English way of life. They belong to the genteel class. The local Pole is the dirtiest creature of all classes and is also the cause for the name "Jew" being used here in an obnoxious sense. The Dutch Jew is by far better and, with all his grossness and clumsiness he is an honest fellow. The Germans constitute the majority among the Jews here; they are very industrious and know how to find their way quickly enough into the life of the community. Among them one finds men of substance, as well as businessmen and manufacturers, as also landowners, etc. The German is haughty toward the Pole and avoids him; in return he is hated by the latter. The Dutch Jew is prone to contest the German Jew's standing and even if the English Jew deems himself above the German, he still has intercourse with him on equal footing. So it is in general and so it is in particular; still, exceptions are not lacking. (Accordingly, splits there too, just as among us everywhere! The Editor.)

Allgemeine Zeitung des Judentums, July 27, 1846, p. 448.

92

The Polish Jews who are mostly from Prussian Poland, have a chameleon nature (act like Orthodox Jews) . . . But they are exactly those who profane the Sabbath most; those who brush aside many a Jewish law for the sake of business . . . The congregations founded by Jewish emigrants from Germany constitute the great majority, and, in their various shadings, are the true bearers of Jewish life in America. There are several elements here which work as a ferment; above all, those brought along from the old country. . . . (Reform Judaism existed in Germany only in large cities, while the emigrants come mostly from small communities . . .) In addition there are the American elements. Most German Jews, poor and without means, were driven to devote themselves to the peddling business, which is not so dishonorable as in Germany, and, making distant trips from which they came back only on holidays, began to lay the foundation for their later prosperity. On these trips nearly all of them were forced to accustom themselves to other than Jewish food; the Sabbath was not observed, and they frequented more and more Christian churches and Christian society. The consequences of this life manifested themselves in various ways. Some, who felt pangs of conscience about it, kept a strictly kosher household at home, and came forward as true zealots at all congregational meetings — merely to show that they yield to the harsh necessity of making a livelihood, but otherwise they are observant Jews . . . A section of this party declare themselves justified in their transgressions, until they shall have acquired an independent fortune . . . (Others are in favor of reform) . . . Others again become indifferent . . . Business is after all the principal thing; money and again money, and the eternal running and driving and chasing does after all take precedence in American life . . .

An open letter to *Die Deborah,* Apr. 4, 1856, p. 244.

93

Dr. M. Wiener's Report from America

One of my acquaintances, an Israelite, traversed the United States as a peddler several years ago. This, by the way, is the chief occupation of every immigrant without distinction of faith, who is not a mechanic and arrives without the means to buy land.

During my sojourn in America, an attempt to stir up Jew-hatred was made in the city of New Orleans; it had its origin in political fanaticism and, as it later turned out, came from a Christian who had emigrated from Germany. (A billboard against the Jewish election candidate: "Make hay while the sun shines! or you will swallow a Charleston Jew!!!)

It assumes a different form when one observes the doings of other (Polish in contrast with Portuguese) sects! Here there forces itself upon one the conviction that all Europe had expectorated the dregs of Jewry upon America . . . In the city of New Orleans there live 700 Jewish families, among these you find no more than four households in which forbidden food is avoided, only two in which the Sababth rest is observed. More than two-thirds of the congregation's members *do not have* their sons *circumcised* . . . This from a rabbi: "This stigma in the ranks of the Jewish ministry eats whatever comes before his maw, never keeps the feast of Passover, indeed, has had none of his boys circumcised! Mr. Markes — that is his name — is, however, also too preoccupied, for, in addition to his post of rabbi, he holds a job as an *actor* at the American Theatre and that of chief of one of the fire-engines. At the *Purim-feast,* the Book of Esther could not be read, since, so the President of the Congregation informed the religious gathering, the rabbi, *i.e.* the reader, was busy at the fire-engine. (Challenged by a pious member of the congregation), the rabbi, beside himself with wrath, pounded the pulpit and shouted: 'By Jesus Christ, I have a right to pray!'

The deceased rabbi was a Dutchman by birth and had a Catholic wife, who could be restrained only with difficulty from putting a crucifix in his grave.

Allgemeine Zeitung des Judentums (1842) p. 290 ff.

94

San Francisco. May. Dear Editor! It is a long time since I have written you; that is due to the fact that in America one can rarely have command over his time and (what generally means the same thing) over one's own self. It seems to me as if everything were in a stupefying eddy, wherein one chases and is being chased and but rarely comes to have a wideawake, self-conscious moment. Here in California this is indisputably the case to a higher degree than anywhere else. A year effects here what it takes decades somewhere else; that is, generations come and go. The shortest space of time here alters the external as well as the internal stage of things. This applies to everything, to families, politics and religion. Everything changes here with astounding swiftness. A man who only yesterday was wallowing in slime, today swims, and one who yesterday thought himself to be on the high seas, the tide suddenly casts back ashore without warning. This is a true picture of California! In their worldly affairs our co-religionists flourish in this state like trees by the waters. Respected by the world as industrious, honest citizens, they have nothing else left to wish for but that at last they, too, might respect themselves.

But the magnificent synagogues, of which the most luxurious possesses an organ and choir — all, all are empty; the schools are crippled and crawl along laboriously. Thus old and young live without a religious revival. Thousands of dollars are being squandered without achieving any other object thereby save that some relative, useless for anything else, is supported in some sort of office at the congregation's expense. Unfortunately the votes are counted and not weighed and thus naturally all sorts of absurdities come to pass. Last Passover everything went as usual. Four weeks prior to the holiday, the houses were turned topsy-turvy by the women. At the first Seder evening the Haggadah was wearisomely "jargoned" (done in Yiddish) and next day was steamer-day. But, ah, you on the other side of the Pacific, you don't know what steamer-day means. It is the calamity which returns every four weeks—to have to send so and so many thousands of dollars and all the while, with hair standing on end, not to know where to get even one-third of that. There ought to be a stipulation for the age of the Messiah that there should be no debts and no steamer-days. If that were true, one could quite quickly make propaganda with the principles of Judaism among the mostly indifferent great merchants.

For the sake of curiosity I must regale you with another trifle, which offers an interesting illustration of conditions. Recently, at a political gala day, to the celebration of which our governor annually invites every good Christian for the purpose of divine eulogy, there was also a big parade in one of our congregations. After the reverend gentleman with a heavy moustache had conceitedly recited chapters of the Psalms without end to the yawning gathering, he finally mounted the pulpit, with the air of a Parisian dude, and in a thousandfold murdered English, whose wailing in the Alsatian dialect rang out through the broad halls incomprehensibly and uncomprehended, said in part the following words: "Ve shus are no langer a beeble nar ave ve some langer an istary pad anyvere is our house and our demble is se natur, etc." (We Jews are no longer a people, nor have we any longer a history, but anywhere is our home and our temple is Nature.) This is a verbatim example of pulpit oratory.

Sinai, vol. iv (1859-60) p. 184.

95

North American Conditions

2. *The Parties*

The great majority of our communities take no part in all this excitement. Most of the members are preoccupied with their business and attend to their commercial affairs from the beginning to the end of the year. The business, which is carried on by many, goes far beyond their resources; credit and America's independent, forward-striving drive them into speculations which are on the increase from year to year. Urged on by the inborn sense of honesty and uprightness, owing to which they intend to meet their obligations punctually, they are constantly obsessed by anxious worries and, accordingly, find little opportunity or leisure to busy themselves with speculative theological wrangles. The few leisure-hours are either devoted to needed recreation or to visiting the numerous secret societies, membership in which has become the dominant fashion in this country.

Der israelitische Volkslehrer, vol. vii (1857) p. 125-26.

96

Our houses of prayer are suffering a dreadful blow due to the dying out of the German language. But both house of prayer and language can be properly sustained. Had the Jews ever given up the Hebrew language in their divine service, they would have also ceased to constitute a people, a nation; their nationality has been sustained only through their language.

Brauns, E., *Praktische Belehrungen für Reisende und Auswanderer nach Amerika* (Brunswick 1829) p. 393.

97

New York, in May (Private communication). If any nation does an injustice to the Jews, it is the German nation, as there exists, indeed, nowhere a truer tribe for Germany than in the Jews. The German *per se* has already in the second generation become assimilated in France and England, but the German Jew holds ever fast to the German language and usage. Let us leave out the so-called Portuguese branch of the Jewish stock. In the steppes of Syria and the Ukraine, as well as on the prairies of America, we hear the Jew speaking German; he carries the German fatherland along everywhere and can never again leave it; that German fatherland, which casts him off so repeatedly and denies him abode and hearth. I am led to this reflection by a small pamphlet before me, bearing the title; *Constitution of the New Israelite Sick-benefit and Burial Society,* New York. Printed by G. A. Neumann, 7 Frankfort St., 1841, and forwarded to me to induce me to become a member. The regulations of this new Israelite burial-society in *New York* are in *German,* and paragraph 4 of article 13 reads: *"All debates and motions must be in the German language."* The motive for founding this society was the existing societies' (chevrot) rigorous discrimination between the "pious" and the "leftist" Jews. This is also expressed in the Preface, which reads as follows: "The motive for founding this society to which we wish to give the name 'The New Israelite Sick-benefit and Burial Society' must be attributed to the narrow-minded outlook of the already existing societies of this sort. Instead of adopting the liberal spirit, which predominates in general in the institutions of this free country, we see prevailing in them an intolerance which is at variance with the present spirit of the time and with conditions. Our society should be independent of the synagogue, and our endeavor, free from prejudice, should be to do good, assist the sick and bury the dead. Charity should be our aim and the spirit that should animate our Constitution."

(Non-religious people are also accepted, new immigrants who have not as yet been 12 months in the country are buried free of charge, or are buried for a small fee up to 20 dollars, if they leave any money.)

Allgemeine Zeitung des Judentums (1843) p. 478.

98

From Bavaria, in September (Private communication) . . . Concerning the foregoing remarks in this journal about the wording of the constitution of the Burial-Society in New York, a correction approximately to the following effect has reached me from a friend who was in America until a short while ago and was a member of this society. The abovementioned friend hopes that through your love of the truth your esteemed journal will accept this for publication:

Those regulations were not drawn up in German out of love of that language or of Germany, but only and exclusively for the reason that the society consists mostly of freshly-arrived German-Jewish immigrants who are not familiar with the English language. But the German Jew, as well as the Christian, sheds his German skin together with his entire German nationality as soon as possible. He seeks distinction in expressing himself meagerly in the English language, and as soon as he can stammer even a few words in English, not for all the world does he ever utter a German sound in the presence of an American; he rather lets himself be railed at as French, and, as to his own disgrace, is ashamed of his language and origin. The above regulations were drawn up in the German language for the reason that as a rule the German immigrant no longer learns to *read* English. He would understand a constitution drawn up in the former language. But the second generation, as a rule, no longer understands a word of German, the German fathers positively do not have German taught to their children, and thus the German nationality dies there quite soon. With the emigrants of other nations it is not so. The third generation of Frenchmen still speaks its mother-tongue.

(Signed KR.)

Allgemeine Zeitung des Judentums (1843) p. 611.

99

In New York *e.g.* there are many small and only a few large congregations, which float around like an island-group in New York without mutual contact, and hence can achieve nothing great. And so it appears in the whole country. First of all comes the main division into German and Polish congregations, existing in well-nigh every city. It should be the task of every good Israelite to break up the Polish congregations, that they may not keep up that atrocious monster and would have to mix with other people and other customs; and to wean the Germans from the ridiculous and insipid prejudices against the Poles. Next come all possible subdivisions, as *e.g.* in Chicago, and particulraly in Cleveland, Quincy and elsewhere.

We cannot understand why the two congregations in Quincy should not unite in a *Minhag* America, as the people after all are neither Poles nor Germans, but Americans.

Die Deborah, vol. xii (1866-67) p. 62.

100

New York, May 2nd . . . For the north-west part of the city *must* have a new German synagogue. All who lay any claim to competence move into that section of the city; and a visit to the synagogues in Clinton, Attorney and Norfolk Streets from Eighth and Ninth Avenues between 20th and 40th St. is a pure impossibility . . . Therefore may the present moment, when the parties acknowledge mutual dissatisfaction, be taken advantage of to leave those East-Side synagogues to the old folks on the one hand, and to build a handsome temple in the more desirable part of the city for the better-situated group, on the other hand, so a peaceful situation may be provided for all parties. As things stand now, the only true and lasting salvation lies in a decisive separation.

Die Deborah (1859).

101

Cleveland . . .

Already in '44, one and a half years before their synagogue was built, their school was commenced, when they numbered only about forty contributing members, most of them poor and new emigrants from Germany. It contained at its commencement, twenty-two scholars, from four to seven years of age. They were instructed in Hebrew and German reading and writing, translating the prayers and the Torah, and in Jewish writing and reading together with exercises in the catechism.

The Occident, vol. vii (1849-50) p. 331.

102

He resolutely objected to speaking German and asserted he had forgotten it. My companions, on the contrary, knew he spoke German, all this — as above all he sought to conceal his German origin — ostensibly because such was his wife's will.

Unfortunately it is a fact that Germans disavow their German origin and hold it more honorable to pass as native Americans—only too frequently, in Texas as well as in the United States in general.

Roemer, F., *Texas mit besonderer Rücksicht auf deutsche Auswanderung* (Bonn 1849) p. 107.

103

Of public theatres the Germans own only one, and in it opera, drama and comedy can be heard in turn; the cast is not always good, and occasionally downright bad, but it enjoys a pretty numerous attendance, namely of the shopkeepers from the Bowery, who are almost exclusively *Jews.*

Teckla, Georg, *Drei Jahre in New York* (Zwickau 1862) p. 100.

104

Jargon

It is a regrettable evil that many children of German parents speak a poor English, so that they are at once recognized as foreigners by the choice and pronunciation of English words as well as by the employment of special phrases and locutions. This is the case not only with the children of uneducated parents, but, above all, with those of educated parents, who are admonished in the parental home to speak a *good* German and to study German grammar.

It cannot be disputed that it is an evil, a material drawback to speak the country's language incorrectly. Thinking Israelites must know what a drawback the jargon (Yiddish) was to the German Jew in the old fatherland; how detrimental it still is for the Jew in Poland and Russia. Indeed Nehemiah of old fought against the linguistic corruption of his people, and the immortal Moses Mendelssohn successfully emulated him in Germany. If we wish to bring up our children to be citizens, to protect them against handicaps and lead them toward a promising future, we must apply the appropriate measure to eliminate the jargon in America.

The causes of this evil are manifold. To begin with, the schools of the Jewish communities, the German schools, the French schools and other institutions contribute markedly to the corruption of the English language. In most of those schools poor English is spoken, the children hear it from their teachers and get accustomed to jargon. What would they say nowadays in Germany, if it were suggested to sensible people to let their children be educated by teachers who spoke a poor German? But here it is an everyday occurrence that in the above-named schools a disgusting jargon is spoken instead of English. This is an argument against the community schools that Mr. Adler has not pondered. According to our view, the youth should be sent only to the state public school so that they should learn to speak the language of the country correctly and be sure to escape the danger of jargon.

"My children must speak only German at home," mothers tell us with special self-satisfaction. This is very fine not because in that way the children somehow learn German, since the two or three hundred words of the home's colloquial language are a tiny fraction of the language, but because the German woman's mind finds comfort in the homeland sounds, because the German mother wants to know that she is loved in German by her children. But the drawback of the matter is that the children's bad English is not heard, consequently, also not corrected, at home, and that every child so brought up is forthwith recognized by the fact that he twists the commonest locutions, the everyday conversational speech and often Germanizes and distorts it to an absurdity. This is the second cause of jargon.

Our object is not to enter into details; we merely wish to direct attention to this evil in a general way. Every Israelite must admit that through fostering jargon we inculcate a detrimental and lasting mistake. The power of language rules the destiny of the country. Accordingly, if we wish to bring up the youth for America, and not for Germany or France, if we do not wish to make them ridiculous to their material detriment and stamp them as beings apart, then we must not tolerate jargon.

Die Deborah, vol. xiv (1868-69) p. 190.

105

The Germanization of the Synagogue

. . .From a speech delivered at Peoria, Ill. . . . we reproduce the essential points . . . To Germanize the synagogue and the Jews in America is an impractical and criminal endeavor. It is impractical because, as we have said, the youth is collectively English-speaking, so that in 10 years Germanism will have reached its end in the American synagogue. He who writes anything in German for the *American* synagogue, writes for the present day. It is criminal, not only because the English language has no equivalent of Hep! and Jew-baiting, but because the German element in America, as once upon a time in Europe, would isolate the synagogue and the Jews, would set it up as a foreign and outlandish institution and completely estrange non-Jews, whereas the native Jew would perceive in it only a mummy, a dead monument of the past . . .

Every teacher and preacher can, should, must learn English, else he will find himself in the same position as the *baal darshon* of old. Only a few will understand him and the few will commiserate with him.

Die Deborah, vol. xii (1866-67) p. 82.

106

As far as concerns the emigrants, it must be observed that the good people are led astray by those journals, which brand everything American as humbug and bamboozle the world as often as they can that in America every preacher, teacher, rabbi can be anything and everything, since those already in office are there for the purpose of humbug, after all; and so everyone naturally imagines he will be the greatest person in America as soon as they hear about him. We have often had opportunity to deplore these views. This, too, can be remedied, the association can do it but first it must come in existence.

The teachers in Germany should learn through every medium possible that there is a prospect for respectable positions here only for those who are thoroughly prepared to write and deliver religious discourses and are masters of the English language, and for no others, unless it be in the public schools of certain large cities.

Die Deborah, vol. xviii (1872) no. 10.

107

The notion that a Jew must necessarily speak German, is on a par with that of the English woman who insisted that Americans live on buffalo-meat.

No people, unless under exceptional circumstances, is willing to be judged by its emigration. A Lasker, Jessel, or Oppert is not apt to seek the fortunes of a strange soil. Yet many cultivated Israelites do swell the Jewish exodus . . . These Hebrews, being foreigners and Jews, are identified by the keen instinct of American society with the ill-bred lounger of the sea-side porch.

The large number of cultured American Israelites in this country do not fear condemnation under the most exacting of etiquette.

Morais, Nina, in *North American Review* (1881) p. 272-73.

108

He is a Jew!

Under this heading the *New Yorker Handelszeitung* prints the following article:

"Immediately upon landing, the German immigrant makes every use of the advantages which the free institutions of this land offer him, but only in rare cases do we find him ready to discard the prejudices which he has brought over from home. *E.g.* when a German is suddenly transplanted from Hesse-Kassel to the far west of the Union, he keeps with him even there his native narrowmindedness. He quickly forgets the oppression he has suffered, he enjoys all the freedom of social and business intercourse but he begrudges his fellowmen this enjoyment. We are moved to this remark by a 'paid communication' entitled 'He is a Jew' in the *Missouri Post* appearing in Kansas City, Missouri; it reads in part as follows:

'A circle of certain people has come into existence here who, it appears, have made it their task to watch the steps of young people as soon as they have begun to make themselves popular through fine and gentlemanly conduct, and if even then they don't find anything to criticize in them, in desperation they whisper into the other's ears: he is a Jew!'

"In itself the statement contains nothing offensive, the baseness lies just in its manner of application. Hardly have certain young people been able to make themselves known, than this one or that one has it mysteriously whispered into his ear: 'He is a Jew!'

Tout comme chez nous, we may add, since notoriously here, too, there is no lack of educated (?) Christian Germans who parade such prejudices. Indeed there is a story about a club in a city less than a thousand miles away from New York in which education, upright character and personal charm do not protect the candidate against being blackballed, if it becomes known that he is a Jew . . . "

Die Deborah, vol. vi (1860) p. 66.

109

New York, Sept. 20. Who would believe that the wild appetite for Jew-baiting crosses over even to North America? And who brings it there? Irish emigrants or rather dregs. . . . The *Weserzeitung* reports the following: A shocking event occurred last Sunday. It was the eve of the great Day of Atonement of the Jews and they all were in the synagogue. The house in which the synagogue is situated is occupied both by Jews and by Irish families. During the gathering of the congregation some one brought a street woman into the rear building: a short time later a rumor spread that the Jews had murdered a Gentile girl for their holiday. About 10:30 a crowd of some 500 men burst into the house, broke down the doors and literally pulled from their beds the sleeping women, one of whom was in childbed next to a sick husband. A most shocking riot was perpetrated; everyone who resisted was knocked down, a little box of jewelry to the amount of 63 dollars was stolen from a peddler. The remarkable thing about the affair is that three Irish policemen were the leaders of this raging mob, and the tumult thereby acquired a sort of official character, whereas, after all, the authorities had remained totally ignorant of this riot.

Allgemeine Zeitung des Judentums (1850) p. 593.

110

"Jewish Folly and American Illiberality"
(Concerning the Tashlich ritual in New York)

Is it not bad enough that these men practice their mummeries among themselves, in their houses of worship and in their private homes, but that they must also in their ignorance bring them prominently in the thoroughfares of a large city with a mixed population, and thus invite a conflict with the lower classes? . . .

The New Era, ed. by Raphael D'C. Lewin, vol. ii (New York 1871-72) p. 35.

111

Among all scandals the most disgraceful are surely the boxing-matches which have again been held very frequently. But that Jews sink so low to barbarity is an outrage that must be most vigorously condemned. We borrow the following notice from our exchange-periodicals:

"A Curiosity in the Prize-Ring

"Among the various prize boxing-matches, which the *New York News* daily records, last week there was one in which not only the boxers, but the seconds, witnesses, referee, etc. were Israelites one and all. The fight took place between Moses Silberstein and Isaac Salomon at Bergen Point for a stake of 200 dollars. There were 26 rounds and finally Silberstein was declared the winner. The two men were woefully mauled and Salomon went through the last four rounds blinded. He immediately sent his victor a new challenge."

Decent people should have no relations whatever with disreputable rabble of this sort; they should be tolerated neither in societies nor in congregations. The place for such riff-raff is in the penitentiary or in the workhouse and it is the duty of every good man to bring them there. But the spectators and the seconds are still worse than the boxing steers, for these the penitentiary would be a reputable place.

Die Deborah, vol. xiii (1867-68) p. 31.

112

North America

From a letter under date of New York, June 16, 1834, of a Jewish shoemaker-journeyman from Bavaria, who emigrated to North America, we glean the following notes not devoid of interest. The writer of the letter advises those who want to go to America to go by way of Hamburg or England, but not Bremen. Says he, the Bremen ship owners promise much and do little. An Israelite, he says, cannot live on the Bremen boats according to the prescriptions of his religion. On the fortieth day after sailing from Bremen the boat arrived in New York, notwithstanding a long-lasting storm by which the boat was driven very far to the north. The correspondent says, that on the third day he fell seasick and remained so during the whole voyage; but the seasickness is of no significance; it consists merely of feeling unwell and vomiting. On his arrival in New York the immigrant immediately came across German acquaintances whom he mentions by name. For a few days he worked for a Frenchman, but soon started a business of his own which pleased him better. A pair of women's shoes can be bought for 2 florins 30 kreutzers; a pair of fine boots stitched with silk—for 10 florins, 30 kreutzers; sole-leather of the best quality costs 30 kreutzers, calf-leather, on the contrary, costs a little more than in Germany. Handworkers, whose trade is not performed by machines, *e.g.* shoemakers, tailors, leather-dressers, joiners, carpenters, masons, get good wages there, but not occupations that can be carried out by means of machines, as cloth-makers, weavers, etc. Hand-tailoring is particularly remunerative: from 15 to 20 florins are paid as the price of labor. And the tailors, moreover, have the finest shops. Therefore, the letter-writer advises his friend, a tailor, most emphatically to go to America. German girls, he says, are very popular there. They find situations easily and can earn from 15 to 20 florins per month as servants; they are also taken in marriage in preference to American girls, as the latter do not work with a will. Any one can marry at will; likewise conduct a business whichever and wherever he pleases; in this respect one is not subject to any police restriction whatever. Wool is very expensive; gold rates very low: a double *louis d'or* is worth no more than 7 dollars (17 florins 30 kreutzer); hence he advises his friend to bring along no gold, but Bavarian kronenthalers (crown-dollars), five-franc pieces or bills. Room and board here are very expensive: the letter-writer pays 7 florins 30 kreuzer a week. The German immigrants are not in good repute here and enjoy little confidence among the Americans; people say they are hard to get on with, deceitful, etc. There are 800 Jewish families living in New York; they have 3 synagogues, 2 German and 1 Portuguese; the last-named was just built and was dedicated last Shevuoth. The writer of the letter made the trip from New York to Philadelphia, a distance of 100 English miles, in seven hours by steamer; such a trip costs no more than 2 florins 30 kreuzer, etc.

Das Fuellhorn, Dinkelsbuehl, January 29, 1835, p. 38.

113

From Altmark, March 31 (Private communication) . . . The above-mentioned Bavarian Israelite showed us a letter received from his brother, who had migrated from Bavaria to New York and had to leave his wife and child, owing to the restrictions prevailing in his fatherland. . . . He highly extols his present situation and his trade (he is a shoemaker) guarantees him an ample livelihood even if not wealth. In his letter he rejoices particularly at the circumstance that his children have an opportunity to learn a lot and that, along with full civil liberty, an Israelite also has an opportunity to comply—unhindered—with all religious prescriptions, as there are three synagogues and all the other Jewish institutions. He invites his brother also to come over, since he will surely find a situation there.

Allgemeine Zeitung des Judentums, Apr. 18, 1840, p. 218.

114

Riches—An Ornament of the Righteous

Grand Duchy of Hesse, September 3. A young Israelite, native of Roedelsheim near Frankfort, had gone to America as a commercial clerk 31 years ago, as the circumstances made it very hard for him to get on at home. Though arriving utterly destitute in the New World, he succeeded in amassing a great fortune by diligence and industry, so that at present he finds himself at the head of one of the first commercial firms in New Orleans, Herrman & Co., and in possession of several million dollars. Some weeks ago he paid a visit to his old home for the purpose of providing for his numerous relatives. He has transferred to them a cash sum of as much as 150,000 florins as capital so that they may expand their business activities, and in addition has made arrangements for those of his family's members, who need a rest on account of advanced age, to be given a considerable allowance regularly during their lifetime by a Frankfurt banking house. He has now gone back to New Orleans.

(SCHW. M.)

Das Fuellhorn (1835) p. 378.

115

Moses Wolf. He was born in Bruch, Kurhessen, on July 4, 1814. When he was twenty-five, the conditions under which his co-religionists

(Israelites) had to live in his old homeland appeared altogether too cramped to him, and the uniformly good reports which came to the old country from Jewish emigrants induced young Wolf to emigrate. In November 1839 he left the coast of the Old World and sailed from Bremen over the blue waves to Columbia's shores, on which he set foot on January 15, 1840. From Baltimore he went to Cincinnati, where he set up house and remained thereafter. His hopes did not deceive him and he died in well-to-do circumstances on Sept. 25, 1875.

Der deutsche Pionier, vol. viii (1876-77) p. 36.

116

Moses Henochsberg. He was born in 1815 in the small town of Fuerth, near Nuremberg, in Bavaria and educated in his youth for the merchant class. However, the oppressive conditions in his home prompted him at the age of twenty-five to migrate to America in order to improve his lot in that new Eldorado. For this purpose he embarked at Havre in the summer of 1840 and sailed to New York, where he arrived in early autumn of the same year. He stayed at first in New York and established himself there in a mercantile business, which he gave up, however, after several years, in order to go on to Cincinnati. In the year 1865 he founded, in the last-named city, a business of his own, a factory of mirrors and picture-frames, first at 283 Main Street and later on Central Avenue. He was a most successful businessman and his factory was in a flourishing condition when implacable death called him away from the circle of his family on Dec. 31, 1875. Henochsberg was ever an affectionate and charitable man, who liberally opened his hand at every opportunity for Jewish societies and lodges, and after his death the Judah Touro Society passed a series of resolutions in which it fittingly emphasized the services of the deceased. In the Pionier-Verein, to which Henochsberg had belonged since May 5, 1874, he was a zealous and welcome member, whose early and unexpected demise will be generally mourned.

Ibid.

117

In Memoriam

Seligmann Harth, born Sept. 6, 1815 at Lauterbach, in the Rhenish Palatinate, Bavaria, where his parents had a small store in which the son helped. But when the war-year 1849 broke out over the Palatinate, it became altogether too uncomfortable for the young merchant in his home. . . . On April 1, 1849, Harth embarked with his family at Havre, later landed in New York on May 2, and thence moved to the West, after having looked around for several days in New York. They reached Cincinnati without any further misadventure and here Harth immediately thereafter found himself again in the mercantile business. . . .

Der deutsche Pionier, vol. ix (1877-78) p. 497.

118

The Grain-King of California

By Paul Oeker

... Isaac Friedlander, the Grain-King ...

For the rest, Friedlander, an Oldenburgian by birth, represented a fine Israelite type. . . . He was one of the Forty-Eighters, one of the Californian pioneers. Having come to New York as a boy, he found himself very early at an office-desk. In his youth he emigrated to South Carolina, and, seized by the California gold-fever, he sailed from there to the new and rediscovered Land of Promise. But the arduous labor in the gold beds did not agree at the time with his delicate health. . . .

Ibid., vol. x (1878) p. 238.

119

Max Thurnauer

Born of poor but honest Jewish parents, on March 14, 1820, at Burgkundstadt on the Main in Upper Bavaria, he spent his youth in the midst of depressing conditions, which still stamped the Children of Israel throughout Europe, with rare exceptions, as a despised class. Only money, a lot of money, could possibly blot out this imprinted stamp of inferiority, and who could find fault with the Jews, that for this reason they strove for the acquisition of the talisman which would qualify them to enter the highly esteemed society. At that time *one* land beckoned them, in which the Jews enjoyed equal rights with the other human beings. That was the Republic of the United States, where all men are free and equal under a liberal constitution, which was won by the liberal-minded fathers of the country and set up for the world as an example to emulate. For this reason Jewish co-religionists streamed here in hosts to find and enjoy the precious boon which is offered equally to all: complete freedom of religion and social equality. But the greatest weakness of the Jews was that here, too, they clung too much to the, one might almost say, disgusting greed of acquisition, still cultivated in the Old World. Through that they kept up the peculiar condition which over there had distinguished them from the rest of society and thus they brought the class-distinction into the New World—and people often pass sharp and hasty judgment!—But Max Thurnauer, whom the above-mentioned conditions had likewise driven to America, clung less to this strongly-marked greed of acquisition than most of his clan, although he, too, strove to raise and improve his monetary circumstances. In later years he may possibly have been somewhat too close-fisted, but his public-spiritedness has been confirmed by more than one example of the opposite sort. It was not the sheer rapid acquisition that animated him—nay, he also knew how to utilize what he acquired for the benefit of the community which he had joined as a citizen. A practical illustration are the magnificent business-edifices redounding to the beauty of Cincinnati City and erected many years ago by Thurnauer and his brothers-in-law at the corner of Fourth and Race Streets.

Thurnauer came to America in the spring of 1842 and lived in this city since July 20, 1842. Immediately after his arrival he went into partnership with his brothers-in-law, Benjamin and Ezekiel Simon, in a wholesale drygoods business at the corner of Main and Pearl Streets. Here it was that through a lucky speculation—as he himself related to the author—he laid the foundation of the great wealth which placed the firm of Simon and Thurnauer among Cincinnati's *wealthiest* mercantile establishments. . . . [Description of the speculative purchase of a cotton warehouse, the value of which rose during the war.]

Ibid., vol. ii (1879) p. 294.

120

. . . It will be an abundant source of consolation for the emigrant: in France itself, however, in the bosom of Judaism people are preoccupied with the Californian question. We learn of a Committee of Israelite Emigration to California at Strassbourg (Lower Rhine), possibly on the pattern of the one whose formation in London (for Australia) we have announced.

J. COHEN

Archives israélites (Paris 1853) p. 220.

121

Bavaria—Upper Bavaria, August 4. We learn that there is a wholesale emigration, particularly on the part of the Jewish population—from Central Franconia, Swabia and Lower Franconia toward the shores on the other side of the Atlantic. Several localities, which a few years ago were inhabited by thousands of Jewish families, are reduced to a few old folks, while the younger generation has settled in the Free States of America. Generally the oldest son departs first, after having finished his apprenticeship; he is provided with recommendations to relatives or friends established in America; shortly afterwards the rest of the family comes to join him.

Ibid., p. 598.

122

From Germany

. . . The emigration-fever keeps growing so fast that anxiety is already overtaking the governments. In Austria an emigration-tax has been introduced and in Rhenish Hesse emigration "to America" has been plainly interdicted without a special permit from the highest authorities. Naturally, the fewer the heads, the fewer the taxes, because the better-to-do class is now emigrating to such an extent. But they will not check this current. *For that* they are too impotent, after all. *They* will in fact only add to the ferment which is predominant in people's minds. The police-system is already so vast that there is beginning to be a shortage of suitable persons, and it is reaching its limit.

Deutsche Monatshefte (New York 1853) p. 64.

123

Bohemian Israelites in Wisconsin

We learn from a reliable source that a number of highly respectable families have just arrived in New York from Bohemia, to form a colony in Wisconsin. There have been for several years past many families from the same country in the neighborhood of Milwaukee; but the present party, we hear, mean to establish a congregation at once; and they came provided, it is said, with teachers and other necessary officers to carry their intentions into effect. We hope to receive more particulars of this enterprise, when we will communicate it to our readers. In the meantime, we wish the colonists all possible success.

The Occident, vol. vii (1849-50) p. 330.

124

(New York)

The amount received, however large it may be, will all be needed in the relief of the distressed Israelites now, or soon, expected at New York, whither the poor of Europe are flocking in great masses, and it is but too likely that the emigration from the overpopulated districts of Germany will continue, and this in an increased ratio throughout the coming summer. We even learn from a late number of the *Orient* that emigration unions are formed in Bohemia, which of course will bring many persons over who otherwise might not find the means of leaving their native land. No doubt many persons with sufficient property to aid themselves will also come; but the majority, we fear, will be the poor, or those who find Europe no longer a field to furnish sufficient support for themselves and families.

Ibid., p. 58.

125

Bavaria. (Rejection of the emancipation-bill in the Bavarian Diet.)
So we may look out for a renewed increase of immigration on the part of Bavarian Israelites into the United States, and we have here another evidence that prejudice dies hard.

The Occident, vol. viii (1850-51) p. 58.

126

Munich, Emigration of Jews.—Accounts, which have reached us from several provinces of Bavaria, agree that, in consequence of the rejection of the Jewish Emancipation Bill by the Upper Chamber, many Jews are on the point of leaving Bavaria, in order to settle in other German states where all civilian and political disabilities have been removed. As this resolution, however, can only be carried out by those possessed of pecuniary means, the amount of capital which will be withdrawn from the country is very considerable.

L'Univers Israélite.

The Asmonean, vol. ii, May 21, 1850, p. 38.

127

Shalom Aleichem once more.—Over 7,000 Polish Jews have passed through Posen on their way to the United States. . . .

[An article in the *Boston Traveller,* which demands a Jewish state in Palestine, is quoted, and characterized as "curious."]

Die Deborah (1860) p. 119, 135.

128

The House of Rothschild and the Jews in Germany

[From the *Grenzbote* no. 22: proposal of J. Kuranda that the House of Rothschild should take over the financing of emigration. . . .]

Has not one the right to say: You who are the richest in Germany, you assist the poorest; not as it were by alms and gifts, you need not part with a farthing—donate to them only your protection, your credit. Place yourselves at the head of a great joint-stock company, purchase the land, charter boats and facilities and ensure the transportation and settling of the emigrants. . . . *Thousands of your co-religionists languish in poverty and under political and religious oppression.* . . . Once Rothschild is at the head of it, then subscriptions of rich Israelites would pour in from all parts, and not from Germany alone. . . . Thus, *e.g.* the agencies which in similar enterprises are paid heavy sums, which, not infrequently, have to be put into unsafe hands, would in this case be run not only on a volunteer-basis, but with a zeal quite different than a paid agent can have, by the clerical and other boards of the Jewish communities, at the most distant points. At the same time these community-boards could exercise the necessary supervision over those desirous to emigrate from their districts, by sending in reports about their character and similar matters to the Central Committee which should have its principal office in Frankfurt or just as well in a seaport. On the other hand, the far-reaching commercial connections of the great Jewish banking-houses would from the very start facilitate the purchase of land and receive the indispensable reports on any land parcel whatever proposed for the purpose, be it in South or North America; and what is more, the political influence of the *Rothschilds* could smooth out many matters which might possibly be an insuperable hindrance for any other, private enterprise.

Der Orient, vol. iv (1843) p. 191

129

Philadelphia [Stern's colonization-plan]. The Lords *Rothschild,* would, at all events, erect for themselves the *finest* monument among their co-religionists through the promotion of a Jewish emigrant-colony.

Der Orient, vol. iv (1844) p. 296.

130

As we hoped from the start, and have confidently expected, the Jews in *America* are beginning to look with less repugnance upon the immigration of Russian Jews. They will do more, they will assist and succor them. On March 13, a meeting for this purpose took place in New York. . . . The idea . . . seems to be finding approval in America; the immigrating Jews should be colonized. Governor Salomon has large land-properties in Washington Territory. . . .

Israelitische Wochenschrift, vol. i (1870) p. 134.

131

In *America,* the attitude toward the Russian Jews immigrating there is becoming better. A committe which will care for the immigrants has been formed in New York. After Crémieux in particular had started corresponding with outstanding men in America and explained to them that there is no thought of sending over beggars and people who are not capable of making a living—the fear of overloading is disappearing and the founding of agricultural colonies in particular seems to have been earnestly taken into consideration. As we foresaw, it is the Washington Territory chiefly which is being considered. . . .

Ibid., p. 153.

132

From *America*—a very distressing piece of news. The executive committee of the Board of Delegates passed a resolution on January 25, to inform Mr. Crémieux that the American Jews are not willing to favor the immigration of Russian Jews, but indeed want to collect money for their migration into the interior of Russia. We are still hoping that the last word has not been said herewith.

As is now well-known, President Grant has promised to use his influence in behalf of the Russian Jews. . . . Here our brethren in America use their influence with their president so that he should use his influence—but they want no immigration of Poles into America. We are speaking of this once more.

In California the attitude is better; Mr. Peixotto in San Francisco has expressed himself to Crémieux warmly in favor of immigration and has raised his voice for it in the press. But the *Jewish Times* also would gladly see the immigration of Russian Jews, so that *through it* they might get far from the rabbis, their Talmud— . . . otherwise we might be rejoicing that at least *one* journal holds that America has still room enough for people.

Ibid., p. 72.

133

The Chief Frontier-Committee of Koenigsberg and Its Accusers

. . . Quite certainly the new arrivals in America, over whose helplessness and uselessness a shout of indignation went up there, *were not, for the most part, sent by the Committee,* but after having raised the money in the previous summer and fall, passed over to doing things of their own accord, in order to go begging again in Germany. However, how was it possible that already in March the American papers should raise such an outcry, after there had been sent there 97 souls all in all until then? But 97 Russian Jews came here every two weeks during the previous summer, what a hue and cry should *we* have raised! Indeed the number would have been still greater, yet the Koenigsberg Committee has nothing to do with that. It is just as *unthinkable* that it should have sent away the sick and the crippled.

Ibid., p. 248.

THE IMMIGRATION OF GERMAN JEWS UP TO 1880

Originally published as Chapter III in Volume I of the *Geshikhte fun der Yidisher Arbeter-Bavegung in di Fareynikte Shtatn* ("History of the Jewish Labor Movement in the United States"), New York, Yivo, 1943

In the 19th century the Germans advanced to first place in the European immigration to America. Simultaneously, the Jewish population of the United States increased from 15,000 in 1840 to 250,000 at the end of the seventies.[1] This increase, particularly noted in the years 1840-60, was due mainly to the German Jews, who were carried along with the general stream of emigrants from Germany. Thus a German-Jewish periodical wrote in 1856: "The majority of Jewish communities [in the U. S. A.] were established by German immigrants. These communities... are the true bearers of Jewish life in America."[2] It is a very significant fact that the German Jews comprised the majority of the Jewish population in the United States, while the Germans themselves were far from constituting a majority of the non-Jewish European immigrants. True enough, they composed the largest single national group from the point of view of numbers, but other peoples (the Irish, the Swedes, etc.) formed an overwhelming non-German majority.

The first general wave of German immigrants, chiefly up to 1860, consisted of "settlers," the subsequent colonists and farmers; the second wave (up to 1880), of "hands," workers in the newly established industrial centers. In certain industries that were altogether introduced by Germans (e.g., the breweries), only German immigrants were employed. The Jewish immigrants from Germany presented an entirely different picture. Those of them who were industrial entrepreneurs employed mainly Jewish laborers; not, however, the new

[1] In the German-American press and literature the number of German Jews in America is frequently exaggerated. Gustav Gottheil speaks of 300,000 German Jews in the beginning of the seventies, and the *Deutsch-Amerikanisches Conversations-Lexicon* puts their number at 600,000! See G. Gottheil, "The Position of the Jews in the U. S.," *North American Review*, 1878; *Deutsch-Amerikanisches Conversations-Lexicon*, New York, 1869-1871.
[2] An editorial "Offenes Sendschreiben" in the Cincinnati *Deborah*, April 4, 1856.

Reprinted from *Yivo Annual of Jewish Social Science*, Volume II-III, 1947-1948.

arrivals from Germany or Prussian Poland (since 1772), but chiefly East European immigrants. The rise of this new group of East European immigrants determined the mode of living of the Jewish population in the United States and also brought to life the Jewish labor movement. But one can understand this process only in the framework of the history of the German-Jewish immigration to America.

How did the German Jews develop the Jewish settlement in North America and when did they begin coming to America? In contrast to the Germans, the German-Jewish immigrants did not have, as the saying goes, to begin from scratch. The foundation for the German-Jewish settlement was laid by the first generation of pioneers, which had arrived as far back as colonial days and subsequently attained a larger competence.[3] Historical studies have not yet sufficiently elucidated the problem as to what extent the earlier colonial immigration had prepared the ground for the subsequent arrivals. The first social positions attained were the closed colonies in Lancaster, Pa., and in Georgia. In 1773, the first forty German Jews arrived in Georgia from London and settled in the newly established colony.[4] These were impoverished Jews, previously supported by the Portuguese Congregation in London. Upon the request of the Congregation, the group was included in a party of emigrants sent from England to North America, and these forty impecunious German Jews had laid, as it were, the foundation for the subsequent German-Jewish immigration. Later, in 1783, we hear of a petition of German Jews to Congress concerning admission to the country.[5] The details of this petition are as yet unknown, but we know that there is mention in it of thousands of German Jews, ready to migrate to America. In the long run, some of these in all probability found ways and means of making the trip to the new world and of establishing themselves there. The itineraries of those days, too, tell of the presence of German Jews in the Portuguese communities of North America since early days.

"Rodeph Shalom," the first German-Jewish congregation, was established in Philadelphia in 1780. In colonial days German Jews arrived in America mainly by way of Philadelphia. In that city, lists

[3] Max J. Kohler, "The German-Jewish Migration to America," *Publications of the American Jewish Historical Society*, Vol. IX.

[4] Henry Necarsulmer, "The Early Jewish Settlement at Lancaster, Pennsylvania," *Publications*, Vol. IX, pp. 29-44; Leon Hühner, "The Jews of Georgia in Colonial Times," *Publications*, Vol. X, pp. 65-95.

[5] *Deutsches Museum*, Leipzig, June, 1783, pp. 558-566.

of passengers of the period have been preserved to this day, and upon scrutinizing these for names of Jewish immigrants we find mainly names of German Jews. In 1790, the Philadelphia German newspaper carried several announcements of a lottery sponsored by German Jews to raise funds for their synagogue. The names of the sponsors of the lottery and of the ticket vendors attest to the fact that German Jews had already attained to a considerable social position in Philadelphia and in other towns of Pennsylvania. One announcement reads: "A lottery to raise eight hundred pounds to the end that the Jewish congregation of Philadelphia might free its synagogue of debts burdening it... tickets are obtainable at..."[6] In the same newspaper we find commercial announcements of German Jews.[7] Of special interest is an advertisement of the well-known Hayim Solomon, appearing as early as 1784. The fact that this advertisement was in German proves that there was already a German and German-Jewish patronage. In this advertisement Hayim Solomon announced that, because of his business connections, he had the "means of transmitting money easily to all parts of the world."[8] The transmission of money to the old homes, at that time one of the chief cares of the immigrants, became a flourishing business.

We are in possession of even more telling proof of the residence of Jewish groups within the German-speaking districts in Pennsylvania. That is the missionary propaganda that was carried on by the German press in America. In this propaganda the missionaries employed arguments that were particularly apposite to the historical and cultural state of the German Jews. Thus, for example, we find in these newspapers a report that Moses Mendelssohn, influenced by the Protestant minister Lavater, had embraced Christianity. The "fact" is described thus:

> Mendelssohn, a man of profound thinking, had reconsidered the arguments of his opponent [that is, Lavater] and his faith began to vacillate. Finally, the power of truth vanquished him completely, and his conscience prevailed upon him to take this significant step. When his coreligionists perceived that they were in danger of losing Mendelssohn, they offered him a large sum of money to dissuade him from his intention. But he replied wisely that he was no poor man and that all their wealth could not appease his conscience.... It is to be expected and all lovers of mankind hope that

[6] *Philadelphische Correspondenz*, 2, Oct. 5, 1790.
[7] See, for instance, No. 52, March 25, 1790.
[8] *Ibid.*, No. 165, June 22, 1784. The *Jewish Encyclopedia* (Vol. X, p. 654) speaks of Hayim Solomon's advertisements in French and English only and fails to mention the German.

> it will come to pass that the example of Mendelssohn will compel many of the lost sheep of the house of Israel to have their eyes opened and recognize that which can bring them true peace.[9]

Needless to say, this story of Mendelssohn's conversion was the invention of the missionaries who sought to entice Jews into apostasy in these out-of-the-way parts.

Max Kohler, the historian, mentions among the very successful German Jews of that period the names of Jonas Phillips, Gratz, Simon, Hyman Levy, and in addition the names of Hart, Sampson, Simon, Isaac Moses, and others. But he doubts that the German Jews comprised a considerable part of the Jewish population of America before 1800. However, his opinion finds no corroboration in the sources now at our dispcsal. If we examine the lists of passengers of the boats arriving in North America from Germany, by way of Hamburg or Rotterdam, in the 18th and the beginning of the 19th centuries, we obtain an entirely different picture. True, it is difficult to determine accurately the names of the Jewish passengers—in those days even German non-Jews frequently had Biblical names. But we may assume that most people with names like Cohen or Levy were Jewish; and there are other names whose Jewishness is no less certain. In general, an expert in Jewish names, and particularly in the German-Jewish names of that period, can find many a Jew in these lists of pioneers. It is important in this connection to examine the original of those lists, since in print the transcription of the names is frequently changed. Thus we can find a considerable number of unquestionably Jewish names in the seven volumes of lists in the state archives in Harrisburg (we have used the photostats of the Pennsylvania Historical Society). Among the signatures in German there are even several in Hebrew.[10] These Jewish names in the lists of Pennsylvania up to 1808 alone comprise a sizable number.[11] It is also necessary to examine the registries of the custom houses, which were preserved in a good many ports. In these registries one can see that many Jews were included among the immigrant groups arriving from Germany.[12]

[9] *Gemeinnützige Philadelphische Correspondenz,* 69, August 20, 1782.

[10] Thus on p. 123, Vol. G (6), under the name "Joh. Abraham Glimpf" and on p. 124, *ibid.,* under the name "Isaac Levy."

[11] Cf. Ralph Beaver Strassburger, *Pennsylvania German Pioneers; A Publication of the Original Lists of Arrivals in the Port of Philadelphia from 1727 to 1808,* Norristown, Pa., 1934.

[12] We have examined in the National Archives in Washington the 6 volumes of *Registers of Passengers* for the years 1820-1826, covering New York, Baltimore, the Mississippi district, the New Orleans district and others, and found a number of Jewish names among the passengers arriving from Germany.

The growing reaction in Germany in the post-Napoleonic period called forth among German Jews a more widespread disposition in favor of immigration than ever before. A reflection of this disposition we find in the well-known letter of Leopold Zunz and Edward Gans in 1822 to Mordecai Manuel Noah in America stating that a section of European, meaning German, Jewry "looks with expectantcy and hope to America and would gladly exchange its sufferings in its native land for the liberty that everyone regardless of faith enjoys there [in America]."[13] That was the time when Germany was engulfed by a tempestuous flood of chauvinism, when an anti-Semitic movement spread throughout the country—in government circles, in literature and the press, in society, and particularly in the universities (the "hep-hep" movement), and when disorders broke out in a number of cities. In the Bavarian Diet shouts were heard: "Banish the Jews to America!"[14] Some German Jews who saw no future for themselves in their native land indeed set out for America. The well-known traveler Benjamin speaks of a "mass emigration" of German Jews, which began in 1836, set in motion by the political reaction, particularly in Bavaria, by the economic depression in the country and the limitations imposed upon the number of Jewish marriages (*vide infra*). The first Jewish emigrants from Germany, he states, "were ordinary artisans, without education or means."[15] From 1840 to 1848, as generally assumed, the number of German Jews in the United States rose from 15,000 to 50,000. But a far greater flow of German Jews came immediately after 1848, after the failure of the revolution and the blighting of all hopes of the German Jews for a full emancipation, particularly in Bavaria, where the Jews obtained no rights whatsoever. The number of German Jews in America was growing continually; according to an inquiry conducted by the Union of American Hebrew Congregations in 1877, the number of Jews in the United States reached 190,000 (more than that, according to other sources). By far the majority of these were Jews from Germany, who had already by that time achieved a considerable measure of success.

In discussions of the economic accomplishments of the Jews in America, the argument was frequently advanced that the Jews in America had not received the aid and support that the Germans had

[13] See *Publications*, Vol. XX, pp. 147-148.
[14] *Zeilungen und Relationen des 15-18. Jahrhunderts.*
[15] J. J. Benjamin, *Drei Jahre in Amerika*, Hannover, 1862, Vol. I, p. 47.

received from their churches and auxiliary organizations in Germany and abroad. This notion that in the first twenty-five years of their settlement in America the German Jews had to shift for themselves is not entirely in accord with historical facts. The German Jews, as we know, came along with the general stream of emigrants from Germany, and together with it they penetrated into the interior of the country. We know that as early as 1815 Germans appeared in Ohio in substantial numbers. In a description of the German settlement in Cincinnati, we find an indication that the first Jewish congregation in that city was founded in 1822.

> Among the 45,000 inhabitants of this city in 1840, 14,000 were Germans. Besides Catholics, Protestants, and Methodists, the number of Israelites too had increased. Their synagogue was located east of Broadway, between 5th and 6th Streets. The warden of the synagogue was M. A. Mähring.[16]

These familiar German surroundings translated to the new world, in part with identical economic functions, provided the Jews with a solid footing in the early years. A second important factor was the German language, which kept the field among the German immigrants in the new home and aided the German Jews considerably in taking root in their first occupations. The German press took into due consideration the Jewish reader and the Jewish advertiser. The German language and the translated German mode of living were a far more cohesive force and united the Germans to a larger degree than the German church organizations, which were frequently at odds among themselves.

The Germans in America are usually described as "latecomers" and "non-pioneers." The historical kernel of this assertion derives in all probability from the fact that the first German emigration was called forth not so much by purely economic motives as by the striving for freedom, after the hopes of a revolution had perished. That was the motto both of the "gray" immigrants of the first revolutionary wave after 1830 and of the "green" immigrants after 1848. In these revolutionary circles the economic motive did not play such a decisive role in emigration as it began to play later. More impressive was the idea of political and religious freedom and of the founding of a free German cultural center in the new world. But

[16] H. H.[einzen], Cincinnati, "Eine Historische Skizze," *Der Deutsche Pionier,* Cincinnati, 1869, pp. 140-168. We find this Mähring also in the membership list of the German Pioneer's Society in Cincinnati published in the *Deutsche Pionier* of 1869. It may be emphasized that prerequisites for membership in the society were a minimum residence of twenty-five years in Cincinnati or vicinity and a minimum age of forty.

for the wide circles of the German population that ideal alone did not suffice. A more powerful influence was exerted by economic motives, by the possibility of establishing oneself in the new land, especially when there was also a possibility of finding familiar surroundings with one's own mode of living and language. Soon after the gold rush in California, maps of the United States began to circulate in Germany, upon which the places where gold was mined were indicated in golden color,[17] and these maps had a greater effect upon the disposition to emigrate than all other motives. After 1860 it is rare to discover another motive for emigration than the economic, save in the case of a small group of active socialists at the time of the exceptional legislation against socialists in Germany (1879-91).

In addition to the general factors of emigration, the German Jews had their own special motives. In the contemporary discussions of Jewish emigration from German lands, these motives were dwelt upon at length. These discussions were primarily an inner Jewish affair, but with a wide window to the neighboring world. They were conducted in the columns of the general German press. Some of the newspapers upheld the arguments of the Jewish press and thereby increased their opposition to the states that had brought about the situation, while, on the other hand, others inveighed against the Jewish arguments as to the causes of their emigration from their native land. However, before considering the specific Jewish motives of emigration the question must be posed: What was the effect of the general German emigration sentiment upon the German Jews?

It would be very odd indeed if the political motives of the revolutionary-minded elements in Germany had not carried along with them also the Jews, who had taken an active part in the struggles of the German revolution. For the Jews suffered not only from the general political regime, but also from special Jewish disabilities. We need not, therefore, be surprised that the general German emigration sentiment—the free man on free soil—had deep repercussions in Jewish life and consciousness, as manifested in the literature and even the folklore of the period. This sentiment was also brought over to the new home.[18] Among the causes that compelled German

[17] *Kollektaneenblatt f. d. Geschichte Bayerns,* Vol. XCIV, pp. 72-86.

[18] Cf. the poem "Der Knabe," published in the *Allgemeine Zeitung des Judenthums,* June 10, 1837, as well as the poem "Die Israelitischen Einwanderer," of similar sentiment published in *Deborah* (Cincinnati), No. 1, 1855. We cite two characteristic passages of these poems:

Mutter, nicht in diesem Lande—Bleib ich, bin ich stark und gross,—Wär's auch bis zum Meerestrande,—Such mir anderwärts mein Loos: —Hab ich Heimat dann gefunden, —Wo ich

Jews to seek a new home overseas, aside from the general disappointment in the hope of a free Germany, was perhaps the concern for the younger generation, which saw no future for itself in its native land because of the special disabilities imposed upon the Jews. This was the case particularly in the small towns and rural districts of Bavaria, which were at that time the main source of German-Jewish emigration. According to the laws or decrees in effect, a Jewish young man could hardly have hoped to become a permanent resident, or to marry in his native place, for he could not obtain the right of citizenship. The number of Jewish inhabitants in each district was restricted, and youth growing up into manhood had to wait for the death of one of the older inhabitants to free a "place," or else leave the district. This subject was frequently discussed in the German-Jewish press. Thus we read in a communication from Bavaria:

> What should our young people do? Having lost a fortune in litigations to gain their purpose (to obtain the right of denizenship) ... what is there for them to do but to seek a new home, where they can utilize their professions and demonstrate their knowledge and abilities? Take this instance: a young, well-to-do artisan applied for protection to the district court and was refused. He made a last attempt to obtain his right, but applied simultaneously for a foreign passport.... He received the passport and is leaving.[19]

Under such circumstances it was more practical from the outset to plan for a new life abroad—usually that meant in America—and use the money for traveling expense and the initial steps in establishing oneself in the new land. In a contemporary German-American periodical we read in a private communication from Southern Germany: "The daily and weekly publications are full of announcements of 'sale of entire stock below cost price....' Emigration this year has reached mass proportions; anyone having relatives or friends in America who are in a fair way hesitates no longer and sets out on his journey."[20] The handicrafts in the small towns of Germany were at that time overcrowded. The young Jewish artisan had no legal or factual opportunity to ply his trade. "In Swabia"—we read in a German-Jewish periodical—"[Jewish] artisans in various trades have recently made their appearance. But many of them have encoun-

frei bin, unumwunden,—Leben wir dann wohl geborgen,—Ohne Schimpf und Angst und Sorgen . . . (*Allg. Zeitung d. Judenthums*, June 10, 1837).
. . . Weit, weit hin gegen Westen,—Da ist ein grosses Land,—Weit über Weltmeer reicht es — Uns seine Bruderhand. — Dort ziehen wir hinüber. — Dort soll die Stätte sein, — Wo Rub wir finden können, — Von Leiden, Schmach und Pein. (*Die Deborah*, Cincinnati, No. 1, 1855).

[19] *Allg. Zeitung d. Judenthums*, May 9, 1837.

[20] *Der Bürgerfreund*, Philadelphia, June 19, 1847.

tered such obstacles in obtaining the right of permanent residence that they have decided rather to emigrate. The majority of them have departed for America." [21] In another instance we read:

> Hamburg, June 22. Last week a group of German emigrants passed through here on their way to America. Among them were some seventy Jews, coming mainly from Bavaria. They have acquired a trade but could not engage in it, since they were not permitted to become residents in their native land; the number of Jewish families in each community must not increase.[22]

In addition to these disabilities, a number of German principalities had countless forms of taxes that only Jews had to pay, and a large share of the income of a Jewish merchant or artisan was consumed by these levies, so that even the fortunate possessor of the coveted rights had no great desire to remain in the old home.

These two causes—the great obstacles in the way of becoming residents and the onerous Jewish taxes—were constantly mentioned in the discussions of the motives of Jewish emigration from Germany. The German press frequently ignored these causes and stated that the Jews were leaving Germany because the country was not rich enough for them, and the Jewish press fought bitterly against that argument. The causes — wrote the *Allgemeine Zeitung des Judenthums* — were entirely different: the local authorities in Bavaria introduced everywhere all kinds of new levies: "protection-money," "goose-money," "horse-money," etc.,

> which imposed a crushing burden upon the Jews, and this at a time when the needs increase and the means are on the decline. This compels the younger and even the older men to seek their fortunes in other parts of the world, where at least they will be exempt from this burden.[23]

The Jewish press was particularly stirred to a high pitch of excitement by the argument of some German publications that the Bavarian Jews emigrated to avoid military service. "Did it ever happen in Prussia that a Jew should leave his fatherland to avoid service in the army? This is a brazen lie!"—wrote the *Allgemeine Zeitung des Judenthums* in indignation.[24]

Such prominent German publications as *Allgemeine Augsburger Zeitung* and *Leipziger Zeitung* participated in the discussion of the causes of German-Jewish emigration. This bears witness to the fact that the Jewish emigration problems elicited a great interest also in

[21] *Israelitische Annalen*, Aug. 30, 1839.
[22] *Allg. Zeitung des Judenthums*, June 30, 1837.
[23] *Ibid.*, Aug. 24, 1839.
[24] *Ibid.*, Sept. 28, 1839.

German circles. As early as 1839 the German press estimated the number of emigrated Bavarian Jews as 10,000.

All the callings that could be acquired in the small towns of Germany were represented among the Jewish emigrants. All over the large cities sprang up societies for the promotion of handicraft among Jews, having in mind the younger generation destined to emigrate. "In thinking of the future"—the introductory report of such a society in Mayence states—"one must call out as loud as possible to the middle and poorer classes: 'Run to the workshops! Learn a trade!' "[25]

As early as the end of the thirties, it was felt in Germany that the emigration was having its effect upon the state of the local Jewish communities and organizations. A number of congregations and organizations realized that if the movement were to continue, they would remain without members. Thus we read in a communication from Würzburg:

> One could have foreseen a considerable emigration this year. But unfortunately it was much more extensive than could have been anticipated. I say unfortunately, because under the present circumstances it will have unhappy results. If the present tendency is to continue, numerous small communities will be compelled to close their synagogues and schools. They will not be in a position to pay their teachers and synagogue personnel unless the state comes to their aid. In many a place, out of a Jewish population of 30-40 families 15-20 people have emigrated, mainly the young and employable.[26]

On the other hand, the necessity of organizing the mass transports was well understood. The newspapers at that time were full of reports on emigration. It was also discussed in special pamphlets and broadsides. These reports give us a clear picture of the way the transports of emigrants streamed into the ports. They also tell us of the provision for *Kashrut* and the other religious requirements on the journey.

> On May 6 [we read in one such report from Würzburg] Jewish emigrants from the Saxon and Bavarian border, some 100 persons, traveling as a unit, assembled in Meiningen. They will travel on one boat and intend to establish in America a small Jewish community. They carry with them a scroll of the Torah, a *megillah,* a *shofar,* etc., and have taken along from Germany men who are capable of fulfilling the functions of *shohet, mohel,* religious teacher, and cantor. They have made all preparations for the observance of their religious duties on their journey overseas. May the blessing of God accompany them and may they safely reach their new home, which is to be their new homeland.[27]

[25] *Ibid.,* 1838, p. 492.
[26] *Ibid.,* 1839, p. 155.
[27] *Ibid.,* May 25, 1839.

The large number of non-Jewish emigration societies were chiefly occupied with providing steamship tickets for their members, protecting them from agents, who were active in the port cities, and also—what was very important—with procuring land in America. But the Jewish communal aid had entirely different tasks: to provide for the emigrants until they reached the boat, and for the religious needs on the boat. They were sure that, having reached America, the Jewish emigrants would be more or less able to get on. Parenthetically, let it be added that all witnesses are unanimous in their declaration that there were no Jews among the swindling agents in the American ports.

> I was particularly assured by the fact [one of these states] that I did not see a Jew among the riffraff and I would have recognized them even aside from their long noses and black hair. Germans of the Christian faith, too, have borne me out in this, that among these bandits they did not encounter a single Jew.[28]

The authorities in Germany and Austria suddenly realized that as a result of the Jewish emigration they were losing more and more taxpayers, and introduced a special tax on Jewish emigrants. Whereas in the emigration of Germans only the loss in population was considered, in the emigration of Jews the loss of income to the state treasury was a consideration, and consequently as much as possible was extorted from them for the right to leave the fatherland. In a communication from Germany, printed in a New York German publication, we read:

> The sentiment in favor of emigration has spread to such an extent that the authorities have become alarmed. In Austria they have introduced an emigration tax; in Rhenish Hesse emigration to America is forbidden save by special permission. And it is quite clear: the fewer people the less taxes, particularly since now so many of the well-to-do emigrate.[29]

In a more concrete form we see this in a communication from Ettingen, published in the *Allgemeine Zeitung des Judenthums*:

> Even some of the older families of Ettingen are now emigrating, but they encounter great difficulties. The European governments, as is well-known, have concluded a treaty with the North American states concerning free emigration up to 1840; but the "Standesherren" [princes] have the right to demand the tenth gulden [meaning a tenth] of the possessions taken along, and a family, let us say, taking 4,000 florins would have to render to the "Standesherren" 400 florins. Wallerstein, the Prince of Ettingen, is patently making use of that right and thereby hinders the [Jewish] emigrants.[30]

[28] *Deutsch-Amerikanische Skizzen für jüdische Auswanderer und Nichtauswanderer*, Leipzig, 1857, p. 23.
[29] *Deutsche Monatshefte*, New York, 1853, p. 64.
[30] *Allg. Zeitung d. Judenthums*, 1839, p. 159.

Just as entire German villages would emigrate in order to settle collectively in America, so there were also Jewish groups that decided to establish in America closed communities of their members, and wished to prepare beforehand for that eventuality. True, in America the fate of the individual members of such groups often varied considerably; nevertheless the emigration by families, with the influx of even distant relatives, helped substantially in the establishment of the first Jewish communities. A number of Jewish communities in America were essentially somewhat larger family associations.

We possess ample information to the effect that German-Jewish emigrants set out to learn new trades before emigrating. Nevertheless, upon arriving in America, practically all German Jews began with peddling. The peddler became the hero of the so-called "Jews Stories." Isaac M. Wise described in his memoirs the various categories of the German-Jewish peddlers of those days: The "basket peddler" who knew no English at all, mostly a young recent arrival; the "custom peddler" who already had acquired a little English; and the peddler who carried a pack of 100-150 pounds on his back and who already entertained hopes of becoming a storekeeper in due time. Among the peddlers arose an aristocracy with a hierarchy all its own: the "wagon baron," with his own horse and wagon for peddling across country; the "jewelry count," who carried around a satchel with watches, rings, and other jewelry; the "store prince," who had attained to the ownership of a store.[31] The German Jews also played a prominent role in the clothing business, first as peddlers of old clothes. In his well-known study of the clothing industry in New York, Professor I. E. Pope[32] states that prior to the Civil War trading in old clothes far outweighed the business in new clothing, and was concentrated in the hands of the Jews. New clothing was made at that time by the Irish, the English, and the Germans. Gradually this industry was taken over by German-Jewish immigrants, who subsequently became the owners of the large clothing shops and stores. We have very scant information on this transition. The few records indicate that at an early period the clothing business came to be centralized among Jews in a special street. Thus we read in a book about life in Cincinnati: "Look, another clothing store, and again the owner is a Jew," said the tailor, "we've passed 33 houses, and this is the fifteenth store. They are settled here densely."[33]

[31] Isaac M. Wise, *Reminiscences*, Cincinnati, 1901, p. 38.
[32] I. E. Pope, *The Clothing Industry in New York*, University of Missouri, 1905.
[33] *Der Erzähler am Ohio*, Cincinnati, 1849, p. 280 ff.

For quite some time it was not noticeable that the Jewish immigrants of that generation had attained to a degree of economic power in certain fields. It seemed as if all leading economic positions were occupied by "Yankees" exclusively, and to the Jews only a very restricted economic field was left. In a German-American periodical a conversation with a Jewish optician-jeweler is cited, saying: "You can make two Jews out of an American, and one Christian will be left yet."

> Jews [says the author of that article], who in Europe have so quickly and so skillfully created huge mercantile enterprises, feel unnerved at the sights of the gigantic American spirit of enterprise. The majority of them become peddlers and petty traders. Possibly they also have the feeling that at bottom many Americans are more intolerant than the Europeans.[34]

Insofar as we can determine the initial careers of individual German Jews who have achieved success, their economic rise began with the accumulation of capital, chiefly in the banking business and real estate.

The rise of small Jewish communities in the Middle West, with the subsequent movement to the Pacific, was in the main the work of the German Jews. Cincinnati was the center of these scattered and distant communities and a mainstay for the satisfaction of their religious needs. Thus we read in a communication from Cincinnati of that period:

> The local community received orders for Matzoh from the entire West; this proves how densely populated the West is with our brethren. Orders came from Indiana, Illinois, Tennessee, Kentucky, and Missouri. This testifies that there are Jewish inhabitants in practically every town in those parts. Judaism has a great future in the young West.[35]

Among the Jewish immigrants from Germany, just as among the German immigrants, were numerous intellectuals. Many of these German-Jewish intellectuals played a role in German-American journalism; some became publishers of newspapers. Thus Joseph Kohn was co-owner of the publication *Der Deutsche Courier,* founded in New Orleans in 1842; only later was this publication transferred to German ownership. It is hard to say whether all the stories about Jews which used to be printed at that time in practically all German-American publications derived from Jewish journalists. Some publications here had (just as in Germany) "Judeo-German" supplements, usually humorous, and undoubtedly the authors of these

[34] Franz Löher, "Am Niagara," *Deutsche Monatshefte,* New York, 1855, p. 458.
[35] *Die Deborah,* 1856, p. 270.

humorous anecdotes were Jews, who wished to curry favor, through these stories, with the German reading public. Some of these "productions," considerably anti-Semitic, smack of self-mocking.[36] On the other hand, neither the better type of German publication, nor the attempts at the establishment of an artistic German theatre in America could have materialized without the support of the German Jews. German theatrical enterprises, at times under Jewish management, took into serious consideration the German-Jewish audience and its press and frequently accommodated themselves to it in their repertory (thus, for example, the comedy *Israel the Long,* produced in Cincinnati, under the direction of Phillip Horwitz[37]). The other German cultural institutions, too, came to count upon the German Jews. German-Jewish educational institutions were considered an extension of Germanism. German public leaders were even dissatisfied with the separate cultural and social activities conducted by the German Jews. A German periodical reproached the Jews:

> A distinct, or better, separate part of the German element consists of German Jews. They possess well-established service organizations and also glee clubs, choral societies, educational associations and good schools. At present they are even engaged in founding a university. In this manner they develop art and science to a higher degree than their Christian countrymen. It is, however, notable that they stand apart [from the non-Jew], while all their efforts in that direction bear such a pronounced German character that the English-speaking Jews even look askance at them, whereof *Deborah* complains bitterly, but notwithstanding calls upon the German Jews not to discontinue their [German] cultural activities.[38]

Thus we see that the Germans defended the German Jews, whereas English-speaking Jewry attacked them for their cultivation of the German language and the German spirit. The former considered these activities a German affair. The Jews who shaped their social life upon a German pattern were very proud of that and considered it a special achievement of the German-Jewish immigration. They emphasized that point in their press, as we read in *Deborah,* the German-Jewish publication of Cincinnati:

> The Queen City has a richer social life than any other city in the states.

[36] In the Philadelphia German newspaper *Die Lokomotive* we find this burlesque of a Jewish participant in the Revolution of 1848, signed "Eisick und Schatzmatz":

"Nu, aner von unre Leit is aach mitgegange(n). Net, dass er's gern gethon hätte! No, no, eh war far die Kaafmannschaft erzoge — die Flint hot er gefercht wie das Feier! . . . er wollt' Offesier werren, — er ist tautgeschosse worren un begrabe." (*Die Lokomotive,* 1853, p. 58).

On the following gem:

"Reb' Itzeg und Reb' Mayer über die türkische Frage . . . England un Frankreich send die Klesmurem un spielen den Tanz, ün der Terrek müss nehbich tanzen, wie sie spielen. . . ." (*Ibid.,* p. 96).

[37] *Die Deborah,* 1855, p. 40.

[38] *Deutsche Monatshefte,* New York, 1856, p. 187.

The blithe German spirit has here more than elsewhere subdued Puritanical rigor and austerity. Our Israelites have a large share in this victory of the joy of life. Not only are they vigorous supporters of the local public [German] theatre, but their own recreation clubs are the best in the city. The "Alemania," "Harmonia," "Phoenix," and "Taglioni" number over 500 members and provide for their membership various social entertainments. The balls, the "socials," the concerts and amateur theatricals bring together every week happy and spirited groups of men and women.[39]

The first generation of German Jews remained faithful to that tradition and saw to it that their children, too, knew German. Here not only the romantic attachment to the old home was operative but also the conviction, held at that time not by Germans alone, that the German school system was the best in the world. The German Jews maintained that they dare not renounce the cultural patrimony brought along from their native land. This patriotism in regard to the German language was expressed in a communication from New York (1845) telling of the establishment of an elementary school at a synagogue of German Jews in New York, and the controversy over the question of the language of instruction. The trustees of the synagogue insisted that the instruction be in German, but this apparently provoked some protests, and the correspondent defended the trustees:

I fail to see why the teacher, a native of Germany, should force himself, or be forced, to teach the children the elementary subjects in English. Why should the German language in general be ignored or thrust aside? [40]

The Germans in America at that time fought for official recognition of the German language and the establishment of a public school system in German, and the Jews supported them therein actively. Just as the German churches were preserved here because of the German service, so the German-Jewish communities and charitable organizations, too, wished to strengthen their position with the aid of the German language. The statutes of the new *Chevra Kadisha,* founded by German Jews in New York, in the middle forties, were written in German. More than that: in the statutes was included a special provision (paragraph 4, art. 93) to the effect that "all proceedings and motions must be in the German language." [41] However, even then concessions had to be made for the younger generation, and for its benefit English sermons were introduced.[42] Notwith-

[39] *Die Deborah,* 1858-1859, p. 126.
[40] *Allg. Zeitung d. Judenthums,* 1845, p. 407.
[41] *Ibid.,* 1843, p. 478.
[42] A correspondent in the *Deborah,* Apr. 15, 1859, from New York relates: "Particularly the younger generation, which no longer understands the German tongue, is gratified with the English lectures of Mr. Cordova" [delivered in a synagogue of German Jews].

standing, the German language survived among German Jews for a comparatively long time. In 1871, the *Deutsch-Amerikanisches Conversations-Lexicon* under the article "Jude" (p. 50) wrote: "In the majority of Jewish communities the German language prevails to this day. However, English is gaining rapidly, and already the majority of Jewish publications appear in English." Jews were freely accepted in the general German societies and were not only equal, but also active members. So it was in the "Pioneer-Associations," educational societies, in the German sports organizations, and particularly in the German immigrant aid societies. Frequently, we hear of Jews in the administration of these organizations.[43]

The later attitude of superiority assumed by the German Jews, of standing apart and above the East European Jews, is to be explained not only on the basis of their higher social and economic position in comparison with the poor green immigrant. From the very outset, the German Jews regarded themselves also as the truest bearers of the Jewish tradition, as they conceived of it. They also looked down upon the Portuguese Jews and even entertained some doubts and suspicions as to their piety. Under these circumstances the German Jews could not acclimate themselves in the old Portuguese communities and soon began to found their own communities, in their own spirit and style. The Portuguese Jews—they argued—have no sense of philanthropy; German Jews can be aided only by German-Jewish charity organizations. The German Jews were quickly seized with the ambition to be acknowledged as the most liberal donors among all the Jews. The number of German Jews depending upon charity became progressively smaller, so that the charitable impulse was diverted to aid the poor East European immigrants. Thus we read in a communication dating from 1856 that "the Jewish community of Cincinnati numbers 6,000 souls; of these, only 150 are in need of aid. The Jewish community of Cincinnati enjoys unusual prosperity and practically all of the Jews belong in the well-to-do middle class.[44]

The growth in competence among the German Jews led to their separation from East European Jews; first, in the matter of residence. At that time the general dissolution of the purely German sections

[43] See the stereotyped "Meldung der Deutschen Gesellschaft" in Baltimore with B. J. Kohn as "Schatzmeister," in Georg Treu, *Das Buch der Auswanderung*, Bamberg, 1848, p. 105.

[44] *Die Deborah*, 1856, p. 302.

of the city began, and the wealthier elements began to move into the more attractive residential sections. The press was of the opinion that the struggle waged in New York between the orthodox and reformed Jews could be settled in the following manner: the wealthier elements, who lived up-town and the majority of whom were reformed, should without contention yield to the "obscurantists" all the synagogues they possessed on the "East Side," since they lived too far away to attend them.[45]

But then something happened. As soon as the Americanized German Jews began to penetrate into "Yankee" circles, the latter withdrew and held aloof from them. The wealthy German Jews felt deeply offended at being regarded as aliens and identified with the immigrant populace. Thus we read in an article about "Jewish ostracism in America" that "no people wishes to be judged by its emigrants." Among the immigrants there are numerous civilized Jews, who nevertheless are identified by the American public "with the ill-bred personages loitering about the wharves."[46] The contempt of the German Jews for the *Ost-Juden* became manifest considerably before the mass immigration of the eighties. As early as the forties, we read in a communication from the United States to the *Allgemeine Zeitung des Judenthums*:

> The Polack [meaning the Polish and, generally, East European Jew] is the filthiest creature of all classes, and because of him they begin even here to use the word "Jew" as an insulting epithet.... The German disdains the Polack and shuns him, and therefore the Polack detests the German.... True, the English Jew deems himself superior to the German Jew, nevertheless, he maintains friendly relations with him.

The paper continues in the same vein:

> The mortal enemies of Lilienthal here are the large number of Polacks.[47] We also have Lilienthal's own opinion of the East European Jews, expressed in his "open letter" in a New York German-Jewish periodical: "The Polish Jews who have come mostly from East Prussia [meaning Posen] have the characteristics of a chameleon.... It is they more than anyone else who desecrate the Sabbath. For the sake of business they disregard Jewish laws.[48]

In the presence of such deep-seated enmity for East European Jewry, the German Jews quite naturally regarded with contempt the mode of life, the culture, and, perhaps above all, the language of the East European Jew. In the German-Jewish press in America we find

[45] *Ibid.*, May, 1859.
[46] Nina Morais, "Jewish Ostracism in America," *North American Review*, 1881, Vol. II. p. 265 f.
[47] *Allg. Zeitung d. Judenthums*, 1846, p. 448.
[48] *Die Deborah*, Apr. 4, 1856, "Lilienthal's offenes Sendschreiben."

many violent attacks on "Jargon," although even then it was quite clear that the German language no longer enjoyed the status it once had, and that it would not survive much longer among the younger generation, which was shifting to English. In order to characterize this attitude of the American German-Jewish press to Yiddish, let us cite a passage from *Deborah* of 1899, attacking Leo Wiener, the author of the well-known history of Yiddish literature in English.

> Leo Wiener suffered embarrassment, as almost all writers do, who come to the defense of the jargon-class [?]. None of the Jewish writers in America was personally so vilified, so pelted with mud and rotten eggs as was he, who wanted to usher into the world-literature this literature without an alphabet [?] or a grammar, and set out to glorify its poets. That is a disgrace, but just as primitive, crude and chaotic as the Jargon on the whole.[49]

Parenthetically, be it remarked here that the German speech of the German Jew himself was not on a very high plane; we find in it many uncouth neologisms, which undoubtedly shocked the true masters and lovers of the language.[50]

Also in the nineties, we hear an entirely different characterization of the two types of Jews, the uncouth Eastern immigrant and the respectable Americanized German Jew, coming incidentally from a German Christian, the son of a village schoolmaster in Schwarzwald, an immigrant in America. The author described his impressions of a synagogue in a poor Jewish section in New York and a reform temple of the German Jews.

> Among these "hooked noses" [in the synagogue of the immigrants] I sensed genuine prayer. There were ordinary Jews, unclean and trafficking, but Jews who never left the ghettos, which are to be found also in the modern American cities. On their prayers poverty has imposed a mark of holiness. This I never experienced in the reform temples, where the hooked noses are turned upward so high. There faith has deteriorated into hypocrisy. The old Jehova is treated to modern opera music. The vacuity of a lost faith is covered up with phrases about humanity and "scientific lectures." There the wives of the notorious bankrupts, the Heavenbridges, Fechbergers, Lichtensterns, and whatever their names may be, sit and display their pomp.... No, I'd rather be with the true orthodox hooked noses. And sickening of the "hep-hep" cries of the anti-Semites, I betake myself to the Jewish synagogue and listen to the song of ancient glory, or I seek refuge in my childhood memories about the Feast of Booths. . . .[51]

[49] *Ibid.*, Apr. 27, 1899.

[50] Here is an example of the corruption of the German language in America cited by the *Deborah*: Er thut a gut Bissnes in the Cauntry. Er kiebt e Stohr in e Willetsch. Sein Keppitel ist zwar nicht gross, aber er ist sehr smart. Sein Bruder ist schon zwei mal gebrochen, und hat immer geseddelt, jetzt hat er doch nichts. Einiger Mann weiss seine Zirkumstenses, und er denied sie nicht. "This is German in America!"—the periodical exclaims. (1855, p. 135).

[51] "Unter Krummen Nasen" in *Der Arme Teufel*, Sept. 9, 1893.

The old "hep-hep" cry, which resounded in Germany in the beginning of the 19th century, began to reach America in a metamorphosed form and gained a hearing in the German-American press. We find it also in the series of anti-Semitic caricatures, that appeared under the caption "Die Physiognomie des Reporters 'Dr.' Schoofle und ihre Wandlungen während der Wintersaison."[52]

Jews in America have fashioned their communities and institutions in a new world of religious freedom, where the external pressure and the political handicaps of the old home were lacking. And in this field, it must be confessed, the German Jews were true pioneers. Without any model before their eyes, under the new circumstances, they fashioned their congregations and institutions, devised methods of raising funds for philanthropic and social purposes and built up a complex cultural machinery. The East European Jews, too, acknowledge the accomplishments of the preceding generation of German-Jewish immigrants in that realm. A Russian Jew, who in Cincinnati had occupied an important position created by German Jews, wrote enthusiastically about the organizational achievements of the German Jews in Cincinnati:

> Even in that time, when generous giving had not yet become a universal habit among the rich, the generosity of the German Jews was proverbial in Cincinnati, and they were the pillars of philanthropies and of the arts.[53]

A kindred study by the author appeared in the *Yivo Bleter,* XXV, 1 (January-February, 1945) and 2 (March-April, 1945). The attention of the reader is also called to a related study by Joseph Kissman, "The Immigration of Rumanian Jews up to 1914," in this volume.

[52] See the German periodical *Schnedderedeng,* New York, Nov. 17, 1873.
[53] Boris D. Bogen, *Born a Jew,* New York, 1930, p. 72.

NOTES ON EARLY JEWISH PEDDLING IN AMERICA

The gifts of Nature, though lavish, are diverse; and not every portion of a country or continent is blessed by her with equal advantages and attractions. The deficiency, however, is often remedied by the efforts of men; and — odd as it may sound — in the task of converting the wilderness to a garden and of accommodating seemingly unpromising areas to civilization, a major role must be assigned to the peddler. Nowhere is this more clearly demonstrated than in the history of the United States. It was the peddler who supplied the early pioneer with those necessities of life otherwise unobtainable in his remote, outlandish settlements; it was, in turn, the necessity of providing the peddler with stock that largely promoted the establishment of commercial houses and factories along the principal waterways, his main means of travel; and it was the subsequent development of the itinerant peddler into a resident storekeeper that laid the foundations of local trade and helped to change primitive settlements into towns and cities.

For the history of American Jewry, peddling is of even more crucial significance. Most of the older immigrants started as peddlers, and it was to the opportunities provided and created by peddling that the small community of colonial times was mainly indebted for its subsequent phenomenal increase and for that radical transformation of its structure and pattern which ensued during the first eighty years of the nineteenth century.[1]

Deductions based on the first U. S. census, that of 1790, indicate that the total number of Jews then engaged in all branches of economic activity

[1] At the end of the 18th century, the Jewish population of North America was between 2,000 and 5,000; in 1880, however, it was estimated at 300,000.

Reprinted from *Jewish Social Studies,* Volume VII, 1945

was less than one thousand. In 1850, however, the number of peddlers in the country was given as 10,669 and in 1860 as 16,594;[2] and that most of these — at least in the last-named decade — were Jews may be reasonably concluded on several grounds. In the first place, the rapid increase during that period coincides with a large-scale Jewish immigration from Germany. Secondly, in the city directories of the time, most of the persons classified as peddlers bear such distinctive appellations as Cohen or Levy, or typically German Jewish names ending in -heimer or -steiner. Thirdly, it is a matter of record that the proportion of economically active persons was larger in the immigrant Jewish communities than among both Jews and non-Jews in 1790.[3]

Moreover, in making calculations from census data, it must be borne in mind that even these do not tell the complete story. The census, after all, is decennial, and therefore registers the status of a person only as it happens to be at the end of a decade. Accordingly, many a man who may have started as a peddler but who meanwhile had transformed himself into a storekeeper, or adopted some other profession, would be entered only in the latter category. Again, owing to the necessity, in most states, of obtaining a license, many peddlers in fact plied their trade clandestinely, and were therefore not registered as such. The number of actual peddlers in any decade would therefore always exceed that recorded in the census.

1. *The Economic Background of Jewish Peddling*

Jewish peddling is generally regarded as little more than an expedient device whereby immigrant "greenhorns" contrived, almost parasitically, to make a living. Nothing, however, could be further from the truth. For while peddling certainly provided the first step in the economic adjust-

[2] Jones, Fred Mitchell, *Middlemen in the Domestic Trade of the United States, 1800-1860.* Illinois Studies in the Social Sciences, vol. xxi, No. 3 (Urbana 1937), p. 63.

[3] The census of 1790 shows that the families of both Jews and non-Jews were then of substantially the same size (six persons) and that there were very few unattached Jews, without families. Both facts indicate that the number of persons economically active was small. This, however, is in marked contrast with the situation at the time of the first large-scale Jewish immigration. Gainfully employed Jews were numerous in the "old immigration" settlements, often equalling and sometimes (e.g. in mining towns) exceeding the total of unmarried males in a family.

ment of the newcomer, it fulfilled a positive economic function in contemporary American life, and its subsequent evolution and with it that of American Jewish life, was dictated by conditions created by the economic development of the continent.

In colonial times, the professional structure of the Jewish population may first of all be characterized by a negative statement; the Jews did not participate in retail trade. They may not all have been wholesale dealers, exporters or importers, but retail trade, forbidden to them originally in New Holland, did not attract them. Doubtless they were active in Indian trade, supplying the Army, and in real estate deals, but the center of their activities was triangular trade between the American colonies and the motherland *via* the West Indies. (The West Indies were the principal link in the chain of Jewish commercial positions.) Historically, these commercial relations were built in the New World by the Sephardic Jews banished from Spain. Part of the Sephardim had immigrated from the West Indies into the North American colonies. This triangular trade was hurt particularly by the Revolutionary War, and its West Indian link completely paralyzed in 1812. The Jews in America tried to meet the new situation, but when foreign trade was restored, it could not serve as a basis for the existence of the new incoming Jewish masses. The newcomers had to follow the strong development of the fresh domestic trade, procuring goods for the frontiersman, doing retail business with the pioneers settling in the interior, the pioneer-merchant following the pioneer-settler, without a possibility of establishing a fixed store. This, essentially, was the role of the peddler.

In American economic history the rise of the peddler marks the beginning of the period when supplying the settler moving into the interior had become a task for expanding domestic trade. After the war of 1812, settlers in great numbers began to stream to the West, where, however, the population was so sparse, up to 1820, that the establishment of general stores could not yet begin. Anything the settler and the frontier-family could not produce in their own primitive home-industry, such as the most necessary articles of clothing and furniture, they had to procure from the only trade that could reach them, river-boat peddling. Later, when roads were established from the rivers to the settlements in the interior, peddlers began to wander from settlement to settlement, and general stores began to appear at points the settlers could easily reach. It is the merit of the peddlers to have emancipated the settler from his economic isolation and forced self-sufficiency. The settler became connected with other sections of American economic life by his contact with trade and goods; he was able to avoid working in home-industry and could greatly increase his activities in agriculture and its several branches. The settler was able to get many things he considered luxuries, varying very much from the rough products fashioned by his home-industry. Descriptions of the pleasant side of home-life at that time report on the contents of the peddler's pack and the things he provides. These "luxuries" were also in the stock of the early general stores in the West. The peddler could not carry heavy articles in his pack and so restricted himself to supply mostly gadgets and knicknacks ("notions") for the housewife. Special wholesale houses provided dry goods and notions for the peddling trade, whereas the general store had to depend on one buying trip a year, during which the store-owner had to plan the whole stock of goods for the principal seasons. In that period, the American retail-store on the Atlantic had not yet developed into a special store, and remained for quite a long time a general store. The peddler, though his stock was small, was very much specialized in the kind of goods he carried, by the sheer force of necessity.

Early reports from the Middle West prove that the Jewish peddler and his activity were well known there, long before anybody tried to open a general store, and when such stores first came into existence, there were certainly many Jewish peddlers among the founders of them. As early as 1758, for instance, the *Pennsylvanische Berichte* carries an advertisement announcing that one Meyer Josephson, "formerly resident at the house of Moses Heyman in Reading," has now opened his own store in the market place of that city and is prepared to exchange goods at regular rates of barter.[4] Similarly, in the following year, a certain Benjamin Nathan, "lately arrived in these parts," announces, in the same journal, the opening of a general store at Heidelberg and declares himself ready to extend credit to potential customers.[5] Of the same general period also is the com-

[4] *Pennsylvanische Berichte,* July 8, 1758.
[5] *ib.,* June 8, 1759.

plaint of one John Beauchamp Jones of Hanover, Missouri, that in seeking to establish a general store he found himself confronted by competition from a former Jewish peddler;[6] while other contemporary records describe how Jews sometimes acquired land for such establishments by paying for it in goods out of their stock.[7]

It is often assumed that the Jewish peddlers crowded out their Yankee forerunners. This, however, is a mistake. The fact is that by the time the Jews came upon the scene to any appreciable degree, the Yankees, two generations ahead in experience, had already transformed themselves, to a large extent, into resident storekeepers. Actual competition was therefore only occasional and shortlived. For the most part, the Jews merely inherited the mantle of Yankees who had "gone up in the world." Moreover, it should be remembered that the Jewish peddler usually catered to a specific market — that of the German immigrants with whose peculiar tastes and needs he was familiar from the old homeland.

To be sure, there were exceptions to this general rule, but these were caused by special circumstances and do not represent the normal condition of affairs. The bustling port of New Orleans, for example, continued as a center of indiscriminate petty-trading until as late as the middle of the nineteenth century, and there Jewish and non-Jewish peddlers certainly rubbed shoulders. An account written in 1851 describes how incoming and outgoing ships were surrounded by the small boats of insistent chapmen crying their wares: "the Jew was there with his hundred-blade penkives, sponges and metallic tablets; the Yankee with his curious knicknacks brought from every auction market in the town." [8] Similarly, the California gold rush naturally attracted its quota of Jewish peddlers, who frequented the mining camps. These, however, were quite distinct from the regular chapmen, with their duly prescribed routes; they were mere catchpenny hucksters operating, from crude shacks, on a "here-today-gone-tomorrow" basis.

> "The Jew-shops," says a contemporary writer, "were generally rattletrap erections about the size of a bathing-machine, so small that one half of the stock

[6] Shortfield, Luke, pseud. [L. B. Jones], *The Western Merchant* (Philadelphia 1849), p. 183.
[7] *ib.*, p. 128.
[8] Hall, A. Oakey, *The Manhattanan in New Orleans* (New York 1851), p. 175.

had to be displayed suspended from projecting sticks outside. They were filled with red and blue flannel shirts, thick boots, and other articles suited to the wants of the miners, along with Colt's revolvers and bowie-knives, brass jewelry, and diamonds like young Koh-i-Noors." [9]

2. *The Evolution of the Jewish Peddler*

The peddler, as we have indicated, usually became a storekeeper, and this development, coupled with the general transition from West Indies to strictly domestic trade, in turn influenced a trend towards "inland business" on the part of Jewish wholesalers, who now became the suppliers of the Jewish retail-merchants. This trend became evident particularly in the West, and Jewish firms in the wholesale centers of the Middle-West and in the seaboard cities became more and more numerous. Following the line of river trade in the Middle West, the most important Western wholesale-center, St. Louis and "wholesaling" New Orleans (specializing in grocery) became considerable Jewish communities, later, Cincinnati, Louisville and Chicago were added. The rising seaboard cities of Philadelphia and New York, in competition with them, saw the successful career of new Jewish wholesale business houses. The peddler could not utilize such facilities as these cities provided for the purchase of merchandise; he had to buy in the next wholesale center, often also in small places, and thus he helped new firms to develop in new cities. Particularly, river trade helped to supply the peddler, who liked to buy in a place where goods could be directly shipped. "The Shylocks prefer to be on the navigable streams," [10] is the complaint of a merchant who seems to evaluate Jewish competition very highly.

This development is well illustrated in the biographies of several men who later attained eminence in American Jewry. Typical is the case of Jacob Seasongut, first president of Max Lilienthal's Reform Jewish congregation in Cincinnati. "Working by day and traveling by night," says his obituary, "he finally sailed up the Erie Canal, in September 1837, and debarked at Chillicothe, in Ohio, then the western meeting-place of the German peddlers. Here he opened an establishment for the manufacture

[9] Borthwick, J. D., *Three Years in California* (Edinburgh 1857), p. 116 et seq.
[10] Shortfield, *op. cit.*, p. 183.

of garments, thereby giving work to many poor and needly families." [11] Similar, but somewhat more detailed, is the necrology of Marcus Fechheimer, a director of the Deutsche Nationalbank in Cincinnati and for many years president of the local Congregation B'nai Jeshurun:

> "Born at Mitwitz, Bavaria, on July 13th, 1818, into a family of fourteen brothers and sisters, Marcus soon found the parental household too cramped, and in the spring of 1837 set out for New York. There he managed at once to stand on his own feet by engaging as a peddler—an occupation which laid the basis for his subsequent successful career. Basket on arm, he spent many years wandering through the highways of New York, Pennsylvania and Ohio, until at length, in December 1839, he settled in Cincinnati. Later, after he had saved sufficient money, he migrated further to Alabama, whither many German immigrants had betaken themselves in search of fortune. In a small town near Mobile he established a garment house, which soon paid dividends. Nevertheless, he later returned to Cincinnati, where several of his brothers had meanwhile opened a business in clothing and materials. This business flourished especially during the period of the war." [12]

Daniel Frohman, the noted theatrical producer, likewise records in his memoirs that his father, Henry Frohman, "was born in Darmstadt, Germany. He came to New York in 1845. . . . For a while he was a pack peddler, and carried his wares up through the Hudson Valley, making the city his headquarters. Later he prospered to such an extent that he was able to purchase a wagon." [13]

The transition mentioned by Frohman, from pack peddler to horse-and-cart chapman, though it often entailed the payment of a higher license fee, was a not insignificant economic development, for it enabled the peddler to supply ready-made clothes to the frontiersman, and this in turn provided new business for the permanent Jewish clothing stores in the West. These now began to sell garments wholesale to the Jewish peddlers, and later to take a hand in actual manufacture. Cincinnati, especially, enjoyed something of a boom in this way during the initial stages of its development. The city's clothing business, at first modest,

[11] *Der Deutsche Pioneer* (Cincinnati), vol. xvi (1884-85), 518.

[12] *ib.*, vol. vii (1875-76), 39.

[13] Frohman, Daniel, *Daniel Frohman Presents* (New York 1935).

became the leading source of supply for the South and, by 1860, both manufacturing of clothes and the clothing trade were exclusively in Jewish hands.

Under gradually stabilizing circumstances, the competition between peddler and store-owner was not so sharp as described sometimes in literature. In that pioneering stage of trade in the Middle West, the peddler had to continue looking for new settlements with which to do business before anybody had a chance to establish there a fixed store. The storekeeper reserved to himself the business operations, like barter-trade and the utilization of goods accepted in barter, as well as extending credit to the customers. The peddler, as a matter of course, had to insist in most cases upon payment in ready cash. In several states, the peddler was forbidden to sell his goods by auction; his greatest chance was to display a well-assorted stock of articles from his pack to his customers in their homes. In that kind of trade, the German-Jewish immigrant was helped by his previous European experience in the same line particularly valuable in his dealings with German settlers.

3. *The Jewish Peddler in the West*

It is an irony of fate that after the Civil War, when the coming of the railroads had done away with peddling in the West, there were still opportunities in the South for the peddler's trade; and these chances were, during a certain period, utilized by Jewish peddlers coming from the Atlantic States, mostly from New York. In the schedule of license-fees according to means of transportation, by pack, horse and wagon, and riverboat, only peddling by boat was not subject to a fee. This fact is referred to by Jones, when reporting his competitor's conversation on the boat: "Sometimes I go in te capin, and dake my chest of jewerly to beddle on. . . . My pusiness is to pe always at pusiness, everywhere. On the steampoat dey ton't make bay licenze." [14]

In the Westward Movement, that creative force which gave its characteristic traits to 19th Century America, migration and immigration, proceeded along the same lines; and peddling was the only trade arising

[14] Shortfield, *op. cit.*, p. 183.

directly from immigration. In interstate migration the composition of the settlers was, on the whole, the same as that of the later developing trading profession, but traders naturally came more often from the Atlantic States, where a fully developed commerce sent clerks and beginners to the West.[15] The situation among the Jews was entirely different. So far as Jews had secured commercial positions in the Atlantic States, they were old settlers and not sufficiently numerous to send beginners to the West. The full and new opportunity was reserved for the Jewish newcomer, mostly from Germany, following the way the German immigrants took. The newcomer was the original creator of the real peddling-trade and peddling remained practically his sole profession.

The Jewish merchants of the West, former peddlers, were entirely different in their ways from the traders in the seaboard states. The majority of the new Jewish population had gone west, had covered that area with Jewish communities at all important communication-points, to a number exceeding that of those in the East. Contemporary observers, when considering the participation of the Jews in the opening of the West mentioned exclusively the German Jewish immigrants, who from peddlers arose to the position of stable businessmen with a large share in the development of all sections of the area in question. Their foes accused them of merely wanting to make money out west and then return to a more leisurely and luxurious life in the Atlantic states, but the Jews repeatedly and energetically denied these allegations and stressed that they meant to stay. At that stage in the formation of a western body of merchants, the Jew was well aware of being a pioneer among pioneers.

4. *Perils of the Jewish Peddler*

The lot of the Jewish peddler was not a happy one. One of his principal difficulties was the necessity of obtaining a license. An interesting account of what this entailed in practical experience is contained in G. F. Streckfuss' entertaining volume, *Der Auswanderer nach Amerika,* published in Zeitz in 1836.

[15] Atherton, Lewis A., *The Pioneer Merchant in Mid-America.* University of Missouri Studies, vol. xiv, No. 2 (1939), p. 19.

"One night in January, 1835," writes this traveler, "I came in deep snow and utterly frozen to Easttown, a pretty little city on the Delaware. Entering a tavern, I found a group of people sitting round the stove. As soon as they set eyes on me, pale and snow-covered as I was, they took pity on me and everyone purchased something out of my stock. I could not complain of my reception and felt that after traipsing around in the cold for an entire day, I was at last getting my reward. While I was transacting my business, however, I noticed an elderly man sitting behind the stove and quietly eyeing me, sometimes with a smile on his lips. He kept quiet and took no part in what was going on. When I was through, he stood up suddenly, clapped me on the shoulder and asked me to follow him. When we got to the door, he turned on me and asked whether I had a license. At that time, I was quite new to the country and could not quite make out what he was saying, particularly as he spoke in a whisper. So I simply stared at him in astonishment. Now, as it happened, I had a ten day growth of stubble on my chin. Noticing it, he next asked if I were a Jew, and when I denied it, seemed reluctant to believe me. Fortunately, however, I had my passport with me, and was able to convince him. He at once softened up, gave me a sympathetic look and said: 'As I see that you're an honest Protestant, I'll let you go, though it's costing me twenty-five dollars. I'm no friend of the Jews, and if you were one, I wouldn't be letting you off so lightly. You would have been fined fifty dollars or gone to jail, and I would have got half the cash for my pains.' . . . When I returned to the company, the innkeeper saw my bewilderment and asked what it was all about. On hearing my story, he praised the constable, laughed at his antisemitism, and bade me deposit my pack." [16]

A statement in Michael Baum's biography of Nathan Barnert, sometime mayor of Paterson, New Jersey, tells much the same story:

"Many times had the press published news of the apprehension of poor Jewish peddlers for selling wares without licenses. Later in the day, Mrs. Barnert's carriage would stop at the police station and the fine of the peddler paid." [17]

Sometimes, particularly in the South, where hatred of the Yankee peddler was apt to be transferred to the Jew, it was not only his property but his very life that was threatened. In 1873, for example, a German Jewish peddler was murdered at Baton Rouge, Louisiana, and three

[16] p. 23-24.
[17] Baum, Michael, *Biography of Nathan Barnert* (Paterson 1914), p. 29.

Negroes subsequently lynched for the crime. The report of the Jewish press, with its unequivocal denunciation of lynch-law, makes interesting reading:

THREE NEGROES LYNCHED

"We reported last week that a German peddler has been robbed and murdered by a company of negroes at Ferry Landing in the western section of Baton Rouge. The victim was a Jew, and burial rites were accorded him by the local Jewish welfare organization. The perpetrators of the crime did not long enjoy their loot. The very next morning, four negroes were detained on suspicion. After a brief investigation, one of them was released. The three others, however, still in possession of the plunder, were hanged in short order by outraged citizens, who strung them up on the nearest tree. Such occurrences, to be sure, transcend the bounds of law. When it is observed, however, that murderers delivered to justice are permitted to go scot-free after a mere day's detention, it is perhaps permissible, in the interests of personal security, even to prefer lynching.

We may add that the victim of the murder was one Jacob Kriss who arrived at New Orleans, from Germany, some three months ago. Thanks to the efforts of Mr. A. Kowalski, he was interred with appropriate ceremonies in the local Jewish cemetery. It has been found impossible, however, to ascertain further details about him. Mr. Kowalski is the leader of the Jewish community and has taken great interest in the entire affair. Neither he, nor any other Jew, however, participated in the execution of the negroes." [18]

On the other hand, there were occasions when the vicissitudes of the Jewish peddler's life were less tragic and, from our point of view, more amusing. As an antidote to the peceding extract we may quote a singular occurrence recorded in *The Israelite* of 1857:

A JEWISH MORMON

"A correspondent at Denmark reports . . . In the meeting of the 1st of September, a Jewish pedlar, no doubt convinced, . . . was immediately admitted into the bosom of Mormonism, and received the usual consecration.

. . . obtained the floor and proposed formally the abolition of polygamy, . . . indignation . . . a large number of women of the lowest classes supported the disciple of Moses, . . . opponents . . . you will succeed no longer in making proselytes. . . . 'If polygamy will cease in our midst,' said a German tailor, 'I

[18] *Die Deborah,* vol. xx (1873), No. 21.

leave immediately the ranks of the Mormons; for I have adopted it with but the intention of marrying so many times, as it will please me.'
. . . more than sixty persons were lodged in the prison. In reporting this scene, we are pleased with the morality and domestic honesty subsisting in a Jewish heart, even when it was carried away to dangerous innovations." [19]

5. *The Jewish Peddler in Caricature*

The familiar figure of the Jewish peddler soon found place in contemporary literature. There are, however, few attempts to describe him in serious vein, and since almost all of these are confined to the German Jewish press, which naturally indulged in a goodly dose of romantic sentimentality, they are of little use in constructing a true picture. Far more illuminating for our purpose are the squibs and satires of non-Jewish writers. Designed solely to "raise a laugh," they naturally concentrate on the more picturesque and bizarre aspects of the itinerant Jewish chapman. Particularly entertaining, in this respect, is the characterization of a lovelorn Jewish peddler contained in a popular songbook of 1839; under the title of *Pretty Sally Solomons.* The song, and its attendant "commentary," run as follows:

Through every place I rove,
A peddler by my trade,
And soon I fell in love
With a very pretty maid . . .

. . . one day, instead of calling my shoestrings, I cried "Sally Solomons, all a penny a pair:" so de people laughed, and I looked like a fool—

And 'twas all for Sally Solomons,
Pretty Sally Solomons,
Oh, listen, love, to me;
Would you be Mistress Ab'rams,
How happy should I be.
. . . No girl in Duke's Place should compare
Mid her to buy and sell:
She made such bargains you would stare,
And so in love I fell.

. . . she got de tings more as twenty per cent, cheaper den her old father Shadriack, who kept a closhs shop and two counters in it. . . .[20]

[19] *The Israelite,* vol. iii (1857), 147.
[20] *Eltone Out-and-Outer Comic Songster* (New York 1839).

It may be supposed that these verses were designed to be sung with accompanying gestures. The resultant performance would therefore have approximated very closely to the characterization of the Jewish peddler in contemporary burlesque. That the American stage had its prototypes of the more modern "Potash and Perlmutter" is evident from several examples. The Jewish peddler, however, was frequently portrayed in the guise of a Shylock.

> "I once see a theater play down to [in New] York," says a writer of 1858, "and there was an old Jew in it, and there was a fellow run away with his daughter and his money puss [purse] and if ever there was a critter ravin', tarrin' mad, it was this old Mister Shycock, or whatever his name was. I never see such work as he made on it; a runnin' up and down the floor, and a pullin' at his wig, and frothin' at the mouth like a 'hoss with the blind staggers'." [21]

Sometimes, to be sure, characteristics popularly associated with the Jewish peddler form the basis for the delineation of Jewish salesmen and showmen who do not strictly fall into this category. Thus, in 1857, Nathaniel Hawthorne could thus portray an itinerant German-Jewish peepshowman:

> "There was other amusement at hand. An old German Jew, travelling with a diorama on his back, was passing down the mountain-road towards the village, just as the party turned aside from it; and in hopes of eking out the profits of the day, the showman had kept them company to the lime-kiln.
> " 'Come, old Dutchman,' cried one of the young men, 'let us see your pictures, if you can swear they are worth looking at!'
> " 'Oh, yes, Captain,' answered the Jew—whether as a matter of courtesy, or craft, he styled everybody Captain—'I shall show you, indeed, some very superb pictures.' So placing his box in a proper position, he invited the young men and girls to look through the glass orifices of the machine, and proceeded to exhibit a series of the most outrageous scratchings and daubings, as specimens of the fine arts, that ever an itinerant showman had the face to impose upon his circle of spectators. The pictures were worn out, moreover tattered, full of cracks and wrinkles, dingy with tobacco—smoke, and otherwise in a most pitiable condition. Some purported to be cities, public

[21] *Piney Woods Tavern, or Sam Slick in Texas* (Philadelphia 1858), p. 37.

edifices, and ruined castles, in Europe; others represented Napoleon's battles, and Nelson's seafights; . . . 'You make the little man to be afraid, Captain,' said the German Jew."[22]

Here the Jewish peddler serves as the model for the swindling cheapjack. Sometimes, however, the satire is less broad and less malicious, the peddler figuring as merely a constituent element in a cultural complex deemed as a whole grotesque and ridiculous. Witness the following description of Germany in a work of 1860, at the height of the German immigration:

"Oh Germany, Germany, land of fiddlers,
Of mad musicians, cabbages and 'sour-krout';
Filled with base Barons and with Jewish peddlers,
Where vulgar dirt at real worth while scout;
A country turning out a host of meddlers,
Like locusts on their first destroying route;
"See, how they come! a smoking, fiddling choir,
With grand pianos bang'd by Smash de Meyer." [23]

Ignominious characterizations of the Jewish peddler were especially common during that later period when, with the development of cities and the opening of stores, he no longer filled a useful economic function in serving frontiersman and pioneer, but had degenerated into an almost parasitic street-hawker. Walt Whitman speaks disparagingly of the "dirty looking German Jews," roaming through New York's Broadway, "with a glass box on their shoulders" crying out "Glass to mend" with a sharp nasal twang and flat, squalling enunciation to which the worst Yankee brogue is sweet music.[24] Similarly, in 1857, a writer on life in New York boarding houses describes how an artist-boarder once incurred the lasting displeasure of the landlady when, on being requested to sketch Moses in the bullrushes, he depicted "a terrified Jewish peddler between two rushing animals of the bovine species." [25]

[22] "*The Unpardonable Sin,* a chapter from an unfinished work," in *The American Literature and Art* (New York 185-) , p. 37 et seq.

[23] *Gotham Ambrotypes . . .* (New York 1860) , p. 15-16.

[24] *New York Dissected* (New York 1936) , p. 123.

[25] Gunn, Thomas Butler, *The Physiology of New York Boarding Houses* (New York 1857) , p. 106.

Sometimes the characterizations took a more serious note. In 1871, for example, *Puck* comments on the case of a Jewish peddler who sold ice cream in the streets of Cincinnati on a Sunday, and when hauled before the bench for this violation of the sabbath, was excused by the magistrates on the grounds that he was an "Israelite." [26] "It pays to be a Jew in Cincinnati."

6. *Later Jewish Attitudes to Peddling*

Of especial interest is the reaction, at a later period, of the settled and "respectable" American Jews to their breathren who still pursued the occupation of peddling. That occupation was now little more than a means of earning a livelihood; it no longer served a real function in the economy of the country. Accordingly, those who had "arrived," or were the descendants of men who had done so, now looked askance on this living reminiscence of their own humbler origins. Typical, for instance, is the staid, almost smug, comment of Isaac Leeser's *Occident* in 1857: Speaking of the problem of accommodating the new Jewish immigrants, that journal observes:

> "Many may perhaps be assisted, as hitherto, by making up for them a small pack of any sort of valuable goods, and sending them into the country to try their luck at peddling among the farmers, and in the small towns; and of these, we acknowledge, up to the present time many have done well and become at length merchants of higher pretensions. Nevertheless, this system must come to an end; it is nearly overdone now; besides which it is illegal in several states; as even could a license for peddling be procured, it will be at such a high rate, and clogged with so many restrictions, as either to be unattainable by the poor, or worthless for all practical purposes if they would strictly comply with the terms of law, often arbitrary and vexatious in the restrictions they contain. The very nature, moreover, of seeking a livelihood by means of small trading of this sort has a debasing influence on the mind." [27]

There were times, too, when those who had outgrown the peddler's existence experienced a notable sense of embarrassment at the suggestion

[26] *Puck* (St. Louis), No. 21.

[27] *The Occident,* vol. xv (1857), 279.

that, for all their wordly success, they might not completely have rid`themselves of certain traits of behavior associated with their ruder antecedents.

> "It is true," complains a writer in 1881, "that the body of rich Jews in America fails to display the culture that wealth demands. . . . With a pack upon his back, or a few shillings in his pocket, the Hebrews contact with Americans culture was exceedingly limited. When die accumulation of wealth introduced him to American manners, he had already become habituated to his particular grooves." [28]

And even as late as 1914, another writer feels constrained to protest that the Jews of the New World were more than peddlers:

> "The German-American Jews are not the vulgar caricatures in which the Jew is painted in the anti-Semitic press; they are far from being the narrow minded, uncultured egotists, always greedy for gold and incapable of higher aspirations, as the prejudiced and relentless traducers of the Jews delight in presenting them to the world . . . ." [29]

7. *Conclusion*

Contemporary authors, when estimating the contributions of the various strata of the population towards the opening up of the country and the transformation of the frontier into a densely populated economic unit, never fail to point out the hardships of the pioneer's life, as compared with the easier existence in already populated states. The pioneers knew they were pioneers, they called themselves so and created their own organizations. Their contemporaries were fully aware of the hard fight these men had to put up in order to achieve economic success, and they knew that the entire nation reaped the benefit of their efforts. The pioneers, in their organizations, had strict conditions for admission of new members. Nobody who had come to a certain territory after a certain date, could join. Modern history, when describing the building of America by its social forces, does not know such deadlines; the historians appreciate the individual function of each group of the population and each profession in the great task of constructing the modern New World.

[28] *North American Review,* vol. ii (1881), 265-75.

[29] Eliasoff, Hermann, "German-American Jews," reprint from *Deutsch-Amerikanische Geschichtsblätter,* 1914, p. 29.

The pioneering Jewish peddler, in his activities in frontier life under a developing economy, had a more difficult time than his precursor, the Yankee-peddler. The organic connection of the Jewish peddlers in the old immigration with frontier-life is demonstrated by constant references to them in American literature dealing with the subject. The Jewish peddler was a pioneer — everybody knew that; as a trader he brought the goods of civilization into the wilderness. The settler, remaining in connection with the outside world through the services of the Jewish peddler, felt instinctively that this was his contact with the advancing civilization that was to follow him.

Literature dealing with pioneer-life stresses the essential function therein of the Jewish peddler, and his figure comes to symbolize the end of the settler's solitude in the wilderness. Stories in American literature of the life of Jewish merchants in the populated East appear insipid and colorless in comparison with those describing the life of the Jewish peddling pioneer in all its adventurous intensity.

The role of the Jewish pioneer merchant in opening the West to commerce, leading to the foundation of permanent settlements around the general store, must not be forgotten. For the most part, the peddlers became settled merchants only after many pioneering years, but in those very years they contributed largely to the strengthening of the trading network. Taking goods in payment, utilizing them, and creating new branches of commercial activity, were among the Jewish pioneer's principal merits. The Jewish trader was certainly equal to all others in the services he rendered towards the development of communal life in the rising cities of the West; and he showed the same qualities which distinguished the typical hardy pioneer-merchants, to whom such a preponderant role is ascribed in modern historical literature. Later, he was one of the decisive factors in the creation of the special store of the West.

The general cultural picture of the Jewish peddler is typically American, connected with the conditions of American economy. Yet, his activities in the period of frontier-life were those of an immigrant. The Jew, coming from Europe and wishing to secure a foothold in the New World, was ready to endure the discomfort and toil of a new existence.

When the railroads finally made an end of his role as a supplier of goods, the peddler was so well experienced in the ways of American economic life, that he found it easy to make use successfully of fresh opportunities. At that time, newcomers could no longer start out as peddlers. But meanwhile, American economy had become strong, the country industrialized and the Jewish communities definitely settled. When the new masses of Jewish immigrants came pouring in, peddling was no longer important; the new conditions of life provided ample economic possibilities for them.

GERMAN JEWS IN NEW YORK CITY IN THE 19TH CENTURY

Beginnings

Scrutiny of the passenger lists of immigrants arriving during colonial days in Philadelphia, then the chief port of entry for German immigrants, reveals the names of a number of Jews. Doubtless some of these moved to New York, which was rapidly becoming the largest American city. As early as 1713, the Rev. John Sharpe wrote of New York: "It is possible also to learn Hebrew here as well as in Europe, there being a Synagogue of Jews, and many ingenious men of that nation from Poland, Hungary, Germany, etc."[1] A document of the New York Sephardic synagogue Shearith Israel, dated September 15, 1728, contains three signatures of men of undoubtedly German origin: Benjamin Wolff bar Jahacob Schwab, Abraham Emden and Baruch bar Jehuda Leib M'Breslau.[2] In 1729 the Sephardic Jew Raphael Jeshurun expressed his concern for the future of the Sephardic ritual in the synagogue, since ". . . the Germans, are more in Number than Wee there."[3]

The period around 1790 is of particular import, for we can compare the numbers of Jews given by Jewish sources with those cited in the first United States census, taken in that year. To be sure, the census did not classify Jews as such, but this fact can be inferred with a degree of certitude from their names. In a congregational register of December 18, 1787, there appear among the names of 35 German Jews the names Moses Homberg and Myer Regensberg.[4] Fifty years later surnames such as these, which derive from the names of cities, became symbolic of German-Jewish immigrants. A later list

[1] *New York Historical Society Collections* (New York 1880) p. 339-343.
[2] *Publications of the American Jewish Historical Society,* no. 21, p. 5.
[3] *Ibid.,* no. 27, p. 3, 4.
[4] *Ibid.,* p. 43.

Reprinted from *Yivo Annual of Jewish Social Science,* Volume XI, 1956-1957.

(covering 1790-1819) of the same congregation, contains such typical German-Jewish names as Leipman, Soosman, Viner (from Vienna), Block and Adler.[5] Likewise, German-Jewish names are to be found in increasing numbers in non-Jewish sources. Among the "Vendue Masters for the city and county of New York" in 1797 were such German Jews as Ephraim Hart, Isaac Moses and Alexander Zuntz.[6] The Custom House registry of June 30, 1820, lists "Simon L. Oppenheimer, Frankfort, dyer"; of December 31, 1822, "Oppeneigher [Oppenheimer-?], 50, merchant, Germany" and "Pollack, 36, merchant, Germany."[7] It is noteworthy that the places of origin of Sephardic Jews are never given in those registers we scrutinized.

On the Road to Independence

As long as the German Jews were few in number and their economic means meagre, they were compelled to depend upon their well-established "co-religionists," the Sephardim, in religious and philanthropic matters. No sooner, however, than they increased in number and improved their lot, they began to establish their own charitable organizations and synagogues. In 1822, the Hebrew Benevolent Society was formed, its leadership consisting largely of German Jews. The Sephardic heads of the old Gemilath Chasadim responded to this audacious step by a notice in the *Mercantile Advertiser* that they had had no part in the formation of the Society and, furthermore, had no personal contact with its founders.[8] The established "Nathan-type" (the popular name for the Sephardim of the older generation) began at this point to be aware of its future competitor, the "Seligman-type"—a fundamental distinction which the non-Jewish world would later seek to introduce.

In short order, the German Jew left the Sephardic Shearith Israel and, in 1825, founded their own synagogue. Nevertheless they felt it necessary to justify this step, writing to the *parnas* and trustees of Shearith Israel as follows: "It is also proper to state that the increase of our brethern is so great and in all probability will be much greater in a few years that accommodations, particularly on

[5] *Ibid.*, p. 45.

[6] *Longworth's American Almanack, New York Register and City Directory...* (New York 1797) p. 56.

[7] *Register of Passengers in Custom-House Books,* National Archives, Washington, D. C.

[8] Camman, Henry I., *The Charities of New York* (New York 1868) p. 292.

holidays, cannot be afforded to all."[9] The foundation of a separate synagogue was interpreted in Germany, however, somewhat differently: "[The German Jews] are undoubtedly more devoted to their religion than the former [the Sephardim], and more conscientious in their observance of Jewish law."[10]

The establishment of the new synagogue apparently made a strong impression on the non-Jewish world. A book describing New York City which appeared three years later, gives the following account of the synagogue:

> It is upwards of a century since the Mill-street congregation was established, and few, if any, of the members then resided above Wall-street. The increase of the city has left few families in that neighborhood, and this, with the great increase, and the continued arrivals from the continent of Europe, rendered it necessary to erect a new temple. Accordingly a *new Synagogue* has been purchased in Elm-street, north of Canal-street, formerly the African church, and has been elegantly fitted up by the German and Polish Jews, whose form of prayers is somewhat dissimilar to the Portuguese.[11]

There follows a detailed description of the interior appearance and decorations of the synagogue.

The number of German Jews continued to grow, and soon tensions and conflicts appeared in the new synagogue. The new arrivals felt that they were victims of discrimination. They complained that the older members behaved as if the synagogue was their personal property, and totally ignored the other members. The frequent quarrels sometimes ended in court cases, and finally led to a split. The following is an account of these developments, taken from a correspondence to a German-Jewish newspaper:

> *Religious Life in New York*
>
> New York. Heretofore we have only had one synagogue, the Elm Street Synagogue.[12] Here sharp distinctions were made between the rights of the old inhabitants of the city, the so-called *baalebatim* [given in Hebrew in the original German text], and the new members, who were regarded as second-class members, with no say in religious affairs. Recently, the latter group has grown so

[9] Goldstein, Israel, *A Century of Judaism in New York. B'nai Jeshurun 1825-1925* (New York 1930) p. 52.

[10] *Der Orient* (Leipzig) vol. i (1840) p. 371.

[11] [Blunt, Edmund M.,] *The Picture of New York* (New York 1828) p. 228.

[12] It is interesting to note how rapidly the Sephardim lost their position of dominance. They are not even mentioned here.

substantially both in number and in cultural level, that it began to press for equal rights in a place where class distinctions do not—or should not—prevail. After more than $5,000 had been spent on litigation, the two groups nonetheless parted ways. Those who felt themselves aggrieved and dissatisfied by the court ruling seceded and, led by Rabbi Isaac, founded a new congregation.[13]

The dedication of the new building of Temple Emanu-El reflected the substantial economic and financial achievements of New York German Jews. Its builders evidenced that they had at their disposal funds which were immensely greater than any that had been expended previously by Jewish institutions in the United States. The general press, too, was struck with amazement. A leading German paper described the event as follows:

Dedication of Temple Emanu-El's New Edifice

The congregation counts the most prominent Jews of New York among its members. Their contributions to the new building, which cost over $650,000, were truly generous. The sale of pews provided an immense source of income. The first twenty pews brought in $140,000. The next score of pews accounted for another $114,000. Though all of the pews have not yet been purchased, the income from their sale has already exceeded the entire cost of the building by more than $200,000.[14]

Economic Advance

By what manner and means did the German Jews achieve this status? Before dealing with this question, it is necessary to note the number of German Jews in New York, as well as in all of America, at various times.

It is estimated that there were about 10,000 Jews in New York in 1840, at the beginning of the mass migration of both Germans and German Jews.[15] In 1877, their number rose to an estimated 60,000.[16] Carl Schurz, the German-American statesman, gives the same figure in his comparison of Germans and German Jews in New York.[17] The most reliable sources of the time maintained that the German Jews constituted two-thirds of the entire Jewish population

13 *Der Israelit* (1845) p. 384.

14 *New Yorker Handelszeitung* (1868) no. 1018, p. 11. This periodical will be referred to below as *NYHZ*.

15 *The American Magazine* (Albany) (1841/42) p. 158.

16 *NYHZ* (1877) no. 1473, p. 11.

17 *Der deutsche Pionier* (1885/86) p. 105-106.

of the United States. This distribution of Jews was, at the time, more or less the same in New York as in the country as a whole. In other words, assuming that New York had 60,000 Jews, 40,000 of them were of German origin. It is estimated that there were then 200,000 German Jews in the entire country. Non-Jewish Germans there were about 180,000 in New York alone.

Though there were artisans among the German Jews, more than half of the new arrivals embarked on their careers as peddlers. In 1840, the firm of Grossheim and Schreiber, of 78 William Street, announced in a New York German newspaper that "German [Jewish] peddlers will find a complete and varied assortment of supplies at the undersigned . . ."[18] The range of the Jewish peddler spread throughout the entire New York area. In 1853, the register of the New York suburb Morrisania refers to one "Loewenstein, Joseph, Peddler."[19] The New York Jewish peddler reached as far as Plattsburgh.

The German-Jewish peddler was an innovator in the annals of peddling. He introduced the practice of installment paying. The following quotation points to the importance, particularly in New York, of this practice: "There are quite a number of time peddlers in New York, and they are most useful members of the community. They are all Hebrews, and sell everything on the installment plan."[20]

In due time, the stereotype of the Jew-peddler came into being. Coney Island, already an important place of recreation, is thus celebrated in verse by an American:

On ev'ry path, by almost every turn,
Industrious Israelites a living "earn,"
By selling colored specs to screen the eyes,
Which would not serve an idiot to disguise.
Purchase by *all* means—yellow, green or blue—
You aid one member of a useful crew;
He *will not work;* he neither starves, nor begs,
But peddles healing-salve for wooden legs.[21]

The stage subsequent to peddling was generally that of dealing in second-hand goods. Usually, this trade became concentrated in one or two streets of the city, whose names later became synonymous

[18] *New Yorker Staatszeitung,* vol. vii, no. 30 (1840/41) p. 3.

[19] *Henry's Directory of Morrisania and Vicinity for* 1853/4 (Morrisania 1853) p. 15.

[20] Smith, Matthew Hale, *Wonders of a Great City* (Chicago 1877) p. 845.

[21] *A Day on Coney Island* (New York [1880]) p. 11.

with bargains. In New York, Chatham Street, which remained famous for almost a century, was the center of the trade in used goods. No literary description of New York could possibly omit reference to Chatham Street. It was on the itinerary of every visitor to the city. The emotions of politicians and reformers of all sorts were raised to a pitch at its mention. As early as 1833, a British traveller described the street as follows:

> Chatham-street . . . The inhabitants of this street are mostly of the tribe of Judah; as any body may be satisfied by going into their shops, as well on account of their dealings, as their long beards, which reach to the bottoms of their waist.[22]

A decade later, an American wrote the following about Chatham Street:

> The Clothing Stores are invariably kept by Jews. A Yankee (cute as they are) shop-keeper in Chatham Street could not exist—it is a physical impossibility. The Jew is gentle—he is insinuating—somewhat even polished; knows at a glance whether you are from the Country or the City, whether you have a monkeyish taste for finery and gewgaws, or want something rough and substantial. He is, too, a great artist, especially in coats.[23]

We find a more detailed description of the Jewish merchant and his salesmanship a few years later. The power of the Jewish tradesmen derives from the fact that he knows how to prepare psychologically the potential purchaser for the decisive moment. He starts out by conducting a pleasant chat with the customer, only parenthetically inserting an aside about a "first-class coat" or trousers. Before long he has enticed him into the store, from which he emerges "in garments of the strangest make, dimensions, and fitnesses."

The writer, not devoid of hostility to Jews, concludes his description as follows:

> This street, reader, was in the old times of this Island, a war-path of Manhattan Indians to the West; civilization hath not affected it greatly. The old red men scalped their enemies, the Chatham Clo'men skin theirs. So little difference have two-hundred years in changing the character of mankind![24]

That these merchants were German Jews is attested to by a

[22] [Green, Asa,] *Travels in America* (New York 1833) p. 43.

[23] [Foster, George G.,] *New York in Slices* (New York 1849) p. 16.

[24] Mathews, Cornelius, *A Pen and Ink Panorama of New York City* (New York 1853) p. 164.

disinterested observer. He suggests that Barnum would do well to buy the entire street and convert it into a kind of museum or circus. He concludes with the remark that "the great mass of the persons doing business in this street are Jews or Dutch[25] Jews, which is nearly the same thing."[26]

At any rate, as far as the German of New York was concerned, the Chatham-Street merchant was a German Jew, a countryman, whose economic rise was really due to his German clientele.[27] From among the thousands of passers-by, this merchant was able to pick out without much hesitation a newly arrived German immigrant, whom he would greet with a hearty "Hello, my countryman." An exchange of a few additional words, and the immigrant was pulled into the store and outfitted from head to toe, at a neat profit for the merchant.[28]

The Chatham Street merchant, however, was ambitious. He would not be confined to Chatham Street. He was also to be found in nearby Grand Street and on the Bowery, and, with the passage of four or five years, on William and Fulton Streets as well, that is:

> . . . he is in business on a large-scale, occasionally imports real woolen goods from Germany, which he sells as Dutch products, employs from fifty to a hundred tailors turning out garments—in short, he has become a wholesale merchant.[29]

In 1853 a volume appeared in New York entitled *New York Commercial List, Containing the Names and Occupations of the Principal Merchants of the City.* Only the names of wholesalers appear therein. On the basis of a name key which we have developed, which includes only such unquestionably German Jewish names as Einstein, Oppenheim, Bernheimer, Bernstein, Hirsch, Rothschild and Schlesinger, we have ascertained that of the 2,751 firms listed in this volume, at least 105 were undoubtedly Jewish. This figure is to be taken as an absolute minimum. There were, in the first place, quite a number of firms which Jews had bought and, for business

[25] The adjective "Dutch" meant in those days German. It was simply a corruption of "deutsch."

[26] *Glimpses of New York City* (Charleston 1852) p. 117.

[27] Evidence in support of this contention is found in such advertisements as: "L. Stein, agent for placement of orders for manufactured goods by German manufacturers" (*NYHZ,* 1859, no. 510, p. 14) or "Philip J. Joachimsen, Deutscher Advokat, Attorney at Law" (*New Yorker Staatszeitung* 1837, no. 48, p. 3).

[28] Griesinger, Theodor, *Lebende Bilder* (Stuttgart 1848) p. 142.

[29] *Loc. cit.*

purposes, had retained their Anglo-Saxon names. Secondly, name-changing was not unknown even in those days. Many a firm called Green, Young, White and even more typically Anglo-Saxon names was owned by Jews. It is noteworthy that of the 105 Jewish firms, 19 were in the clothing industry and 14 were dry goods merchants. Jews were likewise well represented in importing: seven of the Jewish firms were importers, and 15 commission merchants, who considered themselves to be, in part, importers.[30]

The following few years witnessed an intensive economic growth in America. It became necessary to revise the earlier list. In 1859, the *Merchants' and Bankers' New York City Reference Guide* appeared. Here too only established wholesalers and bankers were included. The 3,300-odd recorded firms were listed by industry. The garment industry alone, which included firms in "Dry Goods, Fancy Goods, Straw Goods, Hats, Caps and Furs," contained at least 141 firms with Jewish names.[31] Six years earlier, this category had contained only 51 German-Jewish firms. The following table compares the number of Jewish firms in various lines of trade as presented in the two publications.

JEWS IN SELECTED BRANCHES OF NEW YORK COMMERCE, 1853 AND 1859

Branch	*No. of Firms in* 1853	*No. of Firms in* 1859
Clothing	19	27
Dry Goods	14	41
Fancy Goods	4	20
Laces	3	6
Trimmings	1	12
Total	41	106

One industry other than the garment industry is worthy of note here. In 1853, only two German-Jewish firms were listed under "Jeweler and Watch Import." In 1859, there were 20 German-Jewish firms in "Watches, Jewelry, Gold Pens, Precious Stones."

America began to be thought of as a land of unlimited possibilities. Everyone was a potential millionaire. Commerce and wealth began to be the focus of interest of the American public. Not only did the question of who sells what come to the fore, but many were inter-

[30] Richards, T. P., *New York Commercial List* . . . (New York 1853).
[31] Billard, Louis, *Merchants' and Bankers'* . . . *Reference Guide* (New York 1859).

ested in the approximate position occupied by various individuals in the hierarchy of wealth. A series of volumes entitled *The Rich Men of New York* began to appear in New York. We have selected the following German-Jewish firms from the second series, which appeared in 1861:

SELECTED GERMAN-JEWISH FIRMS AMONG THE "WEALTHY OF NEW YORK"

Firm	*Industry*	*Capital*
Althouse, S. B. & Sons	Iron manufacturing	$250,000
Oppenheim, I. M. & Co.	Furs	200,000
Bernheimer Bros.	Clothing	250,000
Heidelbach	Clothing	150,000
Haber, Isaac	Clothing	100,000
Lillienthal, C. H.	Tobacco	300,000
Frankenheimer Bros.	Importers	100,000
Kessler & Co.	Importers	250,000
Rosenfield Bros.	Importers	300,000[32]

Thus we see that German Jews occupied quite a prominent place in the ranks of New York wealth.

New York German Jews played a special role in the post-Civil War period of economic reconstruction, particularly in the Southern states. There was an intense demand for goods in the South. The local merchants, however, had no cash available, and a new system of credit had to be established. The Jewish merchants in the South contacted the New York merchants, almost all Jewish, and began to resume commercial relations. They understood that they had to meet their old outstanding debts before credit could again be made available to them. Thus a report in a New York newspaper, written shortly after the Civil War, reads as follows:

> While we are informed from Boston that many Southern merchants have arrived there seeking new credit, despite the fact that they have not fulfilled their old obligations, we learn from local importers that many of their former customers have notified them that they stand ready to meet their old debts, including interest for the four years [of the Civil War]. We regard it as important to stress that these are mostly Jewish manufacturer-merchants from North Carolina, Georgia, and other states., who are thus outstanding in their most honorable behavior.[33]

The German-Jewish merchant from the South did not rely solely

32 Vose, Reuben, *The Rich Men of New York,* ser. no. 2 (New York 1859).
33 *NYHZ* (1865) no. 843, p. 10.

upon credit. He engaged in attempts at various exchanges and combination deals. In an article entitled "Trade with the South" in the same newspaper, we read:

> The quiescence in Wall Street stands in sharp contrast to the bustling activity in other commercial sections of the city. New York is full of out-of-town buyers, who are well-supplied with cash or whose credit is as good as cash. The Southern businessmen arrive with receipts for cotton, rice, tobacco and other products. The repayment of old debts by the Southern merchants is proceeding much better than had been anticipated . . .[34]

The role of Jews in New York commerce was so substantial that, for example, observance of a Jewish holiday had a marked effect on business life. On such a day "a strange quiescence prevails in the downtown areas of the city and many of the leading figures on the stock exchange are absent."[35] That German Jews occupied an important role here is explicitly stated in a description of the "Black Friday" crisis on the stock exchange (Sept. 24, 1869) which reads:

> Prominent in the circle around the fountain today was Albert Speyers, a German Jew, a large man now past the middle of life, with a long record as a prominent and wealthy dealer in both stocks and gold. He was now the leader of the bull clique, bidding the price up to the highest point every moment, and buying in untold quantities and acting like a mad man.[36]

A few years thereafter, a book on the old merchants of New York appeared. The author deals with the special role played by Jews, comparing their position at the end of the 18th century to that occupied in 1863. He notes that around 1800 the place of Jews in American commercial life was rather small. He lists some ten names, most of them Sephardim, and adds:

> What a contrast between the commencement of this century, 1800 and 1863! The Israelite merchants were few then, but now? They have increased in this city beyond any comparison . . . There are 80,000 Israelites in the city and it is the high standard of excellence of the old Israelite merchants of 1800 that has made the race occupy the proud position it does now in this city and nation.[37]

[34] *Ibid.*, no. 859, p. 10.

[35] *NYHZ* (1872) no. 1229, p. 12.

[36] *A Life of James Fisk, Jr.* (New York 1871) p. 234.

[37] [Scoville, Joseph A.,] *The Old Merchants of New York City*, vol. ii (New York 1877) p. 121.

Social Advance

In this area of life, advance was much more difficult. American society rigidly observed the principle that it took at least three generations to produce a gentleman, which was, obviously, the minimal prerequisite for acceptance into higher society. German Jews in America at that time could not meet this prerequisite, and they began to seek acceptance through circumventing such requirements. Frequently, the channel adopted was that of German social and recreational organizations, although the doors to these were not wide open either. Typical of these organizations were the Turnverein, choral societies and other such clubs. In the early days, they were quite liberal, and even came out in condemnation of anti-Semitism in Germany.[38] From a report of activities of 1865, we learn that among the participants in an artistic program was a second tenor, H. Rosenthal, representing the New York Liedertafel, a tenor by the name of Cohn from the Uhland Bund, and a singer Cohn from the Williamsburger Quartett-Club.[39] The membership roster of the Deutsche Liederkranz contained an imposing number of Jews.

The place of German Jews was particularly striking in the leadership of these organizations. Even in the choral society Arion, later to adopt an overt anti-Semitic stand, there were Jews among the founders. Among these we find the names of Simon Meyer and Julius Pick.[40] M. Simonfeld Jr. served as president of Harmonie, one of the leading clubs.[41] Quite a number of Jews were even to be found among the founders and leaders of the organization of German war veterans.[42] German Jews were included in the ranks of the Schlaraffia (the kingdom of indolence). Each member of this club had a nickname. The nicknames of the Jews are characteristic: Zobel, the skin robber, Halevy, the rich of song, and the like.[43]

Gradually, the back door was opened to Jews in other clubs in New York. Among the members of the Manhattan Club were Samuel Kaufmann and Adolph Kohn;[44] in the Union Club, J. H. Lazarus and

[38] The anti-Semitism of editors in Germany is ridiculed in the *Bazaar des New Yorker Turn-Vereins* (New York 1880) p. 7.

[39] *New Yorker Musik-Zeitung*, vol. i (1865) p. 161-162.

[40] *Statuten des "Arion" in New York.*

[41] Fairfield, Francis Gerry, *The Clubs of New York* (New York 1873) p. 18.

[42] *Erinnerungsschrift des deutschen Veteranen-Bundes*, 1870-71 [New York] p. 5.

[43] *Chronic der Schlaraffia Nova Yorkia* (New York 1910) p. 9, 16.

[44] Fairfield, *op. cit.*, p. 163.

Moses Lazarus;[45] and in the Palett Club, M. L. Eckstein and M. Eidlitz.[46] There were also Jewish members in the following clubs: American Jockey, Gotham, Manhattan Chess, Travellers Home, Progress, American Fox Terrier—the president of which at the time was August Belmont Jr.—and in the Pavonia Yacht Club.[47]

All this did not quench the thirst for social recognition. Clubs with an exclusively Jewish membership were formed. The Fidelio Club and the Amaranth Society[48] were outstanding among these. Also, a Jewish Readers' Society, a Mendelssohn Society, a Montefiore Society[49] and a Literary Society of "German Israelites" were organized. Precise information is available regarding the latter. It consisted of some sixty members, who met each evening, and maintained a reading room, where books and German, English and other periodicals were available.[50]

These widespread activities inevitably were taken note of in the upper reaches of American society. They could not simply be ignored. This was particularly true since German newspapers continually appealed to their readers to manifest a more intensive degree of communal and cultural responsibility. In doing so, they often pointed to the German Jew in America as a model. Thus, a correspondent of a German newspaper, criticizing the low cultural level of the Germans in New York, finds it necessary to add:

> First and foremost are the Jews, who are among the most intelligent and indefatigable supporters of local artistic, literary and scholarly life. If any segment of the population makes extensive sacrifices on behalf of newspapers, the theatre, scholarly and artistic endeavors, it is first and foremost, among all immigrants, the New York Jews.[51]

The same holds true for communal responsibility. "For the past six years," a German complains, "The German population of New York (now numbering 130,000) has been attempting to establish a fund for a German hospital. Of the required sum of $300,000 only about $30,000 have been collected to date."[52] He goes on to note

[45] *Ibid.*, p. 78.
[46] *Ibid.*, p. 283.
[47] *The Annual Club Book for New York and Vicinity*, 1890-91 (New York) p. 45-155.
[48] *Ibid.*, p. 12, 43.
[49] *Allgemeine Zeitung des Judentums* (1846) p. 553.
[50] *The Occident*, vol. v (1847/48) p. 413.
[51] *NYHZ* (1859) no. 534, p. 11.
[52] Stiger, Joseph Leopold, *Nieder mit der Sklaverei* (Zurich 1864) p. 32.

that New York Jews, far less in number than the Germans, have already had their hospital for quite a while. Let the wealthy Germans take an example from the Jews. The same complaint was voiced elsewhere:

> The Jewish hospital . . . is concrete proof that the followers of the Old Testament have a far keener sense of communal responsibility than the German Christians, who have not yet succeeded in obtaining sufficient funds for the same purpose.[53]

Whereas one campaign for funds for the Jewish hospital netted $115,000, a like endeavor of the Germans brought in the paltry sum of $7,718.[54] Nor did German Jews in New York build hospitals only. The other welfare institutions which they created, such as orphanages and old age homes, were likewise objects of universal admiration.

In 1872, a leading society paper carried a description of a "Fashionable Hebrew Wedding." The wedding took place at the "Orthodox Thirty-Fourth Street Synagogue." Afterward, "there was a grand reception at Adelphi Hall, Broadway." The account then presents a list of the guests, which included a number of leading politicians, and writes that:

> Among those noticeable were: Mrs. S. D. Moss, in blue satin, valenciennes laces, court train and diamonds; the bride, Mrs. David Moss, a beautiful brunette, in white corded silk, valenciennes lace, orange blossoms, and wreath, diamonds . . . Everything connected with the affair was elegant and recherché. Fashionable Hebrew society has been on the *qui vive* for some time in anticipation of the grand event now passed.[55]

Thus Jews had already achieved social recognition. Even lesser events than those cited above are now material worthy of note by the general press. A Purim celebration is written up thus:

> "Merry Purim" was celebrated in the evening by crowds of masqueraders, who drove from house to house in omnibuses and carriages. At the door of a house one of the maskers was requested to disclose his identity and vouch for the rest of the party. The party then entered, and after dancing and jesting with the company drove to another house. Among the houses which were open were those

[53] Pelz, Edmund, *New York und seine Umgebungen* (Hamburg 1867) p. 41.
[54] *NYHZ* (1875) no. 1397, p. 11.
[55] *Fifth Avenue Journal,* vol. i (1872) no. 14, p. 2.

> of Mr. and Mrs. H. Herrman, No. 59 West Fifty-sixth Street, Mr. and Mrs. Herts, of West Forty-fourth Street . . .[56]

Evidently non-Jews also participated in such occasions. Included in the list of guests of this party was "Mr. Theodore Roosevelt."

Joint Political Activity with the Germans

German Jews in New York engaged in no independent political activity. Their primary concern was to establish themselves economically, and politics was a subsidiary interest. In the political sphere they were ready, temporarily, to adapt themselves to the existing German organizations. These groups assumed that a German-Jewish leader, popular within Jewish ranks, could win their votes for the list of candidates supported by the German organizations. Occasionally competition would arise among such "leaders," each priding himself, with inflated figures, on the number of votes he could attract.

Up until the Tweed Ring scandal of 1871, the Germans supported the Tammany machine in New York. In the municipal elections of 1867 German Jews and Germans supported the Tammany candidate for mayor, John T. Hoffman.[57] Subsequently, the same combination endorsed the candidacy of Mayor Hoffman for governor of New York and J. F. Joachimsen for municipal justice. In 1869, the same groups gave strong support to the senatorial candidacy of the "German" Myer Stern.[58] Stern's activities on behalf of philanthropic organizations were stressed in a special campaign biography.[59]

A Nineteenth Ward Jacob Cohen Association was formed to support the candidacy of Jacob Cohen for supervisor.[60] The *New York Herald* commented as follows:

> We are not surprised that Tammany itself is closely watching a curious and interesting movement on the part of the Israelites of New York City to elevate one of their most popular co-religionists to the important post of Supervisor—a post for which they deem him peculiarly well qualified by his integrity, energy and wealth. Now the Germans in general, and the Israelites in particular, are

56 *The Season* . . . 1882/83 (New York 1883) p. 289.

57 "The Mayoralty Contest." *Hebrew Leader,* vol. xi, no. 1 (1867) p. 4.

58 *Ibid.,* vol. xv, no. 3 (1869) p. 2.

59 *Jewish Times,* vol. i, no. 35, p. 7.

60 In connection with his political activities, Jacob Cohen decided to begin publication of a tri-lingual Jewish newspaper, the *Yudishe Nayes.*

> more than ever disposed to exercise independently their rights as citizens.[61]

Jacob Cohen knew very well in whose hands his fate lay. And he did, indeed, do all in his power to gain the approval of both the Germans and the German Jews. Thus we read, for example: "Jacob Cohen, Candidate for Supervisor, has insured his life in behalf of the German Hospital and of the Jewish Orphan Asylum to the amount of $5,000 for each institution."[62]

The German victory in the Franco-Prussian War of 1871 led the German-Jewish press to the conclusion that New York German Jews should cut their ties to Tammany Hall.[63] This brought about a greater degree of independence. Commenting on the resignation of Joseph Seligman from the Board of Education, one paper noted that he "was appointed by the late Mayor Havemeyer as a representative of the German citizens, and perhaps also in his capacity as Israelite."[64]

Cultural Life

We have earlier mentioned the literary circles of New York German life. Almost all the rabbis of German congregations played an active part in these circles.[65] This participation was by no means fortuitous. By and large, these rabbis exercised a major influence on the cultural life of German Jews in New York and perhaps in all of America.

To be sure, the immigration of German rabbis, particularly to New York, began relatively late. Not until 1842 did the first German rabbi, Leo Merzbacher, arrive in New York. This delay is attributable to the fact that the first German-Jewish immigrants to America came from Bavaria. They constituted a conservative element that was not yet influenced by the new currents which had come to the fore in Jewish life in Germany. The limited religious functions, such as those of the cantor, ritual slaughterer, circumciser and teacher, could be fulfilled by the average Jew of Bavaria, as had been the custom in the old country. These activities, of course, brought no compensation. The economic level and spiritual aspirations of the Bavarian Jewish immigrant did not yet permit going beyond this state of affairs.

61 Quoted in the *Hebrew Leader,* vol. xiv, no. 19, p. 5.
62 *Hebrew Leader,* vol. xv, no. 3, p. 4.
63 *Jewish Times,* vol. iii (1871) p. 104.
64 *Ibid.,* vol. vii (1876) p. 472.
65 *The Occident,* vol. v (1847/48) p. 413.

Only when German-Jewish immigration began to include migrants from west and north Germany did rabbis arrive in New York. While some of them remained in the metropolis but shortly, others settled there permanently. Thus, for example, Aaron Messing (arrived in 1867) remained in New York for only three years; Max Lilienthal (arrived in 1845) stayed but six years; and Moses Mielziner (arrived in 1865), eight years. But Rabbis Leo Merzbacher (arrived in 1842), Samuel Adler (arrived in 1853) and Gustav Gottheil (arrived in 1873) remained in New York for the rest of their lives. Both Rabbi David Einhorn (arrived in 1866) and his son-in-law Kaufmann Kohler (arrived in 1869) pursued almost their entire rabbinical careers in New York.

Under the influence of the militant Reform movement, the sermon took on an explicitly cultural character: it was aimed at introducing the public to the broader world of general science, art, literature, theatre and the like. The rabbinate manifested a most serious attitude to these cultural activities. Most rabbis saw to it that their sermons were preserved in printed form. Many volumes of sermons were published. One of the outstanding orators among the German rabbis, in his published collection of 48 selected sermons, included 20 which were delivered in New York.[66] The public was evidently enthusiastic about this type of reading material, for the German-Jewish press would regularly publish the sermons of rabbis even from outside New York, as, for example, a sermon by Rabbi Kleeberg of Louisville, Ky.[67]

In a more limited area—that of religious culture—efforts were already being made to issue a new prayer book. Two schools came to the fore among New York German Jews. One held that the religious sentiments of German Jews in America could only be expressed in the German language. Among the representatives of this viewpoint were Rabbis Einhorn, Kohler and Adolph Huebsch, who came from Hungary. Rabbi Huebsch's prayer book,[68] which appeared in 1872, carried a complete German translation, but not a single prayer was translated into English. A year later the same rabbi issued

66 Kohler, Kaufmann, *Dr. Dawid Einhorn's Ausgewählte Predigten und Reden* (New York 1880).

67 *Hebrew Leader,* vol. viii (Jan. 25, 1867) p. 2-3.

68 Huebsch, Adolph, ed., *Gebete für den öffentlichen Gottesdienst der Tempelgemeinde Ahawath Chesed* (New York 1872).

a hymnal for his congregation, which was entirely in German.[69] On the other hand, there were those who maintained that prayers should be translated into the vernacular of the country, into English. As early as 1855, Rabbi Merzbacher published his *The Order of Prayer for Divine Service.* By 1871, even the German hymns, which had been introduced into the service earlier, were translated into English and printed parallel to the original German.[70] Several years later only an English translation of the German hymns appeared,[71] and the original was omitted.

Closely related to the activities of the rabbis were those of the Jewish teacher. In a letter from America which appeared in an organ of Jewish teachers in Germany, the lot of the German Jewish teacher is described as being unsatisfactory. The small amount of German that was taught in Jewish schools was taught by rabbis. Lest the reader wonder why rabbis were engaged in elementary teaching, the writer states that in America little account was taken of differences in official position. Work was evaluated in terms of its own worth.[72]

Objectively, the lot of the German-Jewish teacher was not at all bad. Great stress was laid on the study of German in the German congregational as well as in the private German-Jewish schools. German was taught even in the New York Jewish orphanage. In an oral examination of the 119 orphans held in 1866, the children "translated from Hebrew into German as well as into English."[73] Hebrew, however, was also taught in these schools. A few hours weekly were devoted to the teaching of Hebrew even in the private schools. Thus an announcement of 1866 relates that "Hebrew is studied from 3 to 4 daily in Dr. Minrath's private school."[74]

One of the serious problems at the time was the lack of adequate textbooks. At first, the practice was simply to take books published in Germany, and attempt to adapt them to American conditions. In 1859, an English adaptation of a biblical history by Rabbi Adler,

[69] *Idem, Hymnen für den öffentlichen Gottesdienst der Tempelgemeinde Ahawath Chesed* (New York 1873).

[70] *Hymns for Divine Service in the Temple Emanu-El* (New York [1871]).

[71] Gottheil, Gustav, *Hymns and Anthems* (New York 1886).

[72] *Der Haus- und Schulfreund* (Muenster 1860) p. 36.

[73] *Hebrew Leader,* vol. viii (Oct. 19, 1866) p. 3.

[74] *Ibid.,* p. 31.

which had appeared many years earlier, was published.[75] Five years later, however, the author found it necessary to issue a guide to the study of the Jewish religion, albeit in German.[76] The innovation of this book was the elimination of the catechism, the question-and-answer form, which was customary in textbooks published in Germany.

The German-Jewish teacher was confronted by a dilemma: on the one hand, his pupils came from German-speaking homes and attended synagogues in which the German language prevailed; on the other hand, these pupils had become part of a predominantly English-speaking environment. Various devices were employed to resolve this problem. In 1869, a textbook for the study of Hebrew appeared in which the text was translated into both German and English.[77] The street, however, was to triumph over home and synagogue. Even in the orphanage, where great stress had been laid on the study of German, the rabbi was compelled to deliver his Sabbath sermons to the children in English.[78]

Among the cultural achievements of German Jews in New York must also be listed Samuel Adler's *Kobez al yad.*[79] Worthy of note among those works of their spiritual heritage, which they set out to render into English, are Graetz's *History,* translated by Gutheim,[80] a work by Abraham Geiger,[81] and various articles on the Science of Judaism.[82] Lest it be considered backward, the orthodox wing published Dr. Drachman's translation of Rabbi Samson R. Hirsch.[83] Of particular significance are the studies in the field of Hebrew language and grammar of Dr. Isaac Nordheimer, Professor of Semitic Languages at New York University, who passed away at an early age.[84]

75 Hecht, Emanuel, Jr., *Biblical History for Israelitish Schools* (New York 1859).

76 *Leitfaden für den israelitischen Religionsunterricht* (New York 1864).

77 Hecht, S., *Prozdor, Elementary Exercises in Hebrew Grammar* (New York 1869).

78 Baar, Herman, *Addresses on Homely and Religious Subjects. Delivered before the Children of the Hebrew Orphan Asylum, New York, 1880-85.*

79 *Sammlung einiger in Zeitschriften verstreuter wissenschaftlicher Artikel* (New York 1886).

80 *History of the Jews* (New York 1873).

81 *Judaism and Its History* (New York 1866).

82 *Hebrew Characteristics, Miscellaneous Papers from the German* (New York 1875).

83 *Igrot zafon, The Nineteen Letters of Ben Usiel* (New York 1899).

84 Nordheimer, Isaac, *A Critical Grammar of the Hebrew Language* (New York 1838-42).

Israels Herold was the first Jewish weekly in New York. Appearing in 1849, it ceased publication after only 12 issues.[85] This weekly was entirely in German. In their later publications, German Jews sought to combine German with English. Thus the weeklies, the *Hebrew Leader* (1859-82) and the *Jewish Times* (1869-79) contain material in both languages.

There were also German supplements to various Jewish publications, such as the *Libanon,* the German supplement of the *Young Israel* (1875), and *Der Makkabäer* of the *Independent Hebrew* (1876). The 13 issues of the *Hebrew News* in 1871 appeared in English, Yiddish and German. Reference is made in the *Jewish Encyclopedia*[86] to 12 such New York publications in the 19th century which included regular German supplements. Actually, there were 14, for the *Encyclopedia* overlooked the *Libanon* and *Der Makkabäer.*[87] There were, moreover, occasional German supplements to Jewish publications, and even the general *New Yorker Staatszeitung,* from time to time, printed reports and articles which were aimed almost exclusively at the Jewish reader.

The bulk of the material in these publications consisted of news of Jewish life throughout the world, but particularly in Germany and in the United States, and of reports of societies, organizations, synagogues and the like. There was also some belletristic work, poems, stories by Kompert, as well as discussions of educational problems.

The German theatre played an important role in the cultural life of the German Jews of New York. The theatre at the time served both cultural and social functions. At first the stress was laid on recreation. Musicals and similar entertaining affairs were presented. The scripts for these presentations were generally written by Max Cohnheim, author of the three popular plays "New York, und Berlin," "Herz und Dollar" and "Der Mord am West Broadway." The music was usually composed by the conductor C. Bergman. The nature of the audience at which the German theatre aimed is seen from the fact that the play "Ephraim Levy" was one of the most successful

[85] Kisch, Guido, "Israels Herold," *Historia Judaica,* vol. ii, p. 65-84.

[86] Vol. ix, p. 640.

[87] Though the *Encyclopedia* did commit this oversight, it was not shared by German bibiliography. In an article on "Die deutsche Presse in die Vereinigte Staaten," *Der deutsche Pionier,* vol. viii, p. 320, *Der Makkabäer* is listed as an organ "for education and the Jewish religion."

in 1856.[88] "Samuel von Posen," a play depicting the success of the German-Jewish immigrants, was also one of the most popular presentations.[89] There were also plays about Jewish life in Germany, and even Jewish historical dramas which glorified ancient Jewish life and suffering.

On the other hand, we come across the following notice:

> The Germania Theatre opened this week with the presentation of "Einer von unsere Leut" by Kalisch. In this play, Mr. Witt, acting the role of Isaac Stern, excels in his charming comic portrayal, which is free of any sort of exaggeration.[90]

It was in this same theatre, whose director was Adolf Neuendorf, that Heinrich Conried, later to occupy an important place in American theatrical life, received his artistic training.[91]

Various groups of amateur actors were also seriously concerned with the theatre. One such group was affiliated with the New York Turnverein. About this group we read:

> In 1856 the group came into possession of a more adequate stage . . . For the first time, Daniel Bandmann, a lively fellow, his friend, Emil Rosenbaum, and others appeared in a drama by Kotzebue,[92] "Das liebe Dörfchen."[93]

The annual Purim balls of the Purim Association, a welfare organization of German Jews, are also to be considered as part of theatrical activity. Over and above their artistic merit, they also reflected the most important events of the day. We read the following about the ball held in 1866:

> The high point of the evening was reached in the masquerade processions . . . The first represented the "victory of the spirit of the times over fanaticism." The centuries of intolerance and religious persecution proceeded in chronological order . . . the medieval ghetto, in which a Jew is being led to the stake, and the young Edgar Mortara[94] in most recent times. At the end of the procession

[88] *Arion New York von* 1854 *bis* 1904 (New York 1904) p. 8.

[89] *New York Mirror,* May 21, 1881, p. 2.

[90] *NYHZ* (1874) no. 1344, p. 11.

[91] Zeydel, Edwin Hermann, "The German Theatre in New York City," *Deutsch-Amerikanische Geschichtsblätter,* vol. xiii (1913) p. 310.

[92] August von Kotzebue (1761-1819) was the author of a number of dramas glorifying rural life.

[93] *Zum goldenen Jubiläum des New Yorker Turnvereins, 1850-1900* (New York 1900) p. 29.

[94] A six-year old Jewish boy who was forcibly abducted from his parents by papal police. A religious Catholic servant girl had baptized him secretly. The incident aroused the Jewish world.

> came the Goddess of Freedom as the standard-bearer of the 19th century, and a Valhalla wagon, on which the spirit of the times trampled fanaticism underfoot. The heroes bore the names of the outstanding Jews of recent times.
>
> The second procession . . . portrayed the triumphal journey of Queen Esther . . . At the end came a tableau which portrayed the fraternization of the Jewish Purim with the Christian carnival...[95]

The "Purim newspapers," distributed on such occasions, presented a mixture of theatre and literature. One such paper is described as being excellently illustrated with pictures of outstanding Jews of recent times, "such as Moses Mendelssohn, Meyerbeer, D'Israeli, Montefiore, etc. The tolerance of the artist is to be seen from the fact that even the Jew-hater Wagner was accorded a place among the pictures."[96]

German Jews were also represented in other areas of cultural life in New York. They served as a bridge between German, or even general European, culture and American culture. Among such men were Georg Adler, Professor of German at New York University,[97] Adolph Werner, Professor of German Literature at City College,[98] Felix Adler, the founder of the Ethical Culture movement, and the world-renowned anthropologist, Franz Boas. Dr. Abraham Jacobi played an important communal role, over and above his notable medical work. In the field of music, the aforementioned Adolf Neuendorf was outstanding. He founded the Germania Theatre, was a composer and conductor, and served as musical director of Temple Emanu-El.[99]

We have deliberately omitted reference to strictly technical or professional fields. We do, however, wish to mention briefly the role of German Jews as patrons of art, literature and scholarship. Among the leading figures here were the brothers Isidor, Nathan and Oscar Straus, James Speier, and the outstanding Maecenas, Jacob Schiff. The latter's activities, however, were largely in the 20th century and hence outside the scope of our study.

[95] *NYHZ* (1866) no. 885, p. 10.

[96] *NYHZ* (1879) no. 1564, p. 12.

[97] Cronau, Rudolf, *Drei Jahrhunderte deutschen Lebens in Amerika* (Berlin 1909) p. 367, 576.

[98] *American Jewish Year Book,* 1904/5, p. 204.

[99] *Dictionary of American Biography,* vol. xiii, p. 434.

Hostility in the Environment

Such outstanding achievements within so short a period of time were bound to arouse emotions of jealousy and enmity in the surrounding population. As early as 1836 a book appeared which characterized the German-Jewish immigrant in unfavorable terms. He is said to think only of money and profit.[100] Even so liberal a man as Walt Whitman referred to the ". . . dirty looking German Jews, with a glass box on their shoulders, [who] cry out 'Glass to mend,' with a stark nasal twang and flat squalling enunciation to which the worst Yankee brogue is sweet music."[101]

Here, as everywhere, the antagonism to the Jew manifests an ambivalent character. On the one hand, cries the anti-Semite, "he [the Jew] will not work";[102] on the other, a critic refers to "bargaining with a degree of ardor and enthusiasm . . . absolutely startling to the uninitiated in the mysteries of this chaos of merchandise."[103] Capitalism is portrayed in golden hues and the capitalist regarded as a hero and benefactor; the Jew, however, is denounced for his pursuit of wealth. While some anti-Semites berate the Jews for being sunk in the morass of materialism, others grant that the Jews are patrons of the theatre and the arts. Of every 100 New York theatre-goers, 80 are Jewish. "The institution could not survive without them." This, however, is not at all to their credit. Why?

> For a paltry few cents he can make himself at home here . . . This is the place where he finds recognition, where no one can make him feel that he is a Jew. And how, the jewelry glitters in the magnificent illumination! Rebecca and Sarah can lean over the balustrade of the first balcony, showing themselves to all. They are on the first balcony! And all for fifty cents apiece! . . . You will, dear reader, recognize them at a glance by the way they carry their elbows. But should your eyes not recognize them—well, then, your nose will let you know in the midst of which species you find yourself![104]

Thus wrote a German in 1848. It is noteworthy that two of the three expressions of hostility presented here refer to relations between German Jews and Germans in New York. Though Jews participated

[100] Bokum, Hermann, *The Stranger's Gift* (Boston 1836) p. 13.
[101] Whitman, Walt, *New York Dissected* (New York 1936) p. 123.
[102] *A Day on Coney Island* (New York [1880]) p. 11.
[103] *A Peep into Catharine Street or the Mysteries of Shopping* by a Late Retailer (New York 1846) p. 8.
[104] Griesinger, *op. cit.*, p. 142 ff.

in the founding of the Arion choral society in 1854, twelve years later the society resolved to refuse further admission to Jewish members. This episode was described at length in the *New Yorker Handelszeitung,* based on a correspondence from the *Illinois Staatszeitung.* This correspondence and the attitude and conclusions of the writer are of such great interest that we would like to quote from it here:

> . . . there are certain people who consider themselves intelligent upon whom, however, the philosophy of centuries and its fruits—spiritual emancipation, humanism and religious tolerance—have left no mark whatsoever. Among the many educated and enlightened members of the Arion society there are those whose fundamental principle is: "We want no Jews . . ." It so happened that a Jew had been proposed for membership in the society. His candidacy was enthusiastically supported by many members. Your correspondent too, who is a friend of the candidate and can only speak of him in praiseworthy fashion, was advised that it would be regrettable to place him in the embarrassing circumstance of failing to receive the requisite number of votes because he is a Jew. Your correspondent stood his ground, and declared that he would leave the society were the candidate refused admission because of his faith. Other progressive members sought to enlighten the benighted members of the society, but in vain . . . My candidate was defeated because he is a Jew. This occurred in the land of freedom of conscience and in the year of our Lord 1866. Naturally I could no longer remain in this society.

Subsequently, the writer adds:

> When one considers that it is precisely the Jews who support German musical productions and the German theatre in New York so strongly and continuously, one must grant that the Jew-haters in Arion compound their stupidity—which compromises the entire society—with sheer ingratitude. But even the gods fight against stupidity in vain.[105]

An editorial note accompanied this correspondence in the *New Yorker Handelszeitung* to the effect that, upon receipt of the communication and prior to its publication, the editors contacted the leadership of the Arion society to allow it an opportunity to reply. This overture was, however, ignored. Evidently, the editors added, the society could find no rational justification of its action. If it wished, therefore, to rehabilitate itself in the eyes of public opinion, it had no choice but to reject unanimously the shameful ballot and accept the can-

[105] *NYHZ* (1866) no. 879, p. 10.

didate. If not, then, the editors hoped, not only would all the Jewish members resign but all the progressive members as well.

It is unknown whether the leaders felt pangs of regret. Before long a second and far more serious incident of anti-Semitism came to the fore. The first was an episode of social life; the second, an economic matter. It concerned not only the Jews of New York, but Jews throughout America.

In 1867, the German fire insurance company Germania joined with three smaller agencies in issuing instructions to their agents that all applications of Jews for fire insurance must be submitted to the general agent for special approval. Since Germania's central office was located in New York, and many of its clients were local merchants, these instructions greatly aroused the Jews of New York. In an article headed "To the Pillory with the Obscurantists" the *New Yorker Handelszeitung* reacted sharply to this incident. Every insurance company certainly has the right, the newspaper argues, to protect its interests and to inquire into the character of the applicant for insurance. What, however, has character to do with faith? The company has only given evidence of its limited spiritual horizons by this procedure, and can only harm its stockholders, for the Jews can take revenge by cancelling all the policies they carry with the Germania. Nor will such action be limited to Jews; the newspaper argues that this is the moral duty "of every enlightened merchant, irrespective of religious affiliation."[106]

The following issue of the paper carried a reply by Rudolf Garrigue, president of Germania. Garrigue employed the familiar device: "All respectable New York Jews are insured with us." The instructions only referred to "second-hand goods dealers, hucksters, adventurers, Jewish war profiteers . . ."[107] "The company will only accept applications," he added, "from Jews who have resided at least five years in one place and who have a good reputation."

Jews fought the policy of the Germania not only through the press, but also by all other means of public communication. A newspaper report reads: "Stormy applause greeted the actor Bogumil Dawison last Monday in the municipal theatre for his extemporaneous portrayal of a rag-picker, in which he delivered a strong attack against the anti-Semitic fire insurance company."[108]

106 *NYHZ* (1867) no. 939, p. 16.
107 *Ibid.*, no. 940, p. 9.
108 *Ibid.*, no. 942, p. 11.

Satire was also often employed. A fire in the Winter Garden, which was completely destroyed, was reported thus:

> The Winter Garden . . . fell victim to flames . . . The president of a certain insurance company is of the opinion that this was the work of Shylock, who recently appeared on its stage . . . Our police officials will surely keep an eye on Shylock.[109]

The Germania incident was, as it were, tailored to suit the choral society Arion. It was used to justify its own policy: Look, we aren't the only ones who are anxious to keep the Jew at an arm's length. A song book published by Arion jested thus: Truly, the Jew seldom blesses "the creator of the fruit of the vine"; but quite often, "the creator of the light of the fire." Elsewhere in the song book we read that the Jew becomes joyous when he sees a fire in his premises.[110]

In later days, the anti-Semitic spirit in Arion was considerably diminished. On the sudden death in New York in 1883 of Eduard Lasker, the Jewish member of the German Reichstag, the Arion participated in the funeral, which took place in Temple Emanu-El. In 1895, when the news came from Germany that a monument to Heinrich Heine was prohibited, the Arion took the initiative in the move to erect the memorial in New York.

The belief, however, that the Jew was wont to set fire to his business in order to obtain insurance money had become deeply rooted in the stupefied minds of the half-drunk Germans of the Arion and in their songbooks, and it was difficult to eradicate it. Years later we come across a gem of this sort, a parody on the language of the German Jews, in a carnival book. For the sake of curiosity, we present it here in the original:

De Feieralarm

Dort wo für weit und breit
Nix wohnt wie uns're Lait,
Dort hält der Isidor
En klääne Notion-Store.
Der Veitel Aaron Stern
Macht dort in Suits für Herrn,
Und Mandel Blumenfeld,
Der wechselt Geld.
Dem Isaak Waslakopp

109 *Ibid.*, no. 941, p. 11.
110 *Arions Gesangbuch* (New York 1868) p. 100-102.

Sein kosch're Butcher Shop,
Liegt an dem nächste Tor
Vun Meyer's Liquor-Store;
Der Moritz Tulpenbeet
Kommt dann mit Real Estate,
Und dann der Moses Süss
Mit Groceries.
Beim Kleiderhändler Leberecht
Do geht's Geschäft schun lange schlecht;
Er geht zu Moses Süss herum
Und kauft drei Quart Petroleum,
Die giesst er dann mit Kennersinn
Uff's ganze Warenlager hin,
Un wie dann vollends leer die Kann',
Steckt er ä Streichholz an.[111]

By and large, the German press in New York was not hostile to the Jews. When it so happened, however, that a Jew was in the forefront of a constellation of interests which the press opposed, it did not refrain from utilizing the Jewish factor in an anti-Semitic manner. On the occasion of the appointment of a Jew to a certain position, a German newspaper reported the event as follows:

> Glory Hallelujah! . . . Rabbi Joseph Gutmann, the discharged customhouse officer, has found favor in the eyes of His Excellency in Albany and has been anointed notary public. Rabbi Schmuhl Bromberg, long live the Republic!—this great patriot, the shining light of the German Whig-Brotherhood,[112] the second Demosthenes of the new Republic—he too gambols about like a kid, for he too has been amply rewarded by High Priest Seward for his great services. Hear, dear readers, Rabbi Bromberg, instead of being appointed to the state treasury, has been named . . . Measurer of Corn . . . Both of the aforementioned gentlemen of the House of Israel are satisfied—and so let us also be satisfied . . .[113]

The newspaper is here hinting at the parallel between Bromberg's role and that of Joseph in Egypt, and stresses the unfavorable characteristics of the German-Jewish grain dealer. Midrashic as well as Biblical motifs are employed in taking cracks at Jews. Thus we read:

> The fallen band of angels of the German Whig-Brotherhood of New York, alias Bromberg, Gutmann & Co., has made one of its

[111] *Der Mainzer Verein in New York,* 1859-1909 (New York 1909).

[112] A political association which opposed the Democratic Party and existed from 1836 to 1856.

[113] *New Yorker Staatszeitung,* vol. vi (1839/40) no. 10, p. 2.

> fallen colleagues an Ariel, presumably because he is superb at getting wind of anything that smacks of a vacant position.[114]

Occasionally emotions reached so high a pitch that they could only be expressed poetically. Thus we read about a meeting of the German Whig-Brotherhood which took place on Wednesday, April 29, 1840, in the Henry Clay House:

> The Jew occupies the front line
> And says: The entire pool is mine!
> In the famous hall,
> In the Whig locale,
> Sat Bromberg, the president,
> Surrounded by the heads of the sects,
> Of various dialects . . .[115]

Hostile attitudes were expressed by non-German sources as well. The writer of the words "Let the reader stroll down Broadway or down any of the leading streets of New York City, and he will find Jewish names plenty as the locusts of Egypt,"[116] is surely not very favorable to the Jews. Even the *Police Gazette* let itself be heard. With few inhibitions, it pointed an accusing finger at the German Jew. Thus we read:

> . . . The developments of almost every day serve to show the extent to which the German Jews are acting as receivers of stolen goods . . . A very general suspicion prevails against this people, and it is not surprising. Many of them are professional lifters, burglars, and swindlers. Those in business find it difficult to effect an insurance upon their stock because of the frequency with which fires occur in their stores and the suspicious circumstances attending them . . .[117]

This "considered statement" appeared in the *Police Gazette* as a supplement to a report about a crime committed by "Moses Breidenbach, a prominent member of one of the Jewish synagogues of this city."

Even when the question has nothing to do with Jews, but an opponent has somehow or other to be insulted, the word "Jew" finds its way into the matter. In 1868 a tramway conductors' strike took place in New York. At a mass meeting of the strikers, the employers

114 *Ibid.*, no. 17, p. 2

115 *Ibid.*, no. 21, p. 3.

116 *The Original Mr. Jacobs* (New York 1888) p. 6.

117 Quoted from *The Israelite,* vol. vi, p. 180.

were referred to as "The Jew-souled excrescences owning the street railroads, semi-annually pocket immense dividends . . ."[118]

If need be, a German Gentile is made into a Jew. The *New York Herald* comes out with an editorial about the coming Jewish millenium, when Jews will rule both the Old and the New World. As evidence of the latter, the editorial points to Carl Schurz, "a German Jew," who was at the time the author of the Republican Party platform.

In 1876, a hotel in Schooley's Mountain, N. J., announced that it would not accept Jewish guests. The *New Yorker Handelszeitung* responded sharply to this in an editorial. But Schooley's Mountain was, in the last analysis, out in the sticks, and not on the map of American higher society. Saratoga Springs, however, was quite a different matter. The crash occurred here in the following year.

In the summer of 1877, Henry Hilton, one of the heirs and the administrator of the estate of the millionaire Stewart, refused to admit the prominent German-Jewish banker Joseph Seligman to one of his hotels in Saratoga Springs. The incident had immense repercussions among the German Jews of New York. The *New Yorker Handelszeitung* referred to it as a "sensation." For present purposes, the incident is highly significant because it constitutes the first time that a distinction was made between the "Seligman-type" Jew, who, Hilton maintained, could not be allowed to mix with better society, and the "Nathan-type," i.e., between the well-established Sephardic Jew and the newly-arrived German Jew. This was the interpretation placed upon the insult by New York German Jews, an interpretation in which the German press concurred, dealing with the issue quite openly:

> In the interests of our Jewish population, would that all were to possess many more of the character traits of the "Jews of the Seligman type." The Seligman family is inferior to none in respectability and education. Its role in communal affairs is highly eminent —nor does its wealth do any harm in this respect. The Seligmans do not deny their faith, nor are they accustomed to flaunt it, except when it comes to contributing to worthy causes even though the donations are not made public.[119]

The German Jews of New York reacted in a most effective manner to the Hilton-Seligman affair. Hilton claimed that the Jewish

[118] 1868. *Scrapbook of Newspaper Clippings on New York Social Life.* p. 22. In the New York Public Library, Sig. IRGC.

[119] *NYHZ* (1877) no. 1475, p. 11.

women who came to the hotel aroused the aversion of his other guests by tasteless, vulgar dress and makeup. He had, evidently, overlooked the fact that Stewart had made his millions from cosmetics. The response of the Jewish population was thus both logical and just, in that "many Jewish firms have broken commercial relations with A. T. Stewart & Co.; others will follow their example. There is also a movement afoot in the Jewish feminine world to cease all further purchasing at Stewart's retail store."[120]

Presumably the Jewish response had hit a very sore spot, for the Stewart interests demanded that all efforts be made to become reconciled with the Jews. Hilton donated sums of $500 to several Jewish charitable institutions in the widow Stewart's name. The donations, however, were refused by the directors of the institutions.[121] Whether the Jewish boycott was the direct cause or not cannot be determined; the fact remains that Stewart's store closed shortly thereafter.

A summary statement of the achievements of the German Jews of New York by the end of the period under consideration, i.e., about 1880, as viewed from without, is to be found in a semi-serious, semi-humorous poem, which celebrates the deeds of "Chakey Einstein, owff Broadway," the symbol and incarnation of the German Jew in America.[122]

In this year of Christian grace
What's your state and what's your place?
Why, you're rich and strong and gay—
Chakey Einstein, owff Broadway!
Myriad signs along the street
Israelitish names repeat.
Lichtenstein and Morgenroth
Sell the pants and sell the coat;
Minzescheimer, Isaacs, Meyer,
Levy, Lehman, Simon, Speyer—
These may just suggest a few
Specimens of Broadway Jew—
And these gentlemen have made
Quite their own the Drygootz Trade.
Surely you're on to-day,
Chakey Einstein, owff Broadway.
Fond of women, fond of song;
Fond of bad cigars, and strong;

120 *Loc. cit.*
121 *NYHZ* (1878) no. 1553, p. 12.
122 *Puck,* vol. xxix, p. 362.

Fond, too fond of Brighton's Race,
(Where you're wholly out of place,
For no Jew, in Time's long course,
Ever backed a winning horse;)
Fond of life, and fond of fun,
(Once your "beezness" wholly done;)
Open handed, generous, free,
Full of Christian charity;
(Far more full than him who pokes
At your avarice his jokes;)
Fond of friends, and even kind
To the sick and lame and blind;
(And, though loud you else may be,
Silent in your charity;)
Fond of Mrs. Einstein and
Her too—numerous infant band,
Ever willing they should share
Your enjoyment everywhere—
What of you is left to say,
Chakey Einstein, owff Broadway?

* * *

Well, good friend, we look at you
And behold the Conquering Jew!

The "Christian world" has the last laugh, however, on the Jew, the author writes: "When your son . . . grows to manhoods years, he'll wed one a Christian born and bred," and his pew in the church "Will bear a name unknown to you . . . Eynston maybe . . ."

The Manhattan telephone directory for 1955/56 does not have a single Eynston . . . and 72 Einsteins.

THE HISTORY OF THE JEWISH COMMUNITY IN NEW YORK

An Analysis of Hyman B. Grinstein's *The Rise of the Jewish Community of New York, 1654-1860**

Originally published in the *Yivo Bleter,* XXIX, 2 (1947)

THE EUROPEAN BACKGROUND

In order to see the development of the Jewish community in America clearly, it is necessary to examine its social and cultural origins in the Jewish community of Europe.

What did the Jewish community of Europe look like? In the era preceding the emancipation of European Jews, and in some cases even in later periods, the Jewish communities not only regulated internal Jewish affairs, but also fulfilled definite political functions with regard to the outer world. The communities were the bearer of the "privileges" that extended to the Jews the right to communal existence, defined their economic functions, and determined the religious and secular rights of the individual. The most important aspect of the "privileges" was economic, and, in a sense, the other aspects of the "privileges" were in the nature of a compensation for these economic responsibilities shouldered by the Jews. Since the economic functions of the Jews were the same in the domain of a king as in the lands of an impoverished knight, the "privileges" were practically the same everywhere. Consequently, the pattern of Jewish life was fairly uniform in all European communities. Thus, a minute-book of a small community reflects in miniature all the problems of the larger communities. A small degree of individuality attaches to some of the com-

* Jewish Publication Society, Philadelphia, 1945, 645 pp.

Reprinted from *Yivo Annual of Jewish Social Science,* Volume IV, 1949.

munities by reason of such purely local events as fires, libels, or epidemics. But even these traits of individuality depended on the time element more than on any other factor. After all, nearly every community had its fires and epidemics, and the differences among them were insignificant.

The situation in America is entirely different. The Jews never constituted a political entity here just as they never fulfilled specific functions as a group. The Jewish community could not expect any support from government agencies in the execution of its enactments. Even if the Jews in America had arrived at a kind of Rousseauan social contract in order to create a centralized community, the government could not have meddled in its internal affairs. Each Jew could live where he pleased, work at the occupation of his choice, and completely ignore the community if he so desired. Since the Jewish community in America did not utilize the power of the state to impose its control over internal Jewish matters, its development was quite different from that of the European Jewish community.

Despite these essential differences in origin, structure, and legal position, the two communities also manifest some notable similarities, mainly in purpose, aim, and function in relation to their constituents. And only in the community organizations of Europe could the founders of American Jewish communal institutions have found a model for their enterprises.

Unfortunately, Dr. Grinstein draws no parallel between Europe and America in this respect. His study begins with the American scene.

The External Character of the American Jewish Community

To begin with, the Jewish community in America was from its very inception a purely voluntary association, which included only some Jews in a given area. Secondly, in comparison with its European counterpart, its functions, at the outset, were rather limited. Moreover, these limited functions were not assumed by a central body, as was the case in Europe, but were distributed among various groups and, on occasion, even among individuals. Thirdly, the hierarchy of the various community activities changed. Activities closely linked with the synagogue were gradually supplanted by such purely social functions as insurance, social service, and rural resettlement. These activities depended to a large extent on local conditions and, therefore, retained their local character. Unity of function and character ceased to exist here. It is hence not surprising that for the period of over two hundred years covered by this study, 1654 to 1860, the author succeeded in finding only fifty-four inquiries and requests that had been sent to the New York community by twenty-eight communities throughout the country, although hundreds of Jewish settlements sprang up and disappeared from the American scene in that interval. These fifty-four inquiries deal with routine matters related to synagogues, cemeteries, or with requests for the loan of scrolls of the Torah and other objects of ritual. The main problems of a small community in the South, for example, could not and did not assume great importance in the eyes of the New York community, and mutual aid could, therefore, not have been expected.

New York had not achieved a central position in American Jewish life in the early years of the period under discussion. The city lacked a dominant personality transcending the limits of the local community, such as we frequently encounter in Europe; there, the prestige of many a small town rabbi often reached neighboring and even distant communities. Furthermore, New York did not become a center of Jewish learning, the influence of which extended throughout the country. Neither did any other American Jewish community attain a position of recognized leadership in Jewish intellectual life.

This lack of a dominant center explains the fact that no body of literature of the type that was current in Europe during the period under consideration, and which to this day serves as a source of information about the Jewish community, came into existence in America. We refer, of course, to the responsa literature. In America, there were few who would raise questions about complex Jewish matters, and practically none competent to answer them. The fact that, in the disputes over the Touro monument, a man of such limited scholarship as the traveler Benjamin II had to be consulted, is a sad commentary on the state of Jewish learning in America at that time.

One thing all Jewish communities in America had in common. They all consisted largely of people who had been transplanted from one continent to another under roughly similar conditions. They all shared a somewhat similar conception of America. They were amazed at the enormous economic possibilities of the new country, and they all began to explore and to utilize these possibilities in a more or less similar manner. Dr. Grinstein believes that the specific American laws about chartering congregations in the United States influenced the development of Jewish community institutions in this country. There is, to be sure, an element of truth in this hypothesis. But the dynamics of American life were of far greater importance in the shaping of the traits common to Jewish communal life than any government legislation.

American reality created a frontier society, and American sociology and historiography have accepted and defined the concept. Whether one follows Professor Turner,[1] the leading exponent of the frontier concept, all the way, or modifies his geosociological interpretations by introducing economic factors, one thing is clear: America would not be what it is if the explorer, the missionary, the soldier, the hunter, and the farmer had not moved steadily westward and thus opened the area of what is now the United States. This frontier society provided the background against which American Jewish life grew. During the period under consideration in Dr. Grinstein's book the most important Jewish communities were found in these frontier areas. But though the majority of Jewish immigrants settled throughout the country and only a smaller number remained in New York, the latter community retained its European character to some extent much longer than the frontier areas. Even those immigrants who eventually moved to the hinterlands stopped in New York for a short time. In addition, those who failed to establish themselves in outlying districts tended to return to New York. A number of questions arise in connection with these developments: To what extent did the Jewish community of New York take the lead over the communities of, say, the Middle West? Was the original development of the outlying communities different from that of New York? What fundamental differences between the two types of communities appeared later?

The Internal Life of the Jewish Community in America

During the period under consideration, especially toward the end, the New York Jewish community began to develop tendencies like those of the European Jewish community. Expenditures for religious and ritual purposes decreased in comparison with the sums spent on social services and education. Thus, the Jewish hospital built in 1855 cost $30,000, and various Jewish charities distributed $18,000 among

[1] Frederick J. Turner, *The Frontier in American History,* New York, 1921.

the needy in 1859. A general feeling arose that the cost of religious services, such as synagogues, *kashrut, mikve* (ritual bathhouse), and other rituals, should be borne by those who made use of them. Thus, the Jewish community began to assume the traditional role of the European community, and the spheres of activity of the Jewish communities on both sides of the ocean came to be practically similar.

The description of this phase of community activity is one of the most successful portions of the book. The author has succeeded in discovering a number of new or little-known facts and in pointing out their significance and proper relationships. He throws light on the development of the synagogues of New York, describing fully the background, controversies, personalities, and forces that led to the founding of new synagogues, such as the B'nai Jeshurun (1825). The administration of the synagogues, their internal discipline, their struggle for democratization, for the general right to vote, the controversies concerning Jewish education, and the attempts at an adjustment to the general cultural milieu are all set forth in detail.

The author describes the duties of the ecclesiastical functionaries —rabbis, reverends, cantors, sextons, religious teachers—their salaries and working conditions. He calls attention to the fact that none of these functionaries received traditional ordination or other authorization. Here, a comparison between the European institution of special gifts presented to the religious functionaries and the American form of emolument would be highly desirable. The author, however, fails to draw such a comparison. Neither does he consider the internal problems of the adjustment of these functionaries to their new environment, to which they had been transplanted from European soil.

The author pays considerable attention to the customs of various synagogues as well as to their liturgies. He considers the role that music began to assume in the religious services. He takes up the development of the choir, the controversies surrounding mixed choirs and the introduction of the organ and group singing, and the competition among synagogues for a larger and more prominent choir. Various customs of the Bar Mitsve ceremony are described in detail. The author devotes a complete chapter to the struggle over the reform movement.

Interment and observance of the dietary laws also played an important role in the internal life of the community. Here, the author takes up the problems that grew out of an influx of large numbers of immigrants. Very often, a poor immigrant died without leaving enough money for burial costs, and the community had to assume the financial responsibility of that rite. The author also emphasizes the social aspect of the problem of *kashrut.* Thus, he tells of the interesting attempt, in 1815, of a well-to-do Jew to establish a fund to help indigent Jews to get meat at a lower price.

We have already mentioned the increased expenditures for social service. Among the Jewish immigrants who came to America in ever increasing numbers, some could not establish themselves economically and had to apply to the charities of the Jewish community for aid. A clear picture is presented of the activities of the Hebrew Benevolent Society and the German Hebrew Benevolent Society. Often, the recipients of these charities were immigrants who had tried their luck in the hinterlands and failed. They usually came back to New York, where they were aided by the Jewish community. Unfortunately, we do not get a clear picture of this movement in and out of New York in Dr. Grinstein's study. New York resembled the Berlin and Vienna communities in this respect. The influx of Eastern European Jews following a fire, a pogrom, or expulsion would suddenly put a heavy burden on the Jewish metropolitan community in Central Europe just as each wave of immigration created a problem for the Jewish charities of New York.

The problem was: how were the large sums of money needed by these institutions to be raised? To begin with, traditional fund-raising devices were used: various types of collection boxes, Yom Kippur collection trays, *mahazit hashekel* (the traditional halfpenny levy), the sale of *aliyot* (the privilege of being called to the reading of a portion of the Torah). Occasionally, a special tax was levied on members of the congregations. These methods were inadequate, however, for the number of the needy was continually increasing, and new methods of fund-raising had to be found. Among the new devices were dinners, charity balls, and similar "benefit" enterprises. Another method, which we do not find in New York but which was frequently used in other communities, was the charity lottery. It would be interesting to examine this method of fund raising: Were these new devices derived from the American environment or were they Jewish inventions? To what extent did other American communities imitate New York or *vice versa?* In general, Dr. Grinstein's study hardly considers the relationship between New York and other American communities just as it considers only superficially the relations between the New York community and its European counterpart, except in one unusual event, the Mortara case, and the instances of the arrival of Palestinian fund collectors.

America did not entirely follow in the footsteps of Europe in the methods of distributing charity, probably because of the milieu. Thus the European *pletn* system, that is, the method of assigning poor transients to individual households, was discontinued, although an individual congregation here and there might have still retained the old custom. The custom of inviting a transient on the Sabbath or a holiday fell likewise into disuse. On the whole, the personal element in charity declined in America greatly; it was replaced by institutionalized forms.

In addition to religious, educational, and charitable functions, another considerable area of Jewish community activity in America was purely social-recreational. This activity was determined largely by the relations between Jews and non-Jews. Even the upper strata of Jewish society were not admitted to non-Jewish circles and, therefore, had to form their own sets for entertainment, intellectual stimulation, and other social relations.

Although the author presents a number of facts bearing on this problem, he does not coordinate these facts or draw the necessary conclusions from them. The cases that the author cites are frequently highly instructive, casting a totally new light on the problem. Thus, he presents facts about attempts to organize the Jews in America and the reaction of the community to these activities, about the problem of intermarriage and conversions, and the position taken by the synagogues in these matters.

Because the Jewish community had to depend on its own resources for social activity, several groupings developed within it. In addition to the usual economic and occupational distinctions, those based on the geographic origin of the immigrants came to play a prominent role. There arose the well-known social cleavages among Sephardic, German, and East European Jews, about which we learn from contemporary Jewish and non-Jewish sources. Although the author makes sporadic attempts to analyze this interrelationship, he limits such investigations to the entry of the German Jews into Sephardic circles by marriage. A detailed study of relations among these groups would be of great significance.

The forms Jewish social life assumed in America were determined by local conditions, but also by the cultural and social heritage that the various groups brought from Europe. In this respect, special stress must be laid upon the groups that came from German-speaking countries. Their homeland enjoyed great prestige in America. Their native tongue, German, was respected in scientific, artistic, and educational circles. All these considerations were bound to influence the Jewish group, especially when we bear in mind the fact that at that time there was a German American community with distinct political, cultural, and social activities in which Jews of German origin were represented and the programs of which served as a model for German Jews.[2] It is to be regretted that the author considers these problems only incidentally, merely recording here and there the dates of balls, bazaars, or theatrical performances, and citing a few instances of Jewish participation in German glee clubs.

The driving force in Jewish social life was, of course, the younger generation. It gave expression to all of the social trends in the Jewish community. Here, the author presents the organizational scheme of the youth groups that arose, reviews their activities, and presents a few samples of their literary and musical programs. Among these groups, too, we must seek the origin and development of that purely American institution, the lecture, which is still important in the social and cultural life of the Jews in America.

In the center of Jewish cultural life was the problem of effecting a synthesis between the older Jewish cultural traditions and the new values of the American scene. This problem was reflected, particularly among Jewish youth, in two forms: in its concrete aspect, as a conflict of languages, and in its more inclusive aspect, as a quest for a broader outlook on life, a new ideology. An investigation of the latter would demand a fundamental study of the press, literature, and art of the American Jews of the time, and this cannot be expected within the limits of the author's work. The problem of language, however, should have received more detailed treatment than the author gives it.

[2] Cf. the author's study published in the *Yivo Bleter,* Vol. XXV (1945), now available in a separate edition in English under the title: *The Jews in Relation to the Cultural Milieu of the Germans in America up to the Eighteen Eighties,* New York, 1947, 55 pp.

He does tell something of the language of synagogue minutes, but we are interested in the spoken language, the language of the home. We should like to know how many Jews spoke German and to what extent German (Western) Yiddish was preserved among the immigrants from those countries. Furthermore, a description of the transition to English would be of great interest. Concerning all this we learn nothing from the book. We are merely informed that there was a contemptuous attitude toward Yiddish. But this very fact demands a more thorough study. In this connection, the question of Anglicizing German-sounding names arises. Here, too, the author's comments are hardly adequate for the theme.

There is a good chapter on education. We see the earnest and concerted effort the community made to transmit the Jewish spiritual tradition brought from the Old World to the generation growing up in America, and it is truly heartbreaking to conclude with the author that the results "were unusually meager." Formal education was limited to the very young. Adult education was, apparently, unknown then, or the author does not mention it. Nevertheless, it would be important to get a picture of the cultural level of Jewish adults. To what extent was the traditional study of the Bible and the Talmud current among the Jews? How active were the various associations traditionally dedicated to this purpuse, such as *Khevre Mishnayes, Khevre Eyn Yankev*? We can learn a good deal about the general cultural level of the Jews from the Jewish press in German and English that came into existence then, and also to some extent from the activities of the different literary clubs very popular at the time.

The author devotes a special chapter to the nonconformists, to those who refused to belong to a synagogue or to submit to community discipline. At first, these people were dealt with quite harshly; later on, a more lenient attitude was assumed toward them. It is a pity that the author allots but a few lines to the cultural background of these nonconformists. We should like to know who these people were, whether they substituted a secular approach to Jewish matters for the religious outlook that they rejected, whether their anti-religious position was rooted in a European ideology or was acquired in America. We should, furthermore, be interested to know the type of institutions the nonconformists created and the general attitude toward nonconformity that prevailed in America.

A Comparison Between the American and European Communities

In spite of the considerable differences between the Jewish communities in Europe and America, it is useful to compare the two in some respects, for there are material resemblances as well. It is particularly worthwhile to compare the Jewish community of New York with the larger communities of Central Europe, such as Vienna or Berlin. The decentralization of the New York community presents no obstacle, because the Central European Jewish communities in the nineteenth and twentieth centuries were also largely decentralized. Thus, in Vienna, although the community was technically unified, of about two hundred houses of worship not even ten were under the community council and about six hundred and sixty organizations were active outside the limits of the *Kultusgemeinde.* Berlin did not even have a compulsory unified community, nor was it necessary for the individual to belong to one of the Jewish communities in order to be recognized as a member of the Jewish faith.

In internal organization, too, the New York community resembled the Berlin and Vienna communities of recent years. Just as the New York Jews were largely newcomers, the Vienna community also consisted in a substantial measure of arrivals from the provinces. Thus, at the beginning of the so-called old emigration to America, about 1815 (the "new emigration" is the one beginning in 1880), the Vienna community consisted of a handful of privileged individuals, the signers of the earliest regulations of the Vienna synagogue. Later, thousands of Jews who had originally planned to make Vienna or Berlin a stopping-place on their journey across the ocean remained there permanently. Thus, as in New York, there were in these communities people who came from different places, and followed various religious customs and folkways. In Berlin and Vienna, a battle was waged over the issue of Reform Judaism just as in America, in general, and in New York, in particular, allowing, of course, for the divergence in circumstances.

To be sure, we know considerably less about New York's immigrants, the founders of the local community, than we do about the signers of the Vienna regulations. The Viennese were proud of their right to live in the capital and of their economic and social achievements. They left considerable information about their lives and activities, on the basis of which Bernhard Wachstein was able to write a fairly comprehensive work about them. The New York Jews considered themselves ordinary folk and left fewer details about themselves. But the "little men" of New York were founders of a community as much as the notables of Vienna, and although they appeared on the scene somewhat later, their structure had a more lasting influence on Jewish life than that of their Viennese brethren.

The author, however, failed to make this comparison, an omission that is truly regrettable. If we had such a comparison between the communities on both sides of the Atlantic, we could set the author's work beside the various monographs on Jewish communities in Europe and draw the necessary inferences from them. In this way, a clear picture of the characteristic achievement of the Jewish community in America and its contribution to the Jewish people as a whole could be obtained. The general American background could be compared with the non-Jewish European background, and all other external conditions could be reduced to more or less equal values. Thus, we could set up a comparative table of amount and sources of income and distribution of expenditures which would be highly instructive. Although the author does not present a complete picture of finance in the community because he lacked detailed figures, it does not necessarily follow that painstaking study would not have discovered such figures directly, or led to other sources whence one could derive the information indirectly.

Sources

In a work of this kind, the author's sources and the use he makes of them are extremely important, both in their own right and from the point of view of methodology. The author's chief contribution is his utilization of the archives of various synagogues and charitable and social service organizations. Although most of the documents relating to the earlier period, as well as some of the later ones, had already been published,[3] these represent but a small fraction of the materials marshaled by the author. His bibliography amazed a Catholic reviewer[4] who is interested in old Catholic parishes in America and who envied the wealth of source material available about Jewish congregations. The author is apparently passionately devoted to details,

[3] In the publications of the American Jewish Historical Society.

[4] Basil L. Lee, *The Catholic Historical Review,* Vol. 32, No. 1, IV, 1946, pp. 106-7.

and he presents his details conscientiously. Thus, the critic who cannot enjoy a book unless he has discovered some inaccuracies in it will fare ill with the author's work.

For his impressive bibliography of sources alone, which is a pioneer enterprise in this field, the author has earned the gratitude of all students of Jewish history in America. His work obliges them to evaluate these sources and, in their light, to revise certain conclusions arrived at by Jewish historiography. To be sure, it would have been preferable had the author himself attempted such a revision or an initial evaluation of these sources in comparison with other sources. His work would have gained immeasurably had he given us a hint of the scope of the information contained in these sources, their reliability, and the extent to which the writers of the various documents participated in the events that they described. The author did not do this, and it is our hope that others will fill this gap.

The mere wealth of bibliographical data, however, is not an unmixed blessing. On the contrary, it may prove a drawback in that one cannot see the forest for the trees. To some extent, this work shows such lack of perspective. The rich archival materials (particularly when they are all of one type, namely synagogue protocols) led the author along a narrow path, with the result that his work is more in the nature of a cross section of a small area than a logically developed account.

This reviewer has studied a number of Jewish community records (not of New York) of the period under consideration, and he can testify to the fact that most of these documents record merely the decisions arrived at in various discussions at meetings. Subjects of cultural significance and of general community interest are almost entirely ignored in these records. At the same time, men of literary talent, both supporters and opponents of the controlling figures in the community, were welcome in the Jewish as well as the general press. There, we find admirable accounts of various aspects of Jewish life, while the writing of community records was left largely to incompetents.

A comparison of the records of an American Jewish community with a minute-book of a European community reveals the great distinction between American and European methods of public protocoling. In Europe, the minutes were written by skilled men under the careful supervision of men who not only read the written lines, but also between the lines. Here, they were written by people of limited information. The large number of protocols in the book, which the author quotes verbatim, clearly indicate that in most cases the writers simply recorded from dictation.

In addition to the protocols in manuscript, there is considerable printed material on kindred topics: regulations, constitutions of synagogues, and the like. These two types, the manuscript and the printed matter, resemble each other and probably go back ultimately to the same source. In contrast to the European synagogue and community regulations, which reflect contemporary life and needs of the hour, American materials are more often than not stereotyped instructions for standard activities, with the result that life, which is in a state of flux, here appears to be fixed and constant. It would be highly desirable to investigate the extent to which New York influenced the rest of the country in the way of recording.

The author frequently provides rich materials in one field of his investigation, as, for example, the table of occupations of 101 candidates for a lodge in 1840-50 (p. 549), from which we learn that among them were thirty peddlers and thirteen tailors, and that nearly all callings were represented. On the other hand, he is often very spare in his discussion of other fields. He does not take full advantage of the Jewish press in this country and of reports on America in the European Jewish press. All important Jewish community affairs were described fully in the Jewish press, because there was a shortage of reading matter, and these activities represented news eagerly awaited by the public. As things stood, the Jewish press could not compete with the non-Jewish press in news of general interest, and sought to attract the reader by special news. Furthermore, the author's sources do not throw any light on other non-traditional activities of the community, such as entertainment.

There is a good and exhaustive chapter in the book on the origins of the German- and Anglo-Jewish press in New York. But the author's failure to utilize the general press is a serious omission. An examination of at least one daily newspaper covering one or two momentous years is necessary in order to see how Jewish problems were viewed by people not active in Jewish community affairs. From the very beginning of the Jewish community here, we find reports about Jews in the general press. These reports, though sometimes naive, are frequently instructive, especially when the fact is borne in mind that the Jewish press often played up matters in order to see the reaction of the general press.

It would certainly have added to the value of the book if the author had made use of contemporary diaries, letters, travel accounts, etc., in which significant aspects of Jewish life are revealed. Such literature gives warmth and color to the period, and the testimony of an outsider always carries considerable weight. It must be said that much information is tucked away in sources of a general nature that have not yet been touched by investigators and scholars.

Interpretation of Sources

The author does not correlate the wealth of detailed facts adequately. He does not coordinate them to show clearly the interaction of the various factors, which led to the creation of one of the largest Jewish communities of the world in New York. The rise of this community took place against the background of the nineteenth-century emigration from Europe. This emigration in the period under discussion was composed largely of Germans, among whom the percentage of Jews was at least twice the percentage of Jews in the total German population. This Jewish emigration is not presented properly in the light of the general German emigration, and the mutual influences of the two communities are not clarified. Above all, the author fails to make adequate use of figures.

Occasionally, he does attempt to speak in quantitative terms. Thus he tries to determine the ancestry of the various Jewish groups in New York on the basis of the number of patients admitted to the New York Jewish hospital. (The material was found in the Jewish newspapers.) But the composition of the Jewish group cannot be determined on the basis of patients admitted to free hospitals, for, as is well known, only the poorest classes of Jews resort to free hospitalization. Such a table can show only the relative economic condition of the various groups of Jews, but not the total figures, and it is by no means possible to arrive at the number of German Jews in New York in 1860 on the basis of their representation among the indigent.

In general, the author's grouping of Jews according to their origin is quite loose. This inaccuracy derives, above all, from the confusion in his use of the concept "Polish Jews," who, according to his estimation, comprised about one-third of the Jews of New York. Occasionally, the term is used as a political concept, referring only to Jews of

Russian Poland, and occasionally it is used in its ethnic sense to include the Jews of all areas that were once Poland. The question arises: if the author considers Poland in its political sense, why does he include Posen, which was then Germany? If he considers it in the ethnic sense, why does he omit Galicia? Furthermore, the author includes English, Dutch, French, and Bohemian Jews in one grouping and does not even attempt an estimate of the size of the respective groups which could have been made on the basis of synagogue membership.

Even where the groupings according to origin are clear, there is no indication of the extent to which these divisions were crossed in community activities. Instead of attempting to present a systematic account, the author presents merely individual features; these, to be sure, are often of great interest. We learn, for instance, that no great help for Palestine was expected from Temple Emanu-El, that German Jews did not attend the dinners of the Hebrew Benevolent Society in great numbers, that Shearith Israel rarely participated in intercongregational activities. Sephardic, German, and Polish Jews are more or less differentiated. But what about the French and Bohemian Jews? Did they join the Sephardic, German, or Polish Jews or did they form synagogues of their own? What happened to the Hungarian Jews? It would also have been worthwhile to consider the relationship between subgroups of a given classification, for example, the Bavarian and North German Jews.

In one case, the author tries to carry out such differentiation and comparison but he arrives at incorrect conclusions. He writes that it was characteristic of the Jewish as well as the non-Jewish immigration that the closer a community was to the ocean the earlier did its members emigrate. In the case of the non-Jewish emigration, this was, generally speaking, true, but it seems that it does not apply to Jewish emigration. French Jews in America came mainly from Alsace and Lorraine, which were farthest from the coast; German Jews came chiefly from Bavaria; North German Jews near the coast began to come in large numbers only later. The same is true of East European Jews. Hence, the inland-seacoast theory of emigration was not a determining factor in Jewish migration. Jewish emigration cannot be understood and interpreted unless specific Jewish conditions are considered.

I should like to raise one more point: the question of utilizing lists of Jewish names that can be found in Jewish or general sources. In examining such sources in an American community quite far from New York, I discovered that in this way more Jewish names can be collected than are found in the membership records of congregations at that time. In other words, only a minority of Jews belonged to congregations, and it is incorrect to deduce the number of Jews in a city from congregation membership only. Is the same true of New York? Are there sources, Jewish or otherwise, from which such a book of names for New York could be composed? Dr. Grinstein does not even raise these methodologically extremely important problems.

Conclusions

In the last analysis it can be stated that the author worked assiduously and presented us with a weighty book, which contains a large number of facts, some of them of great importance. But as a history, the book falls somewhat short of the mark because, except for the last three chapters, a coordinated, continued narrative is lacking.

Reviewers have already pointed out a few of these shortcomings. Harold Jonas[5] says that the book contains excellent material but the organization is weak, largely because the author treats an insignificant fact in a footnote as if it were an important trend in the development of Jewish history in America. Edward N. Saveth[6] concludes that, in comparison with other studies of the type, the work is boring; it neither inspires the scholar nor stimulates the reader. This statement is, I believe, extreme. Every compilation of facts is important to the specialized student even if he must reorganize the presentation of these facts. As for myself, I may say, that in working through Dr. Grinstein's book, my interest never failed, even to the last footnote.

Nevertheless, one must admit that in a study of this kind, the intelligent lay reader cannot be ignored. There are cases of submitting a new thesis for the judgment of specialists where the historian dare not take the non-specialist into account. But the rise and development of the Jewish community in New York could have been presented as a subject rich in interest and implications even for the non-specialist. Such a presentation can be found only in the last three chapters,

[5] Harold Jonas, *New York History*, Vol. 27, No. 2, pp. 238-41.

[6] Edward N. Saveth, "The Immigrant in American History," *Commentary*, Vol. 2, No. 2, p. 184.

where the author considers 1) joint inter-congregational provision for Jewish community needs, 2) the participation of New York in Jewish problems of the world, and 3) the traditional interest of New York Jews in Palestine. In the other chapters, Dr. Grinstein presents a cross section of various aspects of Jewish life in New York at a given time, with marked lack of balance among these aspects, namely, some are dealt with very thoroughly, others merely superficially. Perhaps this was the intent of the author. If so, the title, *The Rise of the Jewish Community* is misleading, and the book should have been called *A History of Jewish Communal Institutions in New York.*

There is still another reason for writing a book of this kind in such a manner as to show the reader the interrelation of facts and convince him of the importance of every detail in the total picture. The significance of Jewish history in the United States has not yet been generally recognized by the Jewish public, and the impression must, therefore, be avoided that history is for specialists only and that the history of a community like New York cannot be told in dramatic fashion. Obviously, such a dramatic account is quite different from "popular" writing or from watering down facts in order to please the uneducated reader. On the contrary, the historian must inspire in the reader respect for details, since accuracy in detail seems to be the real distinction between fiction and history. Every detail must be demonstrable. History is a science, while writing history is an art. We see this in the best achievements of local American historiography; in the Jewish field, Bernhard Wachstein's monograph on the Jewish community of Eisenstadt, near Vienna, can serve as a model.

Apart from its shortcomings, Dr. Grinstein's book represents an important accomplishment. Let us hope that, in the course of his work, the author will achieve a full measure of success in the pursuit of his goal.

THE RISE OF THE JEWISH CLUB IN AMERICA

Social Distinction and Exclusiveness Redefined

In America, club life as an expression of social distinction and exclusiveness was first experienced by the German-Jewish immigrants and the east-European Jews who followed them to these shores. In their old homes social distinctions arose only from historical status, differently conceived by Christians and Jews. To the former, it meant inherited nobility; to the latter, it referred to scholarly attainment. Club life was entirely alien to Jewish experience, in which *shtadlanuth* (intervention through personal contacts) furnished the justification of wealth. In America, wealth per se could both create a social group and perpetuate it through self-segregation without assuming any communal functions. A clearly idolatrous use of money, namely, for sport, travel, gambling, drinking, and frivolity, was outside the range of the experience of the immigrant raised in the Jewish tradition. That the size of such outlandish expenditures could determine one's position in society seemed absurd. Moreover, since the Jewish immigrant was fully preoccupied with his own economic problems, interest in what rich people did with their money had a low priority for him.

At first, there were no leisured rich among the Jewish immigrants to whom the thought of founding clubs in the English fashion could occur. Any attempt by a *nouveau riche* to seek out "clubbable" elements in the Jewish group would have been completely unsuccessful; such snobs were simply inconceivable. With the exception of those few who had spent some time in England, Jewish immigrants had no knowledge of a club system and surely no wish to imitate such an Anglo-Saxon ideal. In addition, very few Jews in America could have suspected that in the British motherland, American "society," including its clubs, was regarded as an inferior copy of the eminent English prototype.

Aspirations for Social Relations with Gentiles and the American Club System

Economic adjustment to the new continent by German-Jewish immigrants created a prosperous merchant class concentrated in selected trades, mainly in the large cities. Material affluence accompanied by leisure awakened aspirations of social relations with the Gentiles. Encouragement for this tendency was provided by the general view, especially widespread during the period of industrialization following the Civil War, that concentrated wealth could assume the role of hereditary

Reprinted from *Jewish Social Studies,* Volume XXXI, 1969

nobility in creating high society. Social status in proportion to one's wealth was pursued; the Jewish immigrants who attained wealth were no exceptions.

At this time wealthy Gentiles were already organized into clubs, and the newly-rich Jewish immigrant encountered the Gentile idea of the club. The leading idea of American Gentile clubs was the patriciate:

> . . . clubbable disposition appears to run in families . . . and an examination and careful comparison of the lists of the great leading associations proves that one half of the club-men of the city are descended from less than a score of the old families. These are club-men in the fullest sense of the word.[1]

Thus, while New York clubs whose officers were elected for life united three generations from grandfathers to grandchildren in common activities, newly-rich Jews first had to become "clubbable" in the judgment of the Gentiles. Acceptance into the clubs had to be sought on an individual basis, and Jews had to submit evidence of a "clubbable disposition." Naively, proofs of "refinement" were imagined as satisfying such demands. A natural result of the pursuit of club membership was competition in the demonstration of refinement and fashionable habits.

At that time, America was a cultural province of England in the realm of club and high society life, and the concept of "clubbable disposition" was an English import having no social relevance. No one imagined that wealth could create an exclusive "society" which would debar the *nouveau riche*. Clubs were regarded as a gathering place of habitués of particular forms of leisure. In addition to the authentic club men there were also those who willingly submitted to the leadership of the club patricians to satisfy their social aspirations.

> There is another class of members who belong merely by way of reference in social circles, and who are members merely because a certain social standing is therewith associated. Club-men, however, in any just definition of the term they are not. Habitués of clubs they are certainly not.[2]

In their most sanguine moments, the Jewish newly-rich could aspire to acceptance only into this stratum of club society, yet this was the kind of social contact generally prohibited to Jews by Gentiles.

The importance of the prohibition is enhanced when one examines the Jewish merchant class for its club qualities. Having achieved opulence, leisure, and full participation in political activity and in all forms of cultural life and philanthropy, this class already had a native-born younger generation which streamed into the professions by way of higher education. Its exclusion from the clubs, while the corresponding Gentile class of businessmen was sure of acceptance, heightened the need of this younger generation for respectability. In 1873, of 50,000 estimated club members in New York, three quarters were married men, "bankers and heavy business men of extensive financial transactions and responsibilities."[3] We may be sure, then, that telling judgments on the Jewish businessman of that time were reached in the clubs.

1 Fairfield, Gerry Francis, *The Clubs of New York* (New York 1873), p. 11.
2 *Ibid.*
3 *Ibid.*, p. 7.

The almost complete exclusion of Jews from Gentile clubs can be easily demonstrated in New York through the end of the 19th century. Club literature is generally restricted to the representative clubs, which do not include the Jewish or even German clubs which accepted Jews. A directory of more than 20,000 club men of 1893 gives complete information on membership in 123 clubs, including political clubs, university alumni clubs, and medical and scientific organizations. The few Jews in the directory are mostly in associations of the latter sort. In the directory the name Cohen appears ten times, Cohn twice, Kohn six times, Levy nine times, and Levi three times.[4] The priestly names Cohen-Kohn-Cohn, common to both Sephardic and Ashkenazic Jewry, account for at least five per cent of the Jewish names in the more complete lists of the time, and already numbered in the thousands in New York in 1893. Of the numerous German-Jewish names at that time in New York, we find Oppenheim(er) and Seligman ten times, Bernheim(er) seven times, Rothschild five times, and Marx three times.[5] All these figures are only a small fraction of those bearing the name and occur only in the aforementioned professional organizations, not the authentic clubs. Political and scientific professional organizations were open to Jews; they were regarded by Gentile club men as civic bodies, not as abodes of social contact.

Unsuccessful attempts to storm the social club barriers, even in the case of Gentiles, left grievous pains. Strong feelings of resentment were aroused whenever people were passed over, as described in an article derisively entitled, "Make All a Stir." The author, *arbiter elegantiarum* of high society, Ward McAllister, was hated as the compiler-adviser of the list of the "400" members of society by those who were rejected:

> To seek membership in a club and be denied it, must be very discouraging, and such a rebuff casts a slur on a man which requires great force of character to overcome.[6]

In blackballing the Jew who made the hopeless attempt, no personal disparagement of the man or his character was intended; it was rather an indication of his ignorance of social mores. Only very few Jews whose names appear in the club rosters of that period succeded in breaking through the uniform barriers of native social clubs on the basis of exceptional personal standing and merit. Such men were greatly envied, but their membership in the clubs did not go unopposed. At least one club scandal of this type was exposed to the public by the effort to exclude further Jewish members. Even attempts by a Jewish father to pass club membership on to his son were frustrated. It was made clear that club nobility by birth could not be handed down by the Jew as it could in the case of the Gentile. The fear subsided that the Jew might penetrate into the patriciate of the generations that ruled the club. The fundamental principle, "two generations make the gentleman" in society was divested of its customary force when applied to the Jew.

Though certain Jews were granted membership as exceptions, candidates who

[4] *See Club men* [*sic!*] *of New York,* (New York, January 1893).

[5] *Ibid.*

[6] Miller, William van Rensselaer, *Select organizations in the United States,* (New York 1896), p. 9.

attempted to hide their Jewish origin were certain of being blackballed as soon as their birth became known.

> About two weeks ago, one of these gentlemen made application for admission into one of our . . . first class clubs. A Jewish member went to the election committee, and told them that the candidate in question was a Jew who denied the fact, and whom it was not desirable to admit. To the would-be-member's great chagrin, he was blackballed, thus teaching him that his measures for admittance into good society were, to say the least, not practical.[7]

In public discussion of such cases of blackballing, Jewish self-esteem and solidarity was first given expression. The objection was made that every futile attempt to achieve friendly relations with Gentiles through such unsuccessful candidacies damaged the image of the Jewish community. Such views were effectively upheld only sporadically. On the other hand, a storm of protests raised against the exclusion of Jews was intended to force clubs to be more tractable in admitting Jews. Such hopes were doomed to disappointment. One salutary outcome, was that it forced the clubs to justify their conduct publicly. However, respectable voices were also found for the official club view, as in the 1893 case of the Union League Club and the Selignam application, when *The Nation* commented:

> . . . It is surmised and it is probably true, that Mr. Seligman was so treated because he is a Jew, there being no other objection to him—that is to say, he has been sacrificed to a prejudice, which, in the main, keeps Jews and Christians socially apart in nearly every city in the country, which excludes Jews more or less from all the leading summer hotels, and would probably prevent Mr. Seligman's entrance into any other non-Jewish club in New York. In fact, there is no social phenomenon of the day more familiar to all New Yorkers, and particularly to the philosophers of journalism, than this prejudice. It may be as sad and reprehensible as you please, but it is as notorious as the sun at noonday, and is of long standing . . . A club is simply an extension of a private dwelling . . . This right to select his guests and associates for reasons best known to himself is one which every man carries to his club . . . It is said, of course, that the Union Leage Club has some sort of public functions, including the care of the Republican party, which makes it rather a political association than a social club. But it was a social club from the very beginning . . . The part of good taste and good manners is to avoid fighting one's way into clubs, private houses, or society of any description in which one's presence would be for any reason objectionable to any portion of the company.[8]

This was essentially a compilation of everything Gentiles thought about the clubbable disposition of Jews. It implicitly regarded the journalistic storm of protests as a disguised "social push" of the Jew into "society." A new principle was expressed for the first time in the case of the Union League Club, namely, that a club founded ostensibly for social purposes, (although it would later undertake political activities) was inaccessible to Jews. This conception of the "Jewish problem" in the clubs was the logical development of *The Nation's* position over the years. It affirmed the "restricted place," warned against "push," and offered advice:

7 "Our Philadelphia Letter." *American Hebrew* (New York) vol. vii (1881), p. 75.
8 "Club Candidates," *The Nation*, vol. lvi (1893), pp. 186–287.

> He is, in fact, a poor adviser of any race or class which is suffering from social obloquy who urges it to right itself by more social "push." Any energy there is to spare for the matter ought to be devoted to the cultivation of the arts on which social success depends, and the art of making one's way into circles where one is not wanted is not among the number.[9]

These words were especially directed against the Seebacher bill which attempted to abolish the restricted hotel in New York state:

> Its author . . . is attacking something which legislation has never cured and cannot cure, and may aggravate. It is not possible, as everybody knows, to open hotels to which people resort for anything more than bare food and shelter to any particular class or grade of persons by legislative enactment. No Jew who feels the present hostility of hotel-keepers would care to make his way into any hotel by the aid of the sheriff, or could enjoy himself after he got there.[10]

For the editor of *The Nation* two parallels were firmly established: the resort hotel, like the club, was an extension of the home, and a proposed law, like articles in the public press, was an attempt at pressure.

Jews in the Club Life of the Germans

Club life as the expression of newly created distinctions became ever more widespread in the 19th century. This practice of Anglo-Saxon circles soon spread to other ethnic groups, above all the Germans. Among them the club achieved its distinctive position much later, inasmuch as their traditional forms of cultural organization—the *Gesangsverein* and the *Turnverein*—already existed and to a marked extent filled the leisure time of the German. The peculiar quality of German inns, reproduced a thousandfold in America, provided an opportunity for private social contacts in a public setting and initially obviated the need for clubs. Nevertheless, the German club made its way everywhere, principally because the need for social distinctions developed with the economic rise of the group. The newer leisure possibilities were obvious to the affluent who desired clubs conducted in German. At the time, a clubable disposition was not generally attributed to the German in the Anglo-Saxon world; he remained "the Dutchman," though he was more successful in breaking club barriers than the Jew. "Society" did not consider the German clubs the equal of native American ones; in club literature, the former were dismissed as "smaller clubs" with occasional comment that social contact was not "the leading purpose of their organizations."[11]

The German club, which filled the demand of *gemütlichkeit,* had its own unique style. Unlike the Anglo-Saxon club with its core of habitués, the German club consisted of a homogeneous group of well-to-do immigrants of the "Grays" and the "Greens" (1830 and 1848) and of later pioneers who were recognized as senior members. This explains the participation of the Jews in the German club world, since the well-established Jewish merchant class and their German counterpart sought social distinction in clubs.

[9] *Ibid.,* vol. xlii (1881), p. 327.
[10] *Ibid.*
[11] Fairfield, *op. cit.,* p. 20.

Moreover, the times were favorable for the symbiosis of Jews and Germans in common clubs in America. Jews took their place in the cultural live of Germans in America by participating in cultural organizations such as the *Gesangsverein* and *Turnverein,* promoting the German theatre and German schools, and reading German newspapers.[12] For the Jew, the German clubs were also a solution to the dilemma created by their exclusion from Anglo-Saxon clubs. Thenceforth, in the cultural circle of the Germans there was also a club for the well-established German Jew. In large cities everywhere, German clubs were founded which accepted Jews and Jewish clubs were able to attract a number of Germans. In fact, some of these clubs were predominately Jewish. In large cities, where more than one German club existed, Jews could concentrate in it and thus this "German club" afforded them social life in an ersatz "society." For this reason a large number of Jews did not join the Jewish clubs in process of formation, while others preferred double membership in German and Jewish clubs and were at home in both. In time the organizations that were dismissed in the club literature as "German clubs" were accorded a more benevolent, ungrudging, and neighborly evaluation. The existence of these "German clubs" diminished the friction resulting from the native clubs barring Jews. Among the Jewish members of German clubs there was satisfaction that they—at least in this indirect way—belonged to "society" and were considered a clubbable element.

Under some circumstances the necessity of sharing a club world with Jews aroused resentment among Germans. Revolts against compulsory partnership with Jews had arisen earlier in German societies. In the case of the Arion *Gesangsverein* in New York, literary evidence of this is extant in the *Verein's* songbook.[13] But such revolts subsided; the Arion club assumed the leading role a decade later in the movement to create a Heine memorial in New York.

Membership lists of certain German clubs give the impression that the acceptance of Jews was avoided, but on the whole the German club in the 19th century remained open to the German Jew. The same standard for social distinction existed in the club for Germans and German Jews, and the social aspirations satisfied by club life were common to both.

Social distinction sought and found by Jews and Germans in America was based on a principle of selection of the highest importance on the new continent —pioneering. In the drive for social distinction, the position of the Anglo-Saxon pioneer was opposed to that of the German club of pioneers in which the German and the Jews were jointly grouped. Eventually, the pioneer was regarded as a figure of the past and accorded first honors. A new nobility, (societies of the local pioneers which excluded latecomers), was created in certain localities. The Anglo-Saxon pioneer barred the "Dutchman" from club membership by imposing requirements such as year of arrival and length of residence in the area. The Germans responded by establishing their own pioneer societies, and imposed temporal requirements for acceptance which made every early German arrival eligible for

[12] See Glanz, Rudolf, *Jews in Relation to the Cultural Milieu of the Germans in America up to the Eighteen Eighties,* (New York 1947).

[13] *Arions Gesangbuch,* (New York 1868), p. 5.

membership. These requirements also applied to the German-Jewish immigrant, who in the main had arrived at the same time as the German. Upon acceptance into the pioneer societies each newcomer was accorded the same social rank. In sharp contrast to Anglo-Saxon club conditions, wealth did not create position and was not a requirement for acceptance. In contradistinction to the gentleman of the club, the pioneer in his society did not boast of generations of ancestors and of the achievement of "refinement." The pioneer societies, a natural selection of the worthy, a "working nobility," were superseded when possession of money became the basic principle in creating "society." At any rate, a hereditary nobility could not be formed from the pioneer class. In the final analysis, money carried more weight than the victorious struggle with nature. The monied class established the continuity of social acceptance which human quality alone could not.

The historic form of German pioneer organization is well exemplified in Cincincinnati; its publication contains valuable material on frontier life.[14] That organization stimulated the founding of numerous pioneer *Vereine* elsewhere, and its members were to a large extent persons who played important roles in German-American life, among them a number of Jewish intellectuals. The following obituary is illustrative:

> M. E. Möhring . . . a German pioneer . . . formerly resident of Cincinnati and one of the founders of the German pioneer verein here. He was born in Danzig, Prussia, May 31, 1795. He immigrated in the year 1828, and in May 1829 came to Cincinnati, where he conducted a clothing business on lower Broadway. Möhring was an educated man. He had studied abroad theology and philology, which he could not utilize here. He was one of the founders of the local Israelite congregation K.K. B'nai Israel, of which he was president for many years. Möhring wrote numerous essays for newspapers.[15]

One had to be at least forty years old and a resident of Cincinnati for twenty-five years to qualify for membership.[16] From year to year more and more Jews became eligible as the continuous acceptance of new members witnessed. The first complete "list of names and members of the German Pioneer Verein in Cincinnati"[17] includes a large group of Jews. Knowledge of the birthplaces of these Jews published there, and in subsequent lists of new members, improves our understanding of the German-Jewish immigration. Still more important, obituaries in later years provide detailed biographies of Jewish merchants in America. In a considerable number of cases we find that members also played a role in Jewish communal life in Cincinnati. We also have reports of Jewish organizations which fostered German cultural values or German instruction. These include the "Literary and Dramatic Association" of Jews in Akron, Ohio, and the Jewish private school conducted by Joseph Goldschmidt in Baltimore.[18]

14 *Der deutsche Pionier* (founded in Cincinnati 1869).
15 *Ibid.,* vol. xii (1880–81), p. 78.
16 *Ibid.,* vol. i (1869), p. 160.
17 *Ibid.,* p. 385.
18 See the following articles in *Ibid*: "Dr. Isidor Kalisch," vol. x (1873), p. 117; "Moritz Bettmann," vol. vi (1874–75), p. 40; "Jakob Abraham Aub," vol. xii (1880–81), p. 35; "Die deutschen Pioniere im nordlichen Ohio," vol. vi (1874–75), p. 276; and "Das Deutschtum in Baltimore," vol. ii (1870), p. 205.

Part of what was felt, cultivated, or only thought to be common to Jews and Germans in the pioneer *Verein* was undoubtedly transmitted to club life, albeit in diminished force.

The Rise of the Jewish Club

Since the native Gentile clubs discriminated against the new, well-adjusted, and wealthy Jewish merchant class, the question of whether to found Jewish clubs soon came to the fore. Numerous Gentile clubs were established in New York in the 1830's[19] when the German-Jewish immigration was slight. If we assume that two decades intervened before later immigrants had become prosperous merchants, the existence of a lively Jewish club life in New York in the 1860's suggests how quick the response of the merchant class was to their exclusion from the Gentile clubs. The answer to the question of whether to found Jewish clubs depended on the degree to which their social aspirations were satisfied by entry into the German clubs. Despite the apparent open admission, in the face of a rush of new applicants the existing German clubs, like all clubs, restricted the number of their members. In addition, though many of the newcomers felt qualified to serve as club leaders, there was no opportunity for them in the old established German clubs.

Last but not least, intangible forces should be considered. The German clubs could not provide the ease and congeniality to be found in Jewish clubs. Moreover, in creating their own clubs, the settled Jewish merchant class was in effect brought closer to Gentile "society" by adopting its social mores. It is thus understandable why there was a springtide of formation of new Jewish clubs, a phenomenon observed not only in the larger cities but also in small localities. It was not expressly clear that it was the social mores of the Gentile world the Jewish clubs sought to adopt. This much was clear: the formation of Jewish clubs entailed no actual Jewish program in the community or specific Jewish educational tasks. The governing idea of the clubs was the creation of "society" through the formation of a closed circle of individuals who considered themselves peers and autonomously determined their club program.

Exclusiveness was the banner of the Jewish club. Even in smaller communities a certain element was not considered suitable for membership. In the larger cities the club was the gathering place for the most prosperous merchants who wished to enjoy privacy. Everywhere the maximum number of members was fixed by statute. In such large New York clubs as the Freundschaft with 800 members and the Harmonie Club with 650, membership was always full and there was a waiting list.[20] In the absence of club rules, we may consider the reported number of members as the maximum allowed by the club's constitution. Yet despite their exclusiveness, the clubs included a substantial number of the Jews in small communities. Jewish affluence at the time was so uniform that many persons of ap-

19 Fairfield, *op. cit.*, p. 10.

20 *The Freundschaft Society of the City of New York. Verein Freundschaft. Constitution and List of Members* (New York 1895), p. 10; *The Harmonie Club of the City of New York, Nineteen Hundred and Four* (New York 1904), p. 22.

proximately the same origin and having similar social aspirations were found in small communities, as the following quotation suggests:

> Another institution is our "Memphis Club." When an Israelite goes to a strange city, the first question he asks is "Which is your best club?" Be he rich or poor, ignorant or intelligent, he will go to no other. Should a stranger ask, then, which is the best club of Memphis, we answer, the Memphis club. It is supported by the wealth and culture and refinement of our Jewish population, and for years their quiet and social gatherings have been a source of unalloyed pleasure to its 100 members.
>
> Our population is variously estimated at about 65,000, two per cent being Israelites—they numbering about 1,200.[21]

Since the first Jewish club generation was unfamiliar with American sports emphasized in the native Gentile clubs, and did not undertake specifically Jewish activities, it fell back on the cultural milieu of its European origins. This meant German forms of sociability—on one hand, literary production, dramatics, and music, and on the other hand, carnivals, card-playing, or bowling. The club language was fixed:

> It is a well known fact that German is the language of these clubs, from the "Harmonie" with its sumptuous mansion on 42nd street, to the "Progress" in its less pretentious quarters on 23rd street.[22]

German was generally the official language of the club, although English was permitted.[23]

In cases where the program of a club is available to us for an extended period, as for the Freundschaft for 25 years, its exclusively German orientation is clear. No Jewish holiday is mentioned even in a purely social context; of the numerous amateur productions, no presentation of a Purim play is revealed; and there is no reference to the traditional *Simchas Torah* ball of the German Jews. The program imitated German forms of sociability exclusively, and those responsible for it prided themselves on their adherence to first principles:

> It was a bold undertaking; it was considered a piece of German idealism to offset the dollar-chasing American idealism.[24]

The club was set up as a replica of the German club. The "small council," or entertainment committee of the Freundschaft Society, was the same as that of the Arion club. It was described as follows:

> The "Kleine Rath" was essentially a German organization; its meetings, its entertainments and its spirit were all German.[25]

The club calendar was geared to carnival time and the highlights reflected German customs. "Foolishness," the "fool's cap," the "fool's prayer"—poetical effu-

21 "Our Memphis Letter," *Jewish Messenger,* vol. lvii (1885), no. 16, p. 5.

22 "Jewish Exclusivenes," *Ibid.,* vol. xx (1886), no. 1, p. 4.

23 "Statuten," *The Freundschaft Society of the City of New York. Souvenir of the Twenty-fifth Anniversary . . .* (New York 1904), p. 1.

24 "Der kleine Rath," *The Freundschaft Society,* p. 61.

25 *Ibid.,* p. 19.

sions of the German carnival time—were part of the inflexible club schedule. (Only in the financial crisis of 1894, usually cited as 1893, did the "Kleine Rath" choose "lustigen Dalless" as its motto.[26] This was realism rather than foolishness.) To the younger generation, the German carnival soon became foreign. With consternation the elders admitted that "all attempts to make the carnival palatable to the young people . . . could not save it."[27]

Several of the clubs expended particular effort on the production of German plays and achieved noteworthy results. Local dramatic critics hailed the produtions of the Allemania and the Phoenix club of Cincinnati. In these productions, unlike the club carnivals, the younger members played roles "for the amusement of the seniors."[28]

Nevertheless, the German cultural atmosphere in the clubs did not discourage the membership of many persons who, as we know from other sources, actively participated in Jewish communal life too.

Public Image of the Jewish Clubs

A building in prime condition creates the first impression of the financial standing of a club. Although clubs occasionally became insolvent, there was no such instance involving a Jewish club.[29] The two elements affecting the public image of a club—the architecture of its building and its financial status by reason of the wealth of its members—always went hand in hand, wherever the club was located. In New York,

> The Allemania, of which A. Wormser has for several terms been president, is probably the most powerful German club in the city . . . The Harmonie . . . under the presidency of Mr. M. Simonsfeld, Jr., is on the other hand, old, wealthy, and prosperous. The Club-house . . . one of the most elegantly appointed in the city.[30]

Similarly, in Cincinnati:

> *Allemania Club,* organized in 1849, occupies the beautiful freestone building erected for the club in 1879, on the northwest corner of Fourth Street and Central Avenue. The building and its elaborate furnishings cost nearly $100,000. In the third story is the Allemania-Hall, with capacity of 500. There is a library of 1500 volumes; and parlors, reading, billiard, card and chess rooms, besides a restaurant and bar. The club, comprising 200 Israelites, gives during the year many entertainments, to which none but members and a few invited by those taking part in the entertainment are admitted.[31]

Cincinnati had an even larger club:

> The Phoenix Club, the Largest and Most Fashionable of the Israelite Clubs
>
> It occupies a fine building on the north-east corner of Court Street and Central Avenue, to which the club removed when its former clubhouse on Walnut Street

26 *Ibid.*, pp. 62, 79.
27 *Ibid.*, p. 63.
28 "Reminiscences of the Theaters of Cincinnati," *Cincinnati Commercial* (Oct. 21, 1877).
29 Fairfield, *op. cit.*, p. 13.
30 *Ibid.*, p. 18.
31 *Picturesque Cincinnati,* (Cincinnati 1883), p. 7.

> was torn down to make room for the new government buildings now being erected. The present building was remodeled in 1874, at a cost of $60,000. It contains, besides a large hall for balls and parties, 12 social rooms, a restaurant, supper-room, billiard rooms, library and reading-room, the whole elegantly furnished. There are 240 members.[32]

The Phoenix Club still maintained its leadership many years later when it obtained a new clubhouse:

> The Phoenix is composed exclusively of Jewish citizens. Its club-house, occupying a fine site at Ninth and Race Street, is the most elaborate in the city. It has a large membership and is a wealthy institution. Its interior furnishings are in keeping with its exterior elegance. A large proportion of Cincinnati's most successful and influential citizens are Hebrews and all the wealthier are members of the Phoenix Club.[33]

The leading Jewish club in Chicago was similarly described:

> The Hebrews have recently completed a massive edifice for their Standard Club. It is built of granite, with an impressive, fortress-like exterior, but containing most luxurious apartments . . . worthy of an intelligent and wealthy membership.[34]

Detailed descriptions of club buildings were often given in the Jewish press such as the one of the Progress Club in New York in 1882, which had 275 members. (A complete list of the thirteen Jewish clubs in New York in 1896 is available.)[35]

The size of initiation fees and membership dues and the manner of admitting guests to club facilities were all indications of a club's financial standing. With the growth of a club and the acquisition of its own clubhouse, capital outlay increased substantially. Accordingly, later entrants were assessed for contributions to the capital investment fund. Initiation fees began to rise perceptibly as a club's net worth rapidly grew. Thus in 1879, in the recently founded Freundschaft club, fees amounted to only $5; in 1884, they had grown to $50, and in 1886, reached a peak of $100.[36] In the Progress Club in 1882, initiation fees were $50, while in the Allemania Club of Cincinnati they were only $25.[37] In general, club initiation fees in different cities were on a par and seldom below $50.

Regular membership dues were subject to corresponding increases, reflecting the more comfortable facilities as well as the greater esteem in which clubs were held. In the Freundschaft Club dues amounted to $16 in 1880, $50 in 1886, and $80 in 1888.[38] In the Progress Club they were $50 in 1882, and in the Allemania Club dues were only $36 in 1883.[39]

32 *Ibid.*, p. 155.

33 McIntyre, Edward F., "The Men's Club in Ohio. The Clubs of Cincinnati," *The Ohio Magazine* (1907), vol. ii., pp. 476–85.

34 Bryan, Charles Page, "The Clubs of Chicago," *The Cosmopolitan*, vol. vii (1889), pp. 211–25.

35 "The Progress Club," *Jewish Messenger* (1882), vol. li, no. 21, p. 2; *The New York Hebrew Select Directory and Visiting List . . . ,* (New York 1896–7), p. 218.

36 *The Freundschaft Society . . . . Souvenir,* p. 13, 22, 25.

37 "The Progress Club," *The Jewish Messenger* (1882), vol. li, no. 21, p. 2; *Picturesque Cincinnati,* p.7.

38 *The Freundschaft Society . . . . Souvenir,* p. 13, 25, 38.

39 "The Progress Club," *The Jewish Messenger* (1882), vol. li, no. 21, p. 2; *Picturesque Cincinnati,* p. 7.

In some clubs, non-residents introduced by members could participate in club activities upon the payment of certain fees, and in others they could enjoy the privileges by paying a monthly fee as long as they remained in the vicinity. In the Allemania Club in Cincinnati, for example, this was possible for $5 a month.

Different clubs in the same city charged different dues. In Cincinnati, for example, dues were $36 at the Allemania Club and $50 at the Phoenix Club.[40]

Club Decorum and Exclusiveness

The idea of extending domesticity beyond the home, a chief ambition of the club, was abhorrent to Jews nurtured in the traditions of Jewish family life. The first contacts of Jewish home and club generated friction. Jewish women reacted to the existence of clubs in the same fashion as Gentile women did:

> With nervous wives and mothers a club is synonymous with extravagance and temptation.[41]

The cultivation of clubs by young unmarried men upset the usual activities of Jewish mothers who had heretofore arranged for suitors to see their daughters at home. It was clear that young men formed a special class in the clubs, with, perhaps, less than praiseworthy motives for belonging:

> There is again a third class of young men who join the club for the mere sake of becoming habitués, and of having an elegant place to lounge and pick up the society gossip of the day.[42]

Since a "bachelor society" might comprise the inner circle of clubs, Jewish women feared the possible voluntary segregation of young unmarried men from decent feminine society.[43]

The reputation of the clubs was especially injured by the card-playing they tolerated:

> By the way, these clubs are called . . . social "and . . . literary," but they generally deteriorate into nothing else than gambling establishments and drinking saloons . . . Our young men need waking up . . . They dabble again in silly fashions, drink and gamble, swear and make bets, go to the club and the races, balls and parties, spend more money in clothing and jewelry for their own persons than their fathers would absorb in supporting a whole family.[44]

Counsels for improvement of the moral climate of the clubs were aimed at preventing the corruption and curtailing the extravagance of young men of limited means:

> More clubs, sectarian in their tendency, are to be provided with elegant apartments in New York, and the surplus money of young merchants, lawyers and clerks is to be diverted from benevolent enterprises to be expended on showy rooms and seductive card tables, including much money that cannot be styled

40 *Picturesque Cincinnati,* p. 7, 155.
41 Fairfield, *op. cit.,* p. 26.
42 *Ibid.,* p. 11.
43 *The Freundschaft Society . . . . Souvenir.,* p. 46.
44 "Clubs in Cincinnati," *Jewish Messenger,* vol. xxxiii (1873), no. 4, p. 4.

surplus, but is needed by its owners for business and domestic expenses. Some of these clubs ought to reform their ways, and not admit anybody as a member who cannot afford to enjoy that expensive honor. A gentleman of means needs occasional relaxation; and to meet his male friend in like circumstances, chat in cozy rooms, enjoy a little game, will do no harm to anyone and will make him enjoy in turn his domestic comforts; but for a man blessed with a good wife and children to abandon them repeatedly for the attractions of a club, cannot be excused upon any ground except incompatability of temper. Let our gentlemen be limited in his income, unable to join this or that charity because of the "hard times," stinging his wife in her allowance for domestic demands; and for him to belong to an expensive club is hardly less than criminal.[45]

In retort to all such reproofs, the constitutions of the clubs, as in the case of the Harmonie and the Freundschaft clubs in New York,[46] officially prohibited gambling on their premise. There was no regulation, however, of the amount of stakes in "legitimate" card playing or in other forms of wagering. Stakes and wagers had to be exorbitant to be regarded as an offense against club standards. In any case, when notices of commercial ruin and suicide appeared in the Jewish press, the clubs incurred censure.

With sufficient experience the clubs learned to avoid unpleasant incidents and public criticism by carefully screening prospective members. Exclusiveness was therefore in the self-interest of the club as well as that of its members. The Jewish club united worthy men on the same rung of the ladder of success.

To enforce exclusiveness safeguards were imposed to hinder the penetration of non-clubbable elements. A five-sixths majority of the ballots was required to confer membership, and a prescribed minimum of members had to be present and voting.[47] It was not sufficient merely for club society to consider itself an elite; it also had to be fully recognized as such by the outside world. This is especially evident in places with only one club. Embracing good society, it afforded all that one aspired to:

Bradford, Pa.

. . . The "Mercantile Social Club"—who does not know the "club?"—the membership embracing the leading lights and best livers of the "dramatic profession" who love to "eat, drink and be merry"—are giving a series of dances at "their would-be-willing-to-have-their-own-hall." They are attended by the "elite" of the city, and by the merriest set of ladies, one not to be found outside of Bradford. The officers of this fantastic club are: "Mr. Reis, President; C. Bartold, Vice President; G. Herz, Secretary; J. Schlesinger, Treasurer."[48]

But here, combining cause and effect, social criticism of the club is interpolated into the report:

. . . it is a shame to confess that for five consecutive Sabbaths no services were held in the synagogue. The minister was compelled, with reluctance, to leave the rostrum for want of attendance, save of a few school children.[49]

[45] *Ibid.*, vol. li (1882), no. 21, p. 1.

[46] *The Harmonie Club of . . . New York* . . p. 37; *The Freundschaft Society . . . Constitution* (New York 1895), p. 37.

[47] *The Freundschaft Society . . . Constitution* . . . 1895, p. 37.

[48] *American Israelite,* vol. xxix (1877), p. 245.

[49] *Ibid.*

Social Criticism of the Club

At the start, criticism of the clubs labored under the naive misapprehension that the exclusiveness of the Jewish clubs was somehow an indication that Jews preferred to be by themselves The advice was freely given that Jews could achieve social parity with Gentiles by opening Jewish clubs to them:

> We object, firstly, to that exclusiveness which prompts maintenance of distinctly Jewish clubs. We object to clubs, *in toto;* but of Jewish clubs, preserving that bitter exclusiveness as to membership and participation which was very well in the middle ages when the Israelites were wont to cleave together, because singly and disunited they were no match for the rapacity and ingenious persecution of their tyrannical masters, but . . . "in our enlightened age" [this] necessarily has the tendency sensible men deprecate. We want our neighbors to know and respect us as *men,* as well as in our capacity of merchants, lawyers, or physicians. We want them to note the purity, simplicity, intelligence, and happiness of our family circles; to observe how we preserve to this day the religion of our fathers, which we do not *intrude* upon them, but practice quietly, zealously and consistently. If clubs mean anything and are better than gambling houses, we should not restrict their social advantages to personages who happen to be born Jews.[50]

Nothing could be further removed from the real cause of the origin of Jewish clubs—that the Jew was not considered clubbable—than this unsophisticated interpretation. The conclusion that German Jews as a group were responsible for the exclusiveness of the Jewish clubs is even more misleading, since as Jews and "Dutchmen" in addition, they had the smallest chance of breaking through the barriers of the native Gentile clubs.

> We say it in all candor and kindness, it is our German co-religionists who do more than others to promote and perpetuate this clannishness . . . It is, again, very curious that those who are most prominent in manifesting their "liberality" in religious questions, who are most vigorously antagonistic to the retention of "old fashions" in our doctrinal practices, who are most conspicuously active in breaking down the barriers between the Jewish and dominant faith, are most vehement and determined in preserving this exclusiveness and social prescription, this intolerance that savors of mediaeval ignorance no less than it does of the ridiculous.[51]

Urging rapprochement did not end the social isolation of the Jewish clubs. The time was simply not ripe for this to occur.

At the time Jewish clubs were mistakenly criticized for their exclusiveness, there was sufficient experience with them to evaluate their role in Jewish social life. By that time clubs were regarded as having positive features, so the criticism was directed against the absurdity of Jewish segregation which negated positive values of club life:

> About Clubs
>
> The growth of clubs is a peculiar feature of recent Jewish history. Not that the club is essentially a new idea, but its adaptation to the wants of society, which prefers to be exclusively Jewish, is at once ingenious and unfortunate.

[50] "Jewish Exclusiveness," *Jewish Messenger,* vol. xx (1866), no. 1, p. 4.
[51] *Ibid.*

> The club serves many good purposes. It is not to be deprecated because of any abuses that have insensibly crept into practice. It is the source of great comfort, contributes vastly to the ease and convenience of members, furnishes a congenial atmosphere for strangers, to whom merely domestic life offers no attraction, and may contribute to the prosperity and progress of a class, or of a whole city.
>
> Not so with the club as understood in strictly Jewish circles. Now the *Harmonie,* the *Standard,* the *Progress,* and other clubs of the like character, disclaim the title of Jewish. They profess to deny the privileges of membership to nobody on account of his religious belief. The Judaism, indeed, countenanced and suggested by these clubs is liberal and harmless. The disciples of Confucius, the devotees of Buddah, would not be offended by any ungenerous strictness of creed or practice. But, in fact, membership is restricted to those of the Jewish race; and upon them lies the responsibility for the misconception of the club idea.[52]

The critic has admitted that the constitutions of the Jewish clubs permits the acceptance of Gentiles, but attributes the restriction of membership to Jews to a misconception of the club idea. Yet, he could not have shown a single case of the blackballing of a Gentile by a Jewish club, so his exposition bears no relation to the facts of club organization. The same critic's view of clubs is influenced by details of Jewish life as it appeared at the time. To begin with, as pleasant a substitute for family life as the club could be for strangers, home life was disturbed by the existence of clubs:

> These Clubs undertake to provide, on the cooperative principle, pleasant social entertainment during the season. Their hospitality is open and hearty to strangers who are fortunate enough to be introduced. But it is clear, that fathers and mothers who would, in deference to social customs . . . receive at home, adopt, the Club as a substitute; and thus, in the first place, the Club superseded family assemblies, which serve to maintain and to beautify the typical Jewish character. Whether it is found more economical or convenient to utilize the somewhat expensive Club receptions, there is no doubt that the season has become more quiet year after year, and because members of the clubs have accustomed themselves to confine their own and their daughters' appearances to the *salon* of the Standard, etc.[53]

Not much later, the social season appeared even more desolate. Efforts to renew old customs were regarded skeptically, though hopes for improvement still were present, as we learn from the following:

> The Coming Season
>
> . . . It is rumored that strenuous efforts will be made to promote visiting which seems to have almost wholly ceased, except among a rather numerous class of loquacious young gentlemen who are just beginning to wear high collars and coat tails. It is to be hoped that no desire will be felt to burn down the club-houses, and no violence used save the customary pouts and expostulations . . . In the lull in amateur theatricals, the best society of late seems to have organized classes for horse back riding and the study of foreign languages, to vary the monotony of the season. Some novelty is undoubtedly wanted this year: theatre

52 "About Clubs," *Ibid.,* vol. xxxiii (1873), no. 10, p. 1.
53 *Ibid.*

> parties, musical receptions, and literary *compots*, seem to have lost their attractiveness.[54]

In the club rooms, the younger generation, instead of getting to know one another to pave the way for marriage, were exposed to bad habits and idle talk. This we learn from a father who forbade his daughter to make further visits to the club:

> Club Receptions
>
> "You see no harm in dancing do you?" Dancing, my dear child, of course not. But the last time I went to the club reception I found dozens of young men, some with hats on, in the supper room, smoking over their last indigestible repast, and dozens of young women, sitting with flushed cheeks in the hot, close room, and listening to the customary twaddle which is repeated on such occasions at midnight.[55]

Thus some fathers found it necessary to shield their daughters from the conduct of young club habitués. It was asserted that older club members were interested solely in playing cards and that this was the prime activity in clubs. Compared to playing at the club, the domestic card table was the lesser evil.

> Another influence for which the club is responsible is the absorption of the older members in card-playing. Of course, every club has a reading room and some well-meaning members contrive to purchase bookcases, and to supply the beginning of a Library. But these are deserted while the card tables are full. That many would while away their evenings in card-playing at home is very likely; but they are weaned from home by the influence of the Club, and how do the nights pass for their wives and children?[56]

The upshot of the criticism was that Gentile clubs were viewed as offering programs of incomparably greater merit than those of the Jewish clubs:

> The Club, as understood in its more liberal signification, encourages art and literature, strives to elevate the taste of its members and the public, exerts a powerful influence for good on popular education, unconsciously leavens the masses and succeeds in directing opinion. In practice, the Century, the Union League, the Lotus, the Arcadian, and other Clubs, furnish at intervals receptions to distinguished visitors, musical entertainment of a high order, exhibitions of paintings, and otherwise contribute to the culture of the people.
>
> At the Jewish Clubs, they continue to dance and to play cards. Occasionally, there are dramatic performances of decided merit. That is the single redeeming point.[57]

To effect reform of the radical sort he deems necessary, the critic reverts to his nostrum of opening the Jewish clubs to Gentiles:

> It rests within these Clubs themselves to progress or to stand still. Their present record is not worthy of their aims, their pretensions, what may justly be expected of their members. Very many of the wealthy, the influential, the intelligent, among New York Israelites, belong to the Clubs. Are they capable of advancing no cause save the dance and the card table?

[54] "The Rambler," *Ibid.*, vol. lvi (1884), no. 17, p. 1.
[55] *Ibid.*
[56] "About Clubs," *Ibid.*, vol. xxxiii (1873), no. 10, p. 1.
[57] *Ibid.*

> It is a mistake, indeed, to maintain the exclusiveness of the Jewish Clubs: better throw wide open the doors to worthy persons, who do not play cards, and would like to vary the evening's amusement by something more novel and intellectual than dancing.
>
> And will it be credited that there are Clubs where card playing is unknown, and where to meet pleasant people and while away an hour in instructive conversation, is the substitution for the inevitable galop?[58]

To assume that the cultural level of Jewish clubs could be raised through the entry of Gentiles is clearly utopian. Moreover, the critic underestimates the cultural achievements of the preponderantly German-Jewish clubs. The published program of entertainment at the Freundschaft club for the first 25 years of its exisence contains a large number of artistic presentations, including the carnivals, which were masterpieces of direction. And, the printed catalogues of club libraries reveal that systematic collections of contemporary works in German, English, and French editions were undertaken.[59]

The Position of the Club in Jewish Communal Life

The club long remained a controversial phenomenon in Jewish communal life. It was acknowledged that the Jewish home was no longer as suitable for social meeting as it had been earlier, and that therefore the club could substitute for the home. Yet the club was not welcomed in communal life. Acceptance of the clubs would have been possible had they cultivated Jewish cultural values, which, in fact, they never even considered. With no specifically Jewish role, many viewed the clubs as somehow hampering Jewish communal life. In addition, there was the question of whether the clubs were a credit to the community. In small localities, for example, the Jewish club was considered by Gentiles as representing the Jewish community.

One form of protest against the lack of content of the clubs was the founding of literary associations of young people. Thus in San Francisco:

> We have a superabundance of so-called Jewish Social Clubs in this city, which are all in a flourishing condition, while there is but one Jewish Literary Society in our midst, which stands on a rather weak footing, owing to the slim encouragement it receives from those who are to be benefitted by it. And this state of things is not confined to San Francisco alone, it is a sad, but true picture of the mental stagnation which seems to have captivated the Jewish mind all over the United States.[60]

Such Jewish literary associations did not become a serious counterweight to the clubs. Here and there, as in St. Louis in 1878, a Jewish women's literary club, in which the club men were usually not involved, played a significant role.[61]

The growing role of the clubs as the sole arbiters of social style aroused the hostility of the more serious elements in the Jewish community. Isaac M. Wise

[58] *Ibid.*

[59] See *The Freundschaft Society . . . Souvenir.*

[60] *The Hebrew* (San Francisco 1878/79), vol. xvi, no. 2, p. 4.

[61] "A Women's Cultural Club," *Missouri Historical Society Bulletin,* vol. vi (1951), p. 109.

described clubs as "an institution for the self-preservation of synagogues, societies," but was contradicted:

> . . . Judaism has always been a religion embodying the highest moral teachings, and it is certainly preposterous to suppose that such a moral religion—if I may use the term—needs as an instrument for its self-preservation an institution which if not immoral, frequently borders on the verge of immorality, and always of necessity has a strong tendency in that direction.[62]

That wing in Jewish communal life which regarded the existence of clubs as a deviation from the historic organizational forms of the Jewish community demanded as a minimum the denial to the clubs of any influence upon synagogue life in America. It eloquently depicted the damage which the clubs could inflict upon the community's undertakings:

> Thus, again, the cause of charity suffers. No longer do we participate in stately or social balls or entertainments, whose delightful object was to aid the needy. So long as the Club circle was comparatively small, these annual festivals proved attractive and successful. With the multiplication of clubs, and their exacting calls upon members, there ensued a draft upon young men who understood the management of these affairs—and good-by to charity balls. Even the "Purim," which shed a lustre on the Jewish population, and astonished all by its brilliancy and respectability, ceased to be a success, when the rival Clubs determined to hold their own masquerades, and thus the good objects which the Association used to help were deprived of a portion of their revenue.[63]

In a period with relatively few problems, the clubs achieved prominence due in part to the role of the press which publicized their events in a Jewish society page. Money that was hard-earned by the first generation of Jewish merchants was more easily acquired by their sons, and the life of pleasure served as the goal of their existence. However, a new seriousness was manifested in Jewish life with the outbreak of pogroms that violenty uprooted the east European Jewish masses. To cope with the problems of the new immigration, older organizational forms had of necessity to be revamped. The social world, above all the clubs, resisted adjustment to the new urgencies. Leadership in Jewish life passed to those organizations which rose to the occasion by adopting deliberate measures to assist the new immigrants. The clubs continued to exist at the periphery of Jewish life but ceased to be a subject of public concern as more pressing issues engaged the attention of the American Jewish community.

62 "Clubs in Judaism," *American Hebrew,* vol. vii (1881), p. 4.
63 "About Clubs," *Jewish Messenger,* vol. xxxiii (1873), no. 10, p. 1.

THE "BAYER" AND THE "POLLACK" IN AMERICA

I

GROUP DIFFERENCES first became dynamic factors within the American Jewish community at about the same time when its members had to relate themselves to other ethnic immigrant groups. Jewish sub-groups were at all times differentiated according to the European countries of their origin. In the Colonial Period, however, when only single congregations existed in the historic communities along the Atlantic—because of the small number of Jews in the country—difference of origin was only a cultural characteristic. Such cultural traits were expressed in the variety of written languages employed (such as Yiddish among the Ashkenazic Jews) or in the various Sephardic and German-Jewish groups of family names, as seen in the first American Census of 1790.[1]

Although these groups were to remain distant from each other for a long time to come, sometimes strikingly so when it came to marriage, the congregations developed a modus vivendi based on the practical recognition of the dominance of the Sephardic *minhag* and rotation of offices, by which Jews, regardless of origin, could attain the highest honors in the synagogue. Parallelism in the sense of establishing institutions by persons of the same origin first arose when the Atlantic migration assumed a mass character. For the first time it brought into America large numbers of Jews from one country—Germany—in the wake of the general wave of German immigration. The need for institutional parallelism, arising out of the mass immigration, is explicitly referred to in the unique letter to the Spanish and Portuguese Congregation of New York which announced the formation of B'nai Jeshurun, the first Ashkenazic synagogue in that city, and which justified the separation by the increase in immigration.[2]

The Jewish mass immigrants in those days, at the beginning of the "old immigration," were the Bavarians or "Bayers." They played the same role in all the countries where the Atlantic migration reached, although nowhere else did they form so close-knit a group as in America—a group distinguished by its numbers, its external characteristics and self-awareness.

The departure overseas of Bavarian-Jewish youth, which began about 1820, introduced a new development in modern Jewish history. It was a transplantation

[1] *Cf.* Glanz, Rudolf, "Jews in the U.S. in the Colonial Epoch," in *The Jewish Review,* vol. iv (1946) 50. The following family groups presumably mainly of German Jews appear in the first U.S. Census in 1790: Aaron, 101 heads: Abraham, 233; Joseph (families listed), 24; Moses, 492; Solomon, 172; and Tobias, 123. *Cf. The First U.S. Census* (Washington 1907).
[2] *Cf.* Goldstein, Israel, *A Century of Judaism in New York* (New York 1930) p. 52.

Reprinted from *Jewish Social Studies,* Volume XVII, 1955

of a young generation of German Jews to a new soil while at the same time the life of the Jewish community in Bavaria continued as before. The new ideals of this young generation were not created by the immediately preceding European revolutions, as was the case in the waves of emigration of the earlier established "grays" of the 1830's and the "greens" of the '48'ers immigration. They were created by the lack of opportunity in the old homeland and the hope in the new American continent. It was only the surplus of population and youthful energy that was drawn off to America. The disproportion between potential and actually accomplished emigration always remained great. Bavarian Jewry numbered 56,158 souls in 1852 in contrast to 53,208 in 1818 when the mass emigration began.[3]

Despite the ever growing emigration, all the old conditions and problems of Bavarian Jewry, which continued to increase in numbers, remained unchanged. Because of the network of tiny communities scattered over the flat land of Bavaria, it was necessary to establish Jewish elementary schools, with the one and only congregational functionary acting as teacher and often also as *shohet* (ritual animal and fowl slaughterer) and *hazzan* (cantor or reader). The number of these schools increased until 1850. There were two different emphases in the education these schools provided. Trades were taught with an eye to the future emigration, and the study of "Jewish writing" was introduced in the public schools and in communal schools in order to enable the potential emigrant to communicate with his parents in Bavaria.[4] Very often the teachers followed their pupils across the sea.[5]

The exodus of Bavarian youth had an immediate effect on the other South German provinces, such as Württemberg and Baden, with which Bavarian Jewry was closely connected. In contrast, Jewish emigration from other parts of Germany failed to increase for some time. The Jews who emigrated in the wake of the Bavarians consciously identified themselves with the first, and were considered as Bavarians by the rest of the world. Such was not the case among the Jews who hailed from the Prussian parts of Poland. They were viewed as "Pollacks." Occasionally we hear of expressions of snobbishness at the cost of Bavarian Jews.[5a] But these failed to affect their standing.

II

The Bavarian, by origin the son of small communities, was considered in America to be the representative of the Jewish village of Europe. Later when he rose to a position of importance in America, it was the village which acquired prestige here as elsewhere. In contrast, the large Jewish communities of Europe were not accorded similar regard, as in this pioneer period they had sent very few of their sons to America. Somehow the growth of large cities in America out of small settlements was connected with the appearance of those men from the

[3] *Cf. Encyclopaedia Judaica,* vol. iii, p. 1182.

[4] *Cf. Allgemeine Zeitung des Judentums,* vol. iii (1846) p. 273-74.

[5] *Cf. Der israelitische Volkslehrer,* vol. ix (1859) 98; *Jeschurun,* vol. i (1854–55) 41.

[5a] To cite: "Does not the Frankfort or the Hamburg Israelite presume to look down on the Bavarian or Bayerische?" *Cf. Jewish Messenger,* vol. xxi (1867) 2.

most insignificant small towns on the map of Europe. America was built by the European village and not by the European city.

For a time the rise of numerous small communities in the newly opened Middle West made it appear that the center of gravity of the Jewish community in America might lie in a network similar to that of rural European Jewry.[6] Such expectations were linked in actuality with the Bavarian Jew, the son of small communities, who brought his wealth of experience with him to America.

Bavaria was thus the symbol of the large-scale Jewish departure for the New World from the Jewish villages of Central Europe. However, no such symbol was attainable for the "old immigration" from Eastern Europe. To be sure, the sum total of this immigration was not inconsiderable when we reflect that even before 1880 at least a third of American Jewry was of East European origin. However, the latter constituted an infinitesimal part of the total number of the Jews from that part of Europe. Thus East European Jewry in America was merely a conglomeration of individuals from the most diverse settlements. As a result, the specific country of origin of the East Europeans remained an undefined geographical concept for America. In city directories the place of origin listed next to the names of East European Jews is shown as Germany or Prussia, as well as Austria, Poland or Russia, or quite often even Europe.[7] A more intimate mental association with the exactly defined district of a province or a definite city never existed. The Jews themselves used the term *Hinter Berliner*[8] to characterize the whole emigration from this area, and the immigrant from the Polish provinces in Russia, Prussia or Austria was called, for short, the "Pollack." The "Russian Jew," as an immigrant, is not heard of until much later after the "Romanian Jew" had been in the foreground for a number of years.

III

Accordingly, the composition of these two groups in America, the Bavarian and the Pollack, was fundamentally different, and the nature of their internal unity and feeling of solidarity quite dissimilar. It was easy to perceive that the former was a family emigration from a homogeneous European Jewish environment, whose strength lay exclusively in small communities. This had already become clear to the European world at a time when mass emigration from Bavaria was periodically reported.[9] The family character of this emigration was underlined repeatedly by contemporaries:

> . . . le fils âine qui part le premier après avoir fini son apprentissage; il est muni de recommendations pour des parents ou amis établis en Amérique; peu après le reste de la famille vient le rejoindre.[10]

[6] *Cf. The Occident*, vol. xx (1862–63) 140.

[7] *Cf.*, for example, Morse, John F. I., *The Sacramento Directory for the Year 1853–54* (Sacramento 1853) p. 31, 51 and *The Western Shore Gazetteer and Commercial Directory for the State of California. Yolo County* (Woodlands, Yolo County 1870) p. 273, 309.

[8] *Cf.* item on San Francisco in *American Israelite*, vol. xxxii (1885) 5, where the expression *Hinterberlinship* is used.

[9] *Cf. Der Jude in Deutschlands Gegenwart*, vol. i (Hamburg 1846) 256.

[10] *Archives Israélites*, vol. xiv (1853) 598.

From emigration reports it is possible to learn the composition of the typical Bavarian-Jewish family and the more intimate circumstances of their lives. The Bayer who came from a village to the New World was usually a member of a very large family. Indeed, this was one of the main reasons that induced him to emigrate. Very often, as we know from the lives of successful Jewish merchants in America, he was a younger child—the eighth, ninth or even eleventh son.[11] Whatever real property there might have been in his father's house, in the young man's eyes, was already assigned to the other children. (Similarly, in the Middle Ages the great warriors were third sons, as the inheritance system generally included only the first-born—at most, the second-born.) When a younger son emigrated in his youth, it was an additional blessing for the family, since further dissipation of the paternal inheritance was thereby avoided. In any case, the young man was equipped with a trade, which he had learned with a thought to future emigration. The selected trade was practical for emigration, easily carried on in a small town or village environment, and was, moreover, expressly encouraged by Bavarian legislation. The recollection of this accomplishment, as if it were his apprenticeship, would fill the Bavarian with pride, even after he rose to a position of importance in America. The employer of more than 2,000 workers in four textile plants in San Francisco boasted in his statement before a government commission:

> I come from Bavaria and there every boy must learn a trade, no matter whether his father has five dollars or fifty million dollars.[12]

The Bavarian Jew looked upon the education he enjoyed as the factor that enabled him to become a self-made man.

In most cases, the Bavarian founded a new family in America before he could think of bringing over his parents, brothers and sisters. For this purpose brides were often taken along or sent for a little later. Sometimes the immigrant would fetch his bride when he had already put behind him his first economic adjustment. Later, the brothers who followed gathered around the original immigrant, who had become head of the family, as it were, by virtue of his experience. These brothers had been brought to America in accordance with a plan adapted to the family's circumstances. The American West, where the Bavarian was an economic pioneer, was built up by groups of two or more brothers, often together with more distant relatives who came over at the same time or not too long after. Nowhere is this so clear as in the personnel of the newly established Jewish firms of the period, which, as some form of family partnership, were represented by resident members in different places, often simultaneously on the Atlantic and Pacific coasts. Business directories of the most important mercantile centers of America reveal this family composition of firms time and again.

Since so many people in the small communities of Bavaria were related to one another and often, in addition, to families in the other South German provinces from which emigration also stemmed, it was not uncommon to find in the newly

[11] *Cf.* "Marcus Fechheimer," in *Der deutsche Pionier*, vol. xiii (1881–82) 501.

[12] *Cf.* statement of Max Norgenthau, in *Chinese Immigration. Report to the California State Senate* . . . (Sacramento 1878) p. 131-34.

created settlements of America several related families in a larger informal family society at the core of the local Jewish population. In many cases, such a comprehensive family society became the nucleus of the first Jewish community.

To give an accounting of the proportions assumed by the transplantation of the small Jewish communities of Bavaria and how the Bavarians from such places were reunited in the New World, one example will suffice. Isaias H. Hellman, who reached San Francisco, was born in Reckendorf, Bavaria, on October 30, 1843. At the time of his birth there were 30 Jewish families in that community. "At least six families, including the Walters, Haases, Greenbaums and Hellmans live in San Francisco." [13] This was in consequence of the emigration of their sons. The firms established by these families were among the largest of the recently founded merchandise emporiums on the Pacific coast. In this manner Reckendorf gained a new, more intimate meaning for the characterization of a group of the most successful individuals on the Pacific coast.

IV

The structure of the group of East European Jews in America summed up by the collective name of Pollack was entirely different, and for that reason its solidarity in the New World rested upon a completely different foundation. The conditions of the East European Jewish emigration were in general in direct contrast to those of the Bavarians. To be sure, the average European family of the Pollack was no smaller than its Bayer counterpart, but unlike the latter only an insignificant part of the former emigrated. On the whole a family produced only a single emigrant. As a result East European Jewry contributed only fragments of families to America despite the fact that the geographic area of its origin was so much larger than all of Bavaria.

A widespread belief that the maintenance of Jewish religious life would be impossible for the emigrant was a prime deterrent to emigration from Eastern Europe. Such a conviction was not widespread among the Bavarians in their homeland; rather, there are optimistic expressions of opinion that they would be successful in maintaining their religion in the New World.[14]

Despite all the restrictions and persecutions of the Jews in Eastern Europe, the absence of strong, direct pressure of governments to force them to emigrate was another factor explaining the difference in the rate of movement to the New World from Bavaria and Eastern Europe. In Russia, Poland and Austria anti-Jewish measures were not promulgated to encourage emigration. A picture of America as the land of the future for large masses of eastern Jews was inconceivable during the period of the "old immigration." The situation in Bavaria was quite different; each successive government regulation destroyed the hopes of those who would have liked to remain, and revealed the veiled intention of the ruling circles to accelerate the emigration of the Jews, even though at the same time administrative chicanery was employed against emigrants. To cite the *Bremer Zeitung:*

[13] *Emanu-El,* vol. ix (1899–1900) 9.
[14] *Allgemeine Zeitung des Judentums,* vol. iii (June 11, 1839) 282.

From Bavaria, July 21. Recently many Jews have emigrated to America again and numerous Jewish families are resigned to following their coreligionists there, as hopes for the mitigation of the legislation of 1813—due to the Frenchman Montgelas—which has been longed for these many years, are by no means being realized. In addition the expectations that were entertained of the new Diet were not fulfilled.

With the law on the books, which, among other provisions, has as a goal the decrease of the number of Jews in places where they have settled, it cannot really be displeasing to the Government when Jews leave the country in great numbers. Nevertheless, this is not the case, as very often obstacles are placed in their path before they obtain permission to emigrate.[15]

Under such conditions the Pollack who had emigrated to America remained here only a fragment of his family. In general, when he was successful in bringing over additional members of his family, it was on a much smaller scale than the Bayer. His progress in the New World was therefore much more difficult than that of the latter. For this reason alone he was hampered in founding a family and partially handicapped in his economic adjustment. The establishment of business firms in pioneer posts, based on the common labor of whole families, was for the most part impossible for him. Where the Pollack could take steps toward founding a community, there were usually no large family circles but rather equally lonely individuals experiencing a powerful nostalgia for the accustomed forms of religious communal life. At least at his start in America his loneliness was so overpowering that his average higher level of Jewish education, as compared to the Bavarian, could not give him adequate inner moral support. German travelers reported that East European Jews sometimes refrained from divulging their origin.

V

An essential difference in the adjustment of the two groups to the American milieu resulted from the economic effects of another circumstance. The Bayer came in the great wave of immigration of Germans from Germany—people among whom he had lived since time immemorial—while the Pollack had no non-Jewish fellow immigrants from his own country. The adjustment of the Bavarian to the new economic life of the American West substantially benefited from the presence of the Germans with whom he jointly undertook the crossing of the North American continent. Peddling in which 50 percent of all new Jewish immigrants were engaged for a time was made possible to a great extent by the fact that new, remote settlements of Germans supplied ready buyers of goods sold by the Bayers. Here the Pollack, because of his ignorance of the German language and customs, was at a definite disadvantage. As the German immigrants became progressively urbanized, the Bavarian Jews remained in their midst, no longer as peddlers but as resident merchants. At the same time the Pollack remained alone, depending entirely on his own efforts. At the beginning he lived in much greater poverty, and later, when economic success came to him too, in much more modest circumstances than the Bavarian.

[15] *Cf.* "Aus Baiern," *Der Jude in Deutschlands Gegenwart* (Hamburg 1846) p. 246. Count Maximilian von Montgelas (1759–1838), Minister of Finance of Bavaria, was the guiding spirit behind the promulgation of the Jew-Law of 1813, which forced the emigrations of younger sons by prohibiting their right to residence as family heads.

VI

The differences in the conditions of emigration operated even more sharply in the cultural sphere. Although he had grown up in the old homeland in the intimate milieu where the Jewish vernacular was used, the Bavarian had acquired the use of the German language for cultural purposes through his public education and his Gentile environment. Hence he could participate immediately in the activities of German, non-Jewish organizations of cultural or social stamp. This was the reason for the great part the Jews later played in German organizations in America. As Jewish emigration from all parts of Germany increased, the Bavarian and all other German-Jewish immigrants established a separate German-Jewish cultural life in literary clubs, choral societies, theatrical productions, etc.[16]

All these forms of social life were denied the Pollack. He was automatically excluded from the social activities of the Germans, and as a natural result the drive to have at least the synagogue for his own became that much stronger. His contemporary critics, who so often reproached him for his passion for congregational secession, understood this spiritual condition of the Polish Jew so little that they could not mete out justice to him in this matter.

The social unity of the Pollack, as a group opposed to the Bayer, derived from two factors. On the one hand, his greater poverty and lower economic status together with his non-participation in the cultural and social life of the Germans established his economic and cultural separateness. On the other hand, he spontaneously created separate religious organizations, often of a sort which scarcely existed among German Jews in America, such as the *Bet ha-midrash,* brought to the Pacific coast at an early period by East European Jews.[17]

VII

The different structure of the two groups, reflecting such fundamentally different religious and social outlooks, was bound from the very beginning to lead to strained relations at various points of contact between Bayer and Pollack. These later developed into genuine antagonisms. The process went so far that finally all conflicts among Jewish groups in America were viewed in terms of the Bayer versus the Pollack.

The spread of Jewish communal life across the continent was accomplished by this factional division. The conflict, moreover, became sharper as new communities arose further west and appeared in a sharp form in California, where after half a century of Jewish settlement it was as palpable as in the beginning, although it had lost much of its edge on the Atlantic coast. The great economic success of the Bavarian contributed to this situation, and invested the whole conflict with new features. In the stage of establishing the first congregation in a locality, the Bayer and the Pollack worked together, even in the large cities along the Atlantic, where both had cohorts of relatives. In Boston, for example, William Goldsmith, born in Oettingen, Bavaria, on June 10, 1810, together with

[16] Glanz, Rudolf, *Jews in Relation to the Cultural Milieu of the Germans in America up to the Eighteen Eighties* (New York 1947) p. 32-43.

[17] *Cf.* "San Francisco," in *Die Deborah,* vol. ii (1856–57) 279.

Jacob Norton, "a native of Poland," founded in 1843 the Congregation *Ohabei Schalom*.[18] However, not much later than this in the West, despite the diminutive sizes of the Jewish communities, parallel congregations of the two groups were common. In 1853 Pittsburgh had a total of 30 Jewish families of whom 14 belonged to the German, i.e., Bavarian, Congregation *Shaaray Shamayim*.[19] At the same time the "Polish" Congregation *Beth Israel* had 12 members. We are expressly informed that it possessed a synagogue with all the necessary paraphernalia and that its salaried congregational official was the *hazzan, shohet,* and *mohel* (circumciser).[20]

On the other hand, it was in the older Atlantic communities, in New York above all, that the early consolidation of all German Jews into larger congregations took place, and the role of the Bayer as founder of congregations receded. This unification was spurred by the antagonism between Germans and Sephardim. In the West, on the contrary, in St. Louis, for example, in 1853, out of an original united congregation, the majority of whom were Pollacks, a second congregation of Bavarians was formed and even a third of Bohemians.[21]

Characteristically, a resemblance between Bayer and Pollack in respect of religious laxity is reported time and again by early observers in the East. Thus Dr. M. Wiener writes in 1842:

> With regret I must confess that the European Israelite, especially the Pole and the Bavarian, becomes accustomed with remarkable speed to walking through the streets smoking, with his cigar in his mouth, on the first Sabbath which he greets in the land of freedom and equality.[22]

The implication of the commentator is most probably that the established Sephardic Jew would not commit such a breach of decorum. In detailed reports of the same period referring to the weakening of Jewish tradition in America, the statement quite generally is made: "This is especially seen among the Poles and Bavarians."[23]

Such observations predominated in the larger Atlantic communities, which were at the same time havens for immigrants. Further west it was not so much a matter of individual liberties with tradition as of a total reorientation. In the train of the movement westward one community after another sprang up, and Sephardic Jewry was no longer strong enough to put its stamp on them. The fresh energy of new immigrants alone could create communal life, and in the overwhelming majority of cases the Bavarian was the pioneer and creator. In this pioneer work the Polish Jew must also be taken into consideration. When it became a matter of taking a stand in communal life, Jews could support only one of the two factions. The Bayer was intensely anti-Pollack, while the sentiments of the latter, who was the weaker of the two, were less frequently expressed; but from time to time they became articulate in characteristic explosions.

[18] *Cf.* text in Schindler, Solomon, *Israelites in Boston* (Boston 1889) [p. 7-8].
[19] *Cf. Occident*, vol. x (1852–53) 317.
[20] *Op. cit.*, p. 414.
[21] *Op. cit.*, p. 56.
[22] *Allgemeine Zeitung des Judentums*, vol. v (1842) 296.
[23] *Ibid.*, vol. x (1846) 553.

VIII

Occasions for conflicts, as in the handling of questions of rite, were never lacking in a united congregation, not even in the period when proposals of Reform did not alarm the adherents of strict observance. A dispute could rage over the person of the *shohet,* be he Pollack or Bayer, and arguments over the order of prayers could be sharpened into decisive questions. Outside of the congregations where both groups still participated in the same charitable organizations, secessions could result if the needy Pole believed himself discriminated against. Such a case was reported in Louisville in 1860.[24] A similar situation occurred in the early communal history of San Francisco. Moses Minz, a Polish Jew, lost everything in a large fire there, and received no help from the Eureka Society, because, the opponents of the Bayers asserted, he was merely a Pollack.[25] Whether this was really the reason in this case, for the truth of which the traveler Benjamin vouches, or if the Bavarians so conducted themselves in general that their opponents could ascribe such bias to them, can not now be determined. However, because of such incidents the conflict between Bavarian and Pole was aggravated. The San Francisco incident had an ironic aspect. The founders of Eureka intended it to prove that the true gold mine was to be found not in the California earth but in the charitable human heart. A mine of an entirely different sort was struck and promptly exploded. We need not wonder that contemporaries, in an oversimplification, attributed the parallel communal organizations of the Bayer and the Pollack solely to mutual antipathy. Thus we read about the secession of a community in Portland, Oregon, in 1872:

> . . . This separation is principally due to the passionate hate which the Bavarian Jews and the Polish-Russian Jews—naturally of the lower classes—mutually cherish.[26]

The true causes of the establishment of parallel congregations by Bayers and Pollacks, common throughout America before the Civil War and especially the West, lay much deeper. It was not a matter of lower class self-expression. The need for separate communal life was a real factor at this time, felt by both groups, the Bayer as well as the Pollack. Secession from united congregations was engineered by the Bavarians no less than by the Poles, despite the fact that critics of the latter ascribe the tendency to separation to them alone. The emergence of Reform tendencies in congregations is not decisive in itself, as even large Polish congregations later went over to Reform and remained the domain of the Pollacks, *e.g. Shearith Israel* in San Francisco. Further, the view that this separation was dependent on the lower classes of the Polish Jews is incorrect. The important element of the so-called English Jews generally belonged to Polish congregations and was considered to be in the upper, i.e., more prosperous, class of every congregation.

The fundamental feeling that was decisive for the attitude of both groups was quite clear. The Bavarian, deep in his heart, preserved the ideal of his youth,

[24] *The Israelite,* vol. vi (1859–60) 315.
[25] *Cf.* Benjamin, I. J., *Drei Jahre in Amerika,* vol. i (Hannover 1862) p. 225.
[26] *Cf. Allgemeine Zeitung des Judentums,* vol. xxxvii (1872) 754.

namely, to bring the whole young generation to the land of freedom. Emigration from Bavaria was the central experience of the life of this generation. The transplanting of their communities to new soil stood clearly before their eyes as the task to which their conscience was committed. And the goal seemed within reach; in jest an emigrant once remarked that America could become Bavaria.[27] In this transplanting, his family, his circle of acquaintances and his community were all one to the Bavarian. In spirit he remained a true son of his Jewish village, and in the depths of his heart he firmly believed in its renewal on American soil. For this reason also he clung tenaciously to his name. These names with endings like *heim, stein, thal, au, wald,* and *bach* reminded the Bavarian of his old homeland and its true fellowship. He desired to bring honor to them in America. The smallest country towns on the map of Bavaria were so commemorated and the Ickelheimers, Einsteins, Frankenthalers, Hanauers and Ansbachers did not change their names.

In the eyes of the Bayer, the Pollack had nothing of the kind to show. Emigration was not the ideal of his generation and there were no signs of his old communities in America at this time. Transplanting them to a land of freedom was clearly not his worry. Therefore he was not accepted as an equal partner by the Bavarian in the building of new communities in the likeness of the old as his efforts were not considered equal. He was only a particle torn off from a far-off whole of which the Bavarian had no image.

In this respect the Bavarian did not fully understand the Polish Jew. Had he been able to do so, he would have conceded that the daring of the Pollack, all alone in the wide world, and as a pioneer in the West, was much greater than his own. Individual effort took the place of what was a jointly conceived decision to emigrate in the case of the Bavarian. If a Pole were not in a position to found a permanent congregation, he could joke about the often merely nostalgic character of his Jewish longings, as in the following:

Leavenworth City, Kansas.— . . . if the Polanders rent a 'shool' and make themselves useful, it is a day or two before 'Rosh Hashana and Jom Kippur,' and as soon as those two days are passed by, their religion is passed by too, and no one thinks of a shool any more until those two days approach again.[28]

Even in Europe Bavarian Orthodoxy lived in seclusion and had no ties with the seats of learning of East European Jewry and its important men. The emigration of individuals from the East did not take place in great numbers at this time and did not touch remote Bavaria, as the "*Hinter-Berliner*" would only pass through Berlin or go directly to German or other ports. The East European, as a human being, remained completely unknown to the Bavarian. Stories that the Bavarian and Polish Jews set out for America together are pure folk lore and not grounded in fact.

This estrangement of the Bavarian lasted as long as he was still Orthodox in the New World. The span of time coincides approximately with the period when his youthful ideal of transplanting the whole Bavarian province to America still

[27] *Ibid.*, vol. ix (1845) 346.
[28] *The Israelite,* vol. vi (1859–60) 250.

persisted. Later, when he recognized that it was impossible to fully carry out this ideal, he was already so far under the influence of the Reform movement that his Jewish communal ideals, above all the yearning for a preacher on the German pattern, again brought him into conflict with the Pole's conception of communal life. The Bavarian in this case merely substituted an all-German ideal for his old one; for the Pollack this substitution had even less meaning than the original. Moreover, the Bayer, who had finally gone over to the Reform movement, found values in his German-Jewish social life that were inaccessible to the Pollack.

The Pollack, therefore, remained in desperate need of Jewish content and he had no way out of the situation when he was confronted with the problem of joining a Bayer congregation. Since he was lacking everything both in the Jewish and the non-Jewish world—he did not have with him his family, his community, his religious authorities, and in addition he did not find the familiar world of the European Gentiles—he needed the *whole* synagogue for himself as the one place for his spiritual self-expression and could not share it with anyone else. Even when the Pollack was well adjusted economically, when, in the terminology of the time, he had achieved the status of an "English Jew," this fundamental feeling persisted together with the need for a separate community that it created.

Reform Judaism did not add anything basic, but it fostered important differences between the two groups. The Bavarian, especially in western communities, succumbed to Reform decades earlier, and at a time when additional immigration from Bavaria had become sparser, the Pollack received reinforcements from the broad territory of his predominant rite. The group of Polish Jews who reached America via England was important because of the additional strength it brought to the Polish congregations. It did not, however, shift the balance of forces in favor of the Pollacks over the Bayers in their communal struggle of almost half a century. On the other hand it did prolong the life of Polish Orthodoxy as opposed to the Bavarian, as the former succumbed to Reform Judaism much more slowly and on a smaller scale. For example, new Polish congregations were continually being formed in the West, while the remnants of Bavarian Orthodoxy vegetated near the Reform synagogues. In Cincinnati an old man was accorded the privilege of sitting next to his children with his head covered while the rest of the congregation was bare-headed. Characteristically these remnants —Bayer individuals who clung to Orthodoxy—rarely joined Orthodox Polish congregations, at least not on any noteworthy scale.

IX

From the broad point of view of the total development of Jewish communal activities in America, it was fortunate that on the new continent, unlike Europe, there was no one recognized communal organization in which membership was compulsory. Secession from existing congregations was always possible. Thus a safety valve existed. Conflicts within a congregation did not reach the bitterness of the disputes of permanent congregational factions—the order of the day in Europe.

At all events, wherever there were large settlements of Jews, a complete parallelism of Bavarian and Polish congregations had been established by 1860. The traveler, Benjamin, found this to be the case not only in the Middle West but also on the Pacific coast.[29] The Polish Jew segregated himself in his separate house of worship even when funds available for the synagogue were very meagre —at a time when the lack of a choir was already construed as an outward sign of poverty.

Later there came a time when a field of communal life remained to the Pollack from which he could not be displaced by the Bayer. In the long run the American need for communal functionaries could only be supplied by the recently arrived Pollack. To be sure the Bavarian had often begun his rise in America through the continuation of his European profession of communal servant; but via peddling he quickly became an established merchant. A sufficient number of individuals with the proper religious training to fill the growing American need for salaried communal functionaries could be found only among the newly arrived Polish immigrants. This field of activity, which in earlier days had been contested by Bavarians of the lower classes, had with the passage of time become a natural monopoly of the Polish arrivals.

X

There was a difference in the rate of economic betterment of the two groups. It enabled the Bavarian to attain leading positions in economic life much earlier and on a much broader scale than the Pollack who attained much more modest positions with greater difficulty. We see this first in business directories which give the origin of the individuals listed. There we find typical cases of the Bavarian listed as "clothing merchant" and the Pole as "tailor." Examination of the lists of wholesale businesses strikingly reveals how much space is taken up by typical Bavarian Jewish names, perpetuating the names of small market towns or cities.

The reasons for this difference are clear. The Bavarian emigration was simultaneously a social movement and a transplantation of family. Many of these Bavarian families brought with them modest capital. Help from relatives who had emigrated earlier gave the Bayer a first start, which was denied the Pollack. His larger family, consisting of energetic young people, enabled the Bavarian to embark upon larger, often ramified enterprises. In the economic sphere too the Polish Jew was dependent on his own efforts alone. Under such conditions the resentment of the Pollack matched the disdain of the Bayer for his economically inferior status.

When economic competition brought individuals of both groups into opposition, they were prejudiced against each other and often exchanged accusations of attempted ruination.[30] Tensions of this kind extended into a period when non-economic grounds for antipathy had lessened. As time passed the antagonism of both groups was transferred to a completely new area, that of social intercourse, social rank and new family alliances.

For the Bavarian this was an entirely new situation, the like of which he had

[29] *Cf.* Benjamin, *op. cit.*, vol. iii, p. 112-25.

[30] *Cf.* "San Francisco," in *American Israelite,* vol. xxviii (1881) 130.

never experienced in Europe. In Bavaria there had never emerged in any appreciable numbers a class of newly successful Jews, able to form their own social circle. In America the Bavarian himself became such a class. The Bavarian *nouveaux riches* laid the foundations for a new form of snobbery in American Jewish communal life in their social relations with the Polish Jews.

Proof of this development became more eloquent than ever at a time when the Poles achieved a higher social status, though much more modest than that of the Bavarians. Instances of snobbery occurred more frequently in the West, reaching their peak a half century after the group conflict had generally begun in America.

With the passage of time the social ladder grew higher and higher and a continually increasing number of new aspirants attempted to reach its uppermost rungs. His economic success enabled the Bavarian, who was the first to arrive here among the German immigrants and the largest in number, to attain the utmost heights of society life insofar as it existed among the Jews at the time. According to their wealth the Bavarians represented Jewish "high" society. Their net worth in dollars, expressed in big figures, aroused the pride of the Jews over their economic achievements. Their exclusiveness came about quite naturally:

> The truth of the matter is that the Bavarians are closed corporations, and in their councils . . . no Polack is admitted.[31]

This applied to high society life and especially to the formation of new family alliances through marriage. The remark was made in one instance in California that it was preferable under certain circumstances to marry a Chinaman rather than a Pollack.[32] For a long time the Bavarians contracted marriages only within their own group, and when marriages between the two groups finally did occur, they were attributed to purely material reasons.

> If a Polack has a daughter that is neither pretty nor classical, and has the money to go into the open market with her, he usually secures a German chasson . . . it is a purely mercantile transaction, entered into between two business men . . .[33]

The party who sought social betterment through such marriages was always the Pollack. Such occurrences aroused the indignation of marriageable daughters of less wealthy Poles. The reverse case, the marriage of a rich Pollack to a Bayer girl, irritated them no less.

Still later, at the time when the mass immigration of East European Jews brought a new poor class to California, the Bavarian was specifically criticized because he did not permit his children to associate with poor Pollack children:

> They don't mix their children with the "dirty Polakim" cause they h'aint got no money, no nice clothes and no nofing.[34]

[31] *Cf. ibid.*, vol. xxx (1883) 5.
[32] *Ibid.*, vol. xxviii (1881) 229.
[33] *Cf.* "San Francisco. Another Miscarriage," *ibid.*, vol. xxix (1882) 90.
[34] *Cf.* "Golden Gate Notes," in *Jewish Voice*, vol. viii (1890) 5.

XI

At this time when the crucial point of relations between the two groups lay in the purely social sphere, a transformation took place in the synagogue life of the Bavarian, insofar as he retained interest in community leadership. Additional new wealthy members were also sought from the ranks of the Polish Jews. The purpose of this approach to the Pollack was not to lessen social exclusiveness but to build up the congregation from the body of wealthy people, to whom all synagogue offices would be open without discrimination. Thus in San Francisco a whole group of Pollacks could be found in a Bavarian synagogue, and with the passage of time Poles served as the majority of salaried congregational functionaries.

> True is that the Bavarians are as wealthy as they are exclusive, and they would rather as a class get beat on a straight flush than lose a solid Polack for a customer but then their rabbi, their hazan, their vice-president, treasurer, secretary and several trustees, besides at least fifty of their members are all Polakim, both water and land Polacks, and while I am not a seat-holder in the temple, to their credit be it said that they would not refuse to take anybody into their council or congregation as long as he has the necessary ducats to entitle him to membership.[35]

The objection to the Bayer that he made his synagogues a domain of the wealthy only, where the money of the members was the sole consideration, harmonizes with general observations concerning him.

For a long time a few old-timers, holding out against the new trend, refused to appoint Poles as salaried functionaries of the congregation. Thus the following humorous account from the Emanu-El Congregation in San Francisco in 1899:

> Then some Bayrische members . . . said: "No Bollack shall ever be our Rebbe nit. God made a Bollack out of mud. A Bollack is the worstest man out of jail. . . ."[36]

Such voices, however, faded away in face of the great, new, common tasks of both groups, which produced a completely new type of communal leader at the turn of the century. In the Far West as elsewhere the Bavarian was preeminent among these leaders. The communal activities of personalities such as Abraham Anspacher, born in Weimar-Schmieden, Bavaria, in 1818, aroused such great admiration as could be accorded only to a man who stood over and above all factionalism.[37]

XII

The peculiarities of the Bavarian immigrant in language and folklore deserve special mention. They did not recur in the generation born in America and passed away in the old homeland. In contrast the Pollack transferred his Euro-

[35] *Cf.* "San Francisco," in *American Israelite,* vol. xxx (1883) 5. *Wasserpollack* was the popular appellation for persons hailing from regions on and near the coast, e.g., Poznania (Posen), Pomerania and Silesia. *Landpollack* referred to persons from the inland communities of Poland, including Russian Jews. These names were applied also to non-Jews.

[36] *Cf.* "Observations," in *Jewish Voice,* vol. xxvii (1899) 16.

[37] *Cf. Jewish Comment,* vol. vii (1898) 4.

pean culture with mass immigration at a time when the rivalry of the Bavarian had already lost its main importance.

The Bayer and the Pollack are often presented to us in their original idiom, in which the differences between the Bavarian-Jewish and Polish-Jewish vernaculars can be still recognized. The Bavarian belonged to the *Aa* dialect of this vernacular.[38] He pronounced the name of his antipode softly, "Bollack," no matter how harshly he might think of him.[39]

In general, it can be said that the old Bavarian, transplanted to the American West, was a true son of the people and retained this character for a long time. The remains of his Jewish vernacular, which are scattered throughout the American Jewish press in direct personal conversations and current idioms, are by no means inconsiderable. In connection with the old vernacular the strange and frequently recurring accounts should be mentioned, in which so many a Gentile tramp, who had learned this language while still in Germany, used this knowledge to levy a contribution on Jewish philanthropy in America by passing himself off as a Jew. Comical descriptions of how such impostors were unmasked are preserved for us. Among the questions, invented by officials of Jewish charitable organizations and put to the petitioner, was: "By what name are you called up to the Torah?" This usually left the tramp speechless. Simpler catch questions could be: "Are you a Cohen or a Levi?"—or simply, "At what age were you Bar Mitzvah?"[40]

In his writing, at least in his private letters, the Bavarian retained the Hebrew script and wrote home in the Jewish vernacular. At the same time in Bavaria as in the rest of Germany the instruction of "Jewish writing" was cultivated in the Jewish elementary schools and explicitly justified by the fact that the children, as future emigrants, would be able to correspond with their parents who remained in Europe only by the use of this writing. In the early Jewish schools in America this "Jewish writing" was also taught.[41]

The synagogue protocols of older Bayer congregations in America are written in the Jewish vernacular and Hebrew script.

In contrast, the vernacular of the East European Jews was preserved among the Pollacks for a much longer period. Its use in American Jewish periodicals is connected with the usual needs of the *kahal* and the traditional *shul* organization as well as the struggle of Orthodoxy against the "Reformers." Its mixture with English was viewed as unspeakably comic by the more assimilated Jews and ridiculed in the press. Thus a San Francisco correspondent reproduces a Yiddish sign-board on Chatham Street in New York with the following comment:

> This style of gibberish beats anything in the decalogue of harlequinades, and . . . would produce a grin on the face of the Sphinx.[42]

[38] *Cf.* Weinreich, Max, "Outlines of Western Yiddish" in *Yidishe Shprakh*, vol. xiii (1953) 42.

[39] *Cf.* "Observations," in *Jewish Voice*, vol. xxvii (1899) 16.

[40] *Cf. American Israelite*, vol. xxix (1882) 42.

[41] *Cf.* "Cleveland," in *Occident*, vol. vi (1849–50) 331. While the teaching of *Jüdischschreiben* in the schools meant the writing of Hochdeutsch in cursive Hebrew script, the letters were usually written in Yiddish in various degrees of Germanization. Teachers in the German-Jewish elementary schools often complained that the children spoke Yiddish.

[42] *Cf.* "San Francisco," in *American Israelite*, vol. xxix (1882) 90.

The older epistolary style of the Pollack is a reflection of the form dominant in Eastern Europe at the time and of the scholarship that in many cases had been brought over to America.

The insignificant origins of the antagonists was represented in a fable with a folklore setting. Bavarian and Pollack, already married to each other in their stage of European poverty, set out jointly on their emigration to America. The circumstances of the re-emigration—husband and wife as a beggar couple—make clear that the inventor of the fable was richly disillusioned by the real conflict of the two groups in American life:

. . . a fellow, with an imposing countenance, a smattering of the Talmud and an idea of how to *bensch* after the *Kugel* finds his way on a schnorring expedition—travelling all the way from Suwalk to Rockendorf to the house of a respectable Bavarian, where he is quartered (*a la* Plett) for the *Shabbas* and where he sings his "*Hashamar Shabbas, Habein im Habbas,*" in the most ancient and approved Polish manner, to the astonishment of the Rockendorffer, Bischoffsheimer and Pfaffenhofener oxenhandler and the Neuburger *Katzovim,* and where he throws sheep's eyes at calf's heads during the few moments of grace that are allotted to him, worms his Polish affections upon the innocent Bavarian maiden until the *Knass* is duly sealed. The parties find their way into this country after awhile, and, as the husband is a native-born *schnorrer,* he schools his wife in his ways, and she takes to it as naturally as does a duck to water. A Polish rabbi remains a mendicant all his life, and as he has more children and more misfortune than any other man under the sun, he is constantly soliciting and in most cases with great success.[43]

The attempt to create a myth of this kind was unsuccessful; any such myth would be exploded by the reality that the meeting of the two parties first took place in the New World, and that the tensions between them were concomitant phenomena of their adjustment in their new country. In earnest and in jest folklore continued to flourish about their conflict: "A Bollack and a Peier . . ."[44] often were opposed to each other as types in stories and constituted a criterion for literary characterization of individuals. A former occupation of the Bavarian in the old homeland is also recalled here: ". . . Bavarian by birth, and a cattle-dealer by education, although by profession a butcher."[45]

Such a biographic observation naturally contrasts with the great pride the Bavarian took in the trade he had learned, as was earlier shown to be the case. And folklore continued to accumulate at every given opportunity:

The Jewish Times is for sale—and the *Progress* says: "Wird er nicht kriegen a bayer (buyer) wird er kriegen a Bollack—Auch gut."[46]

In reality there was no talk here of the Bayer surrendering his position to the Pollack. The former retained his snobbishness on the Pacific coast for a long time to come, and the society page in the Anglo-Jewish press continued abundantly to reflect his "high society."[47]

[43] *Cf.* "San Francisco," *op. cit.*, vol. xxvii (1881–82) 413.
[44] *Cf.* "San Francisco," *op. cit.*, p. 277.
[45] *Cf.* "San Francisco," in *Jewish Voice,* vol. i (1888) 3.
[46] *Cf.* "San Francisco," *ibid.*, p. 3.
[47] At the Hecht-Mandelbaum wedding in San Francisco at one of the city's club-houses, "a chapel of foliage and flowers" erected received wide publicity. Poorer families were victimized by the increasing extravagance. *Cf. Jewish Messenger,* vol. lviii (1885) 5.

JEWS IN RELATION TO THE CULTURAL MILIEU OF THE GERMANS IN AMERICA UP TO THE EIGHTEEN EIGHTIES

1. *The Number of Germans in America*

Before approaching our subject, we have to form an idea of how large was the number of immigrants from Germany and of German-speaking people in the United States in various periods, because this determines the extent of that cultural milieu.

A considerable number of works enlighten us about the German immigration to America. Some of these works deal specially with the number of immigrants and American-born people belonging to the cultural milieu of the Germans.[1]

It is very conservatively estimated that at the end of the Colonial Period the Germans in America constituted one-tenth of the then population.[2] This means that if the first census, that of 1790, showed about three and a half million whites in the United States, it must be assumed that there were approximately 400,000 Germans among them. Considering the names of family heads in that census, this estimate would appear to be a conservative one.

Before the end of the period of the "Old Immigration," we have an estimate (for the year 1873) stemming from a survey of their situation which the Germans themselves made.[3] At that time the German-speaking population of the United States was put at five to six millions. This estimate was based upon the census of 1870, which showed that 1,690,533 inhabitants of the country were natives of Germany. If we add to this number the immigrants up to 1874 and take into consideration the German-speaking immigrants from Austria, Switzerland, Luxembourg, Alsace-Lorraine, and the Baltic provinces, we get a total of about two million German-speaking immigrants.[4] The same German-American source makes this further computation: "The ratio of the German-speaking persons to those born in Germany is rarely less than 2 to 1 in places where Germans live in sizable numbers, while in localities where the Germans constitute a large minority or even a majority the ratio is 3 tŏ 1." Taking into account the Pennsylvania Dutch, one thus arrives at the estimate of 5-6 million German-speaking people.

[1] Of the various works on this subject, we will cite here the following: Albert B. Faust, *The German Element in the United States . . .* , New York, 1927; F. Loeher, *Geschichte und Zustände der Deutschen in Amerika, Cincinnati, 1847;* Marcus Lee Hansen, *The Atlantic Migration . . .* , Cambridge, Mass., 1940; F. Kapp, Geschichte der deutschen Einwanderung in Amerika, New York, 1867.

[2] It is assumed that at the time of the signing of the Declaration of Independence there were 225,000 Germans in the country. Cf. *Dictionary of American History,* New York, 1940, II, 383.

[3] *Deutschamerikanisches Conversationslexikon,* New York, 1869-1874, IX, 286.

[4] This figure is evidently exaggerated, as a careful analysis of the number of immigrants from all the enumerated countries does not warrant the addition of 300,000 to the figure for 1870.

Reprinted from *Yivo Bleter,* Volume XXV, 1947

The extent of the German cultural milieu is also clearly indicated by the fact that among the 400 German periodicals of that period, there were 68 dailies.

2. *The Difficulties Encountered by the Germans in the Process of Americanization*

Among the various cultures which the tide of immigration brought into contact with the core stemming from the British Isles, the German cultural milieu occupies a unique position. The uniqueness was due to the breadth and depth of that cultural milieu and to the peculiar fate of the Germans on American soil. The Germans were not only a closed and exclusive group, but in a certain sense they were also in a difficult situation. The process of Americanization, the transition from Germans to German-Americans entailed heartaches, convulsions, soul-searchings. For many years before the two World Wars the German-Americans had to endure trying inner conflicts. He stood between two worlds, large millstones which slowly ground his unitary culture. His conscience told him at the same time that his "fatherland" was no less to blame than the New World, where he felt that he was not appreciated, although he considered himself in many respects superior to it.

The fact that he was not considered a pioneer was taken by the German as a serious rebuff; the fact that he was accounted a latecomer caused him mental pain[5] and, as a result, his attitude toward the new Americanism was antagonistic.

On the other side, no special love for the German could arise in America to do away with the obstacles to the development of German Americanism.[6] It must not be forgotten that in her seven-year-long War of Independence America had come into conflict with German mercenaries in the service of the British, and since then there remained a mixture of fear and bitterness toward the Germans. There is no better proof of this than the name of that midge, the Hessian fly, which it was assumed without any ground had been brought to

[5] The Germans in America did not come to primeval forests and wildernesses. Even in Ohio and Wisconsin they came after a trail had been blazed by pioneers of other nations. As Marcus L. Hansen, the historian of immigration, says in his book, *The Immigrant in American History*, Cambridge, 1940, p. 67: "The first white man to pioneer in any township was not a Schultz or a Meyer, a Jonson or an Olson. He was a Robinson, a McLead or a Boone. He was a descendant of that old Americanized stock which had learned frontiering in the difficult school that was in session from 1600 to 1800."

In America one must always divide the cultivation of new areas into two periods: pioneer farming and immigrant farming. Cf. Hansen, *ibid.*

The same author points up the fact that nowhere in America did a New Germany arise: "During the succeeding period of colonization when a New France, a New England, a New Netherland and a New Sweden appeared on the map there was no New Germany to delight the map makers of Nurnberg and Cologne" (Marcus L. Hensen, "German Schemes of Colonization before 1860," in *Smith College Studies in History*, IX, Nos. 1 & 2.

[6] See Appendix I.

America by German soldiers: it was destructive, it ravaged the fields, so the fly was given the name of the enemy. So, too, back in Germany, the devil was represented as a limping knight,as a mercenary. But aside from mere feeling, it should be borne in mind that America experienced a real invasion by soldiers: a large number of the German mercenaries remained in the country.

Of course, now, after several generations of spiritual conflicts, Germans in this country may find solace in the cultural contribution they have made to America, but this does not mitigate the pains of the past.

3. *Loyalty of the German Jews to German Culture*

The German Jewish immigrants, the traveling companions of the German stream of immigration, did not go through such a hard struggle between the Old World and the New. The German Jewish immigrant did not experience any inner, painful conflicts. He gladly embraced Americanism, he quickly perceived the beauties and opportunities of the New World, and at the same time he remained steadfast in his will to anchor in America the habits of life he had inherited in Germany. The Jew from Germany was more farsighted and optimistic here than the German himself.

Also, the Jew felt less hurt by public aversion to him, for that had long been his lot in the Old World. Hence he minded it less than did the German, who hovered, as it were, between heaven and earth, between a fatherland he had unluckily lost and unappreciation in a country where he had dreamt of finding a new fatherland.

Nor did the Jewish immigrant who came here from Germany experience any political disappointments. The German did not succeed in creating here a New Germany. The Jew never had any such aspirations; for the Jew, his German heritage was primarily a cultural, a spiritual one. The German Jewish immigrant wished to preserve here what he cherished of his old home and did not find in the new. And that was all!

The Jew's ambition was less far-reaching, but, as against this, he perceived quite clearly that the new America would have to acquire everything good that stemmed from Europe, including Germany. And because he was more perspicacious, the Jew from Germany could also be more unyielding than many Germans, who often, in the foreign, overwhelming environment, soon lost faith in their own worth, immersed themselves in their surroundings and no longer wanted people to perceive the German in them.

All too often the official bearers of German culture in America had to admit that, without the assistance of the German Jewish immigrants, their work would have been of no avail. The optimism of the German Jews in America in appraising the value of the German cultural assets in the new continent was a very important prop at a time when the skepticism of the German-Americanism was already manifest.

4. *Jews as the Companions of Germans*

Accordingly, it is worth while to try to delineate a complete picture of German-Jewish life against the broad background of the historic German-American community. Here meet all points which have meaning and color in the life of the German Jews and of the Germans. Even their economic entrenchment in the new country often runs parallel. Not infrequently there are also the same motives in emigrating on the part of Germans and of German Jews. Before the eyes of the Jew and of the German there hovered the same picture of America which both had obtained in the same language and from the same information in the "Fatherland." The school and trade knowledge which they took with them to the New World gave them the feeling that they would not be defeated by anything the American soil might oppose to them.

In their individual fates, too, the standard bearers of new ideas, Jews and Germans, often united, both during their emigration and their subsequent activity and achievement in the New World. In great things and in small we encounter Jews as the companions of the Germans. When we observe so important a political and cultural phenomenon as the creation of the widely ramified German-American press, we see at the same time the German Jews stream into it. We witness the same thing in the daily routine of societies and organizations. Everywhere the social intercourse between Germans and Jews plays a great part. The Jewish immigrant from Germany remained in the German organizational milieu because he wished to spend his life in the German-American cultural milieu. Regardless of the many obstacles, not the least of them the anti-Jewish prejudice brought along from the "Fatherland," the German Jews in America remained until recently an active element in the whole life of the German-American community.

In his old home the German had been accustomed to rebuffs either as individual or as a member of a particular class. According to modern notions, this might mean that "entire classes" were oppressed, something a German revolutionist of those days could understand. But no German could grasp, and this hit him with unexpected violence, that his whole German people could anywhere in the world be looked down upon by those whose worth he actually doubted. This led to an inner seclusion from the New World, where he began to feel like one ostracised, persecuted. At the same time no German realized that the same feeling had been entertained in Germany itself by a whole people — the Jews — some of whom emigrated together with him. Had he perceived this, the German might have found in such a historical analogy both solace and hope.

To this political nativism and looking down upon him as a newcomer, the German opposed his faith in German superiority. As good must ultimately triumph in the world, he believed that the world's salvation would come through German culture — a belief which is reminiscent of certain contemporary German ideas. In reality, however, the name German was associated in America with beer and sauerkraut (the latter has even become a nickname for a German). Not only was he not regarded as a pioneer, not only did people say, "Where the German comes in, the Yankee goes out,"[7] but they minimized his practical achievements. Thus, for example, they belittled the cultivation of the vine in Ohio, which the Germans had introduced. Previously they had created a scarecrow, namely, that all America was being Germanized. In the end, all that was left to the German was a fight for minor habits of living, which were more or less willingly conceded to him.

The German-Jewish immigrant did not experience this kind of hardship. In the days of the "old immigration" he did not at all feel persecuted in America. He also manifested greater understanding of the pragmatic in German cultural life; he was interested in German organizational life, but not in using German culture for political demonstrations. A "Hebrew vote" never materialized in this country, regardless of the predictions of pessimists or political agitators. Jews did not complain that people were turning their backs upon them, as was more than once the case with the Germans, who always nursed great political ambitions, something which is characteristic of a large and well organized minority.[8] The Germans combated nativism, the Know Nothings, thereby fighting in their own defense.

Herein, too, the course of the German-Jewish immigrant was different. In the political life of America he was first of all conscious of freedom and beheld

---

[7] This was a popular saying. See: Marcus L. Hansen, *The Immigrant in American History*, Cambridge, 1940, p. 62.

[8] The political line of the Germans at the end of the eighteenth and the beginning of the nineteenth century is not quite clear. But it becomes the clear-cut policy of an organized group in the first two decades of the new mass immigration (1830-1850). At that time the Germans were afraid of the nativist movement, which was hostile to all immigrants; accordingly, they voted for that party which had good chances of defeating the Know Nothings. In practice this virtually meant voting for the Democratic Party, which was completely independent of local issues. It was only along about 1848 that the political line of the German-American began to change. The revolutionary immigrants brought along their own ideas. It was realized that no party expressed the ideals of the Germans.

The turning point came in 1856. The nativist propaganda against immigrants no longer played an important part. The center of the stage was now held by the issue of slavery. Here ideological and economic considerations combined to militate against slavery, and the Germans supported Lincoln.

the practical realization of the idea of human equality such as he had not encountered in the old country. Unlike the German, the Jew did not as yet foresee any difficulty in preserving his own institutions.

In order to form a clearer idea of the part played by Jews in German-American cultural life, we must trace it to certain situations in Europe, especially to those connected with the emigration. To begin with, there were the same motives for emigrating. In the second place, they traveled together, they were fellow passengers aboard the same vessels ("ship brothers and sisters"), which in the eighteenth and early nineteenth century meant a great deal more than a hundred years later. From the passenger lists it appears that already in the eighteenth century Jews and Germans sailed together for America on the same ships. During the voyage ties were formed which grew stronger with time and led the Jews to the German cultural milieu.

5. *The Emigration of the Salzburgers and the Jews*

A special factor in the establishment of good relations between German and German-Jewish immigrants was the attitude of the Jews to the Salzburgers. In this the Jews would seem to have manifested a premonition of the great role emigration was destined to play in the life of the Jewish people.

The Archbishop of Salzburg expelled the Lutheran peasants from his diocese. They went to America in groups. The first group arrived in 1734 and settled in Georgia, founding the settlement of Ebenezer on the Savannah River. Before the Salzburgers reached the ports where they embarked for America, they traversed a great deal of German territory. They needed help. And here the German Jews distinguished themselves by their generosity and liberality. This was not an isolated case of a single Jewish community or group of individuals; all the Jews of Germany held out a helping hand to those persecuted for their faith.

The pastors who emigrated with their peasant flocks, observed this; they saw it in the light of the intolerance which the Catholic Germans displayed toward the Salzburgers, and they recorded it:

"So hated are the Salzburgers by the Roman Catholics that the latter deny them the hospitality which they practice toward Jews and other unbelievers. Thus Jews are permitted to pass through Bamberg, although it is known that they do not accept Christ as the Son of God and often blaspheme His Name."[9]

"The priest of Klein-Noerdlingen forbade his congregation to give these people a drink of water or to do them the least favor, as he considered them

[9] *Ausführliche Historie der Emigranten oder Vertriebenen Lutheraner aus dem Ertz-Bissthum Salzburg . . .* , Leipzig, 1732, II, 36.

heretics and dogs. They removed the buckets from the wells and refused to give them water even for money, although the weather was very warm. But the Jews proved to be more compassionate than the Christians. They led the emigrants to their wells and handed them vessels to draw water for themselves and their horses. They also presented them with bread, beer, and a little money, as far as their meager means would permit."[10]

The emigrants traveled through Germany in two large contingents, by different routes, so that their experience in various cities and with various population groups was duplicated. But everywhere the Jews manifest the same attitude. From Hildesheim it is reported:

"The Jews and also a few Roman Catholics were kind to them."[11]

And from the Electorate of Hanover:

"The Jews behaved toward them in such a way that the latter could not praise them enough. Those who live in the landgraviate of Hesse-Cassel collected more than 4,000 thaler for them. The most prominent among the Jews went to meet them when they passed through the country, handed over the money collected to them, and greeted them with these words: 'The situation in which we behold you reminds us of the exodus of our fathers from Egypt. We are full of admiration for the reasons which impelled you to leave your native land. We beg you to accept the money as a token of our sympathy for you in your present plight.' Some of the emigrants were so moved by this that they exclaimed in admiration: 'Is it possible that these people, whom we were taught to regard as enemies, put to shame by their actions the brethren in faith who, like us, believe in Jesus Christ, and yet persecute us and drive us out?' "[12]

The Jews of Frankfort on the Main gave 10 thaler.[13] In Coburg, where a group of 544 Salzburgers came, the following took place: "A Jew who lives not far from the city, sent two Rhinish florins to the town hall with this note: '*A small gift for the steadfast poor exiles.*' The same thing was done by the Jews of Wuerzburg and of Bamberg, who presented several florins and thaler through local citizens."[14]

In Berlin a collection was made in the synagogue. The Jewish women also did their share by collecting linen in the women's gallery of the synagogue. Previously, upon the entrance of the Salzburg group into the city, Jewish men

[10] *Ibid.*, III, 211.
[11] *Ibid.*, III, 226.
[12] *Ibid.*, IV, 79.
[13] *Ibid.*, III, 79.
[14] *Ibid.*, III, 144.

and women had distributed money among the emigrants. This is related in the history of the Salzburgers as follows:[15]

"The Jews, too, displayed their zeal on this occasion. Both men and women gave money to the emigrants as they were entering the city. On the following day they took up a collection of money in their synagogue which yielded 33 thaler and 8 groschen. Both their leaders brought it to the proper place and turned it over together with the following note:

'Whereas, in accordance with the wish of the Jewish community, a collection was taken up today at the synagogue for the Salzburg emigrants, even as we are commanded many times by God in the Torah or Old Testament to assist such strangers, and whereas the said collection amounted to 33 thaler and 8 groschen, we hereby turn over these moneys to the highborn Privy Council von Herolds for further delivery in the name of God. Berlin, May 1, 1732. Samuel and Benedictus Mayer.'

"The Jewish women collected 204¾ ells of linen to be used in making shirts for the old and needy. In forwarding it they enclosed the following lines: 'Whereas the Jewish women also took up a collection for the newly arrived Salzburg emigrants, basing their action on the divine precept, "He doth execute justice for the fatherless and widow, and loveth the stranger, in giving him food and raiment" (Deut. x. 18), the 204¾ ells of linen were collected by them and turned over to the proper place. Berlin, May 7, 1733. Benedict. Mayer.' "

When the Salzburgers, having resumed their journey, passed through Holland, the Dutch Jews gave a magnificent demonstration of their sympathy: "The Jews of Holland made a separate collection and presented 25,000 Dutch gulden, the equivalent of 12,500 of our thaler." [16]

The German papers of those days eagerly wrote about the aid given by the Jews to the Salzburgers. In the Jewish communities themselves this help became a link in the chain of tradition, and succeeding generations pointed to the assistance accorded the Salzburgers as a precedent in succoring outsiders.[17]

A similar tradition developed in the New World, after the Salzburgers had arrived in Georgia. The Jews and the Salzburgers were able to converse in the German language. They had also brought with them certain common habits from the Old World. This served as the basis for personal intercourse. The

---

[15] *Ibid.*, III, 64, 67.

[16] *Ibid.*, III, 27.

[17] "When the donors were asked why they were spending money on Christians, the women answered, 'God helps widows and orphans,' and the men added with an pious look, 'We are strangers like them.' " — Ludwig Geiger, *Geschichte der Juden in Berlin,* 1871, I, 44. Cf. H. Jolowicz, *Geschichte der Juden in Königsberg in Preussen,* Posen, 1867. p. 66.

chronicles of the Salzburgers in Georgia also contain curious bits of information about the Jews of that colony in the middle of the 18th century.[18] Where there were no distinctions in the legal status of Jews and Christians, good neighborly relations developed between the Jews and the Salzburgers.

The Salzburgers were glad that their Jewish neighbors enjoyed in the new country the same rights as they themselves. They praised the Jews for industry. They were impressed by the sight of the Jews in a free country, going through military drills like the British, standing guard with weapon in hand, and lacking only one thing, namely, the fulfillment of their blessing to them: "God grant them (*i.e.*, the Jews) the freedom of God's children in His beloved Son Jesus Christ. Amen." [19]

6. *The German Press of the Eighteenth Century and the Jews*

An important tie between Germans and Jews, in addition to all the contacts in the course of emigration and of getting established in this country, was the German press of Pennsylvania, which in the eighteenth century served the German Americans as the only connecting link with the world at large, and particularly with their old country. The German press had a monopoly on its readers, whom it could also serve old news, as they were willing to wait until it was offered to them in their mother tongue.

Here the German Jews figure not only as readers of the German press, but also as its patrons. They insert advertisements and make use of the newspaper offices for the transmission of mail and for other transactions. Particularly conspicuous are the advertisements in the German papers. Often the advertisements of the Jews are the biggest and the most frequently repeated. Characteristic in this respect is the advertisement which Haym Salomon in 1784 inserted several times in the *Philadelphische Correspondenz*.[20] In it he tells at length about his business as auctioneer and factor of a shipping and banking concern. He also stresses the confidence reposed in him by the Finance Office and the good name of his firm. He announces that in order to be of service to the public, he has opened a branch office in New York. While Haym Salomon inserted only short advertisements in the English and French papers, he spared no money on long ones in the German press.

The community of interests in the press was a reflection of the common interests in life. But the papers on their part enhanced the interest of their

---

[18] See Appendix II.
[19] Kommissarius von Reck, *Nachricht von Georgien*, hg. v. Samuel Urlsperger, p. 184.
[20] *Beylage zum 165. Stück der Philadelphische Correspondenz*, June 22, 1784. The full text of the advertisement is given in Appendix III.

readers in Jewish affairs. The yhad relatively frequent occasion to mention Jews in their reports, in their news columns. To begin with, in doing so they reckoned with their Jewish readers; in the second place, they apparently knew that the Germans were interested in their Jewish fellow immigrants, in their Jewish neighbors. Besides, owing to the fact of Jewish dispersion all over the world, news from any country might involve Jews. Then, too, reporting Jewish news afforded the German paper an opportunity to manifest its liberalism. The press busied itself with instructing its reader how to behave in life, teaching him to be a tolerant, liberal person. In doing so, it also had to give illustrations of how to behave toward Jews. Nor did it halt at printing a story about a Jew as an example to Germans. Accordingly we find in the German press moralistic tales about Jews, examples of Jewish strength of character, maxims illustrative of Jewish wisdom. However, as a paper is always concerned with news, most of the Jewish items were connected with some news report. By way of illustration, we reproduce here a few news items in which there are references to Jews.

BRUSSELS, March 5 . . . . All English Jews in France have been notified that they must leave France. This is a source of great joy to the French Jews, as there are a great many English Jews in France." [21]

Excerpt from the report of a severe earthquake in North Africa:

"Not a single house was left standing in Meniques, and it is estimated that 4,000 Moors and 8,000 Jews, who lived in a separate quarter of the city, were suddenly swallowed up by the earth." [22]

"It was earnestly desired and hoped that, after so severe an earthquake in Portugal, the Inquisition would come to an end in this kingdom; but the people failed to take into consideration that the clergy would not so easily surrender its power, especially as the Inquisition is so profitable. On the 20th of last month another auto-da-fe was held in which a man and his wife were burned alive because they had formerly been Jews and ostensibly become Christians, but had returned to their old faith, having seen nothing better among the Christians." [23]

During the military evacuation of Gibraltar, "Protestants, as well as Catholics and Jews," had to leave.[24] On the occasion of the capitulation of the St. Philips garrison, it is related: "And the English, Greeks, and Jews are to be granted 6 months in which to remove their merchandise and household goods." [25]

In reporting the capture of four British vessels by the American privateer

[21] *Pennsylvanische Berichte,* May 16, 1756.
[22] *Ibid.,* October 6, 1756.
[23] *Ibid.,* October 6, 1756.
[24] *Ibid.,* October 6, 1756.
[25] *Ibid.,* September 18, 1756.

"Rambler," it is related about two of them: "There were 30 English and several Jewish families on board who had left Gibraltar. These passengers said that since the start of the bombardment over 800 persons had died there." [26]

"The Prussian King bought 20,000 ducats' worth of grain in Poland through a Jew." [27]

In reporting about George II's naturalization edict of 1740, stress is put upon a point which is also of importance for the American situation: "Jews must swear allegiance, to be sure, but in doing so they shall not be required to use the phrase, "upon the true faith of a Christian.'" [28]

In reading the German-American press of those days we frequently come upon a comparison between Jews and Quakers. Thus we are told in a correspondence from Boston that Quakers keep their stores open on fast days, just like the Jews.[29]

Thus we find a constant interest in the Jew. The Jew in connection with the most varied places on earth.

This policy of the German press to give "Jewish" news continued also in the nineteenth century. For example, there is a lengthy news item about the Jews in Sydney, New South Wales: "A number of Jews now live in this city. About 30 of them have united, and twice a week they hold divine services and read from the Scriptures. Their only recognized teacher (Levite) is Joseph Markus. . . ." [30]

We have reserved for the last a curious item about an exodus to Palestine:

"WARSAW, Poland, Dec. 30. Many Russian, Polish, and especially Galician Jews sailed from Odessa for Palestine. Most of them are going there in order to be there at the imminent coming of the Messiah." [31]

It also happens now and then that Jews are the bearers of news: "A party of Jews arriving in Salonika from Constantinople brought word that there had been a new mutiny of Janissaries in the Turkish capital." [32]

And since the German papers are well versed in Jewish affairs, they know that many Jews are in the habit of going to the Leipzig Fair. So an editorial advises the London Missionary Society to take advantage of the Leipzig Fair

---

[26] *Gemeinnützige Philadelphische Correspondenz,* No. 29, November 14, 1781.
[27] *Pennsylvanische Berichte,* July 1, 1755.
[28] *Ibid.,* September 18, 1756.
[29] *Ibid.,* July 16, 1756.
[30] *Maryländische Teutsche Zeitung,* Baltimore, 1821, No. 7.
[31] *Ibid.,* 1821, No. 2.
[32] *Amerikanischer Correspondent für das In- und Ausland,* Philadelphia, 1825, p. 74.

to distribute missionary tracts, which the Jewish merchants will take back with them to the East along with their wares.[33]

In Germany itself people were interested in the life of the Germans in America. On the one hand ,the latter were their kinsmen; on the other, there was keen interest in emigration. Accordingly, among the various news reports about Germans in America, the German papers also carried a considerable number of items about Jews in the New World. By way of illustration, we quote the following report about the Jews of New York in 1827:

"The German and Polish Jews have built a new synagogue in New York and on June 1 dedicated it with the traditional ceremonies. After divine service, Mr. Henry Hendricks delivered an address in English in which he reviewed the history of the Jews, enumerated the sufferings of the nation, and praised the free, enlightened institutions of the United States." (*National Intelligencer*)[34]

7. *The Jew in the German Picture of America*

The German people's notions of America were derived from travel books. These played a great role in psychologically preparing the emigrant for the country he was going to. They often told about the freedom of all faiths in the new land; about the unhampered social intercourse between the different elements in the American population; about the positive results in building a new society free from religious hatred. All this could not but have a good effect upon the subsequent relations of Jews and Germans in America. The mere thought of emigrating, let alone the actual emigration (as we have already pointed out), inclined one to tolerance.

The books of travel were in part German translations or adaptations from other languages. But the German is best reflected in the travel books stemming from Germans themselves. And if we find in such works observations, episodes, or stories about Jews in America, they truly afford us a picture of how the Germans looked upon their Jewish fellow immigrants.

In one of the earliest travel books by a German who was in Pennsylvania from 1750 to 1754, conditions there are described as still being in so primitive and barbarous a stage that even religion did not prove to be an organizing force in the wilderness. The lot of the Christian preacher there is compared with that of the Jew. "The most exemplary preachers are often, especially in the country, derided and mocked to their faces, just like Jews, by young and old. I would rather be a shepherd in Europe than a pastor in Pennsylvania."[35]

[33] *Maryländische Teutsche Zeitung*, 1821, No. 8.
[34] *Columbus, Amerikanische Miscellen*, IV. Bd., 1827, pp. 59-60.
[35] *Gottlieb Mittelbergers Reise nach Pennsylvanien im Jahre 1750 und Rückreise nach Deutschland im Jahre 1754 . . .*, Frankfurt u. Leipzig, 1756, p. 51.

Nevertheless there were preachers with the spirit of pioneers who achieved a place for their denominations in the organized life of the American nation then in the making. Fifty years later, under wholly different conditions, the status of the various religions is thus described in the German version of *The United States Register* for the year 1794: "Jews and Catholics were barred from public office, and it is only now that they are free from this handicap, thanks to the new Constitution. And not only they, but all the inhabitants, regardless of their nationality or creed, enjoy absolute freedom of conscience and an opportunity to avail themselves of all the rights and privileges of citizenship." [36]

There also comes to expression the satisfaction felt at the collaboration of men of all creeds and races: "The Indian, the Negro, the Jew, the Christian sectary, by putting aside fierce partisanship, have transformed vast wildernesses into magnificent States. And now they live in tranquility, enjoying every comfort, and having the best prospects for the future." [37]

It also happens at times that the descriptions are interspersed with criticism of the imperfections and inconsistencies which the authors observed in the new society: "In a country of universal tolerance, it is strange that Jews are forced to keep their shops closed on Sunday." [38]

Naturally, the old habit of drawing distinctions and discriminating against the Jews crops up in some of the authors of these works. One observer of the life of Germans in America, who describes himself as a "merchant," begins to rail at the Jews when explaining the expression "to take benefit." [39] He sings the old hymn of hate: "The Jews enjoy an advantage in taking this oath, as they take the same oath as the Christians, which does not mean anything to them. It is no wonder, therefore, that the Jews here are all making money, and it is nothing unusual for a Jew to take his sixth benefit. America is a real paradise for the Jews. All kinds of auctions every day; counterfeit banknotes aplenty, no end of cheating and usury, and finally the benefit: what more beautiful heaven can a Jew conceive of, and what need has he then of his Promised Land?" [40]

The important thing for us now, and possibly also for the reader of those days, is not the appreciation and song of praise for equality, but the mirroring of actual conditions of life and the relations between Jews and non-Jews. The relations which made possible the entrance of Jews into the German-American

[36] *Nordamerikanischer Staatskalender* . . . von J.J.C. Timaeus, . . . Hamburg, 1796, p. 405.

[37] *Frankreich und die Freistaaten* . . . von E.A.W. Zimmermann, Berlin, 1795, II, 484.

[38] *Der Freistaat von NordAmerika in seinem neusten Zustand*, von D. von Bülow, Berlin, 1797, I, 210.

[39] This refers to the oath taken by a debtor in court that, on the basis of his declared assets, he is unable to pay his creditors in full.

[40] *Die Freistaaten von Nordamerika* . . . , von Gustav Loewig, Kaufmann in Philadelphia, Heidelberg. u. Leipzig, 1833, p. 113.

cultural milieu, the participation of Jews in German organizations, are in evidence as early as 1749, as witness the following entry in Pastor Handschuh's Daybook:

". . . On Oct. 5 I baptized the child of an Englishman at his home, in the presence of many English persons and five Jewesses, who behaved quite properly and appeared outwardly so devout that I would never have taken them for Jewish women if I had not been told so afterwards." [41]

The supposed connection between the Jews and the underworld is touched upon by Gottlieb Mittelberger in his account of America. He seems to believe that there is a kind of international of the underworld and a connection between kidnappers in Pennsylvania and forgers of seals and signatures in Holland. He writes: 'I myself have heard from such kidnappers in Pennsylvania that in Holland there are persons — and that Jews — who for a little money will reproduce every seal and perfectly forge every handwriting they are asked to. They can imitate every stroke and letter, every mark and flourish so well that the person whose handwriting they have imitated must himself admit that it is his handwriting. By means of such tricks they deceive even persons who are far from gullible and they are able to conceal their forgeries." [42]

8. *Economic Ties between Jews and Germans*

The common old home, the mutual ties there, the same reasons for emigration, the simultaneous voyage to the new home, the ability to converse with one another in German, the German feeling of being wronged in America — all this was conducive to good-neighborly relations between Jews and Germans on this continent. Both Germans and Jews, like all recent arrivals, were bound by many threads to the old home. This also resulted in an economic interrelationship.

The German press was closely interwoven with the business interests of the immigrants. Complete lists were printed of passengers who had arrived on incoming ships, people called at newspaper offices for letters which these passengers had brought over, and with the help of these offices money was sent to Germany with those returning to the old country. When a new paper is about to be launched, it promises to perform these functions well. In the prospectus of a new paper we read: "Under this heading there will be printed monthly the names of all newly arrived Germans in Philadelphia." [43]

---

[41] *Nachrichten von den vereinigten Deutschen Evangelisch-Lutherischen Gemeinden in North-Amerika, absonderlich in Pennsylvania . . . ,* von D. Johann Ludewig Schulze, Halle, 1787, I, 411.

[42] Gottlieb Mittelberger, *op. cit.*, p. 31.

[43] *Amerikanischer Correspondent für In- und Ausland,* Ankündigung und Probeblatt, September, 1824.

In all the notices in the papers relating to new arrivals and to the economic life generally we find an abundance of references to Jews and Jewish concerns. Here we find news about individual Jews, about money remittances through Jews, about the foreign connections of Jewish bankers, etc. In the *Maryländische Teutsche Zeitung* of 1821 there regularly appears a big advertisement by the Cohen banking house of Baltimore. Mention has already been made of the advertisements by Jews in the German press. It remains to be added that in the economic life of the eighteenth century, Jews were already deeply rooted in the German milieu of Pennsylvania and at the same time making use of their commercial ties with the Old World. This is attested by Pennsylvania German press of the eighteenth century.

Thus we read: 'Goods have arrived in the latest ships and are being sold all the time at low prices by Benjamin Nathan, who has a store at Heidelberg. . . ."[44] Or: "Moses Heymann on Second Street, Philadelphia, where the late Michael Ege used to live, has received the following wares by the very latest boats from London. . ."[45] It happens at times that the advertisement informs the public that the merchant concerned can also be of help in other respects because he knows both German and English. Thus we read: "Lyon Nathan on Penn Street, Reading (near Peter Haass), announces that he recently received the following goods. . . . He also translates German writings into English."[46]

About the mutual trust between Jews and Germans we learn from this advertisement:

"Moses Heyman, who has moved from the house where he previously lived and now lives where Wilhelm Klemm used to live, hereby informs the public that he recently received from London. . . . All those who owe him money for merchandise purchased at his store in Reading, Berks County, are hereby requested to settle their accounts at once through Mr. Martin Kaft in aforesaid Reading, who is authorized to collect the debts and to issue receipts for such payments. Those who fail to settle promptly are hereby warned that they will be forced to do so by the law of the land."[47]

Of still greater importance is the following advertisement of two Pennsylvania Jews who lived in the country and dealt in farm products and in game, and who stated explicitly that they were Jews, which apparently did not hurt their business at all:

"Jacob Levi and Barnet Jacob, who live together on the Muelbach Road, 5 miles past Conrad Weiser's inn and one mile from Saltzgeber, 2 miles from

[44] *Pennsylvanische Berichte,* August 31, 1759.
[45] *Ibid.,* September 14, 1759.
[46] *Pennsylvanische Berichte,* November 11, 1758.
[47] *Ibid.,* April 27, 1759.

Tolpenhacken in Lancaster County, announce that they sell all kinds of haberdashery and buy whatever is raised in the country: all kinds of furs of water and land animals, as well as the hides of neat cattle and calves, linen rags, butter, tallow, wax, hemp, flax, linseed, rye, wheat, maize, and all kinds of other fruit grown in this country. They further announce that they do not trade on Saturday and Sunday because they are Jews."[48]

9. *The German Soldiers and the Jews*

We have already mentioned the German soldiers who, ,as mercenaries of the British in the American Revolution, rendered the German name unpopular in America. About ten thousand of these soldiers remained in the country, and their role as the precursors of the German immigration has not yet been properly evaluated. It is important for us to learn about the relations between these soldiers and the Jews. We must also inquire whether any Jews came to this country together with these mercenaries.

Superficially, if one turns to the records, one may get the impression that Jews did not accompany these Germans. In the great collection known as the Bancroft Archives, which contains a wealth of material on the German soldiers (these archives are in the possession of the New York Public Library), no names of Jews are to be found. But this is understandable, as Jews naturally cannot appear on the crew lists: they were the sutlers, who did not get paid for coming over to America, and so their names cannot be on the aforesaid lists preserved in the Bancroft Archives. References to Jews, however, can be found in connection with the financial transactions between the princes who furnished the troops and England which hired them. Jews lived in all the territories from which the soldiers came, and it is but natural that they accompanied the mercenaries as sutlers. Some of them may have come over with the intention of remaining in America, and others remained here because they found it hard

[48] *Ibid.*, May 11, 1759.

[49] The Charleston Military Protocol was compiled when the Americans recaptured the city. From the *Minutes of Testimony,* dated February and March, 1783, we literally quote the following passages as reproduced in Barnett A. Elzas's *The Jews of South Carolina . . . ,* Philadelphia, 1905, p. 98:

"Henry Moses. Came in 18 months since from N. York, is a Prussian . . ."

"Samuel Levy. Came in 18 months agone. He is by birth a German, came from England to N. York a. from thence here. He has not taken an active part, did intent to go out 18 months agone but had no opportunity. Mr. Cohen says this man came as a suttler with a Hessian General and left him. Thinks him an honest man. Jacobs says same of Levy.

"Levy Solomon. A German, arrived about 2 years since in York and came from thence to this place. He has not not interfered, but has minded only his shop. Mr. Cohen says he came from Germany with a Hessian General, and left him wishing to stay in this country. Jacobs has known petitioner as a child, he is an honest man."

to go back or because they liked the new country. We find clear evidence of this in the Charleston Military Protocol [49] and in the biographical data:[50]

Besides, former Jewish subjects of the princes who supplied the mercenaries, already were in England and America and came in contact with the German soldiers during the expedition. In the "Copy of a Communication from General Staff Adjutant Cleve, dated Montreal, June 23, 1776," we read:

. . ."June 15. Yesterday afternoon I had occasion to come to Portsmouth. . . . It is hard to get along here without a knowledge of the English language, for there are few who can speak French or German. There were only one officer and one Jew who could speak German; the officer had been in Germany in connection with the preceding campaign, and the Jew hailed from Hesse-Cassel. So one has to resort to gestures." [51]

From the time of the occupation of New York by the Hessians there has come down to us an advertisement which may serve as an example of how a Jewish merchant can adapt himself to a given situation. The Jewish merchant announces that he is himself from Hesse-Cassel, that he has imported a great many wares from England and Germany, and that he also has articles for the equipment of the Hessian troops. The same merchant offers the soldiers song books of German origin. They are also offered the brands of tobacco to which they were accustomed in the old country. Apparently, the issue of the paper containing this advertisement was of importance to the soldiers, considering that it was included in the military archives.[52]

In the aforesaid Bancroft Archives we find a number of diaries of German officers. They are for the most part devoted to discussions of strategic and military matters. The language is extremely dry and the range of interests very limited. Reflections of the country they are in are evident only in certain minor sentimentalities, in hobbies of collectors who encounter the objects that hold an interest for them, or in certain observations on nature. There is a total

[50] See, for example, the data on Joseph Darmstadt in Norbert T. Ezekiel and Gaston Lichtenstein, *The History of the Jews of Richmond from 1769 to 1917*, Richmond, 1917, p. 26.

[51] Bancroft Archives, Brunswick Papers, IX, 127.

[52] The paper in question was *The New York Gazette*, Monday, September 21, 1778 (No. 1405), Bancroft Archives, Anspach Papers, II, No. 130. The advertisement ran substantially as follows:

"Alexander Zuntz, from Hesse-Cassel, has imported from London, in the Brig Cornelia, Capt. Smith, and from Germany, in the Britannia, and is now opening for Wholesale, on the lowest terms, in King-street, No. 11.

"From London: Millinery [27 lines listing articles]
"From London: Hardware [23 lines listing articles]
"From London: Hosiery [14 lines listing articles]
"From London: Plated Ware [15 lines listing articles]
"From Germany: Sword knots for Hessian regimentals, elegant canes with gilt heads, Campaign looking glasses of all kinds. . . . Together with German, English, and Virginia cut and Knaster *Tobacco*, and the newest *Music Books*."

absence of any approach to the people of this continent, and hardly more than a few words are to be found here and there about social relations in this country. The only exception is the diary of Conrad Doehla, which stands out by its greater sensibility and human warmth. It is therefore no accident that it is precisely in this diary that we come upon a few passages about Jews. There is even a comparison between the Jews in America and those in Germany. About the Jews of New York he speaks in two places:

"All sects . . . and Jews live in mutual trust and unity. . . . The Jews, however, cannot be told, like those in our country, by their beards and costume, but are dressed like the other citizens, shave regularly, and also eat pork, although their religion forbids it. Jews and Christians, moreover, do not hesitate to intermarry. The Jewish women have their hair dressed and wear French finery like the women of other faiths. Thy are very much enamored of and attached to Germans." [53]

Almost the same thing is stated in another place in Conrad Doehla's diary. There it is added that the Jews, like all the other denominations, have their places of worship in New York.[54]

Concerning Philadelphia we find only a single dry remark in the diary: "The Jews have a synagogue here, too." [55] As against this, however, he expatiates on Newport, and once more on the Jewish women (apparently it was they who stimulated his interest in Jewish affairs):

Newport . . . and the Jews also have a temple and synagogue; they enjoy all the rights of citizenship. But, unlike our Jews, they are not distinguishable by their beards and attire, being dressed like the other citizens, while their women wear the same French finery as the women of other faiths. It is said that the most beautiful women in America are to be found in New York and Rhode Island." [56]

It is a very human trait that, in speaking of Jewish women, he adds praise for the beauty of American women generally. But in the other diaries of German officers this trait is absent. Women, too, are viewed differently by different persons: in a letter to a lady, an officer boasts that, upon his return home, he will bring her a black woman slave.

The characteristically European notion that Jews are recognizable by their beards is to be found in another Hessian officer when he speaks of a certain

[53] "Amerikanische Feldzüge, 1777-1783, Tagebuch, von Johann Conrad Doehla, p. 51, in *Deutschamerikanische Geschichtsblätter,* XVII (1917), 14ff.

[54] *Deutschamerikanisches Magazin,* hg. v. H.A. Rattermann, Cincinnati, 1887; Doehla, *op. cit.* (entry made in 1777).

[55] Doehla, *op. cit., p.* 375.

[56] *Ibid.,* p. 384.

sect in Pennsylvania. "Here and there, especially in Pennsylvania, live many of the Swiss Brothers. They are good and honest people. They let their beards grow, and it seems as though one were living in a colony of Jews." [57]

The treaties between England and the German princes who supplied the mercenaries provided explicitly that "no person of this or any other nation shall be allowed to settle in America without permission from his sovereign." [58] But this proviso proved of no avail. Already during the war there were about 6,000 deserters who settled permanently in the country. And no matter how one tries to find an excuse for the soldiers in order to save their honor as military men, the princes clearly suffered a defeat in that their subjcts ran away at the first opportunity. Those who deserted the princes kept quiet. But even those who returned home virtually held their peace. The dejection which prevailed among them was not apt to give rise to real memoirists in the ranks of the soldiers. Thus an important chapter of German adventures in America was practically lost.

I found the only reference to Jews in an account by Johann David Schoepf, who in 1777 was head of a small detachment of Ansbach soldiers in the British army, but who, however, served in the war as a hospital doctor. He states there that the Quakers refuse to perform military service, "which even Jews in America do not decline." [59] Here we have again the comparison, so often encountered in those days, between Jews and Quakers.

10. *Germans and Jews in the Middle West*

In the storm of the French Revolution and of the ensuing Napoleonic wars, the episode of the Hessian campaign in America was drowned out. To the world at large America remained closed until the end of the great upheavals in Europe, but immigration from Germany continued to trickle in, and along with Germans the ships always brought Jews also. So it was until the eighteenth century gave way to the nineteenth, and so it continued thereafter. We read the names of the German and the Jewish immigrants in the passenger lists, and we even know their signatures.

The great tide of immigration from Europe, definitely marking the end of the Colonial period of immigration, had not yet set in. But even at that time the observer of the German immigrants perceived that a constant, enduring

[57] Tagebuch eines kurhessischen Offiziers vom 7. Oktober 1776 bis 7. Dzbr. 1780, p. 18 (Bancroft Archives).

[58] *Die drey vollständigen Subsidien-Tractaten, welche zwischen Sr. Gross-britannischen Majestät einer Seits / unddem . . . Landgrafen von Hessen-Cassel . . . Braunschweig und Lüneburg . . . Hanau . . . geschrieben sind,* Frankfurt, 1776, p. 11 (Art. XII).

[59] Johann David Schoepf, *Reise durch einige der mittleren und südlichen vereinigten nordamerikanischen Staaten,* Erlangen, 1788, p. 87.

force was driving them to these shores. In an account of a trip made in the years 1804-1806, there is this observation:

"Considering the stability and industry which so eminently characterize most of the German immigrants, I am inclined to believe that things must be very much out of order, in their native land, before men like them would come to the resolution of taking a final farewell of their next connexions and friends, with the peril and inconveniences of so long a voyage before them." [60]

These domestic disorders in Germany were real enough for the Jews and made themselves also felt in that every territory had its Jewish ordinance which made their life miserable and drove the Jewish youth to emigration. Incidentally, the role of the local authorities appears to have been a motive for the exodus. This is most clearly shown in the well-known cartoon on German emigration, wherein the local magistrate asks the assembled multitude of emigrants, "Is there no way to induce you to stay?" To which they reply, "If you go, we can stay."

The tide of immigration at the commencement of the 19th century moved toward the Middle West, and in this the Germans played a very prominent part. The Eastern seaboard already was largely occupied and the Germans were seeking new places. Before long, German settlements sprang up in the Middle West and, along with them, Jewish communities. In the middle of the 1860's there were about 150 communities of German Jews there (according to *Die Deborah*, X, 62.) The *Deutschamerikanisches Conversationslexicon* of 1874 shows that there were then 400 Jewish communities in the United States, and that in a majority of them the German language predominated.

The German immigrants transplanted their culture in this country, organized themselves here in the old-new ways, and revealed themselves by the manner in which they spent their leisure hours and by their hopes for the future. They endeavored to establish here an educational system with German as the language of instruction, and they strove to the end that the German soul might be preserved in the German body, and that a German society might develop and grow in the future. The generation of German immigrants set itself the task of preserving and developing further the transplanted values. This object found expression in the establishment of reading circles, dramatic clubs, choral and gymnastic societies. Leaders came forward who were to lay the groundwork for a political life that would make possible the attainment of the cultural goals they sought to reach. The great aim to preserve his own physiognomy manifested itself in the unwillingness of the German to give up those habits of his which conflicted with the old-established American ways.

[60] Robert Sutcliff, *Travels in Some Parts of North America, Philadelphia*, 1812, p. 266.

Mention has already been made of the German Sunday with its beer-drinking and picnics, which the other inhabitants regarded as a desecration of the Sabbath. Beer, the symbol of German conviviality, but at the same time involving a powerful new position in industry, also became a political issue and figured in the contests between the rival political parties.

The German-Jewish immigrants were in the very center of all these developments and played their part in helping the Germans to organize and to preserve their mode of living. In addition, the German Jews had a special problem: to plant on the new soil religious, educational, and benevolent institutions, all conducted in the German language. The problems of the Germans in their church organizations were easier because they were aided by the general organization of German life, whereas the Jews on the one hand took part in the social life of the Germans and, on the other hand, had to organize their religious and communal life separately.

11. *The German "Pioneers"*

By the middle of the nineteenth century the pioneer had already become the idol of all America. The pioneer was the national hero; the pioneer class took the place of an aristocracy, which does not exist in the country. To be descended of pioneers was a mark of social distinction, and to belong to an organization of pioneers or descendants of pioneers was, naturally, an honor, and also spelled an opportunity to attain a better position in life. When in 1856 a Pioneer Association was formed in Cincinnati, only those were eligible for membership "who had a residence in Ohio on or before the Fourth of July, 1812." [61] When we read the roster of the members of this association, the names sound like those of the census of 1790, with merely this difference that here there is no German-sounding name, not even one that is obviously a modified form of a German name. Afterwards the date was moved slightly forward — to 1815. This was of little help to the Germans, and, of course, no Jew could prove that he had come to Ohio no later than 1815.[62] It was a poor consolation when the organ of the Pioneer Association related: "1817. . . . The first Hebrew, Joseph Jonas, came to reside here. Wealth, worth, and wisdom distinguish them now."[63] The compliment would have done little good if that first Jew had tried to become a member of the Pioneer Association, for he was two years too late to be eligible.

---

[61] *The Cincinnati Pioneer,* ed. by John D. Caldwell, Cincinnati Pioneer Association, No. 1, September, 1873, p. 5.

[62] *Ibid.,* No. 2.

[63] *Ibid.,* No. 4, July, 1874, p. 12.

The Germans had reason to suspect that the year 1815 was set as the deadline in order not to have to admit many Germans into the Pioneer Association. When in December, 1833, the forty-fifth anniversary of the first settlement of Cincinnati was celebrated, there was only one person with a German name among those invited. The circle of the invited guests was so narrowly drawn that the committee in charge of the celebration had to defend itself afterwards against public criticism.[64] At subsequent celegrations, compromises were made and the list of guests extended. Incidentally, at the aforesaid celebration Nicholas Longworth touched upon a German topic: he said that the Germans had accomplished nothing by their attempts to cultivate the vine in Ohio, as it was not suited to the climate of that State.[65]

The Germans formed their own pioneer association, the Deutscher Pionierverein. Here anyone was eligible for membership who was 50 years old and a resident of Cincinnati or its vicinity for 25 years. Such a by-law was apt to favor a considerable number of Germans, but not a few Jews also knew how to prize the title "pioneer" and flocked to it.

Before we proceed further, it must be said in defense of the German, that his exclusion from pioneer organizations clashed with the whole conception of America which he had brought with him from the old country, where there had prevailed a romantic notion of America as a frontier-country where one battled with the untamed forces of nature and with the Indians. The societies of prospective German emigrants had sat over glasses of beer and dreamt of pioneering in America, and the dream had got into their blood. And when they came here, they found only cities and an urban life, and to cap it all, a German was not admitted into a pioneer association! Over here the German often heard himself called a non-pioneer, which particularly incensed him. No wonder, then, that the movement to form German pioneer societies spread all over the country.

Jews also played a role in these societies. Jews were admitted to membership, and enrollment in such an association was an important event in the life of a considerable number of German-Jewish immigrants. In the literature of the German pioneers of Cincinnati, Jews are often mentioned and Jewish life mirrored.

From the viewpoint of the country as a whole, the Jews still appeared such recent arrivals that they were not admitted into the high-ranking organizations of the native stock. But at the same time they could meet the requirements for admission to membership in the then newly formed German organizations.

---

[64] *Celebration of the Forty-fifth Anniversary of the First Settlement of Cincinnati and the Miamy Country, on the 26th day of December, 1833, by Natives of Ohio,* 1834, p. 50.

[65] *Ibid.,* p. 48.

This was of particular importance in the Middle West. A cross-section of the organizations in Madison, Wisconsin, in 1857 shows that there were Jews in the Concordia Lodge, German, or in the Madison Turnverein or Gymnastic Society, whereas no Jews were to be found in the English-speaking lodges.[66] Much more noticeable was the presence of Jews in those pioneer societies which so adjusted their by-laws that they were favorable to Jews. The roster of the Jewish pioneers in Cincinnati shows that all Jews who had attained to wealth or a high station in life wished to crown their success with their recognition as pioneers. As usual, the intellectuals, whether Jews or Germans, occupied a special position.

The leaders of the pioneer societies were educated and eminently practical Germans, often former revolutionists and lifelong liberals by conviction. They sincerely sought to adopt a conscientious attitude toward Jewish affairs, although their anti-Jewish sentiments forced them into a dubious position. They were ready to admit Jewish intellectuals, who had mostly been revolutionists in Germany and who might be of service to the pioneer organizations. But for the most part they had to deal with Jewish pioneers who by dint of hard work had prospered in their vocations but who possessed little education. Toward such Jews they were stiffly formal; one praised them formally, but there was no inner warmth behind the words, as the background and milieu of these fellow pioneers were wholly foreign to one. Why were such Jews admitted at all? These practical Germans perceived that it was precisely this type of Jews who would be useful to their organizations. And they also had in mind the financial contributions of the Jews who had prospered. But the entire group of such members remained foreign to the German leaders. One paid tribute to the cosmopolitan spirit of the age by speaking of the Jews in general, humanitarian phrases, phrases which did not obligate one to anything; but not a single earnest word was said about the plight of the Jews in Germany, which, if uttered emphatically might have been heard overseas also and possibly have done some good.

If the sentiments of the leadership were ambiguous, those of the led masses manifested themselves in undisguised hatred. The pioneer associations were free of organizational anti-Semitism, but in a mass organization like a choral society the anti-Jewish feelings were able to break through and even assume the character of a racist by-law, as is proven by the case of the Arion Society (see below). When dealing with German organizations we must never forget the ingrained anti-Semitism of the German.

[66] *Madison, the Capital of Wisconsin; . . .* compiled by Lyman C. Draper, Madison, 1857, p. 41.

12. *The Ideology of Concord Between Jews and Germans*

Those seeking an ideology for Germanism in America also created the idea of a "higher Judaism" as a kind of companion to Germanism. The Germans with their numerous sects in America were to give the whole world an example of a higher culture, and in this scheme the Jews were included. Nay, more, the Germans in America were to spur this "higher Judaism" to further progress. The quintessence of these ideas is contained in an address which Carl Ruemelin delivered on January 3, 1871, before the German Pioneer Society of Cincinnati:

". . . Germany is an adopting mother and she has adopted children. Among these are the Jews (no mean patrons of German culture) in the homeland and as emigrated sons; she has, furthermore, the Swiss, the Alsatians, the Schleswig-Holsteiners, who love everything German despite their political alienation. . . . In this country, too, there are many such numb remnants of antiquated German culture . . . religious organizations. . . . They derive the idea of their Germanism from the Old Testament by replacing the Promised Land and the Hebrew language with Germany and her tongue. . . . And what the higher Judaism has become for humanity, may Germanism, as moulded by the last century, but in a still more blessed sense, become for the coming generations of man!"[67]

In such a system of thought, the fact of the separate existence of the Jewish group precisely in America acquires a special significance for the philosophizing German when thinking of the preservation of his own existence. Thus we find such a typical statement as this: "The wandering Hebrews bring this question before us in sharpest outline. We ask whether it was wise and right for them to carry their old culture with them everywhere. The rabble answers everywhere, No. The better thinkers say unanimously, Yes. And America as a country takes the affirmative side in respect of such aspirations."[68]

Those were the days when they were not yet talking of "Nathan the Sly" but of *Nathan the Wise,* and Lessing's drama was regarded as a model literary work because in it "kindness of heart, wisdom and tolerance are clearly embodied."[69] Contrary views encountered in the political movements of the country were to be judged only according to the example of the wicked city of Sodom given in the Bible: The nativists of Sodom. Nativism, *i.e.,* hatred for the foreigner, is very old; already the Sodomites were permeated with its spirit and sought to vent their rage on the pious Lot."[70]

[67] *Der deutsche Pionier,* 1871, p. 342.
[68] *Ibid.,* 1872, p. 191.
[69] *Ibid.,* IX (1877/78), 143.
[70] *Ibid.,* VIII, 72.

At that time good relations between devotees of different creeds were highly praised; it was regarded as a model of tolerance when persons of different faiths took part in the same religious ceremonies, as this was a sign of good will and neighborliness: "It is necessary to report another interesting episode, which bears witness to the general harmony and tolerance in religion and politics brought about by the Pioneer Society. One of the older pioneers who has attained the fairly advanced age of 65 years (unfortunately, we did not learn his name) had the youngest of his descendants baptized in one of the private rooms of Bellevue House. And the baptismal ceremony was performed by a pioneer clergyman, Pastor Abele of Marietta. On this occasion the Old and the New Testament met, as is evident from the fact that an Israelite, Leopold Goldschmidt, served as godfather."[71]

The public was likewise told when ministers of religion exchanged pulpits, for example, "a sermon by a Protestant pastor at an Israelitish temple."[72]

So far we have been dealing with Jews as members of German organizations. But an important part was also played by the comparison between Jewish and German organizations, a comparison which was made in both circles. The Jews had a model before them, and the Germans, too, found something to learn from the Jews. Jewish generosity and ability to build and maintain large welfare institutions were held up as an example to the Germans. No less a German leader than Carl Schurz speaks thus to the conscience of the approximately 350,000 Germans then living in New York:

"But first of all consider for a moment the welfare institutions which our *Jewish* fellow citizens have founded and are maintaining in our midst. Here you find an orphan asylum which cost $600,000 to build and requires $70,000 a year to maintain. Here is the Mount Sinai Hospital with its annual budget of $60,000. Next come the United Hebrew Charities, with $59,000; the Home for the Aged and Infirm, with $23,000; the Montefiore Home, with approximately $12,000; the Hebrew Free School, with $26,000; the Hebrew Technical Institute, with $10,000; the Hebrew Sheltering Guardians, with $36,000; the Ladies' Deborah Nursery, with about $14,000, and several other institutions, with an aggregate budget of $25,000 more. I am told that the Jewish population of New York is about 100,000, a figure which seems to me an overstatement rather than an understatement. The majority of them are undoubtedly classed as Germans. At all events, they constitute less than a third, probably no more than a fourth, of the total German population. We thus find a class of citizens, which is not even one third as numerous, giving three times as much for its charitable institutions as

[71] *Ibid.*, XI, 167.
[72] *Ibid.*, XVII (1885/86), 105-106.

the Germans, even if we include the annual budget of the German Association, whose expenditures amounted to $22,350 in 1885, as well as those of the Legal Aid Society (Rechtsschutzverein), and the Polyclinic. Nor should it be overlooked in this connection that the same Jews have assisted in many ways and with a liberal hand the German welfare enterprises."[73]

13. *Envy of the Political Successes of the Jews*

The Jew was readily held up as a model as regards charity, but when it came to the achievement of Jews in other fields, admiration was mixed with envy. This was particularly evident when it was a question of the political representation of the country, where the course of life of the person who gained distinction was looked upon as a career, and the advancement of the Jew was regarded by his rivals as tantamount to their own dispossession.

To be sure, here, too, something worth emulating was found; however, into the theoretical praise for the Jewish leadership, certain insinuations and digs were woven. It was assumed, first of all, that Jews always supported a Jewish candidate for political office. Jewish unity was always stressed and contrasted with German division. Again, it was said that there was something to be envied, even though it was not nice to envy. Even when they wrote about a deceased Jewish leader and had nothing but praise for him (as in an appreciation of Lilienthal), they interwove with it a homily to the Germans on Jewish successes in politics:

"That this is so must be attributed to their inner solidarity and also to the work of their leaders. And it must be admitted that they have leaders who by clever methods know how to achieve that inner solidarity, and also how to secure for their race the full measure of recognition due them. For example, while the German community of this country is today an unknown quantity in politics on account of its disunity—thirty, forty years ago it was different—the Jers are a power which has to be respected and which, in fact, is respected. They, who do not constitute even one third of the number of Germans in this country, hold fully one third of the number of posts of honor and other public offices that the Germans have captured. One should not find fault with them for that, but should rather follow their example and act in unison, like them; envy is only a confession of one's own weakness."[74]

That they could not speak of the "power" of the Jews even in the mildest manner without betraying the envious weakness of the Germans, and that an

[73] *Ibid.*, pp. 315-317.
[74] *Ibid.*, XIV, 162ff.

appreciation of what the Jews had attained in this country had to be coupled with a numerical comparison with the public posts held by the Germans, affords much food for thought. Obviously, the author of the Lilienthal appreciation merely expressed what was on the minds of Germans generally, thereby continuing a literary discussion which had begun earlier in the repercussion of an article reprinted from another paper, the *Deutscher Correspondent* of Baltimore. The article, entitled "The Israelites and the Germans in Political Life," contained this passage:

"The ratio of Israelites to Germans in the United States is roughly one to twenty; nevertheless, their evident influence in politics is almost as great, and as a rule they know far better how to advance themselves quickly. Thus, for example, the first native of Germany to sit in the House of Representatives was not a Teuton, but an Israelite, Meyer Strouse, of Pennsylvania. Long before Gen. Schurz, a descendant of the Patriarchs sat in the United States Senate, namely, the celebrated jurist and later Finance Minister of the Confederacy, Judah Benjamin; and now there is again a Jewish Senator, to wit: Jonas of Louisiana. Along with four Germans, two Israelites sit in the House of Representatives: Morse of Boston and Einstein of New York. If we look over the ranks of government officials, we find mightly few Germans and quite a number of Jews as judges, custom house officials, consuls, and consular agents. And if we turn to the individual States, we find there, too, that the children of Israel know how to make themselves felt in political life; in Cincinnati recently a Mr. Seasongood came within an ace of being nominated Lieutenant Governor."[75]

The significance of such symptoms was certainly not fully realized by the Jews. When Jews replied to such political comments, they did not manifest any awareness of even potential danger. The Jewish politician, Simon Wolf, explains the "riddle" of Jewish eminence in politics by saying, "Yes, it is due to Jewish solidarity."[76] Under different political conditions, this feeling of envy might have led to serious consequences. But the general situation in the country was then such that people worshiped the success of the individual and cared little about his ancestry. The Jews, again, were too deeply rooted in the cultural milieu of the Germans to be able or willing to break their ties with them because of the jealousy evinced by them. The Jewish remedy was—to pretend not to notice it.

14. *The Role of the German Language*

The attitude of the Germans to the Jew was twofold. On the one hand, they could not rid themselves in the new country of the old prejudices against him,

[75] *Ibid.*, XI, 142.
[76] *Ibid.*

and of the added feeling of envy when the Jew attained a high position; on the other hand, they were near to him, they had him in their own organizations where he was made use of, and what mattered most, he could understand them much better than did the other elements of the population. The Jew had brought over with him a piece of Germany and of German culture. He was a partner and co-builder of German culture on this continent. We have already mentioned the unifying and binding role of the German language. But we must dwell here upon a couple of other factors in relation to language.

The Germans in America clearly perceived that the Jews were strengthening the cultural position of the Germans in this country. The German-Jewish periodicals in America were numbered among the German papers; the German-Jewish schools, among the German schools. Thereby, not only were additional items entered in the bibliographies of German periodical publications, but the feeling of entrenching oneself and assuring the future of German culture in this country was enhanced. Well-established German-Jewish institutions won for the Germans local prestige. Thus, a report on "Germans in Baltimore" speaks appreciatively of "the Hebrew-German-English school of Joseph Goldschmidt on Hanover Street, which has existed for fifteen years now and numbers about 150 pupils. It is run with great care, and possesses the merit of being completely independent."[77]

On the other hand, it is noted, apparently with a sense of loss, that the "German Jews, although they are doing so much for the German private schools and theater—indeed, without their patronage, the latter would cease to exist—speak among themselves virtually nothing but English."[78] It goes without saying that the transition from German to English did not take place all at once nor without attendant difficulties. At first, when the religious needs were satisfied through the medium of the German language, the prayerbooks were imported from Germany; the German papers carried advertisements of newly arrived Hebrew prayerbooks, and the publisher of a German newspaper might at the same time be a seller of *siddurim* (Hebrew prayerbooks).[79] Later on the rabbi who preached in German could satisfy only the older members of the congregation and it became necessary to provide for the publication of religious works in an English translation. Whether the German Jews went over to English much faster than the Germans themselves is a separate question, one we have not touched upon.

In passing, let it also be noted that, just as in the City Temple of Vienna,

[77] *Ibid.*, 1870, p. 205.
[78] *Ibid.*, XII, 262.
[79] *Deutsche Schnellpost,* April 26, 1843.

Josef Drechsler composed the choral melodies, so, in Cincinnati, Karl Barus, the conductor of the *Liedertafel* (Glee Club), provided the music for the divine services of Reform Judaism. "He set to music numerous Psalms and Jewish hymns (among them those written by Rabbi I. M. Wise), which are rendered at the Temple on Plum Street and contribute not little to elevate the services there."[80]

This close bond, however, rested upon the common German language. And when the younger generation demanded first the use of two languages (English for the young and German for the older people) and afterwards they went over to English altogether, it represented an adaptation to the new country and a departure from the old. This adjustment, too, did not take place without attendant difficulties. In those spheres which are independent of language (such as music, art), one could keep up for a time the ties with the old country and with the German cultural milieu.

In considering the relationship between religion and language one should not overlook a salient difference between Germans and Jews from Germany. For the German immigrants the German language was a valuable instrument for the advancement of religious life. The Germans brought their church with them. The German church was their first organization, their outpost, and to the church flocked all the newly arrived immigrants. There was mutual aid between church and language. But among a large part of the Jewish intellectuals who came from Germany the very attachment to the German language and culture went hand in hand with the severance of all ties with religion. This kind of Jews who were completely indifferent to Judaism brought with them to this country their negative attitude to religion along with all their other culural habits. From Milwaukee in the year 1856 we have the following graphic account of Jews without Judaism who came here in the immigration waves of the revolutionary years 1830 and 1848.

"It so happened, that some of the most ignorant Jews came to Milwaukee and became a prey to the Atheists. They are the first Jewish atheists I ever saw. I met a philosophical butcher, a superwise rag dealer, an over-learned rum-seller, a sophistical hogdriver, an atheistical servant of a cattle-dealer. . . . There are some men who came from the rudest parts of Germany. . . . Now they are naturally ashamed of all and everything they were or did in Germany, consequently they are also ashamed to be Jews."[81]

Even such elements could have been integrated into the life of the Jewish

[80] *Der deutsche Pionier,* XII, 262.
[81] *The Israelite,* III (1856), 53.

congregations—and so they actually were in the course of time. But the impetus which in religious organizations is precisely what the intellectuals are expected to impart was lacking here. Thus it came about that, while American civilization was largely based on religion, the separate Jewish development in this respect was hampered by the peculiar attitude of many German-Jewish intellectuals.

15. *German-Jewish Cultural Institutions*

The social life of the German-Jewish immigrants was built on two distinct principles: Jewish participation in the cultural institutions of the Germans, and the creation of their own cultural organizations, in doing which latter, however, it was not infrequently intended to preserve and develop their cultural assets and the *same form* of the cultural assets. Participation in a German reading or dramatic circle could mean essentially the same thing as membership in an independent Jewish reading or dramatic club, since the same books were read and the same plays were performed by amateur players. And certainly the foundation was the same in both cases—the German language. The impetus to join such an organization came from the same desire for fellowship.

However, in the different types of cultural organizations, either the German societies with the participation of Jews predominated, or else the independent German-Jewish organization. The former was overwhelmingly the case in the glee and gymnastic clubs, where there prevailed the high standards which the Germans had brought with them from the old country, while purely Jewish organizations predominated in the case of dramatic clubs, literaly societies, etc. For a long time this remained the line of development. This difference was also noted by the Germans, as may be seen from the following appraisal:

"A separate, or rather detached part of the German element is formed by the numerous German Jews. They possess not only richly-endowed benevolent organizations, but also choral, musical, and educational societies, good schools, and are now engaged in establishing a university. They foster science and art in even larger measure than do their Christian countrymen. The only thing strange is their separateness, seeing that their efforts in this respect bear a distinctly German character, so that the English-speaking Jews hate them. The *Deborah* bitterly complains about it, at the same time calling upon the German Jews to hold fast to their aim."[82]

[82] *Deutsche Monatshefte,* New York, VII (1856), 187.

Among the German cultural organizations, Jewish participation was particularly conspicuous in the glee clubs. The German glee clubs enjoyed great esteem in America. They were regarded by the American population as the prototype of German culture, as the special contribution of the Germans to the cultural life of the country. Besides, the Jews had not brought with them singing societies of their own from the old country.

In the eyes of the Jewish public, the Jewish participation in the German glee clubs bore a semi-official character, and it formed a standing head in the German-Jewish papers of America. No less a man than Isaac M. Wise boasted publicly of having helped to organize the first German singing society in Albany.[83] The results of elections in such societies and the composition of their delegations to the annual festivals were reported and commented upon in the German-Jewish press.[84] Stress was put on the participation of prominent Jews in the singing societies. Here is an example:

"AURORA, Ind.—The Fourth Annual Festival of the Indiana Saengerbund. . . . The editor of the *Israelite* has been invited to deliver the principal address, and he has accepted the invitation. The entire speech will in due time be published in the *Deborah*."[85]

Detailed reports on the song festivals were published in the German-Jewish press, and in doing so the general line of German propaganda was followed in full. It was pointed out how disciplined the public was; that there was no need to be afraid of the use of alcohol because it was partaken of in moderation; that the Sunday rest was not disturbed thereby; that the German Sunday was observed in a dignified manner; above all, that German lager beer had every advantage over the straight whiskey of other nations. Here is how the *Israelite* describes a song festival:

"The Festivals of the Song Societies in New York

". . . Here the temperance man saw with bewilderment twenty thousand men, women and children enjoying freely, but with a certain moderation, of God's beautiful gifts, drinking joyously with mirth, fun and love, their cups of wine and lagerbeer without beastly intoxication, without stabbing, beating, swearing and cursing, and perhaps they may have learned, that the Germans at least are

[83] *Der deutsche Pionier,* VII (1875/76), 34.
[84] *The Israelite,* II (1855/56), 3.
[85] *Die Deborah,* 1860, p. 162.

not in need of the prohibitory law, and that beer is not to be included among spirituous liquors.

"To give this article some coloring for the *Israelite* I will finally state, that many of our co-religionists are efficient members of the singing societies, and among the most deserving of the New York associations is one called *Orpheus,* consisting mostly of Jews, who distinguished themselves in the last concert.

"New York, July 4th, 1855. E.B."[86]

Drinking beer was the accepted form of enjoying oneself at more intimate celebrations among German Jews; this fondness for beer they had acquired in the old country, especially those who came from Bavaria. The "Twelfth Anniversary Celebration of the *Israelite* and the *Deborah,*" according to a contemporary report, was simply drowned in beer.[87] Incidentally, the report tells of a wholly forgotten work of art, a "picture by a very talented painter, Mosler," which is described thus:

"In the foreground we see three angry fanatics with horrible faces burning in a large cauldron many copies of the prayerbook newly introduced by Dr. Wise. From the ashes arise, in spite of the zealots, a pair of angels, *Israelite* and *Deborah,* which are protected by their Genius, Dr. Wise, and crowned with laurels. On the right, the towers of the new temple are seen in the distance, and on the left, twelve figures representing the twelve annual sets of the papers."

The report adds that Dr. Bloch was so pleased with the painting that he treated the whole company to a keg of beer. After that they played skittles, a fitting close for a real beer party.

17. *The Aryan By-Law of the Arion Glee Club*

A common name among the German choral societies was "Harmonie" (Harmony), which was intended to express the idyllic relations prevalent among the members. But soon there was a case in a German choral society where the latent anti-Semitism of the Germans burst into the open with elemental force. It is significant that this incident occurred precisely in a glee club of New York, where many Jewish singers took part in all the public concerts given by the German singing societies, as may be seen from the report cited above. A report on a song festival in 1865[88] mentions a tenor named H. Rosenthal of the New

[86] *The Israelite,* II (1855/56), 21.
[87] *Die Deborah,* 1866, p. 19.
[88] *New Yorker Musik-Zeitung,* I (1865), 161.

York Liedertafel, a tenor called Cohn of the Uhland-Bund, another singer of the same name belonging to the Williamsburg Quartet Club, and still another singer, a member of the Germania Club, bearing the same name, which, however, in his case is spelled Kohn (a form of the name which was the subject of coarse jests in German student circles). In the same year, in the Arion Glee Club, "Messrs. Ely and Pick distinguished themselves in the field of comic acrobatics."[89]

But later on the last-named club inserted an Aryan clause in its by-laws. The barring of Jews from membership inevitably created a public scandal, and the club profited by the uproar: its ranks were swelled by an influx of all the elements who thought that they would feel more at home in a *Judenrein* (Jewless) society, and that the genuine German art of singing could be better developed there. The poet's words, "Other times other birds, other birds other songs," proved quite true.

The Arion Glee Club did not content itself with barring Jews from membership, but proceeded to produce appropriate songs about it and perpetuated them in its book of songs. Its anti-Semitic practice was celebrated in song, held up to praise; by constant repetition it was implanted in the mind, and the Aryan clause actually became the foundation of the club. The anti-Jewish sentiments long harbored in the heart but not permitted to pass the lips now burst forth in merry songs. In these songs the Jews are referred to as a pack of "brokers, shopkeepers, ignoramuses, toadies;"[90] and while in this truly German mood, the Arion poets also pay their respects to the "Yankee, cheat, trickster."[91] The anti-Semitic action of throwing out the Jews is constantly defended. In one song the Jew is compared to a dog;[92] in another song it is trumpeted that the Jew spoils good democracy by hs impudence and endless talk.[93] And since it is always more convenient to attack Jews by singling out a rich Jew, songs were composed about August Belmont, who embraced Christianity, rode about in a coach and four in Newport, and was also a most influential figure in the clubs of the rich in New York.[94] In one song the Arion bard makes merry over Jewish parsimony and holds up as a horrible example one August Schoenberg who gives up politics because it cost more than ten percent, and so he has to do only with diplomats and imagines he is an ambassador.[95] But above all, the bards celebrate the story of how the singing society became *Judenrein,* how a certain Doctor Wiesner

[89] *Ibid.,* p. 20.
[90] *Arions Gesangbuch* . . . New York, 1868, p. 5. Excerpts from these anti-Jewish songs are given in Appendix IV below.
[91] *Ibid.,* p. 70.
[92] *Ibid.,* p. 22.
[93] *Ibid.,* p. 39.
[94] *Ibid.,* p. 42.
[95] *Ibid.,* p. 130.

waged war against the society on account of it and became an object of derision, how the masquerade of the Arion Glee Club was a particular success because of the public uproar over the club, so that it was not necessary to spend money on advertising—in short, how nice everything is now, and how it paid to throw the Jews out of the club.[96]

The special significance of the whole Arion affair consists in this, that for a long time one of the foremost German-American organizations openly pursued an anti-Semitic policy and boasted of it in song. Occasional attacks upon Jews were to be found even in periodicals considered radical, but there the anti-Jewish utterances were sporadic, and one cannot divide the German-Americans into pro-Jewish and anti-Jewish camps. Moreover, even in the Arion club itself the rule of the Aryan clause was afterwards completely liquidated. In the first place, two years later the assistance of the Jews was needed in the campaign for the relief of the German sufferers during the Franco-Prussian War; in the second place, the radical elements in the club grew more numerous. As a result, Jewish artists once more took part in the concerts given by the club, and we again encounter Jewish names among its members.

Years later—in 1895—the Arion Glee Club took the initiative in calling upon the German societies to help erect a monument to Heinrich Heine in New York. The response of many German organizations was none too enthusiastic, and "the members of the Arion club ultimately had to make sacrifices in order to enable the erection of the monument."[97]

18. *Jews in the German Gymnastic Societies*

Another characteristic form of organization among the Germans in America was the gymnastic society. The Germans had brought over this type of societies from the old country, and over here the gymnastic movement preserved its traditional forms and became a valuable instrument for keeping the Germans together and providing them with the means for common enjoyment. The gymnastic clubs developed simultaneously with the choral societies and one did not hinder the other.

In those days the Jews in Germany did not yet have gymnastic clubs of their own. Here and there individual Jews desiring to indulge in physical culture and sport found their way into the gymnastic clubs even in Germany. Thus the German Jews did not bring to America their own gymnastic societies. Neither

[96] *Ibid.*, p. 74.
[97] *Arion, New York, von 1854 bis 1904*, New York, 1904, p. 31.

could they join the various American sport clubs because of the language barrier. Besides, the forms of athletics they encountered here were unfamiliar to them. Boxing, for example, was hardly known in the Germany of that period. It took the German-Jewish immigrants longer to accustom themselves to American ways in sports than in any other field.

Accordingly, the Jewish immigrant from Germany was attracted to the German gymnastic societies, insofar as the immigrant had any desire at all for sport after a hard day's work. But young people have energy for everything, and so Jews soon made their appearance among the rank and file and even among the leaders of the German gymnastic societies. These societies were founded on the idea of equality; the membership was liberal. Every gymnast was admonished to "bear in mind that *man* is the main thing, and that Christian, Jew, or Mohammedan is a matter of minor importance."[98]

The periodicals of the German sport movement denounced the reaction in Germany and also any manifestation of anti-Semitism in this country, thereby bringing into relief the free, egalitarian spirit of the gymnastic societies. When, in the summer of 1877, the New York Jewish banker Joseph Seligmann was not admitted into the Grand Union Hotel of Saratoga which belonged to Judge Hilton, there blazed forth the first great "Christians Only" controversy in America with journalistic outpourings, quips, and cartoons. We find an echo of this episode in these lines from a collection of songs of the German gymnastic societies:

"Milwaukee, du bist ein gar herrliches Städchen,
So braun ist dein Bier und so blond deine Mädchen,
Dort beut dem Turner manch gastlich Haus,
Und es schmeisst dort kein Hilton nen Siligmann 'naus."[99]

The friendly atmosphere of the gymnastic societies remained for a long time the place where a militant democracy flourished and imparted liberal impulses to the political life of the Germans in America. But only a few individual Jews could enjoy this atmosphere; to the great majority of German-Jewish immigrants the gymnastic societies did not offer a suitable way of passing their leisure time, especially to those who had become well-to-do, or were no longer young. For them there were other forms of social life.

---

[98] *Turnzeitung der Cincinnati-Turngemeinde,* 1851, p. 32.

[99] *Massenklange aus dem Leierkasten der Chicago Turngemeinde,* Chicago, 1877, p. 8.

For such people there had to be other forms of sociability without physical exertion; they were attracted to intellectual and artistic circles. Societies for the cultivation of literature and the drama could repel no one; there was a great vogue fir literary clubs. Appreciation of the professional art theater began to grow. Everywhere there sprang up groups of amateur players, who organized within the framework of the various social clubs, so that each troupe was at the same time assured of an audience.

The German theater in America was from its inception held in high esteem. When the Germans in this country had attained material affluence, they were able to bring over stars of the stage and opera from Germany for tours of the United States. By this step they popularized German theatrical art in this country, elevated the social atmosphere around the theater, and gained for it the support of wealthy patrons.

Before long people began to notice that Jews formed a disproportionately large part of the public that attended German shows. Jews also began to figure among the patrons who supported the German stage with a liberal hand; Jews were likewise observed among the theatrical producers and the actors. Support for the German professional theater became in Jewish circles almost a semi-official concern, as was the case with the singing societies. Moreover, the literary clubs in which Jews took part often produced amateur theatricals themselves, or helped to make possible tours by German professional troupes. Jewish charity organizations bought benefit performances at the German theater to raise funds for their activities. And even purely literary Jewish societies, which concerned themselves with fostering popular interest in German literature, brought German professional players to cities where there was a Jewish theater-going public. Those players helped to refine the taste of the public, and the heightened interest in the theater finally led to the formation of groups of amateur players within the clubs, which the best elements in these clubs joined, and which offered to the members the best they had to give, namely, the fruit of their leisure hours spent in artistic labors. The difference between the people on the stage and those in the audience was often the difference between two generations. The young played for their parents. When these amateurs felt sufficiently self-confident, they also ventured to perform English plays, so that the older generations gradually began to receive from their children doses of dramatic art in the language of the country.

Literary societies began to spring up among the German Jews even before they came to the new country. We know that as far back as 1837 there were literary societies even in very small localities in Germany.[100] It was precisely those preparing to emigrate who were to be found in such circles,[101] so that one might say that the literary societies on the new soil were a continuation of the development in Germany. But whereas over there the main concern had been to orient oneself to the new country to which one was about to go, over here it was mainly a question of maintaining the spiritual bond with the old country. Here is a typical report about the formation of a literary society of German Jews:

"There has been formed lately among the German Israelites of New York a literary society, who have a reading room where they meet every evening about eight o'clock. We found there several Jewish periodicals, German, English and American, besides other works, and we learned that already fifty-two persons had joined the association. Nearly all the ministers of the German congregations are members of this society, and it promises much good, provided only it be properly conducted."[102]

Even in the poorest circles of the Jewish immigrants, once they had taken the first steps to establish themselves, there was a noticeable tendency to frequent the theater, to support the German stage. The Jewish shop clerks are repeatedly described as patrons of the Bowery Theater and, as such, sometimes also derided:

"In time he becomes a special patron of the liberal arts. The German theater, in particular, enjoys his patronage. Here he can spread himself out—and how he spreads himself out! For this is one place where he is received. A place where no one can make him feel that he is a Jew. And that gold chain of his, how it glitters in the bright light! And his Rebecca and his Sarah, how they can bend over the railing of the first gallery, at 50 cents apiece! Among every 100 theatergoers in New York, there are always 80 Jews. Without them the theater could not exist!"[103]

What even the scoffer had to admit appears even more evident to the serious observer:

"The German-American stage is generally a very shaky institution which is subject to every metamorphosis imaginable. In New York, to be sure, it is fairly well established, thanks mainly to the patronage of the Jews. But in the other cities of the Union it leads a miserable and precarious existence, and no season ends without a deficit that cries to heaven."[104]

---

[100] *Allgemeine Zeitung des Judentums,* I, 424, 453-54.
[101] M. S. Hansen, *The Atlantic Migration,* Cambridge, Mass., 1940, p. 150.
[102] *The Occident,* V (1847/48), 413.
[103] *Theodor Griesinger, Lebende Bilder aus Amerika,* Stuttgart, 1856, p. 146.
[104] Karl Knortz, *Amerikanische Lebensbilder,* Zürich, 1884, p. 125.

The Jewish press was an outspoken champion of the German theater. Even before the opening of the season, nay, while new troupes were still in the process of formation, it wrote about the coming theatrical events and prepared the public for them. Here is a typical theater notice in the press:

"Reopening of the Germania Theater. A cable dispatch announces that all the artists engaged by Director Neuendorff for his theater are aboard the Hamburg steamer "Suevia" and will reach New York in a few days. To all the friends and admirers of German art the announcement of the reopening of the Germania Theater, which is to take place on September 15, will be welcome news. Inasmuch as the Jewish New Year falls at that time and it is our custom to exchange good wishes on that occasion, we should like to wish the new artists that they may make an instant hit with the public; the Germania Theater, that its boxes and reserved seats may be occupied every night and sold out three evenings in advance; finally, we wish the enterprising, gifted Director Neuendorff Rothschild's income."[105]

Such a New Year's wish was in the spirit of the many Jews who patronized the German theater. But Jews were not to be found only among those who enjoyed the theater passively; they also figured among those who wrote the plays for it, among the actors and the producers. Foremost among those who supplied the German stage with melodramas and farces was Max Conheim.[106] Among the actors who particularly distinguished, mention must be made of Heinrich Conried, son of Joseph Cohn of Bielitz, Silesia, whom Neuendorff had brought over.[107] The fact that there were a considerable number of Jewish players and, what is more, that the Jewish part of the audience particularly applauded the Jewish actors aroused the ire of certain critics. Here is what one of them wrote about the Jewish actor Daniel Bandmann:

"His entire fame is the product of systematic puffery and the lucky accident that he is an Israelite. The last factor, in particular, can hardly be overestimated, considering the local theater-going public. A disproportionately large part of this public consists of Jews (to their credit let it be said), but they display more feeling for their countrymen than a taste for art when they go into ridiculous raptures about Jewish roles and plays. Even the comedian L'Arronge, who is now guest-starring here, benefits very much by it; otherwise his horribly coarse

---

[105] Libanon, III, 144.

[106] "Max Conheim . . . the most active and successful of the local authors . . ."—Fritz A. H. Leuchs, *The Early German Theatre in New York, 1840-1872*, New York, 1928, p. 96.

[107] *Deutsch-amerikanische Geschichtsblätter*, Bd. 13, 1913; Edwin Hermann Zeydel, *The German Theater in New York City*, p. 310.

and low comedy would not have scored such a great triumph immediately after Dawison's appearance."[108]

Daniel Bandmann's accomplishments are little known today, but L'Arronge lingered long in the memory of the general public as the prototype of a popular actor, the critics to the contrary notwithstanding.

It was only natural that the Jewish public should flock to the theater when a humorous Jewish role could be seen, as was later the case with the play *Sam'l of Posen,* when two-thirds of the audience, according to one reporter, consisted of Jews.[109]

The buying of benefit performances by Jewish benevolent organizations was often connected with the hope of keeping certain troupes for a long time in the cities concerned. In a report of the year 1877, the complaint is voiced that Philadelphia can no longer maintain a German troupe because the Jews of that city no longer took sufficient interest in the German stage:

"In order to brighten our spring mood and at the same time to benefit its treasury, the Family and Orphan Educational Society of the local Temple brought here from New York Neuendorff's Troupe, which played the farce *Castles in the Air* at the Academy of Music on the 14th of this month to a well filled house. . . . It seems rather strange, one might say shameful, that *it is necessary to bring* a *German* troupe from *another* city for such a purpose, at a not inconsiderable cost. The local German population is large enough, yet no worthwhile theatrical enterprise has been able to maintain itself here. Whether this is due to lack of the necessary intellectual interest, or whatever the reason may be, our city lags behind the other large cities of our country also in other fields of German thought and art. At least among the local Israelitish German-Americans there is little interest in fostering German culture, as is proven by the fact that among their societies there is not one which makes this its task."[110]

---

[108] *Neue New Yorker Musik-Zeitung,* 1867, p. 649.

[109] *New York Mirror,* May 21, 1881, p. 2. The hero of this play is a Jewish peddler who comes with his pack to a jewelry shop. There he meets Rebecca Dreyfus, with whom he already was in love in the old country. He exhibits a great deal of ingenuity and shrewdness, uncovers thefts in the shop, helps the good and brings the evil to justice. In the end, there are several happy matrimonial matches, among them one between the peddler and his Rebecca. The Jewish audiences consisted largely of peddlers who had prospered or hoped to prosper, and the peddler made a great hit with them.

[110] *"Kaleideskopische Briefe,"* Libanon, III (1877), 59.

The Jewish amateur theatricals in German penetrated deeply into the life of various societies everywhere. Even in the small Jewish settlements of the Middle West we find groups of amateurs who perform plays in German. But apparently the model in this respect was the city of Cincinnati, where the Jewish population prospered in a relatively short time, was large in number, and exercised an influence over the entire German cultural milieu. The following press notice is illustrative:

"CINCINNATI—The Queen City is unsurpassed by any other city in the Union in social life. If puritanic stiffness and coldness has anywhere given way to the cheerful German disposition, this is certainly the case here. Our Israelites have greatly contributed to this happy victory. They patronize in large measure the local public theater, and their recreational societies are among the most attractive in the city. Allemania, Harmonie, Phoenix, and Taglioni number more than 500 members and afford them the most varied social diversions. Balls, banquets, concerts, amateur theatricals,—these unite men and women week after week in gay, merry circles; and rivalry among the societies results in very fine entertainments."[111]

In Cincinnati itself these achievements of Jewish society were recognized. In a printed guide to the city, after mention of the Jewish community, there is the following statement: "In addition, their clubs, Allemania, Phoenix, and Eureka are the best, one might almost say the only successful clubs in Cincinnati."[112]

When one praised these clubs, one had in mind mainly the accomplishments of their groups of amateurs who used to perform plays for the club members and their guests. In Appendix V the reader will find a more detailed appraisal of the above-mentioned three clubs together with the names of their principal members.

Neither the clubs generally nor the amateur circles within them were inferior to the German clubs and the German amateur circles. As we have just seen, this had to be acknowledged. Nevertheless, the Jewish amateur theatricals were not infrequently the target of mockery and caricature, which, by virtue of the law of inertia, tended to return where it had once before found a target. The humorous periodical *Puck,* which German immigrants founded and which always

[111] *Die Deborah,* IV (1858/59), 126.
[112] *Der Führer von Cincinnati,* Cincinnati, 1875, p. 70.

had its eye on the German-Jewish immigrants, gives this derisive picture of Jewish amateur theatricals:

"The drama at Dinkelspiel's . . . There are some things of which he ought to steer clear if he wants to avoid trouble in the family. One of these is private theatricals. If he must go into the amateur dramatic business, he had better steer clear of 'Camille'.

"They gave 'Camille' the other night at our friend Dinkelspiel's, with disastrous results. Almost every young lady with theatricals ambitions yearns to play *Camille;* and Miss Rebecca Dinkelspiel was no exception to this rule. Mr. Oppenheimer, her betrothed (fancy goods, Grand Street), likewise saw a future before him as *Armand*, and nearly all of the members of the Kosher Dramatic Club expressed a willingness to take the subordinate parts. The play was presented, after long and careful preparation, at Mr. Dinkelspiel's residence, in 73rd Street."

Here follows a caricature of the performance and of the audience, and the writer concludes as follows: "The Kosher Club is dissolved; the engagement of Miss Dinkelspiel and Mr. Oppenheimer is off."[113]

Obviously, the name Kosher Club is a thrust at the high-sounding names of clubs and circles among the German-Jewish immigrants. We also detect here echoes of a number of stereotyped and familiar ways of ridiculing Jews which were brought here from the old country.

21. *Card-playing*

Lower forms of social diversions than amateur theatricals also sprang up under the influence of the German cultural milieu. Hand in hand with private playacting went card-playing. It was soon noticed in America that the vogue of card-playing spread along with the immigration from Germany. The German-American Jews introduced card-playing among all American Jews and devoted a very large part of their leisure to cards. Soon it was realized what danger there lurked in the vice of card-playing, which took up all the leisure hours, leaving no time for more serious social activity and for the higher forms of sociability. The following is a quotation from an article on the theme of card-playing which paints a picture of this social evil:

"A sin. American Jewry is making a great mistake which is bound to have

[113] *Puck,* IX, 211.

evil consequences later on: it *reads* very little and *plays* very much. Young people who have enjoyed all the advantages of the public schools, and who enter into practical life between the ages of 16 and 18 years with a good school education, very soon decline intellectually because the society about them is busy playing theater or cards. . . . Once business hours are over, we play theater or cards, or attentively watch others play, and we refuse to be disturbed. . . . It is no exaggeration to say that card-playing is the worst and most besetting vice of American Jews, who, though no gamblers, devote all their leisure hours to it. . . . Not all of them, but a good many, play; not all of them go to ruin but a good many do, so that it makes itself keenly felt in all public affairs. . . . The lust for card-playing was brought to these shores by the tide of immigration and, like other diseases, it has become hereditary. . . . They try to excuse themselves by saying that there is nothing else to do on the Jewish Sabbath (Saturday), which they cannot or will not observe; however, those who go to business on Saturday play on Sunday and on all the other days of the week. The lust for card-playing pushes Judaism and the Jewish spirit aside; the rabbis fight against it in vain. . . . In our opinion, this is a vital question which should be discussed and settled before everything else."[114]

Card-playing is a typical pastime among Germans; cards are part of their Sunday and of their weekday evening. The Jews had already acquired the habit of card-playing back in Germany. Here in America the Germans popularized the playing of cards. "The population of the city of Cincinnati, which in 1800 had 750 inhabitants and now numbers more than 50,000, mostly Germans, possesses no fewer than 800 cafés and saloons, 450 card-playing parlors, 30 pool rooms, and 30 bowling alleys."[115]

No doubt the number of Germans in Cincinnati is greatly exaggerated here, but apparently the other figures are correct. Be that as it may, the card parlors and bowling allays must be wholly credited to the Germans, who indulged there in their favorite evening and Sunday amusements, just as it it certain that cards were diligently played in German homes and clubs. The invasion of Jewish private homes and clubs by card-playing proves that, with growing affluence, the ways in which different people spend their leisure moments tend to become the same.

---

[114] *Die Deborah,* XXVI (1881), 268.

[115] *Amerika wie est ist. . . .* Hamburg, 1854, p. 144.

Underlying every public activity, among the Jews from Germany as among the Germans, was the use of the German language in mutual intercourse. The common tongue imposed a certain community of interest, which manifested itself both in the school and in the press.

The generation of immigrants from Germany desired to hand down their cultural possessions to their children. They wanted the children to understand their parents. For this reason Jewish religious instruction had to be imparted in the German language. Insofar as they intended at all to transmit the values of Judaism to their children, they again employed the German language as the medium. Here we have a parallel between the endeavors of the German Jews and those of the Germans, and the efforts of the Germans to preserve the German language in this country aided the German Jews in their striving to retain German as the language of instruction for Jewish subjects. On the other hand, the Germans were greatly pleased by the fact that Jews were establishing on this Continent private schools with German as the language of instruction, or were supporting such schools. In their reports on the cultural situations, the Germans often spoke of the schools in the German language maintained by the Jews or of the aid received from Jews for German schools.

A kind of lingual pluralism developed in the school system of the German Jews. Besides German, some instruction was always given in Hebrew also. Presently there arose the added competition of the English language. Thus we are told about the Talmud Yelodim School of Cincinnati at the beginning of the 1850's: "The primary classes were examined in English and German, also in Hebrew . . . the higher classes were examined in German."[116] And a later report from Cleveland tells us of a similar situation in the school there, and speaks of a split among the parents and of concern over the future of the school. We quote in part:

"Only here also exists the evil of a mixed language at school, parents being in many instances desirous that religion and scriptures should be taught in German, which we consider a great wrong, as a perseverance in this course will keep up a wide breach between the natives and those who speak English on the one side, and the exclusive Germans on the other. To our view, the sooner all residents in America unite in the use of English, which sooner or later must become the language of all born here, the better for all parties."[117]

---

[116] *The Occident,* II (1853/54), 49.
[117] *Ibid.,* XV, 305.

On the other hand, the champions of the German language in the school system of the immigrants did not readily lay down their arms. They endeavored to overcome all difficulties and cling to German. Below we quote a report written by one who favored a compromise, namely, that it was necessary for the children to know English well, but that it was likewise necessary to learn German and also to teach Jewish subjects in that language:

"NEW YORK, May 14 . . . Yet I fail to see why the teacher of German origin should force himself or be forced to teach the children elementary subjects in English, why the German language should be neglected at all, nay, rejected. The plan of the board of trustees of the Temple to introduce German as the language of instruction in the school for children to be established by them would also have miscarried if those at the head were not men of insight, and still others who had full confidence in the leaders."[118]

In announcements of the opening of new schools we often find "English, German, and Hebrew" listed among the subjects taught. Such an announcement was published when a school for boys and girls was opened at the German Institute.[119]

A general appraisement of the prevalence of the German language among American Jews, dated 1871, states:

"The German language prevails in a majority of Jewish congregations; however, English is rapidly gaining ground, and already a majority of the Jewish periodicals are published in English."[120]

23. *The Jewish Press in the German Language*

When German-Jewish immigration was at its peak, even Jewish papers printed in English had to give part of their contents in German. An explanation for this is found in the following:

"The Asmonean in German.

". . . This is done purely with a view of ascertaining if it be the language which has restricted our circulation. We are told that all that prevents the Asmonean being found in every Jewish in the Union is the fact that the majority

[118] *Allgemeine Zeitung des Judentums,* 1845, p. 407.
[119] *Die Deborah,* IV (1858/59), 39.
[120] Art. "Juden" in *Deutsch-Amerikanisches Conversationslexicon,* Vol. V, New York, 1871.

of the Hebrew population are German, and that they require a portion of the paper in that language."[121]

As readers of the German newspapers in America the Jews were sufficiently important to assure a generally liberal editorial policy. Besides, Jewish intellectuals from Germany often became editors of and regular writers on the German press in this country. In some cases Jews were part owners or even sole owners of newspapers.

Nevertheless, there were cases when one paper was feuding with another and in connection with it the Jewish issue was injected. This happened once when the *Judenrein* editorial board of a German paper taunted a rival paper about the Jews on its staff. In one instance, even the name of Carl Schurz was dragged into the attacks, who, in European fashion, was mocked at as a "slave of the Jews" who had finally turned Jew. Let us pause a while on this incident.

There were two German dailies in St. Louis, *Die Westliche Post* and *Der Anzeiger des Westens,* which were engaged in a feud. A couple of Jews were employed on the editorial staff of the *Anzeiger,* and the *Post* could not forgive its rival for it. A contemporary periodical,[122] writing about the long-standing conflict, points out that in that fight the *Post* displayed an article imported from Germany, namely, *rishus (i.e.,* Jew-hatred) and that from time to time, it sounded the Hep, Hep cry (anti-Semitic war cry). So, for example, when the *Post* was fighting the Democratic Presidential candidate, Samuel Tilden, it always referred to him as *Schmuhl* (contemptuous German name for a Jew). And thus it came about that an ultra-Democratic German newspaper thereupon attacked Carl Schurz, the editor of the *Post,* publishing the following notice about him:

"The news that Carl Schurz embraced Judaism last Saturday and was circumcised will surprise even his most intimate friends. We must confess, however, that we were not wholly unprepared for such news. Judged by his principles, Carl Schurz was always a Jew; he never acted otherwise than as a Jew; he was the representative of European Jewry in America. So we do not care if Carl Schurz is no called a Jew."[123]

The only thing true in this notice is that Carl Schurz was not afraid in certain cases to tell the Germans that they ought to learn from the Jews, as we saw above, when we quoted his remarks on the Jewish welfare institutions of New York.

[121] *The Asmonean,* Vol. 4, April 25, 1851, p. 44.
[122] *Israelitisches Wochenblatt,* 1876, p. 365.
[123] *Ibid.*

In the news reports about the German Jews in America the Jewish readers found things that displeased them, or did not find the news they expected to come upon in the German press. There was a feeling that the German press was deliberately ignoring Jewish achievements. As an illustration, we will cite the story about the collection of money for aid to the German victims of the Franco-Prussian War. The German Patriotic Relief Society of the United States conducted a country-wide campaign to raise funds with which to help the widows and orphans of soldiers killed in the war. Linked with the drive were demonstrations held in honor of the German victories. The Jews played a big part both in the collections and in the demonstrations. The sum of $180,000 was raised in San Francisco, a sum the Germans of that city, without the assistance of the Jews, could not even have dreamt of. The Germans knew who gave the money, and the local campaign leaders expressed their gratitude to the Jews.[124] But the German papers ignored the great Jewish part in the relief drive and did not tell their readers about it.[125] The German-language Jewish press complained bitterly about this.

The German-American press also steered clear of the Jewish question in Germany. It did not want to appear in the role of educator, in the matter of equal rights for Jews, either to the Germans in Germany or to the Germans in America. In short, the press did nothing to keep the Jews within the cultural milieu of the Germans nor promoted the rapprochement of the two elements in the population of the United States whose common language was German. Subsequent tragic developments in the fortunes of the Germans in America found the latter alone, as the German-Jewish immigrants were already separated from them nor shared their life.

But the main cause which separated the German-Jewish immigrants from their cultural partners was the great wave of Jewish immigration from Eastern Europe. The German Jews gradually became part of the great Jewish community in the United States, insofar as they were not lost to Jewry in the process of adaptation to the non-Jewish environment.

Beginning with the 1880's, the influence of the Germans upon the life of the Jewish immigrants assumed a wholly different character and calls for a separate study.

APPENDIX I

On the Reaction of the Germans to the Negative Attitude Toward Them

The Germans encountered antipathy toward them on the part of the Anglo-

[124] Theodor Kirchhoff, *Californische Kulturbilder,* Cassel, 1886, p. 20.
[125] *Israelitische Wochenschrift,* 1871, p. 236.

Saxon core of the country. True, the Germans also became aware of regional animosities and of the sentiments of the Southerners about the Northerners. They saw that the Yankee of the New England was hated in the South, but they realized that regionalism would resolve itself into a common nativism, and the hatred would be directed against the "latercomers".

We find this clearly expressed in the following dialogue in Emil Klauprecht's *Cincinnati oder Geheimnisse des Westens,* Cincinnati, 1854, I, 26:

"Ein Yankee, Wilhelm? Du weisst, dass meine Frau eine Virginierin ist, und solltest wissen, dass in ihrem Staate Antipathie gegen das verknöcherte Yankeetum herrscht."

"Eine Antipathie, so um hundert Prozent geringer als die Gesamtabneigung der Amerikaner gegen die Deutschen."

While the difference between the Anglo-Saxon and the German was represented, often quite caricaturally, as one between whiskey and beer, there were sufficiently salient differences in real life. They concerned primarily the manner in which Sunday was kept: whether it was observed in a strict Puritanic way, without going anywhere, but staying home and reading the Bible, or merrily, with outings, with song, with amusements. The battle between Sabbath and Sunday went on for decades. We have an echo of it in some verses printed in *Die Fehme,* St. Louis, 1869/70, No. 38:

DER YANKEE-SONNTAG

. . . Blieben auch beim Gelderwerbe
Unsere Hände nicht gar rein,
War der Sonntag uns nur Sabbath,
Schauten wir nur sauer drein.

The German certainly felt offended when continually twitted about sauerkraut and beer, and he boasted that in the end he had left his impress upon American life. We quote again from a poem in the same German magazine, No. 21, p. 7:

EINER AUS CHICAGO

. . . Doch was hilft alles Schreiben Euch,
Ihren armen Yankeeseelen,
Germanisiert wird Euer Reich
Ja doch, es kann nicht fehlen!

Jetzt esset Ihr auch Sauerkraut,
Trinkt Bier und Saft der Reben,
Und unsere Lieder singt Ihr laut,
Wir lehrten Euch zu leben.

The German fancied himself to have been the real pioneer in the forest primeval:

Bald tönet mit gewucht'en Hieben
Die Axt der deutschen Pionier,
Hei, wie sie auseinanderstieben,
Die Riesenbäum, des Urwalds Zier.
Und wie im Urwald es sich lichtet
Zieht schaffend ein der deutsche Geist;
Um jede Hütte, die errichtet,
Beglückend deutsche Sitte kreist.

(*Der deutsche Pionier,* I, 3)

APPENDIX II

On the Relations between Salzburgers and Jews in Georgia

From the reports about the Salzburgers in America we cull a few characteristic passages which incidentally tell of the Jews and their life in general:

"Anno 1759 May . . . Es gibt zur Zeit noch einige Juden in Savannah. Weil diese wenigen Familien aber sich leicht und wohl naehren, und den Engellaendern und anderen Einwohnern in allen Stucken gleich gerechnet werden; so ist wohl zu vermuthen, es werden sich nach und nach mehrere einfinden. Sie ernaehren sich als Kaufleute in der Stadt; zwey Brueder handeln mit den Indianer, haben auch mit indianischen Weibern Kinder gezeugt; eine Familie haelt ein Wirthaus, eine stehet mit einem teutschen Metzger in Compagnie, und schlachtet auf dem Markte zu Savannah u.s.f. Eine einzige Familie, die schon ueber 26 Jahre im Land ist, haelt steif an dem juedischen Gottesdienst, Feyertagen und Aberglauben. Der Hausvater reichte mir vor einigen Tagen, da ich bey seinem Hause vorbeyging, eine Englische in Pennsylvanien gedruckte Monatschrift, das Amerikanische Magazin genant, mit dem Begehren, die Predigt zu lesen, welche ein vornehmer juedischer Rabbi gehalten. Ich fragte ihn, ob es denn wahr sey, dass die Juden (wie in der Predigt erzehlt werde) im Gebet auf ihre Knie fallen; seine kurze Antwort war, sie bueckten sich, und das hiesse so viel, als auf die Knie fallen etc. etc. Er machte so viel aus dieser Rede, als waere ihres gleichen noch nie zum Vorschein gekommen; ob ich gleich in der That gar nichts besonders in ihr antraf. Die Juden hier geniessen alle Vorrechte des Landes mit, und leisten auch alle buergerlichen Pflichten, wie andere Einwohner. Sie werden auch in die Bruederschaft der Freymaurer aufgenommen. Ihr Toechter haben einen recht aergerlichen Kleiderpracht." (*Amerikanisches Ackerwerk Gottes,* hg. v. Samuel Urlsperger, 1744, IV Stueck p. 45.)

"Den 22. (November 1752) Eines Juden Sohn aus Savannah brachte mir einen Brief von dem Schulmeister der Negers, Names Joseph Ottolenghe, darinnen er meldet, dass er am vergangenen Sonntage die Stelle des verreiseten engellaendischen Predigers in der Kirche versehen und von der geistlichen Wiedergeburth gepredigt habe. Er brauchte dabey solche Ausdruecke, die von einem demuetigen Sinne zeugen. Er ist ein gebohrener Jude und vermutlich gar ein Rabbi in Italien gewesen; . . . Es sind nur zwey Familien Juden in Savannah: einer haelt ein Wirthaus, und der andere naehrt sich mit einem kleinen Kram. Sie sind beyde deutsch. Ob es gleich nur zwey Familien sind, so sind sie einander doch in einigen Stuecken ihrer Religion zuwider. Die Juden geniessen mit den Christen hier einerley Vorrechte." (*Ibid.,* III. Stueck, Augsburg, 1745.)

Characteristic of the social and business relations of that period is the following item, dated July 19, 1740:

"Ich empfieng heute einen Brief aus England, welcher ins Couert eines Juden in Savannah eingeschlossen gewesen." (*Siebente Continuation der ausfuehrlichen Nachrichten von den Saltzburgischen Emigranten,* hg. v. Samuel Urlsperger, Halle, 1741, p. 565.

We have this story about relations of another sort:

"Es kam noch ein anderer unangenehmer Handel vor. Eine Magd, Papistischer Religion, welche auch zu diesen teutschen Leute gehoeret, hatte mit einem Juden Hurerey getrieben und nachdem ein Kind bekommen, und von dem Englischen Prediger taufen lassen, war sie weggelaufen, vermutlich nach St. Augustin zu ihren catholischen Glaubensgenossen und hatte das Kind in des Juden Haus liegen lassen. Der Jude will sich zu dem Kinde nicht bekennen, ob er wol ausser Zweiffel Vater ist, daher er es fast verderben und verhungern lassen; darueber wurde er vor der Obrigkeit gefordert, und angewiesen, fuer das Kind zu sorgen, und soll er dazu aus dem Store-Hause einige Beyhuelfe bekommen."—Diarium Anno 1739, Mai. (*Continuation der ausfuehrlichen Nachrichten von den Stalzburger Emigraten,* hg. v. Samuel Urlsperger, Halle, 1746, p. 87.)

APPENDIX III

Haym Salomon's Advertisement in the Philadelphische Correspondenz

"*Haym Salomon, Mäckler des Finanzamts,* hat einen Freiheitsbrief erhalten, um das Geschäft eines Versteigerers in der Stadt Neuyork zu treiben, hat nun zum Empfang aller Arten von Waaren sein Haus in der Wallstrasse, Num. 22, eröffnet, es hat solches letzthin Herr Anton L. Bleeker besessen (eins von den besten Lagen in der Stadt) und jedes Geschäft, welches im gerinsten zu den Geschäft eines Faktors, Versteigerers und Mäcklers gehört, wird mit derjenigen Redlichkeit, Eilfertigkeit and Pünktlichkeit vollzogen werden, welche bis daher seine Geschäften so berühmt gemacht haben. Das Haus ist in Ansehung der Bequemlichkeit und Lage sehr wohly zu den verschiedenen Arten des oben angeführten Geschäfts eingerichtet; und er denkt es fast unnöthig zu sein, diejenigen, welche ihn mit ihren Befehlen beehren wollen, zu versichern, dass die genaueste Achtung und die äusserste Sorgfalt wird angewendet werden, ihr Interesse zu befördern.

Sein Geschäft setzt ihn in Stand, sehr leicht nach jedem Teil der Welt Gelder zu übermachen, und dieses hoffet er wird ihn mit denjenigen begünstigen, welche entfernt wohnen.

Ein Verlangen, dem Publico mehr nützlicher zu werden und allgemeine Vergnügen zu geben, sind seine Hauptbewegungsgründe, dieses Haus zu eröffnen, und werden beständig der Leitfaden in allen seinen Handlungen seyn. Indem er Mäckler des Finanz-Amts ist, und mit dessen Zutrauen beehrt, so sind alle diejenigen Geldsummen durch seine Hände gegangen, welche die Grossmüthigkeit des Französischen Monarchen und die Zuneigung der Kaufleute in den Vereinigten Niederlanden angetrieben haben uns damit zu versehen, und uns dadurch in Stand setzen, die Kriegskosten zu ertragen, und welche so viel zu dessen baldiger und glücklicher Endigung beygetragen haben; dieses ist ein Umstand, welcher seinen Credit und Ruhm festgesetzt und ihm das Zuvertrauen des Publici erworben hat, ein Zutrauen, welches er sich beständig bestreben wird, durch heilige Erfüllung seiner Verbindlichkeiten, zu verdienen und zu vermehren. Das Geschäft wird auf das rühmlichste nach einem ausgebreiteten Plan geführt werden, unter dem Namen von Haym Salomon und Jacob Mordecai. Philadelphia, den 7ten Mai 1784."

APPENDIX IV

Excerpts from the Songbook of the Arion Glee Club

1

Unser Comite
Sich stolz erhob in kleinen Rat,
Ein Narr, der seine "Länge" hat,
Er tat es laut verkünden:
Dass sich ein Narr von Israel
Thät unter uns befinden.
So wandert bald an Freundeshand
Ein Pintcher aus gelobten Land,
Ihn wartet er auf im Witze:
Aus angeborener Höflichkeit
Mit reserviertem Sitze.

2

Als August Schoenberg liesse ich
Von Politik die Hand,
Die Spesen sind zu fürchterlich,
Wohl mehr als "10 perschent."
Mit Diplomaten nur allein,
Blieb ich noch im Verkehr,
Und bildete mir lebhaft ein,
Ich sei Ambassadeur.

3

HAW MER KEIN FREUD
. . . Der Doctor Wiesner, sonderbar,
Vor kurzem sehr entrüstet war,
Weil ein beschnitt'ner Candidat
Durch im Arion fiel.
Schellt mit den Kappen . . .
Er gleich im Zorn nach Hause lief
Und schrieb 'nen wilden Schreibebrief,
's war lauter Phrasenbrei.
Schellt mit den Kappen . . .
Allein ein wackrer Handelsmann

Nahm sich der Sache wacker an,
Und er erhob ein gross' Geschrei,
Wie alle Helden tun.
Schellt mit den Kappen . . .
O! Meier, liebes Meierchen!
Sei doch kein solches Schreierchen!
Du bist kein Held, bleib friedlich bei
Der Handelsmeierei.
Das ganze Volk von Israel,
Das fing nun gleichfalls an Krakehl,
Und es beschloss in Zorn, nicht auf
Den Maskenball zu geh'n.
Schellt mit den Kappen . . .
Der Moses, Purim President,
Kam zu dem Schindeler gerennt
Und bracht zwei Tickets ihm zurück,
Verlangt sein Geld retour.
Der Moses lacht sich in den Bart:
Hab sswanzig Dollars nun gespart;
Gott! was für Stuss. Ja, was gemacht.
Schellt mit den Kappen . . .
Du braves Volk von Israel,
Sieh uns darob nicht an so scheel,
Dieweil ein Mann von deinem Stamm
Durch im Arion fiel.
Nimm Weinstein ein mit Schwefelblüth,
Das wird besänft'gen dein Gemüth:
Denn Glaubenssache ist es nicht,
's ist Sache des Geschmacks!
Schellt mit den Kappen . . .
Doch diesen danken wir ganz fein,
Dem Doctor und dem Meierlein,
Dass sie uns für den Maskenball
's Annoncengeld erspart.
Schellt mit den Kappen . . .

APPENDIX V

Concerning the Jewish Clubs of Cincinnati

(From "Reminiscences of the Theaters of Cincinnati, "*Cincinnati Commercial,* Oct. 21, 1877)

"*The Allemania.*—This is a strong and time-honored Jewish organization. They have the lease of Melodion Hall, which they have fitted up in beautiful style. The general object of the club is sociability and good fellowship, and its membership is very large and wealthy. The younger members give dramatic and operatic entertainments for the amusement of the seniors. Those participating in the plays are privileged to invite one guest, but beyond this limit none but members are admitted.

"Among the principal members are Messrs. Isaac M. Simon, M. J. Mack, Fred. Rauh, Theo. Adelsdorfer, Alex. Labold, Ben Rice, D. Heinsheimer, Jr., Hermann Mack, Abe Newburgh, Mrs. G. Mendel, Miss Esther Stern, Miss Monheimer and Miss Loewenstein. The season has not yet been opened, but the club has in preparation the 'Two Orphans.' Mr. Simon, mentioned above, is a capital actor in such parts as David Garrick and Elliot Gray, in 'Rosedale.' We also recall a fine rendition by him of Landry Barbeaud to the Fanchon of Miss Oppenheimer, a few years ago, at Mozart Hall. Mr. Rise is a dashing comic vocalist as well as a good actor. Mrs. Mendel has already been noticed as a member of the Davenport Club."

"*The Phoenix Club.*—Boasts the superb theatre and club-rooms on the corner of Court and Central Avenue. It is similar in purpose and organization to the Allemania. Among its principal dramatic members are Chas. Mayer, Lew. Wyler, Lewis Strasser, Ben. Strauss (the late excellent comedian of the Allemania), Justis Thorner, Misses Freiberg, Holstein and Thorntr, and Mrs. Kahn. The photographed group of the male members, now on exhibition at Clarke's, shows a body of gentlemen of whom any club might well be proud. How in the world they forced such a modest fellow as Eg. Johnson into that front rank is, however, one of those things that no fellow can find out."

"*The Eureka Club.*—Is another prominent Hebrew organization, meeting on the corner of Ninth and Walnut. They give occasional entertainments, both musical and dramatic. Prominent members are Mr. and Mrs. Victor Abraham."

JEWS IN EARLY GERMAN-AMERICAN LITERATURE

The life of the Jewish immigrant from Germany of the last century has invariably been depicted through the symbolic figure of the Jewish peddler, who with his pack on his back betokened the department store of the future. "It was this type which inspired so many American 'Jew stories' and the stage character of the vaudeville houses."[1] In a similar vein many historians have been concerned only with the material success achieved by these immigrants. They have not realized that unless an explanation of that success were attempted in proper historical terms, the result would be a caricature which would leave unclarified the role German Jews have played in American history. Errors and omissions of this sort are directly responsible for the great contrast between the level of the historical study of German immigrant life in America and that of its Jewish aspect. This is all the more regrettable since the Jewish records are extremely rich and the periodical literature of German Jewry in America has been preserved far more completely than the corresponding non-Jewish material.

The Jews not only followed in the footsteps of the Germans in making their economic adjustment, but by virtue of their participation in German cultural life and their knowledge of the language they were able to assume their Old World functions in and around the German settlements in a new world of opportunities never dreamed of. Apart from this cultural "pack on the back" there was an even more important item, namely, the conception which the German had brought with him

[1] Wittke, Carl, *We Who Built America* (New York 1939) p. 329.

Reprinted from *Jewish Social Studies,* Volume IV, 1942

of the Jew who shared his fortunes on both continents. It was in this conception that the "Jew story" had its origin. Sometimes it is merely a literary manifestation, a story like any other, in which the life of the times is portrayed. At others true events are described for the purpose of instructing and edifying the reader. Occasionally the object is purely literary; in a mild spirit a writer might dispense praise and blame among his people citing the classic example of the children of Israel or admonishing them against following the examples of Jews. In certain instances the purpose was simply to caricature; the amusement evoked by the caricature of the particular faults attributed to the Jews would serve as an effective warning of its evil effects.

At a later stage of German-American literary development, when the revolutionists who had been exiled from Germany (1830-48) began to publish magazines, many features which had served to entertain German readers in their homeland were automatically retained, including the humorous "Jew-stories" in dialect. This type of literature often embodied the satire of *Jewish* writers in the ranks of the German revolutionists whose co-operation was welcomed in the new literary ventures. One receives the definite impression that the editors of these periodicals, desiring to present a familiar picture to their readers and to give them the sort of entertainment which they had enjoyed in the Old World, deemed it advisable to print humorous stories about Jews. These stories may be profitably consulted to explain the economic function of the German Jews as well as their success in the New World.

I

The world for the German of colonial times was colored by his religion. To him the people of Israel were God's living witnesses whom he knew only as they were described in the literature with which he was familiar, namely, the Bible. He more often than not bore a Biblical name, he re-lived the episodes narrated in the scriptures and from them derived his precepts and ideals of human character. His preachers were his "scribes" and the "true Israelite" was one who did not deviate from the paths of evangelical Christianity. This characteristic expression appears frequently in the tales of the immigrants from Salzburg. "Master

Kiefer (a good Israelite in whom there is no guile)"[2] is cited as an example of loyalty, but when the evangelical immigrants go astray they are described as victims of that contrary spirit which made of the children of Israel an impatient and stiffnecked people.[3] At a later epoch business prosperity is compared to the manna which fell from heaven and fed the children of Israel in the wilderness.[4]

Nevertheless, it is not merely the Jew as a literary symbol who is portrayed in the literature. The children of Israel in the flesh wander through its pages on American soil together with the Germans of colonial times. We find here the first appearance of true literature with the human factor as the important element aside from any other purpose. Encounters with Jews are described and stories recounted in order to depict their character concretely. This type of German-American literature usually ends with the description of Jewish behavior and the moral to be drawn therefrom. The Salzburg literature records these encounters with Jews during the eighteenth century in great detail. The tales of travels which were printed under the name of Samuel Urlsperger were in effect the combined diaries of various preachers and thus embody the testimony of many different persons.

> A Jew who obtained land here lodged the Saltzburgers and gave them a fine rice soup for breakfast.
>
> March 21: The Jew, of whom we have spoken before, presented himself and he and his wife showed no little kindness to the Saltzburgers; he has great honesty and sincerity which are qualities rare to find in others of his race, or for that matter in many Christians, as the following example shows: By mistake and because of the darkness the Jewish woman accepted a whole crown instead of half a crown from a Saltzburger woman who gave her the coin thinking that was all it was worth. The next day when the Jew saw the money and learned that the woman had not known that it was a crown, he came running to the tent of the Saltzburgers and asked for the woman who had received too little change and he paid her the other half crown, exclaiming that God forbid that he should keep that which did not belong to

[2] Urlsperger, Samuel, *Amerikanisches Ackerwerk Gottes* (Augsburg 1767) IV. *Stück*, p. 242.

[3] *idem*, *Ausführliche Nachricht von den Saltzburgischen Emigranten* (Halle 1744) p. 11. Sealsfield, Charles, *Das Kajütenbuch oder nationale Charakteristiken*, in his *Gesammelte Werke* (Stuttgart 1845-47) vol. xii, p. 174.

[4] "St. Louis, Mo. im April 1854," in *Meyers Deutsche Monatshefte*, vol. ii, p. 78; published in New York.

him; it would bring him no luck. His wife had done it unwittingly and without intention, and so forth. This event made a very strong impression on the Saltzburgers. These two Jews bear us great love and have promised to visit us often in our settlement. We hope to preach the Gospel of Jesus Christ to these folk not in vain. (Travel diary of the preachers Boltz and Gronau.)

April 3: The Jew whom we have often mentioned before has shown so much helpfulness and friendliness to us and the Saltzburgers that no one could ask for more. And though we wanted to give him a piece of gold for his trouble, he refused to take it; so the Saltzburgers who are still here decided to plow his land for him and help him clear the trees from his soil, so as to repay him for what he did for them. We have had much interesting discourse with him regarding Judaism and have made clear for him one and the other important point and comment in Holy Writ at which he was somewhat amazed. The brotherly conduct which the Saltzburgers practice and their Christian way of life impressed him and his wife greatly;[5] . . .

It was a strange coincidence which brought these Germans and Jews together again on American soil. Both had been sent to Georgia, the Jews by the London Portuguese Synagogue, whose wards they had been, and the Saltzburgers by the London Protestants, whose protégés they were.

In the absence of a secular literature the German-American press fulfilled a double mission in the colonies by bringing news from home and abroad in the form of simple moralistic stories. The life and fortunes of the Jews throughout the world were considered sufficiently interesting news items. There evidently was someone in the background whose interest it was to gather these items and disseminate them among the German public. We see further how these publications were used to further the economic interests of the Jews in the German settlements of colonial America. The quaint advertisements of Jewish merchants, bankers, land agents, etc., make diverting reading and provide us with data of great social interest.

It is noteworthy that the stories about Jews are singularly free from any reproach of self-seeking. The *Germantowner Zeitung* of September 6, 1785 printed "A remarkable story" describing the gratitude of a Jew who had been rescued at sea and who never forgot the man to whose feet

[5] Urlsperger, *op. cit.*, p. 82, 90, 97.

he had clung as they climbed on a mast after shipwreck. The *Gemeinnützige Philadelphische Korrespondenz* of June 1, 1784 carried a report of the Offenbach floods in which a Jew is portrayed as a hero:

> Finally a Jew dared to row over in a boat and succeeded in bringing back bread, flour, meat, etc., and when the people wanted to give him the promised reward, he refused it and all he would accept was the price he had paid for the food.

It was considered appropriate for a writer to protest against injustice done to the Jew and console him by turning the tables on his adversary:

> From Hesse. . . . A Jew came along with an assortment of fancy goods which he offered to some of the guests who knew him and jested with him. A stranger turned him away with a curt "Begone, rogue!" The Jew retorted, "That I am no rogue all the gentlemen present know, but who the gentleman is, I don't know." The stranger pointed to his decoration; the Jew quickly pulled a box from the bag around his neck and displayed three decorations: *"They are all for sale!"* A shout of laughter went up; the man with the decoration hurriedly got up and left with evident annoyance.[6]

The remarkable thing here is that the words of the Jew are set down in his own dialect without any intent to produce a humorous effect, in sharp contrast with the later "Jew stories," as will be shown below.

The Jew as the bearer of a praiseworthy spirit was a popular figure and was cited as an example for German youth. A juvenile story, "Honesty in Dire Distress," filling three of the eight columns of a juvenile publication describes an honest peasant and a generous Jew living in harmony. It ends with a pleasing picture: "Always at fair-time the grateful Jew visited him and never once did he come without bringing a gift for the peasant and his family at whose home he always spent the night."[7] In one parable concerning wisdom as the greatest good the Jew is depicted as the embodiment of that virtue. Many simple stories of the schoolbook type were written about famous Jewish personalities. "The Ways of Providence" is the title of a story about Rabbi Akiba[8] and in

[6] *Amerikanischer Correspondent für das In- und Ausland* (1825) p. 121, published in Philadelphia.

[7] *Jugend-Zeitung*, published in Pittsburgh by Carl Weitershausen (October 5, 1844).

[8] *l.c.* (June 21, 1845 and August 24, 1844).

the publication entitled *Der Deutschamerikanische Kinderfreund*[9] we find pieces entitled "Moses" and "David." The spirit of these stories is well illustrated by the following instructive tale of the Jewish philosopher of the eighteenth century:

> Moses Mendelssohn was a clerk serving a merchant who was not a very intelligent man. Moses was a very religious and wise man. He was, therefore, held in great esteem and was beloved by the learned men of his time. That he was content with his lot is proved by the following anecdote. One day a friend came to him and found him laboring over a difficult computation. "What a pity, good Moses," said he, "that a man as intelligent as yourself must work for another, and one who is not worthy to serve you a glass of water. Is it not true that you have more sense in your little finger than he in his entire body?" Any other man would have let such praise turn his head, would have left his pen and inkpot there and then and have given his master notice. The wise Mendelssohn, however, merely stuck his pen behind his ear and viewing his friend calmly said, "That is a very good arrangement. Providence has managed matters very well; my master profits by my services and I earn a livelihood. Were I the master and he the clerk, he would be of no use to me."[10]

The authority of Moses Mendelssohn's name was invoked at an early stage in the German-American press of the eighteenth century. The missionaries who saw possibilities in the large number of Jews who read German, based their arguments on personalities and events culled from German-Jewish life. Thus one story spread the false report of Mendelssohn's conversion to Christianity by Lavater:

> Mendelssohn, a man of reflective spirit, examined his opponents' arguments anew and then doubt of his own faith crept into him; he was finally convinced by the force of the truth and his conscience compelled him to take the important step which we reported above. When his co-religionists saw that they were in danger of losing him they conferred together and offered him a large sum of money in order to turn him from his purpose; he replied, however, that he was not a poor man but a rich one and that all their treasures would not suffice to still his conscience. It is hoped and ardently desired by all friends of mankind that his example will have a good

[9] (St. Louis 1861) p. 433-36.
[10] *ibid.*, p. 36.

influence on the lost sheep of Israel by removing the bandages from their eyes so that they may see where their true salvation lies.[11]

The reproach of materialism, implied by the offer of money which the Jews made to Mendelssohn, was clearly interjected by the missionaries for their own purposes although it also served to emphasize the nobility of Mendelssohn's character. Nowhere else do we find a reproach of this kind in the German-American press of that day.

II

The simple humanitarian aim to show the Jew as he really was had to give way as times changed. It was no longer an individual, isolated phenomenon which the writer wished to explain or use as an example, but a distinct social group was involved. During the mass immigration from Germany, which swept the Jews along in its wake, there was a general discussion regarding the motives operating within this group and particularly the causes which led them to emigrate. The early German-American press had devoted its attention to the reasons which had motivated the Germans to leave their homes and this inquiry led them to ask likewise what had prompted the Jew to come to these shores. The political literature, daily press and magazine articles all mirrored the burning questions of that time: economic stress, the reproach of evasion of military service, inequalities, the difficulty of founding a family in the homeland. In the course of the bitter polemics the newspapers all but ignored the purely human aspect. It was left to inventive fantasy to banish within the confines of a short story the human element bound up with the German-Jewish emigration. An excellent illustration of the manner in which the German did justice to the humane instincts of the Jew is given in the tale entitled "The Noble Robber."[12] The story begins by describing how a duke while on his homeward journey from London was attacked by a band of six robbers who took his wallet but strangely enough left him £500 of the £2,500 which it contained.

The duke had long forgotten the story and was in London again some two years later, when one day he received the following letter: "My lord:

[11] *Gemeinnützige Philadelphische Korrespondenz* (August 20, 1781).
[12] *Jugend-Zeitung* (December 2, 1844).

I am a German Jew. The prince whose subject I am drew the blood from our veins and used it to bait deer whose blood he then gave his dogs to lap up. I escaped to Great Britain with five other Jews in order to save my life. On the way across I became very sick and the boat which was to carry us from the ship to land capsized in the storm. A man I had never set eyes on sprang into the ocean and saved my life at the risk of his own. He brought me to his house, let me rest there, nursed me and called a doctor. He was a wool worker with twelve living children. I recovered and he refused to take payment from me, asking only that I visit him occasionally. Some time later I came to his house and found him grievously unhappy. Trouble had broken out in America; he had sent goods worth £8,000 to Boston and the merchants there refused to pay him. He told me that he had a draft falling due in four weeks, that he was unable to meet this draft and that he would be ruined unless he paid it. I would willingly have helped him but I was not in a position to do so. I reflected that I owed him my life and I decided to sacrifice it for him. I gathered together the five Jews who had come with me from Germany, all of whom loved me as I loved them. We waited on the street which we knew you, my lord, had to pass; the rest you will remember. I took from your wallet two thousand pounds and in your purse there were one hundred and ten pounds. I wrote a letter under an assumed name, sent the man the two thousand and fifty pounds which he needed and I told him that I would ask him for it again as soon as I thought he had it. By that act I saved the man's life; but the Americans did not pay later either and he died a week ago penniless. However, fortune smiled on me that selfsame day and I won four thousand pounds in the state lottery, and I am sending you, my lord, with this letter what I robbed you of plus the interest. You will find one thousand extra pounds. I beg you to send this sum to the F . . . family in S . . . . Also have the kindness to inquire about a poor Jew whom they once tended. With the remainder of the money I am returning to Germany together with my fellow Jews and we will try again to see whether they will permit us to live there in peace. I swear to you by the God of my fathers that none of our pistols was loaded when we attacked you, my lord, and that our cutlasses were rusty in their sheaths. Save yourself the trouble of looking for us. When this letter reaches you we shall already have been on the high seas several days. May the God of my fathers watch over you!"

The duke made inquiries about the wool worker's family and also about the Jew. Everything the letter said was true. The duke sent the family all the money the Jew had enclosed in his letter and he also helped them be-

> sides. "I would give a hundred pounds," the duke used to say, "to him who will show me the Jewish rascal's face and a thousand pounds to him who brings that Jewish rascal himself to me."

Through all the divergent opinions of the many writers who treated the subject runs one general conclusion: the Jews left their German homeland because they were not permitted to live in accordance with the dictates of their conscience whereas abroad, despite all the hardships and hindrances, they were able to safeguard their ethical spirit and bring it to fruition. The recurrent theme of German-American poetry, "We shall return if the reformed fatherland will allow its estranged sons to live a decent human life," has its counterpart in the decision of the noble-minded robber to try Germany once again and see whether it will allow him to live there as a Jew.

The incorporation of the large masses of German immigrants into the economic life of America, particularly in the Middle West, coincided with the industrial development of the entire country. Functions of greater or lesser importance were assumed by various immigrant groups who remained associated with such activities for many years. Long before the Jew had become America's tailor, when the great clothing industry of today was still unborn, the German mind identified the Jew with the dealer in clothing both old and new. The vast possibilities of this field were scarcely envisaged by any of the German-American business men of that day and even as late as the nineteenth century the economic activity of the Jews was regarded as of an inferior order:

> I purchased something from a jeweler and optician who was a Jew and a merry fellow. In reply to my question whether he did good business in America, he said, "Well, I say as do the rest, you can make two Jews out of one American and there will still be a Christian left." It is truly remarkable that the Jews who in Europe can always dig up business are intimidated by the American business man's acumen and a great many of them become peddlers and clothing dealers.[13]

This concentration of the Jews in the clothing business provided German-American writers with material for stories, and since groups rather than individuals were now in view these stories were not free from

[13] Löher, Franz, "Am Niagara," in *Meyers Deutsche Monatshefte* (1855) 458.

remnants of transplanted antisemitic prejudice, to which was added the opposition on the part of the tailoring gilds. Much of this literature was written to supply a demand on the part of readers since already in the mid-nineteenth century there existed about 150 German newspapers and periodicals in America. The following, culled from "Travels and Experiences of a German Immigrant," gives us a picture of the city of Cincinnati, Queen of the West, destined to become a great German-Jewish center. We see the beginnings of the Jewish clothing trade already standing out in the local scene:

> They sauntered slowly along the wharf or the so-called "steamer landing" and passed one of the numerous clothing stores. A young lad, his hair marvelously curled and wearing very shiny boots, popped up from the cavernous depths of a cellar, stepped close to the four men, looked at them searchingly, and then suddenly grasping Schmidt around the middle, pulled him into the entrance, all the while pouring out a volley of English of which Schmidt understood not a word. "Let me be!" he cried at last angrily, "or else tell us in a language that we can understand what it is you want."
>
> The young man, however, refused to utter a single word of German although it was plain that he understood it. When he saw that his English availed him nothing, he invited our four travelers in a very good German dialect, although mixed with Yiddish, to come and inspect his wares. "We are in need of nothing," said Schmidt, who was embarrassed at being clasped by a stranger, "our clothes are still good."
>
> "Still good?" echoed the young Israelite mockingly, "still good? Then I would like to see what you would call *bad;* and in *such* a coat you dare walk about the streets of Cincinnati? And you allow respectable people to see you in *such* trousers? And you dare wear a hat like *that* on your head? If I had a garden I would willingly exchange your suit for a brand new one, on my honor I would, it would make a fine scarecrow to frighten away the birds—upon my word of honor."
>
> "Say, now," Schmidt interrupted, starting to get angry, "that is none of your business. I don't want to get vulgar but in our country we have a special word for such things."
>
> "Don't get angry, kind sir!" cried the youth. "Your clothes would look all right on someone else, but such a fine figure of a man like yourself should not wear such rags. Look now," he interrupted Schmidt who was fast becoming furious, "I will sell you this suit for—." "Thanks," said Schmidt

and made an effort to free himself from the merchant's grasp, "I do not need anything." However, it was easier said than done. The young Jew held fast and let flow a stream of compliments over poor Schmidt, telling him how foolish he was to disfigure his fine limbs in such unshapely garments, until poor Schmidt, rendered helpless, asked the price of a pair of trousers just to get rid of his tormentor. He was saved by the brewer who had become thoroughly annoyed by the proceedings. With his big fist he punched the skinny little Jew so hard that he cried out aloud.[14]

At a still later period when the pioneer achievement of the German Jews in the sale and manufacture of clothing had been acknowledged by all, the German reading public still clamored for humorous treatment of this great forward stride. To please readers stories were written such as "Bowery and Fifth Avenue, or Jacob and Joseph. A romantic tale without any antisemitic prejudice—on the contrary" by Carl Hauser.

> When one compares the America of even two hundred years ago with today, how the Indians ran around half-naked, while today even the poorest is clad in the latest fashion, one cannot help but give credit for this service to mankind to that race, whose only aim in devoting itself to the clothing business was to fulfill one of the most important and far-reaching cultural missions. We cannot, therefore, blame the missionaries in this field when they call attention to their ready-to-wear clothing in blaring advertisements and disfigure all street corners, rock walls, cemeteries, etc., with their accurate and hence not always very decorative likenesses.
>
> . . . Jacob Abrahams may well proudly call himself "the American tailor" for he more than any others of his gild was active in spreading the *Kleider-Cultur* and it was seldom that one of the barbarians was allowed to pass his store in the Bowery without either Abraham or one of his missionaries pulling him almost by force in order to make of him a bearer of culture.[15]

In all cases where the author's name or the lexicon of German-American anonymous writers, which is unfortunately far from complete, seems

[14] *Der Erzähler am Ohio* (1849-50) 280; published in Cincinnati. One of the characters in this story remarks, "We have passed 33 houses thus far and there were 15 clothing stores." To balance the picture it should be noted that in the middle of the nineteenth century the local German population monopolized the amusement trade, consisting of 800 cafes and beer saloons, 450 card-playing rooms, 30 billiard parlors and 30 bowling alleys; see *Amerika wie es ist* (Hamburg 1854) p. 20.

[15] See *Puck Kalender* (1883) 89-96; published in New York. This Jewish tailor advertised himself as "Ther ohnly Abrahams" and "Ther troo Jacob."

to indicate a Jewish writer, the literary product is considered here for its informational value. If anything the Jewish writers were even more sensitive to the readers' needs and were conscious of the material they could contribute. The majority of the Jewish journalists, who ranked as emigré revolutionists, had spent their youth in small German towns and utilized their familiarity with the lives of rich Jews who lived there. We find numerous references to Jews in the period when the German-American press and periodicals were in the process of adapting their contents to the masses which the great wave of immigration had brought to these shores. There was an abundance of reading matter with Jewish themes taken directly from European literature as well as original short stories. Beside Spindler's "Der Jude" we find "The Count and the Jewess. . . . A Tale of the 16th Century"[16] and "Der Silberne David. Eine Ghettogeschichte."[17] These banalities, however, seldom contained any social criticism of the Jew. Occasionally one finds stories such as the novel, "Eleanor oder Sklavenfang in der Quäkerstadt," by George Lippard[18] where the slave trader is a Jew and the highlight of the story is the appearance of the Jew at the slave market. In stories such as "Der Jude. Eine Erzählung. (Für die Monatshefte)"[19] an idealized portrait is given of the Jew as the standardbearer of humanity.

III

The earliest literature in America aiming social criticism at the Jew originated with groups representing the European masses whose custom it had been to read stories in which the Jew was criticized for one thing or another. Running through these writings like a red streak is the reproach contained in the older German antisemitic literature and caricatures, namely, that the sole aim of Jewish education was to teach the young to count money and keep accounts because that was all they would need to succeed in life.[20] "Education for Practical Life, or How to Become a Money-making Gentleman" is the story of a Jew who is unhappy

[16] *Deutsche Monatshefte* (1856) 161.

[17] *l.c.,* (1854) 421.

[18] *Die Lokomotive* (1853-54) 250; published in Philadelphia.

[19] *Deutsche Monatshefte,* vol. v (1855) 257.

[20] See the caricature, "Israelchen hat einen Dukaten verschluckt," (about 1820) in Fuchs, Eduard, *Der Jude in der Karikatur* (Munich 1921) p. 104.

because his son is unable to learn arithmetic and has strange attacks of human sympathy which must surely hinder him from becoming a wealthy merchant like his father. Everything is done to cure the boy and a cartoon of "Father and Son at the Phrenologist" shows us the efforts of the frantic father to liberate his son from these handicaps. The story ends in a Philadelphia clothing store where the son is being outfitted in the latest fashion. The happy ending reads: "Jack Will, the aforementioned genius of the fine art, as German as his taste, made a perfect gentleman out of the dirty little urchin."[21]

In time this transplanted social criticism crystallized into opinions and attitudes which the German reader readily accepted as representing life among the German-American population and as reflecting the typical role which Jews played within that group. Previously the economic function with which the Jews were commonly associated, viz., the clothing trade, which in fact formed but a small part of their activities, was used as a literary subject, sometimes in the form of pure satire for the sake of local color. Now, however, a conscious effort was made to describe the place the Jews occupied in American and particularly in German-American life. The Jew is always treated as a phenomenon of literary interest rather than as a concrete factor and is not discussed in a political vein. This makes the conception which Germans had of Jews all the more interesting since it was so utterly out of harmony with the broad humanitarian ideas current in America at that time.

The primary reproach levelled at the Jews was their materialistic view of life, wealth being their criterion, which prevented them from appreciating true spiritual values. They were believed to be dominated solely by a desire for gain which left no room for reflection and precluded any form of higher life. They esteemed people with money and celebrities from whom they hoped to derive profit rather than men of real worth. The Jew was criticized not only for embodying such attitudes but for propagating them among others. In short, we have here a whole collection of reproaches which, although incorporated in descriptions of American situations, might have been lifted bodily from the pages of German antisemitic literature. There can be no mistake as to the meaning of such expressions as "ubi business, ibi Jerusalem" and "Misadel-

[21] *Die Lokomotive* (1853-54) 230.

phia."[22] This criticism reaches its greatest force, however, when the literary figure of Shylock is made to represent the materialistic philosophy of life with which Americans in general were taxed. Thus we find the following "literary report" of a masked ball held in New York in 1867:

> Art follows bread— Shylock (represented by Mr. Truchsess) who walked between two sacks; one sack bore the inscription "Broadway" and the other "Bowery." Having arrived in the center of the hall, he picked up the Bowery sack from under which there emerged a scrubby little fellow with sidewhiskers and a bashed-in hat; Shylock sharpened his knife, cut out of the Bowery fellow's coat the section under which the heart usually beats, and withdrew a bag of gold which he laid on one of the scales; he then pulled off the Broadway sack and a natty little fellow with a lorgnette appeared.
>
> He performs the same operation on him and throwing the bag of gold on the other scale finds that it weighs less than the other. He then takes the little Bowery chap on his arm and gives the other a kick. Whence comes this Shylock scene?[23]

The answer to this question may readily be supplied by a student of social history. It was the notion of the Jew's character in vogue among the Germans which inspired this literary fantasy. Such a conception of the goal of the Jews in the New World led writers to put a special construction on the immigration to America. The social historian will find a twofold interest in the combination of both types of antisemitic literature: the charge of Mammon worship directed at the Jews in Germany, living in a vanishing and helpless Europe, as well as at those in the New World with its rising sun of wealth and prosperity.

My friend Isidore

He was born in Germany somewhere near Diedenhofen, where his good father is a merchant who sadly recalls the days when there were as yet no Prussian spiked helmets there. And it was the "terrible" respect which both father and son had for those spiked helmets and the state which they represent, that was the cause of their separation and prevented the youth, rapidly approaching military age, from exercising his distinct talent in all that concerned calves, wool and other fine points of the paternal business.

[22] Rittig, Johann, *Federzeichnungen aus dem amerikanischen Stadtleben* (New York 1889) p. 237; *Deutsche Monatshefte* (1854) 182.

[23] *Neue New Yorker Musikzeitung* (1867) 555.

> After they had sought in vain for some physical defect to enable Isidore to ask for classification in the reserve, and the military doctor had turned a deaf ear to the most delicate hints regarding the close relationship between the general debility of the youth and the moneybags of the old man, it became clear that flight was the only means of salvation. With his father's blessing Isidore safely crossed the French border and when he boarded the ship at Le Havre, which was to take him and his fortunes to New York, all at home knew that he had emigrated secretly and against his father's will.

To this there is added a slight correction to the effect that "he carried his inheritance in the lining of his vest in the form of a good draft on a New York house." The further adventures of our hero manifest the familiar characteristics: already on board ship he began to trade in small wares which he smuggled into New York; he studied English diligently and dreamed of becoming a millionaire.[24]

It is interesting to note that the author was repeating a contention current in the German press, namely, that German Jews, particularly from Alsace, emigrated in order to evade military service and that they therefore sailed from Le Havre rather than from a German port. A careful study of the literature of Swiss emigration, which followed the same direction as the movement from southern Germany, shows that this French harbor was chosen by immigrants from all German parts simply in order to avoid the rough Channel crossing. The reproach of evasion of military service and lack of patriotism was added chiefly in order to underscore the materialistic view of life attributed to the Jews.

The rise of the German Jews to affluence and the accompanying desire to wield social power furnished the theme for a good deal of satirical writing. For example, "I Invite a Celebrity! A satirical piece in three prologues, one act and an epilogue" by E. Knotser; "Place—An American City in the West." The names of the hosts, Mr. and Mrs. Samuel Lemberger and Miss Sarah Lemberger, and those of the other guests provide an unmistakable clue to the setting. The host declares that his house is always open to guests, "and do not Abeles and Deutsch, Singer and Steiner and the ladies of the Russian Immigrant Aid Society, of

[24] Stürenberg, C., *Klein Deutschland. Bilder aus dem New Yorker Alltagsleben* (New York 1886) p. 110-17.

which you are the president, come?" These names explain his urge to invite a "celebrity" for once and contain the tacit admission that these bearers of German-Jewish names are not "fine society." The second scene gives us the usual comments on the invitation through the mouths of Mrs. Silbermann and Mrs. Cohn. The climax of the play is the sumptuous dinner graced by the celebrity and the indispensable report in the newspapers, all this spiced with caricature.[25] Since parties given by German Jews, about which we have abundant archive records at least in one case,[26] were generally marked by excellent taste and their wide circle of guests, satire had to be directed against those who had not yet attained a social position.

What strikes us most in the references to Jews encountered in the remaining German-American literature is the prominence of the element of amusement. There was a large mass of readers to be entertained and both the lighter magazines and the corresponding sections of the more serious papers had to include sufficient humorous material. The Jew, therefore, was an indispensable figure in the comic papers to which this public had been accustomed in Germany. This material often contained important social observations and even in purely antisemitic criticism there was always a humorous rather than a propagandistic point. This is quite apparent in a satire on the Jew as a journalist in a series of caricatures entitled "The Physiognomy of the Reporter, 'Dr.' Schoofle, and Its Transformations during the Winter Season." Had this appeared in contemporary Germany it would have to be viewed as antisemitic propaganda rather than satire:

Sieh, Leser, hier das Angesicht,	See, gentle reader, here the face
Das Dir gewiss zum Herzen spricht,	Which is surely one to your taste,
Und denk dabei, wies Jeder tut,	And remember as all do,
"Der Anfang Jud, ist alles Jud."[27]	"Once a Jew always a Jew."

The flood of Jewish anecdotes printed in the comic papers of Germany flowed through the columns of the German-American press as well. Again and again one meets echoes of stories read long ago, which alternately stress the Jew's cunning and tickle the reader by showing how the Jew is often

[25] *Puck Kalender* (1883) 34-40.
[26] In the Cohen archive of the Maryland Historical Society.
[27] *Schnedderedeng* (1873) no. 25; published in New York.

foiled by his own shrewdness. "The Lost Wallet" tells about a Jew who took the wallet but left its owner, a young artisan, lying;[28] another anecdote is about the Jew who cheats a peasant and gets a beating but when he complains, he not only obtains no redress but is forced to pay the court costs.[29] Under the title, "The Charitable Samaritan," we find the hoary story of the Jew who in the false guise of a benefactor gives a man some forged ducats.[30]

If most of this satire were not intended to satisfy the public's taste for amusement, it would have to be taken as representing the actual commercial practices of the Jews. Such an assumption, however, would hardly be plausible for we know that the Jews operated within the economic sphere of the German-Americans. In this connection we find the following effusion:

> The humbug of the so-called linen Jews has often made one laugh when reading the newspaper articles during the Leipzig Fair. One has come into a great inheritance and as a result of this lucky stroke wishes to sell his goods for a song. Another has decided to go to America and so will sell at a sacrifice. In Berlin one of them really goes too far. This Schmul claims that he is an Hungarian count who is forced to trade in linens because he incurred the enmity of the Windischgrätz and had to flee.[31]

What is of particular interest in this article is that it was written at a time when Ohio was first settled by Jews and when the German papers were full of advertisements inserted by gentiles who desired to sell their merchandise before emigrating. Despite that fact it is the Jews who are singled out as resorting to such tricks to sell their goods, very likely inspired by envy of the success achieved by them in Cincinnati. The same periodical, it may be noted, carried reports regarding the local clothing trade.[32]

It was not only anecdotes concerning Jews which were reproduced from the German comic papers. The political field, too, came in for its share of attention. Under the title, "Schulze and Müller at the Weissbier Club," one reads: "We hail the press order which appeared on June 29,

[28] *Die Lokomotive* (1853-54) 112.
[29] *Der Erzähler am Ohio* (1849-50) 432.
[30] *l.c.* 316.
[31] *l.c.* 559.
[32] *l.c.*, 280.

ordering suppression of insolent writers, bums, Jews, Frenchmen, Poles and emissaries."[33] The popular comic characters also voiced their observations on America and the influence of the Jews. Thus the century-old classic figures of Prussian officers, Sprudelwitz and Prudelwitz, state in a two-page long correspondence: . . . "Real 18-carat republic without any Semitic alloy. . . . Is it true, as I hear, that Socialists have also been imported? Am thinking of crossing them with blacks. Red and black make brown. . . ."[34]

The creators of German-American representatives of German wit were in some instances Jews, as the following notice in familiar style shows:

> Notice of birth. Le Kladderadatsch is dead! Long live the Bumsvallera! Since Providence saw fit to cut down my first-born, Kladderadatsch, in the bloom of his youth, my dear wife, "sweet Temper," née Humor, presented me today with a new healthy boy who was christened Bumsvallera. The editor of Bumsvallera, Max Cohnheim. (Price of the weekly number, 6 cents).[35]

The introduction of Jewish dialect in the comic section of the German-American press represented a real concession to the public since there were comparatively few humorous writers in that language. The fact, however, that so many newspapers and periodicals featured this brand of humor proves that the public had been used to it in Germany and insisted on getting it again in the new country. The pseudonyms of the German-Jewish humorists have been identified only in part; it has been found that several pseudonyms were used by a writer for his humorous writings, while another was signed to his other brain-children. In his *Deutsch-Amerikanische Schriftsteller und Kunstlerpseudonyme* H. A. Rattermann indicates that "Hersch Mennubel" was the pen-name used by Carl Hauser for some of his humorous stories, while others were signed "Federmann Jeremias,"[36] "Pinneberg," "Schnacke" and "Shoddy." Other pseudonyms used by German-Jewish humorists, such as "Dobbljew Zizzesbeisser," "Carlchen Miessnick," "Schatzmatz," "Eisick" and "Hugo am Damm" (Hugo Naphtali?) cannot be assigned with any certainty.

[33] *l.c.*, 713 ff.
[34] *Puck Kalender* (1882).
[35] *Amerika, wie es ist*, p. 53.
[36] *Deutsch-amerikanisches Magazin* (1887) p. 144 ff.; published in Cincinnati.

Although not pertaining directly to Jews, a piece such as "The Jewish Moorish Prince, a Parody on Freiliggrath," was considered worthwhile by its author.[37] Other stories were also written by "Dobblejew Zizzesbeisser," which although containing no allusion to events of the Jewish year 5639 (1879) contained considerable folklore in addition to old and new jokes. "Der Tog vun *Esther*—un dorum *esst er*" appeared in the same form in a *Purimspiel.* The same author also commented on an antisemitic occurrence in Saratoga: "The situation has often recurred in which our people have been thrown out of Paradise—in Saratoga as well as Manhattan Beach—but Hilton and Corbin did not have any cause—."[38] Minor events were often reported in this vein. We find the account of a fancy dress ball of the Choral Society, which took place in Philadelphia, under the heading, "A letter found: Dear Itzig! . . . it came to my mind among so many of your people . . . I am only a Jew—but righteous God! the Choral Society is not particularly Christian either."[39] Thus the writer mimicked the Jewish imitation of polite society; this mimicry was brought to even greater perfection in the later European satire. "Schatzmatz" reported a harmless political discussion as follows: "Reb Itzeg and Reb Meyer on the Turkish question . . . England and France are the musicians and play the dance-music, and the Turk *nebbich* must dance to their tune."[40] The large number of German-Jewish contributions to this literature, which contains considerable autobiographical material,[41] would well merit more detailed examination in order to sift important data on the period from what is mere fantasy. In this connection a study of the vocabulary would yield a no mean by-product.

Of even greater importance and having more far-reaching effect were the references to Jews which appeared in polemical and propaganda papers published in Germany, which reappeared in America in the form of humorous "Jew stories." The vilification and caricatures of Jews in

[37] Hugo am Damm in *Puck Kalender* (1883) 113-16.

[38] *Puck Kalender* (1880).

[39] *Die Lokomotive* (1854) 168.

[40] *l.c.,* (1853) 96: "Reb Itzeg und Reb Meyer über die türkische frage . . . England un Frankreich send die Klesmurem und spielen den Tanz, un der Terrek muss nebbich tanzen, wie sei spielen."

[41] Cf. the autobiographical note by "Hersch Menubbel" in *Puck Kalender* (1881).

military service are directly traceable to the satirical treatment of the report of the death of a Jewish soldier on the battlefield in 1848: "Schmul stood up and said . . . Well, one of our people also went, not that he did so willingly, no, no, he had been raised to be a merchant—he feared the musket like fire—he wanted to become an officer—he was shot dead and buried." This effusion followed by the parody of a funeral oration is signed "Eisick."[42]

Our survey would be incomplete if we did not include one of those rare instances in which a German sincerely tried to give an honest account of his experiences with Jews. There is nothing more touching than the nostalgic memories of the son of a schoolmaster of the Black Forest who found again in an East Side synagogue the beloved figures of his childhood:[43]

Among The Crooked Noses

Since Max Nordau pushed his good Jewish vulture's nose into the Promethean body of young German poetry, I had dreamed in my feverish nights of the Eternal Jew, who in my childhood memories walked side by side with the Christ child to bring joy into the land of the Germans. For I am too good a Christian for the evil which the aforementioned peddler disseminates in his books to make of me an antisemite. On the contrary, it moves my soul to charity and love and awakens loving memories of the strangers who live among us.

A village in the Schwarzwald would have preferred to give up its minister or its schoolmaster rather than the regular visit of the Jewish peddler whose inexhaustible boxes were filled not with conventional truths and "paradoxes" but with silk ribbons, gold rings, and pipes decorated with silver as well as Christian calendars. Among the peasants of the Schwarzwald the Jew was not yet playing the role of Shylock, rather was he their intermediary with the outside world and their heads and state officials; he was a comedian who was all the more beloved because he never minded a joke at his own expense and above all he was the children's friend. Schmul, whom I remember so well, was a true Santa Claus for me; it was he who gave me my first knife! and he praised me for my knowledge of the Bible when I asked him whether that was the knife with which Abraham wanted

[42] *Die Lokomotive* (1853) 58.

[43] Published anonymously in New York in *Der arme Teufel* (1893) 324 ff.

to sacrifice Isaac. My mother, of course, thought the world of him and even my father, who seldom departed from his schoolmasterly reserve, did not think it below his dignity to bring out a bottle of the better Markgräfler for him. He was the "Eternal Jew" who did not spread dismay but love and one could easily understand that he was a near relative of the Christ child. Bishop Johann Peter Hebel, who would view present-day anti-semites as a Korah band, has immortalized the wit of these village Jews. Rosegger in particular has with great love and understanding unearthed a mine of gold in the minds and hearts of these wanderers.

I became conscious of the poetry of Judaism for the first time, however, when I celebrated their Feast of Tabernacles with them. How much truer is this poetry which grew out of the history of this wandering folk than the poetry of our Christmas celebration, which was forced on us Germans and is nought but an oriental fairy tale which we have vainly tried to graft on the magic of our forests with their pale winter sun! I know of nothing nobler than the celebration in the booths, even amongst the poorest Jewish family. What had come over this Schmul, who laden like an ass jogged along the road and like an ass patiently accepted beatings and privations, now became a patriarch and enjoyed every bounty like Job in his happy days; and the sorriest female becomes a Sulamith with a shining countenance. Lights and faces shine, there are autumn flowers and fruits and in the grape arbor juicy grapes hang overhead. Today I am a guest of the chosen people, but not merely "tolerated" as is the Jew when he sits in a corner of the hearth in the house of the peasant. No, I sit in the seat of honor and I drink wine out of the goblet of the prophet Elijah. Aye, it's pleasant to bide among the crooked noses, and when the oldest among them intones an ancient song about the lost homeland which rises to a song of triumph in its longing and pain, I realize that our Lord is also a Jew and cannot be pictured otherwise than with a Semitic nose.

Thus lost in the contemplation of time and space, he finds in an orthodox "Schul" in New York the memories of his childhood years and the experiences of his adult life:

I felt reverence among those crooked noses. They were very ordinary Jews, dirty, bargainers, but they were Jews who had lived all their lives long in the ghetto which can be found even in the modern American city, and their child-like prayers put the stamp of dedication on their poverty. I have never experienced such a feeling of prayer in the Reform temples, where the crooked noses are carried so high. In those temples faith has turned to pretence and in the same way as old Jehovah is attacked with modern opera music and humanitarian phrases and "educational lectures" are substituted for a discarded faith. There sit the haughty wives of the great bankrupts, the Heavenbridges, Fechbergers, Lichtensterns and whatever their names may be, their riches impressing a stamp of vulgarity on the service. No, I would a thousand times rather have the true orthodox crooked noses; and when the *Hepp, Hepp* of the antisemites becomes too much for me, I will ask one of the old men in the Jewish Schul to sing me the song of the lost glories, or I will take refuge in my childhood memories of the Feast of the Tabernacles.

GERMAN-JEWISH NAMES IN AMERICA

German-Jewish Names as a Category

The appearance of a group of distinct German-Jewish names in clearly recognizable economic occupations or whole branches of the economic system indicates the penetration of German-Jewish immigrants into the economy of the New World. This holds for the displacement of Yankee peddlers by the German Jews about 1835 and of individual tailoring by mass clothing manufacture which was entered upon by pioneering German-Jewish wholesale houses throughout the country. In other commercial fields in which Jews concentrated in the course of time, such as dry goods, tobacco, export and import trade, and auctioneering, the listings show a similar trend. Conversely, typical German-Jewish names are missing in such fields as beer brewing in which Germans, but not German Jews, predominate.

The recognition of a distinct group of German-Jewish names was an insight of American wit, humor, and popular literature, foreshadowing the later results of scientific nomenclature research. American folklore accepted on faith the fact confirmed by this research that German-Jewish names give the geographical origin of their bearers. Among Germans personal names or paternal occupations transformed into family names predominate, while among German-Jewish immigrants names of geographical origin are characteristic.[1] It is a bitter irony of history that these names, rather than bespeak their bearers' ties to German soil, actually came to characterize a whole emigrant group in a new land. Moreover, they were the mark, not of the Germans, but of German-Jewish emigrants whose number, to be sure, surpassed their proportion to the German population in general and exceeded by far their proportion to the population of South Germany.

In American folk humor one name-group in particular which retained the essence of the German landscape—the group of -heim(er)s and -stein(er)s—came to represent German-Jewish names in their pure form. The unknown humorist who wrote, "Where the -heimers are, the -steiners will follow," expressed a prescientific appreciation of an objective historical fact. Just before the beginning of the German-Jewish mass emigration of the early nineteenth century, the process of assigning family names to the Jews had ceased throughout Germany. As a result

[1] Kessler, Gerhard, *Die Familiennamen der Juden in Deutschland* (Leipzig 1935), p. 30.

Reprinted from *Jewish Social Studies,* Volume XXIII, 1961

of this process the German Jew was differentiated by the geographical element of his family name. The -heimer and -steiner endings referred to Jews almost without exception, while the use of these endings among the Germans in America was negligible.

The -heimers and -steiners first attained importance with the mass immigration of German Jews from southern and western Germany in the early nineteenth century. Few examples of these name-endings are to be found in the German immigration to Pennsylvania in colonial times, and they almost never were attached to the geographical place names characteristic of German-Jewish names. Among the names of 30,000 immigrants on passenger lists of 1727-1776, names ending in -heimer and -steiner play practically no role. On most of these lists there is not even one name belonging to these groups.[2] In the roster of German names included by the first census of 1790 in the enumeration of Pennsylvania family heads not one name of both these groups occurs in a number of sections designated by letters (*e.g.*, A, C, I, K, N), although thousands of names are listed. The name Oppenheimer, which was widespread among German Jews even before the official assignment of names at the beginning of the nineteenth century, is also missing. The number of -heimer and -steiner names included in the first census is negligible.[3]

The number of -heimers and -steiners is insignificant among the many thousands of German immigrants to Pennsylvania from 1791 to 1808. There is not one instance of these name-endings among immigrants in the years 1790, 1793, 1795, 1796, 1800, 1801, 1805, 1807, 1808. In 1802 one arrived, in 1803 three, in 1804 there were seven out of 900 arrivals, among whom we accept an Elias Salomon Pappenheimer as a Jew.[4] It is especially noteworthy that in those cases—a fraction of the total—in which the passenger lists indicate the place of birth, there predominate localities ending in -heim. However, the passengers do not bear these place names. Thus in one list of 1806, among 43 places of birth given, 9 end in -heim and -stein, but there is not one person with either of these name-endings.[5]

Official German name-research failed to recognize the significance of this phenomenon. Under heim and stein Heinze[6] lists only a small frac-

[2] Rupp, Daniel, *Chronologisch geordnete Liste von mehr als* 30,000 *Namen von Einwanderern in Pennsylvania . . . von* 1727-1776 (Philadelphia 1876).

[3] *First Census of the United States* 1790 (Washington 1901).

[4] Egle, William Henry, *Names of foreigners who took the oath of allegiance to the province and state of Pennsylvania* 1727-1775 . . . With the foreign arrivals 1786-1808 (Harrisburg 1892), pp. 536-627.

[5] *Ibid.*, pp. 655-57; the following places of origin are recorded: Freinzheim, Pfaffenschwabenheim, Mühlheim, Witgenstein. (Jewish family names did not originate from these place names).

[6] Heinze-Cascorbi, *Die deutschen familiennamen,* etc. 7th edition, edited by Paul Cascorbi (Berlin 1933), p. 75.

tion of the names which German Jews brought to America in the form of -heim(er) and -stein(er). Kessler designates as "Jewish place names" from the old German territory of west, south-middle and northwest Germany a total of 119 names ending in -heimer and -steiner—again only a fraction of the whole.[7]

We must also consider the fact that as early as in colonial times both German Jews and Germans came to Philadelphia, the greatest immigration center of that century, and contributed to the few -heimers and -steiners of the period. For even Ottenheimer, Eckstein and Epstein could have been Jews at a time when these name elements were still inconsiderable and devoid of social reference.

In general, however, German Jews who came to America in the colonial period had name-types which they shared with the Germans—predominantly personal names transformed into family names. Thus, in the first census we find the Joseph group with 24 heads of families, the Aaron group with 101, the Salomon group with 172, the Tobias group with 123, the Moses group with 492 and the Abraham group with 253. These names are among the most common for Jewish communities. While Germans still bore these names at this time, we conclude on the evidence of internal Jewish sources that these names belonged to a substantial number of Jews. In Charleston, which had the largest Jewish community in North America at the time, the Abraham group included 10 families from 1800 to 1810, the Moses group 23 families from 1800 to 1818, the Joseph group 11 families over the same period, the Salomon group 18 families from 1800 to 1819, the Tobias group 3 families from 1800 to 1811.[8] These families constitute a considerable percentage of the bearers of these names in America before 1820.

In the Pennsylvania lists of the eighteenth century there appear a number of names which later are often found to be the names of Jews. In some individual cases, such as the following, this can actually be shown: Ancker, Beerends, Bachrach, Bamberger, Donat, Gerson, Gottschalk, Heineman, Heller, Herzog, Hirsch, Hirschfeld, Infeld, Israel, Joel, Jonas, Kann, Kaufman, Lazarus, Leib, Mintz, Pappenheimer, Riess, Rosenthal, Schein, Seligman, Strauss and Weil. While already in the eighteenth century these names of German Jews who ventured to America identified their bearers as such, they nevertheless still remained also names of Germans who emigrated at the same time.

At least one name reminds us of the historical occasion when German soldiers, "the Hessians," arrived on American soil during the Revolu-

[7] Kessler, *op. cit.*, pp. 34-36.

[8] Glanz, Rudolf, "Jews in the U.S. in the Colonial Epoch," *The Jewish Review* (New York), vol. iv, no. 1 (April-June 1946), 40 (in Yiddish).

tionary War. As the following reference has it: "Joseph Darmstadt was, as his name imports, a Hessian and came to this country as a sutler . . . established himself in Richmond . . . "[9]

Names of German-Jewish Pioneers in America

The most important facts concerning the assignment by German authorities of names to German Jews before their mass emigration may be summarized as follows: 1. Jewish family names used prior to government action referred for the most part to local origin. Dietz found this to be true among 65.5 per cent of the family names of Frankfurt Jews in 1802.[10] 2. When names were officially assigned, authorities practically everywhere preferred a geographical name—a place or a country. Hence the preponderance of these names.[11] In Baden alone 20 per cent of all names ended in -heimer, not including names ending in -steiner.[12] 3. Among names of geographical origin, places and territories in German provinces were used which lay outside the places or territories of actual residence. Thus of the geographical names of the Jews of Baden only 32 per cent are from Baden itself; the rest were taken from other German territories, mainly southern and western Germany, or even from abroad.[13] 4. The artificial formation of names after the pattern of place-names, although the places did not exist, increased the number of -heimer and -steiner endings.[14] 5. In the exceptional case of the kingdom of Westphalia, Jews were forbidden, by the law of 1808, to choose names after places located within the territory. Instead, they used outstanding geographical features such as mountains, valleys, and forests near their homes. In this manner they increased the number of -heimer and -steiner endings. In other cases, the -heim was tacked on to a place name so as to modify it: Soest, *e.g.*, became Sostheim, Bevern became Beverstein.[15]

It was not until the Civil War that the German-Jewish immigration, side by side with the German immigration, had spread over the whole of America and especially the newly settled West. Thus it became possible to compare lists of names of the two immigrant groups.

For the German-Jewish list we use the 1860 roster of German-Jew-

[9] Ezekiel, Herbert T. and Lichtenstein, Gaston, *The History of the Jews in Richmond from* 1769 *to* 1917 (Richmond 1917), p. 26.

[10] Dietz, Alexander, *Stammbuch der Frankfurter Juden* (Frankfurt a.M., 1907), p. 7.

[11] Occasionally adoption of names in foreign territory was denied.

[12] Dreifus, Erwin Manuel, *Die Familiennamen der Juden unter besonderer Berücksichtigung der Verhältnisse in Baden* . . . (Frankfurt a.M., 1927), p. 98.

[13] *Ibid.*, p. 97.

[14] *Ibid.*, p. 52.

[15] Samuel, Gustav, "Die Namensgebung der westfälischen Landjudenschaft von 1808," *Zeitschrift für die Geschichte der Juden in Deutschland*, n. s., vol. vi, no. 1 (1936), 47-51, p. 49.

ish California pioneers who were members of the Jewish welfare organization Eureka. This list is to be preferred to the membership lists of the German-Jewish synagogues of the period; for such synagogues, even when they were characterized as Bavarian, had an admixture of members who were not German-Jewish. The Eureka society was clearly German-Jewish both by the circumstances of its origin and by its sphere of activity. It arose as a counterpart to the First Hebrew Benevolent Society which had been founded earlier in San Francisco and which embraced all non-German Jewish elements. Its purpose, as well as its actual practice, was to help German Jews only, a policy which created a crisis when aid was denied a Polish Jew who had sustained losses due to a fire.[16] Eureka also had an auxiliary, the "German Hebrew Ladies Benevolent Society," whose avowed purpose was likewise to aid only German Jews.[17]

San Francisco in 1860, moreover, offers an ideal ground for comparing German-Jewish and German names. Of a population estimated at about 50,000, approximately 20,000, including the German Jews, were of German-speaking ancestry. The Jews numbered about 5,000. Their participation in organizations and undertakings of the German-speaking cultural circle was extensive enough to make possible the comparison of names along various lines. In addition, the *City Directory* of 1860 lists all important business relationships from different aspects as well as local organizations of all kinds with the names of their officers. This list of pioneers in the Far West is much richer in its cultural-historical implications than similar lists in the interior or on the Atlantic coast.

The 393 names on the Eureka list[18] include the following German scenic-geographic name-endings: -land, -wasser, -burg(er), -ach(er), -hof, -dorf, -wald, -stadt(er), -baum, -feld(er), -au(er), -thal, -bach, -stein(er), -heim(er), and finally, -berg(er) and -ing(er). Such endings are represented by a total of 78 names on our list. In addition, there are 12 individual place and city names and 15 names of territories.

These figures indicate the dominant position of scenic-geographical endings among German-Jewish names in America. From this point on, it is easy to grasp the difference between German-Jewish and German names in America.

Thus, the -heim(er) group with 14 representatives is the largest in our list and comprises almost 18 per cent of the 78 names that have scenic-geographic endings. The -stein(er) group is next with 8 names, about 10 per cent. This includes the independent name Stein, which oc-

[16] Benjamin, J. J. II., *Drei Jahre in Amerika*, 1858-1862 (Hanover 1862), vol. i, p. 225.
[17] Langley, Henry G., *The San Francisco Directory for . . . 1860 . . .* (San Francisco 1860), p. 442; Benjamin, *op. cit.*
[18] *Ibid.*, pp. 243-46.

curs once. By contrast, German names in America in 1860 include only a vanishing proportion of -heimer and -steiner endings.

Another major difference between German-Jewish and German names is the small number of -ing(er) endings in our list, three in all. It is these that occur most frequently among family names taken by Germans from localities; in Baden, for example, the ing(er)s and the berg(er)s constitute two-thirds of the family names derived from localities.[19] Our list has 13 -berg(er)s and) -ing(er)s, a total of about 20 per cent.

German names ending in -burg are especially frequent because of the importance of the old German families who lived in or near the seats of nobility—the old towns. In our list there are five burg(er)s, including Regensburger which, according to Kessler, never occurs among Jews.[20] Nonetheless, it appears three times or about 4 per cent. The stadt(er)s, generally more frequent among German-Jewish names than the burg(er)s, occur four times.

For the rest, the -feld(er) endings occur seven times; -thaler and -baum, each six times; -wasser and the sole river name, Rhine, twice; -ach(er), twice; -land, -hof, -dorf and -wald, once each; -au(er), twice and -bach, likewise, twice.

Better-known cities, Worms, Triest, Eger, among others, occur 12 times or about 11 per cent of the combined total of all geographic names. Names of territories or states, Frank, Böhm, Sachs, Hess, Unger, Schweitzer, Engländer, Elsasser appear 15 times or about 14 per cent.

Viewed historically, the cultural significance of names that refer to great cities and states is slight. Even the name "Hessian" made no impression on American popular literature, wit, and humor. While America preserved "Hessian fly" as a designation, the family name *Hess* remained as colorless as all other names of great cities or states. In general, the man from the great city with his great name was not so close to the pioneering spirit of America as the men from small communities with their unknown names places on the German map. The German-Jewish provincial, transplanted to the New World, saw his role as the builder of giant cities out of small settlements, particularly in the West.

> Once we moved about in slow, deliberate, proper and pedantic Germany . . . Quite suddenly we were transplanted into the vortex of youthfully ardent, unbridled, rushing American life . . .
>
> We grasp the nature of this revolution and quickly make use of it in our

[19] Heintze, A., *Die deutschen Familiennamen* (Halle 1914), quoted by Dreifuss, *op. cit.*, p. 98.

[20] Kessler, *op. cit.*, p. 33.

business pursuits, because the satisfaction of physical needs and the longing for possession drives us on . . .

Many of us were born and raised in villages or small towns . . . And now we live mostly in great cities, where palaces rise from the earth in four weeks, one invention displaces another, each day the whole history of a small German town unrolls and he who moves slowly is run down.[21]

To what extent the German-Jewish province was transplanted may be seen wherever emigration data are available. Thus, 329 emigrants left Jebenhausen and Göppingen from 1830 to 1870. The 317 who went to America included 39 Einsteins, 38 Rosenheims, 23 Ottenheimers, 12 Bernheimers, 9 Fellheimers, 9 Lauchheimers, 1 Mannheimer, 1 Adelsheim, 9 Löbsteins, 9 Erlangers,[22] 9 Dettelbachers, 5 Dörzbachers, 6 Massenbachers, 12 Rohrbachers, 6 Rosenfelds, 2 Rosenthals, 6 Hesses, 52 Arnolds, 7 Kohns or Kuhns, 10 Levis.[23]

One notes that even the venerable, priestly names of Kohn and Levi —retained at great sacrifice by German Jews in the face of forced name changes—are submerged in a flood of -heim(er), -stein(er) and -bacher endings.

In the New World, the name *German Jew* acquired a new significance: " . . . prosperity increases from day to day; those who were beggars when they arrived are rich men after 6 to 10 years, and the name *German Jew* has here become a name of honor, a sign of uprightness and honesty."[24]

The concept of a distinctive German-Jewish name extends also to Jewish social life. The names of German-Jewish societies form a special category both for the images they evoke of the homeland and for the tradition of activities which they represent: " 'San Francisco Israelite Women's Society.'—Under this name there was constituted the German Israelite society of women and young women. . . . The society is German and its chief aim is to assist those who speak the German tongue."[25] There is certainly a difference between a "Hebrew Ladies Benevolent Society" and an organization that could name itself the "Israelitischer Frauenverein."

If we now compare the San Francisco list of German-Jewish pioneers with the names of Germans in the same city, we find all the characteristic differences. The 1860 *City Directory* contains 4 Muellers, 8 Webers and 25 Schmidts,[26] together with a large group of German given

[21] *Die Deborah* (Cincinnati 1855-56), vol. i, no. 2 (August 31, 1855), "Zeitfragen."

[22] Tänzer, Aron, *Die Geschichte der Juden in Jebenhausen und Göppingen* (Leipzig 1927), p. 89.

[23] *Ibid.*, p. 89.

[24] *Wiener Jahrbuch für Israeliten* (Wien 1846), vol. v, p. 52.

[25] *Die Deborah*, vol. i, no. 2, p. 40.

[26] Langley, Henry G., *San Francisco Directory for* . . . 1860, pp. 233, 316, 276.

names that had become family names. There is nothing that corresponds to this in our list of pioneers.

The situation becomes even more clear when we compare occupational lists. The brewers are overwhelmingly German. Of the 24 names in this list, not one is of geographic origin.[27] On the other hand, there are 5 such among the 25 names in the wholesale clothing group and 20 names of scenic and geographic origin among the 108 in the retail clothing list[28]—or about the proportion in which they occur in our list of pioneers. These facts regarding names prove the full penetration of German Jews into the San Francisco clothing business.

In the cigar trade, the directory lists 6 names of geographic origin among the 25 importers and 9 among the 89 retailers.[29] In dry goods, 6 out of 43 importers and jobbers and 8 out of 77 retailers bear names of this type.[30] Thus in both of these lines there is significant penetration by German Jews; but it is only a little more than one half of that found in the clothing business. Scenic-geographic names make up 20 per cent of our list of German-Jewish pioneers. If we assume that the same proportion holds for the rosters of individual occupations, we obtain the following figures: wholesale and retail clothing business, 125 German Jews out of a total of 133; cigar importers, jobbers, manufacturers and retailers, 75 out of a total of 114; dry goods importers, jobbers and retailers, 70 out of a total of 120.

A few words should be added regarding the priestly names Cohen and Levi and their variations. The San Francisco *City Directory* lists 40 Cohens, 65 Cohns, 10 Kohns, 3 Kahns, 16 Levis, 39 Levys, 3 Levins, 1 Levinger and 6 Levinsons.[31] Obviously, we cannot assume that all of these designate German Jews. In Germany itself Cohen and Levi belong to the basic stock of Jewish names; but in America they are not specifically German-Jewish, since they occur also among Sephardi and east European Jews.

The Eureka Society roster includes 2 Cahns, 4 Cohns, 1 Kahn and 9 Levys.[32] Thus a significant proportion of German Jews bore the priestly names despite the efforts of the German state authorities, on the occasion of the assignment of names to Jews, to eliminate particularly the Hebrew names. Moreover, it is likely that the 143 priestly names in the directory included many employees of large German-Jewish firms and others who were unable to pay the not inconsiderable membership dues of the Eureka Society.

27 *Ibid.*, p. 348.
28 *Ibid.*, p. 351.
29 *Ibid.*, p. 350.
30 *Ibid.*, p. 353.
31 *Ibid.*, pp. 96, 190, 180, 198.

Under the circumstances, the names Cohen and Levi by themselves could not serve as a cultural characteristic of German Jews in America. For this reason these names play practically no role in American popular literature and anecdotes, although in Europe they play a major part. In American wit and humor, the German scenic name-ending must first be added to obtain a full representative of the German-Jewish type in popular literature—Kohnstamm, Cohnheim, Cohnstein, along with Leviheimer and Levinstein.[33]

German-Jewish Pioneer Names as American Place Names

Along the frontier a constant search for appropriate new settlement names was under way. Worthy local pioneers, German Jews among them, were often honored by the use of their names as names of localities. Thus in many instances German-Jewish scenic and geographic names came to designate settlements on the new continent.

This process began quite early. Indeed, even before the Civil War the point had been reached where place names had lost their association with their roots, and the American public had to be reminded of them:

> 'Local names.' . . . there is a small number which express the country or original place of residence of the assumer . . . Germaine [sic] . . . Holland . . . Poland . . . [34]

In the search for names on the frontier moral and aesthetic considerations played an important role. The following report from the Oregon Territory in 1848 is eloquent testimony:

> 'What's in a Name?' . . . There is more incongruity and positive ugliness in the names of places, perhaps, than in any other species of names, which is intolerable and unbearable . . . We know of but few handsomely and appropriately named town-sites in the Territory . . . [35]

Where the complaint was aimed chiefly at the preference for Indian words in the naming of places, the sound of a German scenic or local name could scarcely be objectionable. Moreover, the mark of honor fell to men of reputation who stood in a special personal relationship to the places named after them.

We begin our list with Ehrenberg, Arizona, founded in 1854. This town was named after Hermann Ehrenberg, the German-Jewish mining

[32] Benjamin, *op. cit.*, pp. 244-45.

[33] *Puck*, vols. i-xxxvi, offers the richest collection of all these names. Those of special significance for stereotypes of wit are: Hosenstein, Geldstein, Grabbenstein, Burnstein and Failinstein.

[34] *Life illustrated* (New York), 1855-56, vol. i, n.s., "Something about surnames," 201.

[35] *Oregon Free Press* (Portland 1848), vol. i, no. 16, 2.

engineer who, after fighting in Texas, settled in Arizona.[36] Such places as Heidenheimer, Oppenheim,[37] Bamberg,[38] Gratz,[39] express direct geographical connections, while Heinemann, Heller, Seligman,[40] Goodman, Jacoby,[41] are only a few of the names of German-Jewish pioneers of modest rank that were so perpetuated; likewise, Schleisingerville,[42] Heppner,[43] Goldstein,[44] and Rheinstein[45] carry over into our times.

Among widely known German-Jewish figures, the name Börne was transferred from the old homeland to Texas.[46] August Belmont (who was still referred to by his enemies as August Schönberg[47]) gave his name to localities in Missouri and New Hampshire.[48] The name of Isidor Busch is perpetuated in Busch and Buschberg.[49] The record, however, is held by Adolph Heinrich Joseph Sutro after whom there were named forests, heights, and a mountain peak in California,[50] as well as a village in Nevada.

In most cases these names establish the fact that a German-Jewish merchant-pioneer was one of the first settlers in a locality and usually opened the first general store. This recalls a special function of such stores. For example, Jacoby Creek is named after the proprietor of a brick store in Union, California, in which the inhabitants gathered when attacked by Indians.[51] We also know of other German-Jewish merchants in California whose brick-stores served a similar purpose since they were the most secure buildings in the locality.

Aaronsburg, Pennsylvania, occupies a special position in respect to its name.[52] It is named after Aaron Levy who founded it on the basis of advance planning and acquired all the land needed for the purpose.

American state or regional directories and older local histories

36 University of Arizona, *General Bulletin,* no. 2, p. 141.

37 Och, Joseph, *Der deutsch-amerikanische Farmer* . . . (Columbus, Ohio, 1913), p. 230.

38 Gannett, Henry, *American Names* (Washington, D.C., 1947), p. 35.

39 *Ibid.*, p. 142.

40 Och, *op. cit.*, p. 230.

41 Gannett, *op. cit.*, pp. 139, 167.

42 Settled in 1845, and named in honor of B. Schleisinger Weil, the name was shortened in 1921 to *Slinger.* Hunt, John Warren, *Wisconsin Gazetteer* . . . . (Madison 1853), 202; Wisconsin. *A Guide to the Badger State* (New York 1941), p. 329.

43 McArthur, Louis A., *Oregon Geographic Names* (Portland, Oregon, 1952), p. 297.

44 Gudde, Erwin G. *California Place Names* (Berkeley 1949), p. 130, "Goldstein Peak."

45 *Ibid.*, p. 283, "Mount Reinstein."

46 Och, *op. cit.*, p. 230; Gannett, *op. cit.*, p. 50.

47 Glanz, Rudolf, *Jews in Relation to the Cultural Milieu of the Germans in America up to the Eighteen-Eighties* (New York 1947), p. 53.

48 Gannett, *op. cit.*, p. 50.

49 Och, *op. cit.*, p. 230.

50 Gudde, *op. cit.*, p. 348, "Sutro Forests, Sutro Heights, Mount Sutro," Gannett, *op. cit.*, p. 294.

51 Gudde, *op. cit.*, p. 164.

52 Settled October 4, 1786, this was the first town in America named after a Jew. Rosenbach, Isabella H. and Abraham S., "Levy Aaron," ***Publications of the American Jewish Historical Society,*** vol. ii, pp. 157-63.

contain many other references to German-Jewish pioneers for whom scenic points, parts of a city, streets and buildings were named.[53]

German-Jewish Names in the German-American Cultural Milieu

While the German-Jewish name group is readily identifiable in general lists, such as American business directories, this is not true in equal measure of the German name group. In the first place, German family names, formed largely from personal names, were shared with many other immigrant groups. Secondly, German craft names were easily and early anglicized—Müller became Miller, Schmidt became Smith, Schuster became Shoemaker—and in these forms were common to other immigrant groups, too, as well as to Anglo-Saxon stock. On the other hand, even when a personal name became a family name among the Jews, its Jewish cultural character was retained, as in the Abraham group. The same can be said for craft names like Goldschmidt, which occurred so frequently as to become a symbol of the German-Jewish craftsman.

Since German names are not generally identifiable, it is not possible to sort out and compare German and German-Jewish names in a general American list. But this can easily be done where there are lists confined to these two groups, and fortunately such lists do exist.

Owing to a cultural symbiosis of Germans and German Jews, which developed in America throughout the entire period of their common adjustment to the New World, the German-Jewish immigrants joined German cultural circles. They are, therefore, to be found in all German societies, statewide, regional or local, and in all cultural, athletic, choral, and literary societies, as well as in organizations based on common ties with the past, such as pioneer societies and even organizations of veterans of the Franco-Prussian war. The membership lists of these organizations provide all that we need in order to contrast the German-Jewish name groups and the German names.

The membership list of the German Pioneer Society of Cincinnati is ideal for our purpose. By its very formation, the Society gave expression to important aspects of the historical and cultural development in America of Germans and German Jews alike. Cincinnati, the wholesale center of the West and the seat of the great Jewish clothing industry for the entire Southwest, saw the emergence of the first Jewish community in the West. At the same time, it was the undisputed cultural center of the Germans who early constituted a considerable proportion of the popula-

[53] Popperton, a fashionable suburb of Salt Lake City, was named after Charles Popper, and developed from the Popperton Plot of 140 acres. Fohlin, E.V., *Salt Lake City, Past and Present* . . . (Salt Lake City 1908), p. 147.

tion: "In the year 1840 the number of Germans in a total population of 45,000 already equalled 14,000. In addition to Catholics, Protestants and Methodists, the German Israelites also were increasing."[54]

Raised in the cultural customs of the old homeland and still imbued with its spiritual ideas, the German Jews took a very active part in German cultural institutions. The German Pioneer Society, at the time of its founding, had 500 German and German Jewish members. Membership was restricted to those who had resided in Cincinnati or its vicinity for 25 years and were over the age of 40.[55] Even the first printed membership list of the society in 1869 contained a sufficient number of German-Jewish names to form a distinct group.[56] Salomon Oppenheimer, born in Hamburg, Bavaria, is the only *heimer* on the list and Isaak Lichtenstein, also born in Bavaria, the only *stein*. But there are also representatives of many family names deriving from family symbols—a type which becomes increasingly important among members admitted later—such as Adler, Wolf, Strauss, and Rothschild. In this connection, we note that the same family-symbol names are strongly represented in our San Francisco German-Jewish pioneer list. There we find five Adlers, four Wolfs and eight Strausses.[57]

The bearers of these names and of others that appear on later lists can be clearly identified as German Jews. For the lists show the place and date of birth and the date of arrival in the United States, and the obituary notices in the Society's paper regularly indicate the Jewish descent of the deceased.

In the lists of new members one finds an abundance of German-Jewish names derived from places of origin and geographic-scenic names: Rosenberg, Eppinger,[58] Frenkel,[59] Heinsheimer,[60] Weiler,[61] Bamberger,[62] Wolfstein,[63] Hamburger,[64] Seinsheimer,[65] Ronsheim,[66] Löwenstein,[67] Goldberg, Rosenthal and many others. Along with them, there are the most important family names formed from personal names, such as Moses, and additional family-symbol names, like Schiff, Stern, and Hecht. None

54 *Der deutsche Pionier* (Cincinnati, August 1869), 168.
55 *Ibid.*, p. 160.
56 *Ibid.*, p. 385 ff.
57 Benjamin, *op. cit.*, p. 245.
58 *Der deutsche Pionier*, pp. 385 ff.
59 *Ibid.*, 192.
60 *Ibid.*, vol. v, 1873, 328.
61 *Ibid.*, 1873, 328.
62 *Ibid.*, vol. vii, 40.
63 *Ibid.*, vol. viii, 128.
64 *Ibid.*, 168.
65 *Ibid.*, 516.
66 *Ibid.*, vol. ix, 48.
67 *Ibid.*, vol. viii, 352.

of these German-Jewish names find bearers among the Germans on the same lists. However, they do meet their counterparts, however, in our San Francisco list of German-Jewish pioneers where, for example, we have two Sterns and two Weils.[68] Further, the Cincinnati list includes German-Jewish occupational names—Wechsler, Glaser and Golschmidt —which do not occur among the German members. In the San Francisco German-Jewish pioneer list, Glazier occurs once and Goldsmith eight times.[69] We find the common and incontestably German-Jewish name Marx on the Cincinnati as well as on the San Francisco list.[70]

Conclusive inferences may be drawn from the appearance of names on two clearly defined lists, the one solely German-Jewish, the other German with the inclusion of German Jews: 1. German-Jewish immigrants everywhere brought with them distinctive names in no way paralleled by the German immigrants. These names form a clearly recognizable group wherever German-Jewish immigrants arrived in sufficient numbers. 2. In the "old immigration," these names remained for the most part unchanged, except for minor adjustments like Goldsmith for Goldschmidt. From the very beginning, these names signify the arrival of a new group under circumstances which especially single out their names and put them into circulation. This is the case in particular with the names of merchants. From the standpoint of American public psychology, such names become "good" or "bad" depending on what their bearers contribute to the whole. From the standpoint of the bearer himself, the German-Jewish name carries with it both a pride in the distinctive name and a general pride in possessing a "good name" among the American public. This pride in "the good name of German Jews in America" marks the whole group of German-Jewish name bearers.

3. Individual and group consciousness of names becomes possible only when there is a frequency that permits an association to grow up between these names and certain typical images. Such is the case in our Cincinnati list; the names accumulate as new members are admitted from year to year. The jest, "where the -heimers are, there the *-steiners* will follow," literally comes true in the membership rolls of the Cincinnati German Pioneer Society.

The membership lists of the German Veterans Organization in America, 1870-1871, provides a control case. Among the members alive in 1896, we find J. B. Stern, L. Herzheimer, Max Rothschild, and Wil-

68 Benjamin, *op. cit.*, pp. 245-46.

69 *Ibid.*, p. 244.

70 *Der deutsche Pionier,* vol. i, p. 192; Benjamin, *op. cit.*, p. 245.

helm Stern.[71] The total membership is much smaller, but the German-Jewish names come to the fore just as distinctly.

The picture remains unchanged even when we examine the large German cultural and philanthropic organizations in America. A good example is the German Society of Pennsylvania in the year 1876, when its membership numbered approximately 2,700.[72] Members with scenic-geographic names include: Bacharach, Bamberger, Guggenheimer, Löwenthal, Newberger, Reitzenstein, Rosenheim, Rosenstein, Rosenthal, Sinzheimer, Weyl and Thalheimer. Among the names derived from family-symbols are Stern, Adler and Rothschild; Fleischer and Goldsmith represent occupational names; and Cohn and Levy, among others, perpetuate the Hebraic stock of names.[73]

The Success of the German-Jewish Name

The success-story of the German Jews begins from the earliest period with one of their names.

In the shadow of the titans, of the "House," under Rothschild's vine and fig tree, lived his brothers-in-name—all the Rothschilds who form one of the most important name groups among German Jews in America. Their success-story began already with the fact that they bore the fortunate name. Many names in America carried weight and many who bore them failed to live up to the expectations associated with them; but the name of Rothschild held fast in American cultural history.

At the start, we find Rothschilds as resident merchants all over the continent. In its full glory, we find the name appearing 33 times on a select New York society list. It follows Kohn (Cohn) and Levy (Levi) in numerical importance, but far outnumbers all other names—even the 24 Oppenheimers and 13 Einsteins.[74] In Germany itself, Rothschild was still in twelfth place among Jewish names from 1914 to 1918.[75]

In the last analysis, however, the great battles of names are won not by the generals with great names but by the noncommissioned officers who train the multitudes. In the end, the glory reflected by the Rothschild name on the bearers of other German-Jewish names was dimmed

[71] *Erinnerungsschrift des Deutschen Veteranen Bundes,* 1870-1871 *zum* 1. *Stiftungsfeste in der New York Turn-Halle, . . . am. . . .* 19. *März* 1896.

[72] Seidensticker, Oswald, *Geschichte der Deutschen Gesellschaft von Pennsylvania* (Philadelphia 1876).

[73] *Ibid.,* "Namens-Verzeichnis der Mitglieder der Deutschen Gesellschaft, mit Angabe des Jahres ihrer Aufnahme."

[74] *The New York Hebrew Select Directory and Visiting List* (New York 1896-7), p. 155.

[75] "Die 60 häufigsten jüdischen Familiennamen," Meyer-Erlach, Georg, *Jüdische Familienforschung,* vol. viii, December 1932, pp. 501-3.

by the American democratic process—by the rise of innumerable individuals bearing modest names recalling the homeland. It was all these names together that put their stamp on the German-Jewish immigrant and produced a unified image, the image of success. The conviction was created that the German-Jewish name would not disappoint. It is significant that of all population groups in America, the German Jews alone received no nickname. Their names could be used directly for the psychological types created in popular literature, anecdotes, and humor. Hence it was unnecessary to devise a general type through resort to a nickname; to do so in this instance could only have meant restricting the literary possibilities. German-Jewish names were "good" for literary purposes.

"Statements of good standing" for names are very difficult to obtain whether in the world of business or of literature. Experience taught that names could deceive. Even the Puritan predilection for biblical names encountered doubt in America:

> I never knew a man named Job that possessed an uncommon share of patience, though I could point to many a Job that possesses all his troubles. Show me a man named David that is distinguished among the sons of music, or the daughters of song; or show me a modern Solomon that has wisdom . . . Show me a modern Judas without treachery, and I will yield the point at once. I never knew a person named Moses or Aaron, or Abel, that was not meek and very devotional.[76]

Despite the scepticism, it was acknowledged that some names are bad per se and should be avoided: ". . . give a dog a bad name is to ruin him. Do you suppose that names are of no importance? Name your next son then Caligula or Judas . . . "[77]

The German-Jewish names of the mass immigration—occurring with such frequency as to necessarily impress themselves upon memory—achieved their "good standing" through the life work of numerous German-Jewish merchant pioneers who as individuals often remained lost in obscurity. We can trace the stations along their road of life, thanks to the painstaking, detailed work of local and regional historians. Only later, when social success is added to business success, does the full picture of this immigrant generation emerge. Then German-Jewish names appear as an indication of the state of affairs in the country. They express much more than could be conveyed by the names of individual heroes of capital. For they signify the lasting adaptation of the German-Jewish immigrants to an America that in their lifetime was changing before their very eyes.

76 *New England Magazine,* vol. iv (1833), 272-74, "An Essay of Names."
77 *Harpers Bazaar,* vol. iii (1870), 482, "Manners upon the road."

Through these names we can follow the course of economic adjustment to the New World pursued by the sons of small Jewish communities in Europe: their rise from peddler to proprietor of the general store, the transition to the specialty shop, to wholesale trade, regional banking, the department store, and to the beginning of industrialization. We can follow their social success: from immigrant without influence, ignorant of the language of the land, moving only among fellow-immigrants, to the cultivated Jew making claim to social exchange with Gentiles, to the beginnings of the salon and of acculturations in regard to American sports.

Economic rise was rapid. The large number of characteristic German-Jewish names on lists of merchants—general and specialized, national and regional—is proof that by the second decade after their arrival the basic economic adjustment of German Jews was well advanced. Thus, a New York Commercial List of 1853, which includes only the most important merchants, records 13 -heimers and -steiners. There is an abundant selection of other scenic-geographic names as well as a number of family-symbol and occupational names, priestly names and the Germanized Kohnstamm.[78]

The speed of this rise becomes even more clear when measured in relation to the whole American scene. A "Catalogue of the Most Important German Firms in the United States" (1855) reveals the large number of firms that bore characteristic German-Jewish names:

German Firms	City	Firms with German-Jewish Names
24	San Francisco	12
8	Boston	3
2	Buffalo	1
1	Niagara	1
15	Milwaukee	3
2	Highland, Ill	1
4	Belleville, Ill.	1
1	Galena, Ill.	1
35	Detroit	11
15	Chicago	5
35	New Orleans	12
2	Houston	2
2	Cleveland	2
34	Cincinnati	11
2	Louisville	1

78 *New York Commercial List. Containing the Names and Occupations of the principal Merchants in the City* (New York 1853). Compiled by Richards, T. P., Stock Exchange and Bill Broker, No. 1 Hanover Street.

In many western localities the German-Jewish establishment was the only important German firm.

In St. Louis both distillers bore German-Jewish names, as did 2 of 7 dry goods merchants, 3 of 9 novelty dealers, 2 of 3 shoe leather merchants, 2 of 3 hardware dealers, 3 of 4 tobacco dealers and the only wallpaper dealer. We find the same proportions in the lists for communities along the Atlantic coast—especially New York, Philadelphia and Baltimore—and in the South.[79]

The rise is best expressed if we consider the list of merchants of a single western city, St. Joseph, Missouri, in 1860. Among the relatively small number of local merchants, we find Oppenheimer, Westheimer, Eppstein, Weil, Hineburger, Rosenblatt, Sulzbacher, two Schwabachers, Kahn, Lehmann, Schlossman, Levy, and Waterman. In addition to the general German landscape names, two of the Bavarian -bacher place names were transplanted to St. Joseph; from Bavaria only Ansbacher is missing.[80]

In 1859 in New York, we can find the whole gamut of German-Jewish names among the large firms in a single branch of business, excluding retailers. And for this purpose we need not select the Jewish-dominated clothing business. The dry-goods, fancy goods and light furnishings, hats and straw goods provide the following scenic-geographic names: Ahrenfeldt, Althof, Arnstein, Bernheimer, Wolbach, Dinkelspiel, Einstein, Aschenberg, Frankenheimer, Geismar, Halle, Hamburger, Heidenheimer, Hirschfield, Honisberger, Katzenberg, Lithauer, Michelbacker, Neustädter, Ottinger, Goldstein, Oppenheim, Pinner, Pollak, Rosenfield, Rosenblatt, Rosenheim, Schlesinger, Stettheimer, Mehringer, Speyer, Steinberg, Lichtenstadter, Strakheim, Stursberg, Sulzbacher, Thorn, Wachenheim, Warburg, Weinberg and Wetzlar. In addition, there is the usual percentage of German-Jewish family-symbol names, occupational names, and personal names that had become family names.[81]

To be sure, it took a while before the German Jew was ranked among the moneyed men in America and counted as one of the "successful American men of affairs."[82] In time, however, such an enumeration for New York alone, to take one example, contains Ansbacher, Bernstein, Bamberger, Boskowitz, four Bernheimers, two Einsteins and other typical German-Jewish names.

The full glory of these German-Jewish names first becomes appar-

[79] Meyer, Moritz, *Der Handel New York's im Jahre* 1855 (New York 1856), pp. 70-3.

[80] *The Missouri State Gazetteer and Business Directory . . .* (St. Louis 1860), pp. 246-55.

[81] *Ballard' Merchant's and Bankers New York City Reference Guide* (New York 1859) Compiled by Lewis Ballard.

[82] Hall, Henry, ed., *American Successful Men of Affairs* (New York 1895-96), I.

ent in Jewish social life when we compare them with Jewish names that were regarded at the time as not having achieved distinction. For example, the New York Hebrew Select Directory and Visiting List of 1896 records Horwitz only 3 times and Goldberg only 12 times,[83] even though these names were also born by east-European Jews in New York and should therefore have occurred most frequently, outnumbering the 33 Rothschilds. But here it was a matter of social standards, not numbers. In the same list, the -heim(er)s are very strongly represented: 24 Oppenheimers, 6 Oppenheims, 9 Guggenheims, 4 Guggenheimers, 19 Bernheimers, 10 Bernheims, 13 Ickelheimers, 3 Minzesheimers, in all 88. The heim(er)s exceed the 69 Levi(y)s and the 81 Cohen, Cohn, or Kohns; and not all of the bearers of priestly names are German Jews. Among the -stein(er)s, Einstein is best represented.[84] It occurs 13 times, more than any other name of that group. Dinkelspiel appears six times and Hamburger seven.[85]

Einstein is the most common German-Jewish name-symbol in American popular literature and humor. On the serious side, it should be noted that it occurs everywhere, from New York to San Francisco and along the Atlantic from the North to the deep South. The name is "here to stay." Isaac M. Wise wrote in 1862 about Philadelphia, "Einstein is still Parnassus, the indestructible, eternal Parnassus."[86]

That the name Einstein was not content with such a role, however, may be seen from the fact that it furnished a Civil War general.

The German-Jewish Name in American Popular Literature, Wit and Humor

In the richly endowed lists of nicknames used for immigrant groups in America, we look in vain for one that pins down the German-Jewish group as "Sauerkraut" does for the German "Michel."[87]

Thus, in retaliation for the Paddymaking of the Germans on St. Patrick's Day (putting up a puppet dressed as St. Patrick), the Irish, at the beginning of the nineteenth century, would hang a wreath of *Sauerkraut* around the neck of the German patron saint on St. Michael's Day.[88] Such mutual deriding inspired pictorial symbols. The struggle of the Germans against the Irish for the leadership of city administrations was

83 *The New York Hebrew Select Directory and Visiting List* (New York 1896-1897), pp. 65-91.

84 *Ibid.*, p. 50.

85 *Ibid.*, pp. 46, 73.

86 *Die Deborah* (Cincinnati 1864), vol. x, p. 30.

87 *Atlantische Studien. Von Deutschen in Amerika* (Göttingen 1853), vol. vi, pp. 107-19, 183-98; vol. vii, pp. 14, 118, "Spitznamen in Amerika."

88 Kercheval, Samuel, *History of the Valley of Virginia* (Winchester 1844), p. 239.

presented in caricature as the struggle of the beer barrel against the whiskey bottle, with the inscriptions "Lagerbier" and "Irish Whiskey" providing additional flavor. The German Jew was excepted from these pictorial symbols. "Dutchmen" and "Dutch," as invectives, derided certain traits attributed to Germans, such as drunkenness, but these traits were never attributed to German Jews.[89]

In short, no term was applied to the German-Jewish immigrant equivalent to "sheeny" or "kike"—expressions which came into use later at the time of the east-European Jewish mass immigration. The popular reference to the "porkhating" Jew was directed not alone at the German Jew, who indeed was often accused of failing to observe the dietary laws, but at all Jews as a group.

In the absence of a single set of psychological facts that might serve to designate the whole German-Jewish group, the typological evaluation of German-Jewish names in American popular literature and humor assumes great importance. For a similar use of names as types took place with regard to no other immigrant group.

As the city began to dominate intellectual life, even fabled Sam Slick, the Yankee peddler, and the numerous stories about the "Jew-peddler" failed to survive. Humor turned to the world of the merchant. In so doing, it leaned on European humor which was urban and in which the Jew carried a large assignment. Jokes about Jews were imported from Europe and were adapted to American conditions—in particular by Germans who even published their own *Fliegende Blätter* in America. The essential process in the literary consciousness of America, however, was original; it dealt only with changes in American social life and not with Europe.

Types drawn from mercantile life, with which broad acquaintance could be assumed, were found in the world of German-Jewish names. The mirror of humor was held up to the element of undependability in business practices in a series of stories, the hero of which was a *Mr. Schaumburg* ("castle of froth"). Through his person, whatever was not genuine and much exaggerated among asserted qualities of commodities was treated to a brilliant example of the later "art" of advertising; the actual difference between the commodities was only "half a tollar."[90] And the element of mercantile risk as such was well portrayed by *Mr. Hoffenstein* ("stone of hope").[91]

89 "Zur Geschichte der Scheltnamen Dutchman and Dutch," *German-American Annals* (1905), p. 19.

90 Sketches from "Texas Sifting," by Sweet and Knox (New York 1882), p. 11.

91 Abe, Joe C., *The Tales of Rube Hoffenstein* (New York 1882).

Both writers and readers of humor knew very well who were the originals of this swarm of literary -heimers and -steiners, to be used as prototypes for urban life in America, the sons of the large Jewish families from rural Bavaria. Numerous biographies of Jewish merchants who achieved success in America confirm that they came from large families; cases in which the tenth or eleventh son was the first to emigrate are not rare. The larger the families, the smaller seem to have been the places of origin. In most instances, they were small towns with names that sounded too improbable to justify the trouble of searching for them on a map. Nothing was easier than for humor to deck out the figures of its fantasy with these seemingly imaginary place names. (The real places that served as names for German-Jewish immigrants were for the most part tiny Bavarian communities—so small, indeed, that they could be counted as branches of other Jewish communities, themselves quite small.)

The romantic propensity to invent a world of names for the figures of humor found strong support in the -heimer and -steiner designations and the other scenic-geographic names. These designations appealed to the sense of the specific and the sense of place in American humor. Moreover, they directed attention to the special process by which the man from the small European community was so suddenly transported to the bustle of American urban life. What was novel about the German Jew in America was precisely his position as an immigrant; on the other hand, the existing settlement of Sephardim had long been familiar and was only occasionally mirrored in humor, as when in the colonial period its community was designated "the synagogue."

In this context, it is obvious why the simple names Cohen and Levy in European stories about Jews were regarded in America as inadequate. To the extent that they were used at all, they were touched up scenically and became Cohnheim, Kohnstamm, Cohnstein, and Leviheimer, Levinstein, or Löwenstein. In these cases, the humorous name draws on the existing German-Jewish names which are regarded as fantasy names.

The formation of German-Jewish names in American humor varied with the function that the humorous figures were to perform. Thus Isaacstein and Kohnstein merely indicate the appearance of the German Jew, whereas Einstein characteristically is the successful German-Jewish merchant with all his problems of acculturation. Just as this name was most frequently encountered in American life, so it was used most frequently in jokes. The rhyme of the two syllables -ein and -stein was thought to be very funny, while -stein by itself was not.

But the -heimer and -steiner names that enjoy the most currency in folk humor are not the ones that occur most frequently in reality. Oppenheimer, for example, rarely turns up in humor. A special case is

Bernheimer, who becomes the Burnheimer of the insurance joke. On the same model, Bernstein is transformed into Burnstein.

On the other hand, fantasy takes certain -heimer names, which actually occur infrequently, and makes them leading figures of humor. Thus countless jokes are told about Ickelheimer and Minzesheimer; dialogues between the two and alliterations on the sound of their names are legion.

There is almost no reference in popular humor to large cities; we encounter Mannheimer as seldom as Berliner or Hamburger. Instead, small, unknown places are favored; for the improbable becomes more plausible when attributed to the man from the small place. It is for this reason that the name Dinkelspiel enjoys such great popularity in humor—the more so since the real place, Dinkelsbühl, is no longer easily recognized in this garbled form.

At the same time, purely imaginary -heimers and -steiners occur in folk humor, each serving a special function. Geldstein and Diamondstein symbolize cash and its related form, jewels worn for show. Grabbenstein calls to mind the ways and means of moneymaking; and the unfailing Mr. Failinstein signifies what happens when money is lost, when the bankrupt places himself under the protection of the law and reaps the "benefit." The close connection of the -steiners with the role of the Jew in the American clothing industry is represented by Mr. Hosenstein who thus reflects the thoughts of the American when he imagines the German Jew and his world. This "trouser" role of the -steiners did not last long; they were replaced on the stage of life by Mr. Misfitsky, representing the east-European Jewish immigration, by profession an actual tailor and not merely an "old clo's" dealer.

Nevertheless, there are also authentic German-Jewish imaginary names that can stand alone as regards their comic effect and yet unmistakably indicate the presence of the German Jew in America. This is true of the name Morgenthau where it comes into use.[92]

Changes in the Stock Names and Changes of Names

As a result of the emigration of German-Jewish provincials to America in the first decades of the nineteenth century, especially from southern and western Germany, the whole stock of names in the homeland was quickly changed. So many bearers of typical scenic-geographic names emigrated that we can also speak of an emigration of names. Instead, rarely if at all were many of these colorful names to be found in Germany in later years, while in America they lived on in another gen-

92 Names contained in the files of *Puck* and other humorous magazines.

eration. This is explained above all by the fact that the youth emigrated and married in America, and no new bearers of the names were born in Germany. If we examine the names of Jewish soldiers in the German army of 1870-71, we find that the Schildsheims, Heinsheimers, Fechheimers, Löwenheims, Seinsheimers, Wertheimers, Hoffheimers, Heidenheimers, Reinsheims, Mendheims, Kuppenheims, Bodenheimers, and all the other -heimers, who were so plentiful in America, were already dying out in Germany. Among some 3,000 names on this list, there are only 47 -heimers.[93] And of these, the large majority are Oppenheimers.

The Jewish province of southern Germany was emptied of its youth. Only where an occasional community remained untouched by the emigration do we find the old names. Thus Betra in Hesse which numbered 35 families, supplied 4 -heimers as soldiers; all 4 soldiers from another small Hessian locality were -stein(er)s. The total number of -stein(er)s on the list was only 62.

When we consider that at the time of the legal assignment of names in Baden, for example, 20 per cent of the Jewish names ended in -heim-(er),[94] we can see how far things changed during the intervening years. Naturally, the 1870-71 list is dominated by names from middle, north or east Germany, so that the proportion of names like Hamburger—derived from the names of large cities—is considerable. In fact, this list differs little on its face from the list of soldiers of 1914-18, mentioned above. On the other hand, it differs enormously from our pioneer list for San Francisco, enlarged by the Jewish names from the *City Directory* of 1860.

In the New World, the same forces worked in the opposite direction to change the stock of German-Jewish names. South German names increased as the young immigrants married and raised families; but this was offset by the later Jewish immigration from other parts of Germany. The result was a stronger representation of names from large cities and from provinces outside of south Germany. For example, the name Rothschild appears less frequently on the emigration list of Jebenhausen than most of the heim(er)s and is exceeded by Einstein 39 to 10; but on the New York Visiting List of 1896 it outnumbers Oppenheimer 33 to 24 and Einstein 33 to 13.[95] At the same time, since the Rothschilds did not emigrate in such numbers as those with -heim(er) and -stein(er) name endings had earlier, they also came to the fore in Germany. Our list of 1914-18 ranks them twelfth; Löwenstein, in twenty-fourth place, is the

93 *Allgemeine Zeitung des Judentums.* "Gedenkbuch an den deutsch-französischen Krieg für die deutschen Israeliten."

94 Dreyfuss, *op. cit.*, p. 98.

95 *The New York Hebrew Select Directory and Visiting List* (New York 1896-7), pp. 39 ff.

highest ranking -stein(er) ending and Oppenheim, in twenty-seventh place, the highest ranking -heim(er) ending.[96]

We come next to the question of the changes in German-Jewish names made by their bearers in the course of their Americanization. This is best considered against the broad background of changes in name on the part of Germans in general and of American Jews in general.

To begin with, we note that the established German-Jewish names still flourished in New York in 1897—at a time when New York's German Jews had taken what they believed to be their most important step toward Americanization by moving "uptown" and leaving the East Side to the east-European Jews. Name-changing in America often signified entering into family ties with other ethnic groups, a course which German Jews widely avoided. Meanwhile, Germans who had come to America in colonial times had been so completely transformed through intermarriage that extensive research is necessary to establish the original German family names. Thus a study in Louisiana reveals that the original German name Weber already exists in twelve different forms. These reflect the cultural interaction of the language circles of the main population groups.[97]

Such a transformation did not occur with respect to typical German-Jewish names. Above all, the scenic-geographic name endings remained. Very rarely was -heim changed to -ham; it just does not fit the most frequent -heimer, Oppenheimer. Somewhat more frequently -stein was changed to -stine, but more to anglicize a familiar name than to flee from it. Most -stein(er)s, however, retained the ending. A striking example is the wrong prediction of the nineteenth-century humorist who foresaw that by the next generation all Einsteins would be transformed into Eynstones. Hundreds of Einsteins are listed in the telephone books, but the monstrosity that was forecast is entirely absent. Moreover, general and selective lists for present-day America, even before the Hitler emigration, record all the well-known German-Jewish names in proportions that demonstrate the retention of these names by the young generation.[98]

96 *See* note 75.

97 "Zum Kapitel der Namensänderungen," *Deutsch-Amerikanische Geschichtsblätter* (Chicago 1909), vol. ix, p. 154.

98 *See* the Telephone Directory of Manhattan for 1955-56 which lists 72 Einsteins. In the Manhattan Telephone Directory for 1952 the number of listings for the five most popular *-heim, -heimers* names include: 193 Oppenheimers; 121 Oppenheims; 21 Bernheimers; 39 Bernheims; 25 Mannheimers; 31 Manheims; 22 Manheimers; 4 Mannheims; 24 Bodenheimers; 4 Bodenheims. Of pre-World War I lists of the twentieth century, the membership list of the Freundschaft Society in New York contains 45 *heim-heimers* and 24 *stein-steiners* out of a total of 773 names. Die Freundschaft Society of the City of New York. Souvenir of the Twenty-Fifth Anniversary (New York 1904), pp. 110-23. In the New York Telephone Directory for 1914 (Manhattan, Bronx and Brooklyn), the following are listed: 131 Oppenheimers; 60 Oppenheims; 34 Bernheimers; 42 Bernheims; 12 Mannheimers; 6 Mannheims; 27 Manheimers; 11 Manheims; 6 Bodenheimers; 5 Bodenheims; and 27 Einsteins.

Which names of German Jews were changed and how far did these changes go?

First come those of little consequence: Goldschmidt becomes Goldsmith, Blum becomes Bloom. Even the more singular cases do not change the linguistic form very much, and it is mostly the singular cases that are cited in the older literature. There has been a tendency to exaggerate this theme in the German-American Press, which reacted unfavorably to the extensive changes of names among Germans:

> Our Jewish neighbors are especially eager to change their family names into English sounding ones. They not only change the spelling, such as *Krouse, Trounstine, Wyler, Dowman,* etc., but they change them further to make them easy to pronounce in English. *Blum* becomes *Bloom, Goldschmidt* becomes *Goldsmith, Gutherz* becomes *Goodheart, Marmelstein, Marblestone, Süssengut, Seasongood;* or they translate the name into English, like our deceased fellow citizen, founder of the beautiful opera houses in Cincinnati and New York, Mr. S. N. Pike, whose original good German name, which he brought to America as a five-year old from Schwetzingen, near Heidelberg, was Samuel Nathan Hecht. In New York, the German *Hecht* changed into an American *Pike,* although with equally good preparation and provided with an equally tasty sauce the fish would taste the same under the one name as under the other . . .[99]

In addition, legal problems could result from large-scale changing of names by immigrants. In cases of inheritances and other family matters, family ties with the old home had to be proved. The author quoted above gives a particularly amusing example of the unforeseen incidents that could arise from careless changes of names:

> Another interesting case occurred several years ago in Richmond, Indiana. About 1824 a young Israelite, David Feuerstein, emigrated from Fürth, near Nuremberg, to New York, where an uncle of his operated a profitable clothing store in which young Feuerstein found employment. After the young man had become familiar with the new country and new language and had acquired the knowledge necessary for a clothing merchant, his uncle gave him the opportunity to establish himself as an independent merchant in the then young and flourishing town of Richmond in the new state of Indiana. Young Feuerstein moved out there, but left his old name back in New York and took on its English translation, *Flint.* When Feuerstein or Flint, as he was now known, reached middle age, his uncle in New York passed away. At that time in Richmond it happened that a notorious horse thief, who likewise bore the name of Flint, was condemned by the tribunal of "Judge Lynch" and sentence was carried out immediately by means of a hempen noose. From that time on, our good David "Flint" suffered a good deal from the inquisitive "Hoosiers" who came daily to ask him if he were not a brother or at least a relative of the man who had been lynched. He was so annoyed that he decided to change his name

[99] Rattermann, H. A. "Die Entstehung und Entwickelung der deutschen Familiennamen," *Der Deutsche Pionier,* vol. x, 218.

a second time. And as he had learned in the meantime that a German Flinte was an Englin *gun,* he had the painter do over sign with the inscription, "David Gun, Clothier." Once more many years passed and the newly made Gun was as good as completely enfranchised when suddenly something happened which threatened to become very troublesome for him. Another uncle of Feuerstein, alias Flint, alias Gun, died without direct heirs in the East Indies, and David Feuerstein was one of his indirect heirs. The report of the inheritance reached him, but now he was in great distress for he could not legitimize himself. A protracted suit in the court of Wayne County ensued, which cost the good David much, much money, which the snickering attorneys divided. And the facts of the case were slowly developed until he finally succeeded in adducing incontrovertible proof that Gun, alias Flint, was really a German Feuerstein.[100]

Such undesirable contingencies explain the rare cases in which a change of name is advertised in the American-Jewish press—a Freudenthaler, living in faraway Mackinaw, advertises that from now on he will use the name Lewis L. Leopold.[101]

Otherwise, changes for the most part were sought in those names which, at the time of their original distribution, were regarded as derisive or degrading:

> What's His Name?
> Wonder why *Rindskopf,* assistant superintendent of the Metropolitan Life Insurance Company now lets himself be insulted as Reno?[102]

German Jews never developed a flight from names such as a paper like the *New York Sun* thought it could establish in 1905 on the East Side: "McCarthy has been for a long time a popular choice on the East Side among the Hebrew immigrants who abandon names."[103]

For the well-versed Jewish observer of the time, name changes among Jews were by no means a German-Jewish phenomenon. He was concerned about arbitrary changes in the Hebrew language endowment that damage the spiritual quality of a name—changes made by all Jews in America, not especially by the German-Jewish immigrants:

> . . . Biblical names are frequently "modernized." The custom, we fancy, arises generally from a feeling of false shame, which is certainly culpable; for names of themselves express nothing, and it is altogether ridiculous to suppose that the change of one or more letters will whiten the moral character or raise one's reputation, save among a community of the silliest and most depicable. Thus Abraham becomes Braham, Abrahamson, Bramson, Baruch, Bar-

100 *Ibid.*

101 *Asmonean,* vol. ii, p. 13.

102 *Die Laterne von New York* (New York 1870), vol. ix, no. 18, p. 2.

103 *The Hebrew* (San Francisco 1904-05), vol. lii, no. 18, p. 4, "How the New York Jews come to take Irish names."

row; David and Davidson, Davis and Davison; Elias, Ellis; Emanuel, Manuel; Jonas, Jones. Levi is made to undergo several transformations, appearing successively as Lewis, Levey, Levett, Lieber, Levin; while Levison is transmuted into Levinson and Leviberg into Lavenberg. Moses is americanized into Moss, Mosely and at times Morris; Solomon is transformed into Salomon, Salmon, and Sloman; Zacharias is changed to Zacharie; Jacob and Jacobson appears as Jacques and Jackson.

Scriptual names are frequently altered by the insertion or omission of one or more letters, the bearers thereof becoming correspondingly glorified. Thus Aaron and Aaronson blandly beam upon you as Aron and Aronson; Esther, "the star," loses all its significance when turned into Estelle; Eve would not know herself as Eva, nor Hannah as Annie; nor Elkanah as Elkan; nor Joseph as Josephi; Judah is shortened into Juda, and Sarah into Sara. On the other hand, Rachel is lengthened into Rachael, and Samson into Sampson.[104]

The present generation of American Jews—now for the most part descendants of east-European Jews—is acquainted with name changes that testify not to the legal difficulties of the German-Jewish immigration, but to difficulties of a purely social order.[105] All the greater then is the inspiration to be drawn from the loyalty of the German-Jewish immigrant to his hereditary name.

Loyalty to the Hereditary Name

The psychology of the bearer of a typical German-Jewish name—of the -heim(er)s first of all—is that of the self-made man who more strongly than others is conscious of having brought honor to his name. His capacity for self-analysis strengthens his love for the lack of pretension of his name. For he, too, was once unnoticed, like the tiny hometown which he has since made great with his name. The Berliners, Potsdamers, Spandauers, Hamburgers, Frankfurters, Mannheimers, Poseners and others named after large cities may often feel the pomposity of their names. But the typical great man of provincial origin—the -heim(er) above all—is a man who made his small name into a world. Nothing overshadows him, not even the name of Rothschild. For he embodies the democratic nature of America's rise, a rise in which the Jewish immigrant masses from Europe participated. The single financial potentate of the European model recedes before the new rise of -heim(er)s and -stein(er)s and other bearers of unpretentious names. It is the vigorous, vital Jewish province of the Old World which, transplanted to America's

[104] *Jewish Messenger* (New York 1871), vol. xxx, no. 16, p. 1.
[105] Friedman, Lee M., "American Jewish Names," *Historia Judaica,* vol. vii, no. 2, pp. 147-62.

fast growing cities, became the source of the Jewish achievement in the great cities.

This democratic feature lends a certain popularity to the names. The force of the German-Jewish name spreads especially in the American West and in the smaller communities throughout the land, where the main weight of the German-Jewish immigration lay until the Civil War.

As to the extent of name changes, the scenic-geographic groups showed strong resistance to change. Aside from occasional small distortions, these groups—and foremost the -heim(er) and -stein(er)—preserved their paternal heritage. An elementary feeling for the eternal is evident in this perpetuation of scenic-geographic and, often, pure place names. And there is no doubt that the sons of the small towns and villages felt a closer attachment to the places of their birth than did the sons of the large cities of the homeland. This is testified to by the large gifts bestowed upon their old-world native towns by those who later became wealthy. The present author can cite a typical case of loyalty from his own observation: of two business partners, the -heim retained his name, while the man from a great city exchanged Breslau for a name taken from the film world.

The -heim(er) names, representative of the whole group, further suggested the aspect of permanence in the German-Jewish emigration. The emigrants were not pitching tents and planning to return to the old home with the wealth that they accumulated. They were building a new home for themselves and succeeding generations—a characteristic which is expressed symbolically by the name Bodenheimer.

A great many of these German-Jewish names won leadership in the larger Jewish community of America. And in the new American industrial society they attained in the course of a single generation an intellectual and spiritual importance precisely in those fields of endeavor in which the new continent led the whole world.

JEWISH NAMES IN EARLY AMERICAN HUMOR

I. MOTIVES IN THE SEARCH FOR APPROPRIATE HUMOROUS NAMES

IN THE culture-historical study of literary names, the primary concern is to find out why certain distinctive names were given to certain literary characters. In the case of humorous names, the motive at first appears simple: by holding a crooked mirror before literary figures, the simple meaning of given names is comically deflected, and laughter is produced. But actually our questions start exactly at this point: What real situation does the humorist want to depict by using a specific name, and how is his own tension vis-à-vis the reality he is viewing relieved by creating a humorous name for a person in a given situation? How is the created name to be analyzed in its constituent parts? What forces, what conditions of time and place around the humorist's literary age determined the selection of specific components for a name? Furthermore, how can the reader, accustomed to the finished literary product, be made to understand the creative process involved in the humorist's search for a distinctive comic name? Mere anecdotes of an author's lifelong search for suitable names for his literary characters may illustrate the course of the author's thinking. They do not give an overall culture-historical picture on which a satisfactory interpretation may be based.

This essay attempts to give a historical interpretation of the origin of a distinct group of comic names for Jews in the humor of an already vanished America. This interpretation is closely interrelated with important developments in a newly evolving society whose institutions were being shaped when these humorous names were first applied. At the same time, however, the old European world continued to exist and in its humor conventionally comic names for Jews persisted. For a while the ideas of this co-existent old world continued to influence the formation of names for Jews in American humor.

Reprinted from *Max Weinreich Festschrfit,* 1964

II. THE FIRST FUNCTION OF THE JEWISH NAME IN AMERICAN HUMOR

Aging Europe, appropriately, saw the Jew only in his time-worn image. The humorous names for Jews lacked the dynamics usually at play in the creation of names for people involved in new social phenomena. Essentially the comic names were based on the old priestly names: the *Kohn* with a *K*, in Oskar Kraus' immortal *Meyrias* called *Kohnus vulgaris* permeated most of the stale jokes about Jews, embodying long familiar situations. The Jew himself was not seen as acting in any new situation; his general station in life was considered to be known and established. Not even in its humor did Europe assign him any new role.

This was quite different in America, where popular imagination and literary creativity were from the beginning focussed upon the unbelievably new. Here, the traditional position of the Jew in European humor soon gave way to new situations worth symbolizing and caricaturing. These new situations were characterized first of all by attributing to the Jew a belief in incredible and unreliable events. Like the *credat Judaeus* of the classical world, this idea, too, proved in the New World an unfailing initial impetus to popular humor. But a distinction ought to be made. The American tall tale about the vast powers of nature, a genre so dear to the popular imagination which produced it, reached a dead end as soon as the nation achieved a certain intellectual level. At this point the incredible could be believed only by a new humorous character, and was then attributed to the Jew, as in Rome of old.[1] Thus, the Jew, introduced into a new world of satirical design, was at first, characterized by vague and poorly contrived humorous names which crystallized in time as the situations were more concretely perceived.

Early in the history of American humor, Biblical names as a source of humor were possible because of the widespread knowledge of the Bible in America. The humorist readily assumed the public's familiarity with many Biblical figures. Thus, the earliest humorous names appeared in the joking application of Biblical names to certain situations which resulted in a comically incredible effect. These situations were made believable by the additional comic notion that the Jew in his present situation still personified the Biblical name. For instance, Elisha's mantle in the clothing store put the comic question of the customer: "Who is the Elisha who'll wear it?"[2]

By comically juxtaposing the contemporary period with the patriarchal age, the humorist expected the contrast immediately to create its grotesque effect. This expectation increased with the application of broader strokes. For example, Abraham's readiness to sacrifice his son was given new meaning:

[1] Horace (*Sat.*, I. 5.97-103), cited in Harry J. Leon, *The Jews of Ancient Rome* (Philadelphia, 1960), p. 12. The name Apella which Horace gave to the Jew was used by the humorist in a letter to Mrs. Grundy containing a complaint about the swines on New York's streets. The letter is signed "Judaeus Appelles". *Mrs. Grundy*, I (1865), p. 34, "Pigs".

[2] *Swingin' Round the Circle* ... (Boston, 1867), p. 55.

"Abraham's Sacrifice.
Entire Stock of Clothing of Isaac a. Co's at a Sacrifice by Abraham."[3]

Or, longevity in the Bible served as a pun on contemporary bargaining methods:

"From a stock market point of view.
No, Jacob, no! The Lord isn't going to take me at hundert when he can get me at 70."[4]

Associating the stock market with the Biblical concept of man's 70-yaer life span would be comical enough, even without introducing the point about bargaining. (The humorist must have felt justified in not selecting for his joke the 80-year life span eventually conceded by the Bible, for the added ten years would not provide such a satisfying margin for speculation).

Occasionally, even a tall tale, already ascribed to German Jews, was supplied with Biblical names showing Abraham playing a dirty trick on Isaac. To pinpoint his German origin, the latter was equipped with the family-name *Finkerhaus* and the story (1853) was removed to Santa Fe, a Western trade center used by German Jews.[5] Here, only the transfer of the story's locale to the Far West strained the imagination. In other stories, the newness of the business world was symbolized by the appearance of the Jew, and he was endowed in folk humor with every feature capable of reflecting people's astonishment at the new things around them. Peddling showed up under romantic circumstances. Symbolic meaning was attached to the appearance of the peddler with horse and wagon; in the store, the wares for sale were given the veneer of rarity or antiquity; and the situation was further characterized as extraordinary by the use of farfetched Biblical names for the persons involved.

Wherever a Gentile whose Puritan parents gave him a Biblical name moved onto the humorous scene, the addition of the epithet "Jew" to his name was not unusual, especially if he was a money-lender: "Old Jeremiah Jenkins, the Jew" (1855). The pawnbroker as well as the note-shaver were, as a rule, tagged with Biblical names.

Although Biblical names, especially patriarchal ones, were appropriate equally to Sephardic and German Jews, their use in comic situations suggested Sephardic rather than German Jews, perhaps because Sephardic Jews were more commonly known in the Anglo-Saxon cultural milieu and associated with familiar financial situations. Shylock on the Rialto had penetrated from the stage into the American language, but it took some time before he was seen as hailing from Frankfurt. After 1848 German Jews, preponderantly from Bavaria, had begun to emigrate in large numbers to America, but for some time their names as well as the unpretentious names of the places of their origin remained unnoticed by the American public.

The traditional position in which American humorists first observed the Jews in

[3] *Sinai and Olympus* (New York, 1899), p. 41.
[4] *Puck*, XLV, No. 1152, p. 4.
[5] *Yankee Notions*, II (1853), p. 164, "Turning the tables".

the New World at first resembled the way European popular humor saw the Jew. But this attitude did not long persist. American humorists must have felt intuitively that the old stereotypes of the Jew were being changed in America by new phenomena.

These new phenomena were shaped primarily by America's urbanization. The Jew was viewed as a moving force of this urbanization and began to appear in entirely new situations to the observer, and, because of the newness and strangeness, the Jewish attributes stuck. When situations appeared irresistibly comic, a Jewish name, in its actual form or humoristically transformed, became a useful mark of these situations. When German Jewish immigrants appeared on the American scene, Jewish names had already begun to be applied in comic situations bearing on urbanization and the new arrivals could therefore continue to serve in this capacity. So fast was the pace of this urbanization that it was not easy to accept the insignificant, at first unnoticed son of a European province, as the motor of the sweeping change that was visible everywhere. The humorous potential of his implausibility was increased by the unlimited possibilities of using and transforming his name. The very pattern of the German Jewish name was new and therefore useful in expressing the humorist's reflections on the new times. This was true even in the first phase, when these names were used and their bearers were not yet fully recognized and stigmatized as Jews. Nevertheless such names already served to cast a humorous light on situations. In this phase, and in later humor, too, family names like *Sulzbacher*, *Woermeser*, and others based on places of origin were used. But they were reduced to minor importance as the need arose for characterizing new humoristic types.

A popular concept already existed then about which names were regarded as German Jewish. The suffixes *-heim* and *-stein*, *-bach*, *-feld*, indicating geographic origins in German lands, were commonly considered to indicate that the names were those of German Jews.[6] The frequency and intensity of the new situations subjected to humoristic evaluation were seen in the multiple use of such names, whether real or contrived. The hundreds of comic names for German Jews outnumbered and far exceeded in variety the humorous names for Germans (*Hans Breitmann*), Irishmen (*Flaherty*, *Finnegan*), and other minorities. The designations for occupations or professions then current in traditional American humor (*Sam Slick* for the peddler, *Smooth⁵onöue* for the preacher) were also outnumbered by the references to the stations of life of German Jews. These German-Jewish names constituted an entirely new world of names to the American public, as strange and surprising as the new situations from which they emerged. In the earlier use of Biblical names, the imaginary situation covered by the name could be laughed off because the name did not fit it. Now reality itself seemed incredible since all these meaningless names, without

[6] The humorous names quoted in this study have been taken from the more important humorous periodicals and from joke columns of American newspapers, the most important of which are *Spirit of the Times*, *Puck*, *Life*, and *Judge*.

any hold on the historical memory of America, nevertheless affected American reality. The reaction to this situation was sharp enough to stimulate the humorist to invent new names and, when the situation had become static enough to be satisfied with already existing stereotypes, new variations. This drying up of the sources of humor indicated the humorist's helplessness vis-à-vis the pace of life in which the unaccustomed quickly turned into the familiar. The same march of time also created an inner emptiness in humorous literature because the familiar ceased to be funny. In the subsequent use of comically outmoded Jewish names, long obsolete comic figures sometimes still appeared in humorous journals or in joke columns of newspapers as space fillers but no longer expressed any social tension or evoked laughter.

III. THE NEW WORLD OF BUSINESS

Conquest of nature and the human embodiment of its giant forces were long the nearly exclusive preoccupation of the American popular imagination. Later, an idealization of the real Yankee – ingenious, inventive, playful with these forces of nature but also intellectually superior in man-to-man confrontations – became a major folkloristic theme. The two situations were associated with each other: the Yankee moved in nature and among people at the same time. Only the new world of business was regarded as entirely separate from nature. The milieu of business then became its own natural atmosphere populated only with human beings. These people, conceived as humorous types, could not be imagined as moving about in unconfined nature. Wherever humorous names contained references to nature and open spaces – geographical endings like *-baum*, *-tal*, for example – they were not perceived as such.

Business, normally seen as a gainful occupation in its appropriate setting, became a subject of American humor only when the farmer and peddler ceased to be effective comic figures. The humorist needed new names to designate the business milieu. At that time German Jewish names fulfilled this purpose and thereby actually introduced a period in American humor business.

At first the mere insertion of real German Jewish names was apt to give a joke, story, or anecdote its flavor of business and to create a specific business atmosphere. Seen as a group, the names symbolized a business milieu and instantly suggested the thoughts and motives of the business world. Names like *Goldstein*, *Silverstein*, *Lowenstein*, *Rosenbaum*, and many others, especially when used for the first time, implied that the Jew had arrived into a milieu which suited him. Even then, one could rarely find the real name of a Gentile business-partner who might have shared the Jew's fate in humor.

This depiction of the Jew in business, or as its epitome, was made even more pointed by the selective use of real names, with the specific intention of giving a special flavor to the humor about business. In this regard names combined with *-heim* and *-stein* must have appeared specially strange and comical to the English reader: *Einstein*, with its rhyming syllables, was in the forefront, followed by *Dinkelspiel, Morgentau, Rosenheimer, Eckstein, Rothstein, Rosenblum, Rosenstein, Rosenzweig, Rosenbaum.* All these were real names, but took on a special tone in the humor of business.

When the saturation point in the use of such names was reached, it became necessary to invent new names, after the earlier ones had lost their attraction. The first invention in the field – and in the long run the most fruitful – was the combination of the suffixes *-heim* and *-stein* with parts of real names, thereby giving a fanciful air to the new combinations. The old priestly names *Cohn* and *Levi* were the favorites and combined to make *Cohenstein, Cohnstein, Cohnheim*, and *Leviheimer*. Nor did Biblical names escape this composition: *Isaacstein* and *Mosenstein*. Then, one step further: the suffixes *-heim* and *-stein* were combined with invented, nonexistent names, with words for elements essential to the comic conception of the world of business:[7] *Geldstein, Loanstein, Silverheimer, Geldheimer, Goldfinger* symbolize the role of money, particularly cash, in the operation of business. Words for conspicuous riches were also used as components for names: (Miss) *Sparklestein, Silverbaum, Blinkenstein*, and *Diamondstein*.

a. *Business Motives Expressed in Names*

When Calvin Coolidge said "The business of America is business", he frankly acknowledged the motives of the commercial world. There is, first of all, the acceptance of the profit motive. The name *Gettstein*, for example, adhered to this neutral line. But *Grabbenstein* and *Grabbenheimer* already introduced criticism of the way money was made. (*Shylock Graspall*, pawnbroker, appeared in even older illustrations).

The desire for gain, as intensified by dishonesty, was embodied in the names *Swindleheim* and *Swindlebaum*. Where mercantile transactions are not trustworthy, Mr. *Schaumburg*, whose price quoting was uncertain and Mr. *Wogglebaum* with his maneuvering were blamed.

In the world of dishonest business, insurance and bankruptcy took first place. Note the following joke:

> "The cause of the fire: Insurance.
> "The cause of the business failure: The benefit."

In the innumerable variations of the insurance joke, fancy played on name composition as on a piano. The real-life names *Bernheim, Bernstein* and *Bernheimer* were

[7] *New Yorker Lustige Blatter*, I (1892), II (1893) were an imitation of the *Fliegende Blätter* published in Germany.

transformed by a comic exchange of *e* for *u*, into *Burnheim*, *Burnstein* and *Burnheimer* (even abbreviated to Burns), to emphasize the fire-insurance joke. The next step in these jokes was the invention of names in which suffixes were added to the fireworks, for example *Blazenheimer*, *Smokenstein* and *Flamberg*.

In the world of business failure one name stands for all: Mr. *Failinstein* seeking the benefit.

b. *Economic Station in Life*

Marking a Jew's place in economic life by a fitting name was already a standard device in European folklore. America followed European ways by adopting notions from English literary style. *Shylock dealer in old clothes* and the use of Biblical names for fictitious clothing stores in Chatham Street (*Moses Abrahams a. Co.*, *Benjamin a. Levi*, *National Clothing Store*) were early expressions of the ubiquity of Jews in the clothing industry and trade. With the rise of readymade clothing in America and its identification as a Jewish industry, jokes about clothing became flooded with Jewish names: *Cloakstein*, *Hosenthal* and *Hosenstein*. Comic allusions to Christmas sales played on names like *Seasongood* and *St. Klausenstein*. *Fleckenstein* became a symbol for all that is worn out, whether in pawnbroking or in old-clothes trade. For goods other than apparel in the pawnbroker's shop, the outstanding names were those which expressed changing colors, spuriously glittering like *Himmelstein*, *Rubinstein* and *Sapirstein*. Invariably the pawnbroker's son was *Ikey* or *Jakey* and he was assumed to wear all the treasures of his father's store on his private sprees, especially at the race-track.

c. *Pretensions to Social Intercourse*

According to the social axiom of American aristocracy, at least two native generations and, more often, three were required to make a man "clubbable", eligible for America's "good society". The idea that the Jew was as intent on his standing in society as others struck the humorist as a comical notion. This subject, then, became a vehicle for humor by depicting the Jew's unsuccessful attempts at social climbing. The self-rhyming *Einstein*, funny in itself, led to *Zweistein* and even *Dreistein*. Other exaggerations satirizing the effort to show off are *Augenstein*, *Doppenheimer*, *Woolfenstein* (dandy), *Heavenrich*. Jewish sentimentality was derided by such names as *Morgenlicht* and *Abendrot*. Generally, the names ridiculing social aspirations created their comic effect by their senselessness, without indicating any distinct quality of the name's bearer. Some of the most widely used were *Ickelheimer*, *Ickelsteiner*, *Ickelheim* and *Ickelstein*, followed by *Mitzelheimer*, *Ipzenheimer*, *Minzesheimer*, *Hinkelheimer*, *Hockenheimer*, *Hundsheimer* and *Pickelstein*.

Characterizations of Jews by giving them such names became more elaborate as they advanced upward in society. *Benjamin Franklinstein* was a Jew laying claim to social intercourse with the Gentile, a *Feldheimer* when he took up golf, or a *Summerpanz* when he intruded into vacation resorts. In adapting himself socially he was prepared to change his name ("How he won the Silverites"); *Goldstein* became *Silverstein.* Despite his pomposity (Schönheimer), he was socially suspended, without firm ground under his feet, a *Bimbelstein* or *Wigglestein.*

d. *The Newcomer as a Substitute*

The humorous name loses its meaning and comic effect when the object of humor has changed his station in life. Such was the case with the German Jews in America, who in several decades rose more rapidly than any other immigrant group. Previous notions associated with Jews became obsolete. It became less plausible that the expanding business and industry in which Jews were engaged could gain from incendiary insurance tricks or bankruptcy. The sober reality of the Jewish presence in the world of mercantile credit went far to destroy the derisive names that had been coined to depict him.

New objects were required on whom to bestow humorous names. These were provided when East European Jewish immigrants followed the German Jews to America. This new Jewish immigration, of incomparably larger numbers than the German Jewish migration and of greater socio-economic variety, became the new object of humor.

Almost immediately, the suffixes *-heim* and *-stein* which had previously characterized the comic German Jewish name were replaced by *-ski* (from this, the pejorative *kike* was later derived). At first the *-ski's* referred generally to the new mass of immigrants. As with the earlier *Einstein*, assonance increased the humorous effect: *Schinski, Minski.* Biblical names were then introduced into the combinations: *Isaakski* and *Levinski.*

But soon this device was refined to reflect more specific social and economic functions. To indicate that the Jew was unskilled in his work, hes was called a *misfitsky* when he followed in Mr. *Hosenstein's* steps. As a furrier he was *Skinninsky*, a name intended to contrast the quality of his work with real craftsmanship. As a cut-rate competitor, he was a *Markdownski.* He then acquired the art of fireworks and *Burnstein* changed to *Burnupski.* Nor was he a stranger to bankruptcy: *Failinstein* became *Failinski* and *Failupski.*

Socially the East European Jewish immigrants could not be located on the status ladder. They gave no sign of aspiring to social intercourse with Gentiles. The crudest derision thus served well, on the model of the European *Judenschwein*, which dated back to medieval times. Besides the archaic *Sheeny* – in all probability derived from *swine* – Mr. Piginski appeared. Other names reflected other qualities of the Jews' adaptation to new surrounding: we find an *Allrightsky*, a *Hurryupsky*, and an argumentative *Buttinski*.

IV. CONCLUSION

The unchanging names for Jews in European humor mainly stressed their inadequacies in social life. In the European jokes about Jews the names themselves remained static (*Kohn*, der kleine *Kohn*, Moritz). In contrast, the wide use of Jewish names in American humor testifies to the variety and change of the position of Jews in an urbanizing country. This contrast was dramatized by the attempt to publish *Fliegende Blätter* in German in America. It was a purely European comic paper with all the old European jokes, without any relationship to developments in America. On the other hand, jokes about Jews in America originated at a later time and belong to a different category. In these, the urbanization of America is assumed to be complete. Comic criticism of this state of affairs has often blended into criticism of the Jews.

JEWS AND CHINESE IN AMERICA

I

In the history of the relationships between Jews and other important ethnic-national groups in this country, the Chinese played the smallest role insofar as direct connections are concerned, in contrast to the broad contacts with Germans or Irish, which led directly to intense tensions. The Jews generally came with the Germans or followed them as part of the "old immigration" and they concentrated in the big cities in proportions comparable to the Irish. Hence there followed a mutual attraction and repulsion between these groups because of varied cultural and religious backgrounds, economic rivalries and aspirations to political leadership. There were elements of clash and differences also in the case of smaller groups with lesser contacts, as for instance with the Mormons, who were concentrated in a specific settlement area.

Of a similar character were the contacts between the Jews and the Chinese, involving as they did, in physical terms, small numbers and a limited geographic area, namely, California. However, the significance of such contacts and the parallel in the situation of both groups as seen from certain angles extended beyond the regional limits of settlements and economic relations.

When the Chinese newcomer arrived in California, the American Jew already had a decisive social experiment behind him in that area. It had become clear that the newly created society on the Pacific could not deny the Jew equal rights. Like other Americans, Jewish adventurers and pioneers came to California during the gold rush. Within a few years (1855-1860) the estimate of the Jewish population in San Francisco was 5,000 out of the city's total of 50,000, constituting about the same proportion as that of the Jews in New York City to the metro-

* On the Chinese problem in America, see, *Bibliography of the Chinese Question in the United States* (San Francisco 1909); Gibson, Otis, *The Chinese in America* (Cincinnati 1877); and Gompers, Samuel and Gutstadt, H., *Meat vs. Rice* (San Francisco 1908).

On relations between the Jews and the Germans, *cf.* Glanz, Rudolf, *Jews in Relation to the Cultural Milieu of the Germans in America up to the Eighteen Eighties* (New York 1947); *idem*, "Jews in Early German-American Literature," in JEWISH SOCIAL STUDIES, vol. iv (1942) no. 2, 99-120.

On relations between Jews and Mormons, *cf.* Watters, Leon L., *The Pioneer Jews of Utah* (New York 1952). My study, *Jew and Mormon*, is still to be published.

Reprinted from *Jewish Social Studies*, Volume XVI, 1954

polis' number of inhabitants. There was much prejudice against members of different races and nationalities in the mining camps during the formative years of the new commonwealth, and inequality of status carried over later to their social position in the cities. However, throughout that early period in California, the various "foreigners" had no lowest common denominator. The Mexican still had to await the coming of the Chinese so that he might have his whipping-boy. In those days, before the Chinese became the lightning rod for all the evils of Pacific society, the status of the Jews and their relationship to other groups on the West Coast by and large followed the pattern of coexistence that prevailed in other parts of America. They lived predominantly within the German cultural sphere. On the whole, the Jews of California felt less the tensions existing in American group relations.

Non-Chinese usually accepted the view that unlike members of other nationalities who came to California as a matter of free individual decision, the Chinese were imported wholesale by their societies, and remained, subject to the discipline of the societies in their work; that they were slave laborers even before they became sweated labor. That this was not the case is shown by the unimpeachable testimony of a contemporary Jewish manufacturer of San Francisco, as reported in the *San Francisco Chronicle* of April 15, 1876:

> A. Altmayer, a member of the firm of Einstein Bros. (manufacturer of boots and shoes, who have, until late, employed Chinamen of the Hop Wo Co.) testified that "He did not think that the men were the slaves of the Company for they drew up their contract when they chose and left without opposition."[1]

Nevertheless, the view of the Chinese as permanent slave laborers underwent no change for many decades.

The Chinese, though latecomers on the West Coast, did not develop all the typical resentments against the earlier arrivals that were characteristic of the other newcomers. Other groups intensified their resistance to hostility by such resentment. In contrast it was commonly held that the Chinese had an immunity to the emotional weaknesses that beset the other groups, but that very immunity eventually made them all the more vulnerable when everyone else rallied against them.

II

The first known Chinese servant of a California Jew was also the first Chinese in Los Angeles. He was hired by Joseph Newmark for $100 a month and board, some years before full-scale Chinese migration to the west coast began.[2] Later, with the concentration of Jews in

1 Quoted from Layres, Augustus, *Facts upon the Other Side . . .* (San Francisco 1876) p. 17.

2 Newmark, Harris, *Sixty Years in Southern California, 1853-1913* (New York 1926) p. 123.

certain branches of industry, there developed mass employment of Chinese in California Jewish enterprises, a fact which itself throws light on the position of those industries. Statistical studies of the San Francisco enterprises in which Chinese were employed reveal that it was precisely in the fields in which Jews had concentrated that the number of Chinese workers was incomparably greater, above all in the shoe and clothing industries.

In boots and shoes we find in November 1876 the following: Levinsky Bros.—60 Chinese, 28 non-Chinese; Buckingham & Hecht—40 and 60; O. Porter & Schlesinger—54 and 130; Rosenthal, Feder & Co.—16 and 100; S. Wolff & Co.—25 and 10.[3] Among the clothing firms: T. Alexander & Co.—35 and 11; Ash Bros.—20 and 14; E. B. Elfeld & Co.—45 and 38; L. Strauss & Co.—180 and 50.[4] Higher percentages of Chinese workers at that time were to be found only in laundries, where they appeared as employers, and in the gunpowder industry, where the element of danger was decisive (80 Chinese as against 28 others).[5] Thus, at a time when most of the country was under the impression that it was being clothed by Jews, the prevailing opinion in California was that "the Chinese have a monopoly, in San Francisco, of what is termed 'plain sewing'."[6] How near the truth this was can be seen from testimony by Max Morgenthau, a Jewish clothing manufacturer in San Francisco since 1850, who had four plants employing 2,000 workers, nearly half of them Chinese. When asked why he used Chinese labor so extensively, he explained that white workers were generally unreliable and tended to absenteeism, and that he was therefore compelled to turn to the Chinese.[7]

The number of Chinese workers was also disproportionately high in the cigar industry, another point of Jewish concentration. In this field, as in laundering, the Chinese attained a position of independent entrepreneurship at an early date. "The Chinamen, who at first made only second-rate cigars, now make the very best of 'Imported Havanas'." As for Chinese cigar makers, "in 1862 they numbered between four and seven thousand, and nine-tenths of all cigars and cigarettes used on the Pacific coast were made by the Chinese."[8] The Chinese began to displace the whites in laundries even earlier.

3 Brooks, B. S., *Appendix to the Opening Statement and Brief of B. S. Brooks on the Chinese Question Referred to the Joint Committee of the Senate and House of Representatives, Consisting of Documentary Evidence and Statistics Bearing on the Questions Involved* (San Francisco 1877).

4 *Ibid.*, p. 111.

5 *Ibid.*, p. 106.

6 Frost, J. B., *California's Greatest Curse* (San Francisco 1879) p. 18.

7 *Report to the California State Senate on Chinese Immigration* (Sacramento 1878) p. 131-34.

8 The quotations are from Gibson, O., *The Chinese in America* (Cincinnati 1877) p. 109; and McLeod, Alexander, *Pigtails and Gold Dust* (Caldwell, Idaho 1947) p. 93.

The economic rise of the Chinese in California can be largely traced to their early experience as immigrant laborers in the light industries in which Jewish entrepreneurs specialized. Here is how one contemporary saw the process:

Stealthy and cautious in his approach, but naturally tractable, the Chinese soon gained a knowledge of our mercantile, manufacturing and agricultural enterprises, which makes them powerful and dangerous competitors, but mostly in small trades, or rather in trading in small wares and in light manufactures, such as cigars, matches, slippers, boots and shoes, various articles of underwear, peddling fruit and vegetables, pins, needles, Chinese toys, matches and other small wares.[9]

The threat of competition was obvious, and the Jewish press published the facts with a comical twist, impelled by self-irony, somewhat sweetened with the humorous notion that the Chinese would not only one day wipe out the Jews, but had also become serious competitors for the very Yankees who had imported them.

. . . . The Chinese have got the Jews by the horns, in the matter of cheap clothing, boots and shoes, and even shrewd Yankees, who are a sort of cross between a Scotchman and a Slavonian, are apprehensive that John Chinaman will soon get the better of them. I am glad of it. The Yankees preached for and prayed with the Chinese lepers, and now they whine that they have been instrumental in importing a race that can outyank the shrewdest manufacturers of nutmegs and wooden hams.[10]

The new situation in California's commerce is described much more concretely in the Jewish press two years later. By this time a considerable reversal had occurred, with some Jews being employed by Chinese.

The Chinese merchants have not only copied after their former white employers in the matter of manufacturing clothing, underwear, shoes, cigars, ruffles etc. but they have also imitated their manner of doing business, and engaged recently white drummers—mostly Jews—to travel throughout the length and breadth of the coast, clear into Mexico and Central America to place their goods upon the market . . . .[11]

One correspondent even reported on the practical joke that Chinese were selling matzoth in San Francisco and depressing the price:

. . . . Matzohs are to be had here in town at the lowest rates, on account of Chinese competition and Irish labor—and the Matzohs are as kosher as "Chaser fuess."[12]

Along with these new developments there always remained the original area of the Chinese advance, the laundry, where the Chinese was the entrepreneur from the smallest to the largest establishments.

9 Frost, *op. cit.*, p. 16.

10 "San Francisco," in *American Israelite*, vol. xxviii (1881) 86.

11 *American Israelite*, vol. xxix (1883) 422.

12 Argus, "San Francisco," in *The Jewish Voice*, vol. ii (St. Louis 1888) no. 14, p. 5. "Chaser fuess" means pigs' feet.

Jewish merchants who arrived in California at an early date were witness to the failure of the first laundries, opened by whites and subsequently forced out by Chinese competition.[13]

Typical occupations of the Jew and the Chinese were linked in American popular humor not only on the surface but also deeply in the unconscious. The street cry of "old clo'" was supplemented by the laundry, and honorable characters in popular humor declared one to be as necessary as the other as symbols in political whitewash. At a time when the Jews were already clothing a part of the nation, the Chinese were brought to the big eastern cities, where there was enough dirty wash in municipal politics. Cartoonists gladly exchanged them for the Irish, who were held responsible, through the party machines, for all municipal dirt. And in the east, Chinese immigration was considered to be truly useful, although here the Irish built the railroads and for this purpose it was not necessary, as in California, to import Chinese wholesale. It was because of this western importation that the West Coast Irish became the sworn enemies of the Chinese. Men who had exact knowledge of the anti-Chinese societies of San Francisco have assured us that they were under Irish leadership.[14]

We must remember, too, that regardless of the common view of the rise of the Chinese as immigrant labor in California, Chinese merchants had also settled in San Francisco in large numbers, and relatively early, so that they became noticeable as a distinct group. The Jewish traveler Benjamin estimated the number of Chinese in California as 8,000 and added that "in the city there is a good number of respectable and wealthy Chinese merchants."[15] In consequence, purely commercial dealings between Jews and Chinese began very early.

III

The experience of the California Jews with the Chinese made them more immune to the cry, "The Chinese must go," that was so popular among other sectors of the population and that met with the opposition of the thinking people. There were no Jewish names on the rosters of the leaders of the anti-coolie clubs. Nevertheless, there can be no doubt that in the end they, too, fell for the anti-Chinese psychosis to a considerable extent, thereby earning bitter reproach from their brethren in all other regions of the country. It was the Jewish press of California

13 Newmark, *op. cit.*, p. 79.

14 *Memorial of the Six Chinese Companies* (San Francisco 1877) p. 15-17.

15 Benjamin, Joseph Israel, *Drei Jahre in Amerika*, vol. i (Hanover 1862) p. 312.

that succumbed first, and its hostility eventually filtered into Jewish publications elsewhere in America through their California correspondents. All the more noteworthy, therefore, were those leading voices among California Jewry that stood up for full equality for the Chinese, unpopular as that position was. Judge Solomon Heidenfeldt, for example, after twenty-seven years residence in the state, and after five years service on the State Supreme Court, declard it to be the quintessence of all his experience that "California owes its prosperity very much indeed to the industry of the Chinese . . . . I think we would not have had as many white people if the Chinese had not come." They "give white people homes and employment." Without them, the Southern Pacific would not have been built. And as for their moral qualities, said Judge Heidenfeldt.

> I think they are the best laboring class among us . . . . Give the Chinese a chance and they will assimilate with us . . . . I see no reason why he is not equal . . . . Taking the classes that we have here before us, the Chinese are something better; I think they are more faithful, more reliable, and more intelligent . . . . [They show] more industry than the corresponding class of whites.[16]

Without a doubt, in their hearts many California Jews thought no differently than this judge, who enjoyed the highest trust among his co-religionists, and the expert testimony of Jewish industrialists, appearing before public commissions on their experiences with the Chinese, usually was a sober statement of the realities of the situation.

Even before Jewish industrialists employed Chinese in such large numbers, Jewish merchants in the mining camps had already had considerable experience with Chinese, who liked to buy from them, and their relations were generally satisfactory.[17] Then came the manufacturers, and they too worked in part for the Chinese consumer.[18] That was an answer to the common anti-Chinese argument that the Chinese were not consumers.

For a considerable time, "The Chinese must go" was a slogan issued solely for California. Its echo on the east coast met with disbelief, and then, when it developed that the whole nation would be compelled to take a condemnatory position on the anti-Chinese agitation, American Jews found it altogether unbelievable that so many of their brothers in California joined this cry. And there can be no doubt that they did:

16 *Memorial . . ., op. cit.*, p. 18-19.

17 McLeod, *op. cit.*, p. 45.

18 *Report to the California State Senate on Chinese Immigration* (Sacramento 1878) p. 133. Morgenthau's statement (*cf.* note 7) can be viewed as representative of the opinion of Jews who employed Chinese laborers. On the other side, I have come across a statement by Adolph Sutro that he never employed a Chinese worker as a mattery of policy. *Cf.* Ms. Adoph Sutro in Bancroft Library.

It has been supposed that a good many of our people deeply sympathize with the alleged necessity of excluding these so-called "celestials" from the universal, God-given rights of American freedom.[19]

These Jews honestly believed, as did other Americans, that the Chinese were cheap labor and non-consumers—arguments of witnesses who were free from the bias of economic antagonism to the Chinese.

These arguments were repeated in detail by some California correspondents of Jewish publications and thus brought to the attention of all American Jewry. Unfavorable descriptions of San Francisco's Chinatown, with lurid tales of the opium dens,[20] became part of the account of the situation of the Chinese in California, and all the prejudices of the time provided ample room for them. Not even the passage of time, between the beginning of the anti-Chinese propaganda and the eventual adoption of the Chinese Exclusion Act (1882) tempered the language of such correspondents. And some outbursts continued even after the law was passed.

The way in which one journalistic excess was answered should become part of the permanent record, for it reveals all the implications of the anti-Chinese agitation against American Jewry. In reporting on an explosion in a powder mill, the San Francisco correspondent of the *American Israelite* wrote:

We do not mind the China-men—they should all be employed in powder-works—and enjoy periodical explosions, but we mind the two white superintendents.[21]

The reply, in a letter to the editor from D. Lelewer, read as follows:

"Am vielen Sprechen erkennt man den Narren" may justly be applied to your worthy San Francisco correspondent, especially in his communication in your last week's issue. Shocking as the calamity is which befell the Russian Jews, persecuted with a spirit of intolerance which brings gloom to the hearts of all sympathizers with suffering humanity, and to us Hebrews in particular, he forgets himself as a co-religionist of the same unfortunate class so far as to express himself in a very intolerant spirit toward the Chinese, and in a manner unbecoming an Israelite. Ridiculing their mode and habits of life, and justifying the cry: "The Chinese must go." Their expulsion or limitation in the United States, he thinks, is "none of his funeral."[22]

IV

The indignant letter writer not only struck the right emotional tone, but, undoubtedly without being aware of it, he also brought out the essential quality of a basic discussion then in the air; for everything

19 "Chinese Judaism," in *Jewish Voice*, vol. ix (1890) no. 10, p. 4.

20 *Jewish Voice*, vol. iii (1888) no. 30, p. 4.

21 "San Francisco," in *American Israelite*, vol. xxix (1883) 270.

22 "The Chinese," *ibid.*, vol. xxix (1883) 399.

in the situation was ready for a linking of the Chinese question with the fate of the Jewish immigrant, the large stream of Jews from Eastern Europe having already begun to enter in force. And this discussion would of necessity touch on the status of American Jewry and might influence the attitude of the Jews themselves towards the continuation of Jewish immigration.

Soon the anti-Chinese propaganda in the Jewish press began to take a precautionary, apologetic tone, designed to acquit the Jewish immigrant, in advance, of the evils charged to the Chinese:

The Russian, Polish, German and all other Jews, and, for the matter of that, all other immigrants, assimilate with the dominant race, settle down for good, raise families and take a deep and kindly interest in the body politic. The Chinese are as disgusting as the lowest type of the digger Indian, as treacherous as the greaser and as unprincipled as the Lazaroni. They do not come here to stay. They drive white labor out of cities, they monopolize every industry that requires physical labor, and contaminate the atmosphere where they are packed like sardines in tiers to the depth of thirty feet underground.[23]

And on the other side, defenders of the Chinese recognized from the very beginning that they were being accused of things which were held with equal falseness against the Jews:

Now the Jew resembles the Chinaman in just this one characteristic of thrift and frugality, and if this be a crime he is guilty; and how much of the antipathy to and prejudice against him is due to this cause is a question. Unfortunately, in this country, in the second and third generation, we begin to fall into the ways of our Gentile brethren, namely, out of every dollar we make, never to spend more than one hundred cents![24]

One commentator went over to the offensive altogether, showing how unworthy the whole situation had become in the country with the shift from aid for Russian Jews to persecution of the Chinese:

The Chinese are to be excluded because they do not assimilate with the whiskey drinking class of sand-lot politicians who form the American variety of communist! . . . To conciliate "the Kearney Party," the Senators would deny to an intelligent and industrious foreigner of another race the right of residence in this republic. To "conciliate" the German vote in some other section of the Union, these same politicians would doubtless be ready to check Irish immigration. As for Italians, Swedes, Swiss, and others who come hither to labor and to prosper, how can these people "assimilate" when they save for their families the wages which the voting foreigners who demand their exclusion,

23 "San Francisco," *ibid.*, vol. xxviii (1881) 357. For Jewish objections to the immigration of Russian Jews, see item 132 in my "Source Materials on the History of Jewish Immigration to the United States," in *YIVO Annual of Jewish Social Science*, vol. vi (1951) 155. *Cf. also* Szajkowski, Zosa, "The Attitude of American Jews to East European Jewish Immigration (1881-1893)," in *Publication of the American Jewish Historical Society*, vol. xl (1951) 221-80; and Mandel, Irving Aaron, "Attitude of the American Jewish Community Toward East-European Immigration," in *American Jewish Archives*, vol. iii (1950) 9-33.

24 "Christian Charity and Jewish Wrong-Doing," in *Jewish Messenger*, vol. liv (1883) no. 2, p. 5.

regularly waste upon whiskey? . . . America, . . . which sympathizes with industrious and innocent Hebrews plundered and maltreated in Russian cities, must henceforth drop into the rank from which Spain is emerging . . .[25]

Among non-Jews the parallel between Jews and Chinese was drawn first only in terms of the treatment of the Jews in Europe. Such a comparison was made in defense of the Chinese as early as 1860:

In Austria, Jews have been long incapable of giving legal testimony; but even Austria, as I perceive by a recent notice, has found this disability a little too barbarous for the present age, and has removed it. Is it any compliment to California to compare her social institutions with those of Austria?[26]

After his criticism of the legal disabilities of the Chinese, the same writer went on to consider the human side, and again he drew a comparison with European Jewry, this time in anecdotal fashion:

Really, our objection taken in connection with our treatment of them, is about as rational and consistent as the discipline of Old Fritz, of Prussia, when he caught the Jew trying to get out of his way. The poor fellow confessed that he did so because he was afraid; whereupon Fritz administered to him a most unmerciful caning, exclaiming at every blow, "Do you hear, you scoundrel? I want my subjects to love me and not to be afraid of me!" Our lessons of love to the Chinese are certainly not wanting in impressiveness.[27]

V

However, as the anti-Chinese campaign in California became intensified, less emphasis was placed on comparison with European conditions, and instead, it became more and more embedded in the general framework of American immigration problems. Insofar as American Jews were thereby affected, it was a historical accident which was decisive. It was pure chance that the period when the door was closed to the Chinese in 1882, coincided with the greatest mass entry of Jews into the new world, in consequence of the Russian pogroms. Analogies and contrasts between these two migration situations, basically so different, entered the public mind, at first almost unnoticeably but soon as the subject of sharp public discussion.

Almost instinctively, American Jews understood that on this point certain voices of the press had significance far beyond their actual circulation figures. The average reader remained silent at first on the immigration problem and so did most of his newspapers, but people began to believe that their secret views were to be found in the occasional out-

25 *Jewish Messenger*, vol. li (1882) no. 11, p. 4. The "Kearney Party" was the Workingman's Party of California, organized by Dennis Kearney in 1877.

26 *On the Contact of Races Considered Especially with Relation to the Chinese Question* (San Francisco 1860) p. 8.

27 *Ibid.*, p. 21; "Old Fritz" was of course Frederick the Great.

burst of a rabble-rouser. Such ideas could give rise to new realities. And soon it became high time for self-assertion, as American papers began to attribute similar causes to the persecutions of both Jews and Chinese, and to justify both.

> There is much similarity in the reasons for the persecution of the Jews in Russia, and the Chinese in California. They live off the country and leave nothing to it. They are clannish, do not assimilate, hoard money and spend nothing.[28]

Such charges were only a part of nativism's arsenal. To them were added stereotypes about Jews and Chinese alike. It became necessary for the Jewish press to consider this development when coming to the defense of the Jews. It recognized that the idea was spreading, for obvious reasons, that Jews and Chinese were comparable point by point.

> As the *Scientific American* remarks, one need but read any argumentative article in a California paper against the Mongolians, substituting "Hebrew" for "Chinese," and he would imagine that he was reading an anti-Semitic article written in Berlin. This able contemporary attributes the wicked agitation, both here and in Eastern Europe to an epidemic craze, generated perhaps by an accumulation of sun-spots.[29]

An energetic campaign began in the Jewish press to combat the spreading tendency of equating the two groups and to deny any possible adverse similarity between the situations. Optimistic views were expressed that the comparison would not stand up under close scrutiny. Hence the Jewish counter-arguments concentrated on a denial of similarity through a point-by-point examination of the immigration itself and of the economic and cultural adjustment of the two groups in their new home, a procedure in which, unfortunately, there was room for enough prejudice against the Chinese:

> But we venture to suggest that the comparison between Hebrews and Chinese will not hold on closer examination, so that there need scarcely be any fear, even if the iniquitous Chinese Bill should become law of the land, that any such discrimination against Hebrews would be made. Whatever may be said in envy of the success of our people, no one will deny that they spend liberally as well as they acquire largely: thus making money and setting it afloat again. Not so the Chinese. Then our people stay here, when affluent, and help to build up the country, where they have grown. The Chinese are not so. Finally, the Jew immigrates today, as Moses insisted he should in Pharaoh's time, "with wife and child and belongings." His family life contributes to the elevation of the moral tone of the society in which his lot is cast. The Chinaman, on the contrary, leaves his kith and kin behind, and rejoins them with his fortune in the Flowery Land. These are still further reasons why grave differences will ever be drawn between the son of Palestine and the descendant of the Tartar.[30]

28 *Indianapolis Journal,* quoted in *American Israelite,* vol. xxviii (1881) 302.

29 *American Hebrew,* vol. x (1882) 61.

30 *Ibid.*

In short the heart of the argument was the same "live and let live," which American Jews have put forth so often as a social device. The stress on Jewish family immigration automatically pointed to the absence of women among the Chinese immigrants, and to the implications which many contemporaries liked to draw therefrom. And then there was reference to the unity of western culture, with its substantial Jewish elements, to be defended against the Asiatic interloper.

The clearer minds among American Jews, however, did not share this faith that even the passage of the "iniquitous Chinese Bill" would give Jews nothing to fear. Further, they recognized that, as a matter of conscience, they were obligated to combat the threatened legislation and do what they could to hinder its passage. They saw in the Chinese not only the age-old parallel to the oppressed of all peoples and all ages, but also the contemporary parallel to the persecuted Russian Jews.

"The Chinese today: why not the Jews of tomorrow?" This is the reflexion that must have arisen in many minds on reading that the combined legislative wisdom of this Government has decided to set restrictive limits to the immigration of the Chinese to this country. A few courageous members of the press have raised their voices in protestation against this authoritative repudiation of the fundamental principle of our Union, "that all men are created equal," and the supposition is not far removed that the same jealousy of commercial success, the same unjust restiveness under competition, which animate the "Chinese Bill," may come some day to be applied to "limit" the in-coming and activity of the Hebrews.[31]

After the "Great Massacre" on the west coast, the voice of Jewish public opinion was raised sharply, and with a clear understanding of the international implications:

Who are the Chinese? They are settlers in the United States, invited hither and protected by treaties ordained solemnly by the Government of the Oriental Empire and this great Republic. They are pursuing their humble vocations, and are more sober than their neighbors, and necessarily more industrious. They are eccentric, perhaps, in their mode of life. Some of them are no better, morally, than some of their neighbors. They do not live extravagantly—indeed, it is probably "a true bill" that they save as much money as they can, and send the surplus to China for the support of needy relatives. They are human beings, seeking to pursue in peace the means of livelihood at their command. Apparently this very meekness of bearing furnishes occasion for inhospitable treatment, for persecution. Such a condition of things might be understood of Russia and Rumania . . . . But the plunder and murder of the Chinese took place in a mining town in Washington Territory, within reach by telegraph of philanthropic Boston, New York and Philadelphia.[32]

31 *Ibid.*

32 "The Chinese Question," in *Jewish Messenger,* vol. lix (1886) no. 11, p. 44. The riot of September 2, 1885, in Rock Springs, Wyoming Territory, is known as the "Great Massacre." There were also anti-Chinese riots in the Washington Territory in the middle eighties. *Cf.* Works Projects Administration [W.P.A.], *Guide of Wyoming* (New York 1941) p. 245, *idem, Guide of Washington* (New York 1950) p. 49; and Bromley, Isaac Hill, *The Chinese Massacre at Rock Springs, Wyoming Territory, September 2, 1885* (Boston 1886).

The Jewish press demonstrated that the Chinese lived under exceptional circumstances, even as compared to other persecuted minorities, the Mormons, for example, who were treated incomparably better.[33] Similar arguments appeared in the general press, where the Jew was used for purposes of comparison, which must have made the Jewish press uncomfortable, since the Jews' own position was thus thrown into question.

One thing I am certain of, namely, that if the Press of England, Germany, and other Eurepean countries were as largely in Chinese hands as it is in Jewish hands, we should have heard much more than we have heard about anti-Chinese action in America and much less about anti-Jewish action in Russia.[34]

That was a wound which hurt, and it helped still further to clarify the Jewish position on the Chinese question. It was unthinkable to the sense of justice of the overwhelming majority of American Jews that their brothers in California could have donned the garb of the California anti-Chinese, even though it was conceded that they may honestly have come to believe the anti-Chinese arguments. The difference of opinion between the Jews on the Pacific and all other American Jews reached the point where public demands were made that the Jews of California do not defend the anti-Chinese bill. In the course of the dispute, the arguments of the Jewish opposition to the measure were clearly worked out, dictated primarily by the viewpoint of the immigrants. The Jewish press of California was told bluntly that, by its anti-Chinese position, it had isolated itself not only from the Jews of most of America but also from the best spirits of the country generally, and that soon enough it would find itself morally isolated in California, too.

The *Jewish Record* very properly takes to task our San Francisco contemporaries for their un-Jewish but Californian attitude in the Chinese question. The best religious weeklies of all denominations are unanimous in opposition to anti-Chinese legislation.[35]

When the Jewish press of California reacted against this jibe, another paper wrote:

Our San Francisco contemporaries cannot forgive the *Jewish Record* for its righteous opposition to the Chinese Bill. They claim that there is no similarity between the anti-Chinese crusade in America and the anti-Jewish crusade in Russia. Let us see. In Russia it is claimed that the Jews are foreigners, that they do not adopt the manners of the country, that they do not mingle with the general community, that, although they are thrifty and economical, they do not contribute to the common weal. Not a syllable of these charges need be altered in order to be a repetition against the Chinese here. If today antipathy

33 See *Jewish Messenger*, vol. xlvi (1879) no. 7, p. 1; vol. liv (1883) no. 25, p. 1.

34 "Mr. Freeman's View" (from *Fortnightly Review*), in *Jewish Messenger*, vol. lii (1882) no. 12, p. 5.

35 *Jewish Messenger*, vol. li (1882) no. 13, p. 4.

to the Chinese can legalize enactments against them, what guarantee have we that legislation may not be enacted against the Hebrews, if that irresponsible and dangerous standard, popular prejudice, be the criterion of right? The Chinese Bill has become a law, and so far as that is concerned, discussion is useless. But the Jews cannot afford to stand before the world in the character of oppressors. They have felt the rod too often, not to know the keenness of its application, and if there is any lesson for us in the last nineteen centuries of our history, it is that we must be liberal, talented and catholic, that we may not be guilty of the crimes that have been practised against us.[36]

The California press only stiffened in response, and for that it was criticized particularly.

Still unrepentant—the attitude of our Californian contemporaries on anti-Chinese legislation. Strange that Jewish editors can be so short-sighted and illiberal. Shall Russian bigotry find its supporters in America? The mob that plunders Chinese laborers because they are Chinese, and the press that fails to denounce the un-American spirit of class and sectarian legislation, is on a par with the lowest moujiks, and Ignatieff's salaried journalists.[37]

No Jewish paper could go further than this comparison of a Jewish colleague with the Russian journalistic defenders of pogroms. Nevertheless, the California press remained unrepentant for years, and continued its efforts to win over the rest of the American Jewish press, through direct personal contact when the occasion presented itself:

During a recent visit to New York, en route to Europe, Mr. A. Seligson, of the San Francisco *Jewish Progress*, explained why the anti-Chinese agitation exists in California. The fact that all classes unite in the resolve that the Chinese must go indicates that it is no narrow feeling, but one arising from the spirit of self-preservation. It is impossible to compete with the Chinese . . .[38]

If such old arguments maintained their potency for years, there also remained the inner compulsion to seek all kinds of assurances that the Jews would not meet a similar fate in America. Characteristic in this respect is a statement solicited from W. Phelps, American ambassador in Vienna:

. . . . And finally we have yielded, and now for ten years we shall let in no Chinese . . . . But don't you fear that we shall treat the Jews so. They are a gain, and we are too thrifty to throw away an advantage . . . . let the Jews come . . . .[39]

For the California Jews, at least, the argument that the coming of the Jews was not to be compared with the coming of the Chinese, was well-timed. The years were long gone when the charge could be leveled that the Jews had rushed to the Pacific coast only to get gold and then to

36 *American Hebrew*, vol. xi (1882) 1.

37 *Jewish Messenger*, vol. li (1882) no. 18, p. 4. Nikolai Pavlovitch Ignatieff (1852-1908), Russian Minister of the Interior, approved of the pogroms.

38 "A View of the Chinese," *ibid.*, vol xlix (1886) no. 16, p. 2.

39 "An Intelligent Opinion," *ibid.*, vol li (1882) no. 25, p. 5.

return to the east with this new wealth. The permanence of the Jewish settlement in California was no longer questioned by anyone. But such was not the case in other parts of the country, specifically on the east coast. Here every ship was bringing more Russian Jews, who, according to the older settlers, had to be dispersed and whose poverty and difficulties in economic adjustment raised doubts and provoked hostile reactions in so many cities. It should not be cause for surprise, therefore, that it was in these areas that the full implication of the anti-Chinese attitude was felt, whereas it was almost entirely ignored in California itself.

Hence it was looked upon as an anachronistic curiosity when one newspaper recalled that in 1866, at a San Francisco banquet celebrating the arrival of the Chinese, one speaker made the point that, just as the expulsion of the Spanish Jews had eventually enriched America, "the Chinese would similarly benefit the Union." But it was not lost on the Jewish editors in the east, who could challenge their western colleagues:

> How do our Jewish friends who have failed to show any sympathy with the Chinese, Jewish editors on the Pacific coast whose abuse equals Kearney's, apply the lesson?[40]

VI

In retrospect, the fact is that the whole discussion of the Chinese (now a thing of the past), despite all the excitation of public opinion, failed to produce in the public mind a pairing of Jew and Chinese. But there is no proof that such a possibility did not exist at all; its failure to mature lies in American developments entirely outside any group relationships, real or fictitious, between the Jews and the Chinese. With the march of industrialization, begun after the Civil War and based on the great immigrant masses, America entered a period of colonial expansion, in which the "manifest destiny" to imperial expansion took in Asiatic peoples, too. The old anti-Chinese struggle became then much too insignificant, and the comparison of the Jews with the Chinese no longer had a basis in the actual conditions of an expansionist country, which was rapidly attracting working hands from Eastern Europe. On the West Coast, the anticipated population of thirty millions proved a mirage; migration to the west was stagnant, particularly so, that of the Jews.[41] Under the circumstances, the anti-Chinese struggle died in its tracks, the Jewish-Chinese parallel was mentioned only sporadically,

40 *Jewish Messenger,* vol. lxiv (1883) no. 16, p. 4.

41 Between 1850 and 1860 there were at least 10,000 Jews in California. However, its Jewish population did not exceed 28,000 in 1901. *Cf.* Voorsanger, J., in *Jewish Encyclopedia,* vol. iii (New York 1912) p. 513. During the same period the number of the Jews on the Atlantic coast grew from approximately 50,000 to approximately 1,000,000.

and the coexistence of the two groups in a very limited sector of the national economy lost all significance.

A new economic relationship arose, that of Chinese servants in Jewish households. Could they eventually replace the Irish and Negro maids, now that German domestics were scarcely available—that became the question. And the irony is enhanced, in the light of the earlier conflict within American Jewry over the Chinese, by the fact that the servant problem found its expression in discussions between East and West, in which the West charged the East with retaining old prejudices.

> The Chinese are not nearly so perfectly awful as Eastern people believe, but are bad enough, after all, and then if they are just too wretched for anything, it is quite the thing to say, "my Chinaman, you know" . . . . There, now, I guess you will see that the Chinamen, like the colored people, soon learn to be excited and uncontrollable, yet they are more steady than the darkey and not so tricky. People from the East do not like Chinese help at first, but soon get accustomed to them and generally find them good, clean and faithful servants.[42]

And if, from a moral viewpoint, some Chinese were still evil, the same could be said of Jews:

> . . . . Just as the Chinaman and others of his race have acted, so have also a number of miserable so-called Jews, who have gone over to Christianity merely for gain, with no scruples as to the honesty of their acts.[43]

Time renders life-habits as powerless as ideologies. And yet, one human group retains the historical power to wait for a new day. The Chinese also found his day with respect to the American Jew. Long after anything that suggested the earlier comparison between Jew and Chinese had become meaningless, came the time when the Jew was the most visible of all minorities in America. When the hostile feelings were no longer hidden, when there were no scapegoats to receive the blows intended for him, when even the Negro could not serve as his lightning-rod, the Jew became the focus of nativism. Even the Chinese could see clearly and could assert that "all combine against the poor Jew."[44]

It is demonstrable that the Chinese acquired their own insights at an early date into the contradictions in American society, and had learned to repeat the saying that the Jew had killed the Christian joss. Contemporaries were of the opinion that "Christ-killer" was heard more frequently on the Pacific coast than elsewhere in the country, and not

42 "Los Angeles," in *American Israelite*, vol. xxxii (1885) no. 31, p. 2.

43 "San Francisco," *ibid.*, vol. xxxi (1884) no. 40, p. 6.

44 "As a Chinaman Saw Us," in *The Jewish Outlook*, vol. i (1903-4) no. 41, p. 3.

rarely from the mouths of Chinese and Japanese.[45] In popular humor, the Chinese showed his superiority over the Christian American on this very point:

. . . . Several years ago a Christian missionary was laboring to convert a heathen Chinese . . . . So your God got killed—who kill him?" "The Jews." "Me got a God a tousand eyes! Ten tousand arms! No d - - Jew kill him!" The Chinaman would not renounce his God for one that got killed.[46]

Actually, Jews and Chinese were not often brought together in American humor, whether written or drawn, although an occasional cartoon did point to the future, for example, in satirizing Jewish efforts to enter the overseas trade with China.[47]

45 "Echoes from the Pacific," in *Jewish Voice*, vol. ix (1888) no. 52, p. 3. *Cf. Jewish Times*, vol. iv (1872) 245:"When the Chinese could think of no other epithet, he exclaimed, 'You Jew, you killed Mellican man's Joss.' "

46 *Jewish Voice*, vol. ii (1888) no. 25, p. 2.

47 "A World Grabber," in *Puck*, vol. lii (1902) 6.

JEW AND YANKEE: A HISTORIC COMPARISON

Viewed in historical perspective, not the least significant feature of the great American Immigration of the last century was the fact that it was the first movement of its kind which involved individuals rather than groups. It was the fancies and prejudices, the experiences and reactions of the individual newcomers that subsequently dictated the patterns of civilization in the New World. These conceptions and impressions were of twofold origin. On the one hand was the immigrant's view of the world he had left; on the other, his picture of that to which he had come. Europe was to him a continent of economic and political oppression; America loomed as a land of golden opportunity, a fantastic fulfillment of his secret hopes and dreams, an almost miraculous relief from a chronic condition of social inferiority. Based mainly on the first, and often premature reports of earlier forerunners (who later ceased writing home), his initial picture of America was one of new *material* conditions. Not until he had struck roots did he come to realize that life in the New World involved also a new *spiritual* climate and new cultural patterns. Then he began to take note of his neighbors and, having but little contact with the American Indians, his attention was naturally concentrated upon that dominant element of the population—his own white predecessors. These he characterized roundly, if inaccurately, as Yankees, extending to all Americans the sobriquet which native usage had reserved for the New Englanders.

The immigrant's delineation of the Yankee, the comparison of him with other men, forms an interesting and diverting item in the development of his thinking, a stable topic in his general idea of the New World. Sometimes the picture is arbitrary and capricious; at other times, it is inspired and informed by actual conditions, reflecting and keeping pace

Reprinted from *Jewish Social Studies,* Volume VI, 1944

with current tendencies and streams of thought. Utterly distinct from native characterizations such as appeared on the purely American stage or in purely American literature, this foreign portrayal of the Yankee was nevertheless of considerable cultural significance; for it was this that contributed most to the European estimate of the American and to his subsequent emergence, in the European mind, as the economic leader and savior of the world.

In general, the immigrant got away from his old-world ideas about men, but certain mental pictures were taken over insensibly into the new way of thought. One of these was the picture of the "eternal wanderer," the Jew (with whom he very often had no personal contact), and this led him inevitably to a comparison between Jew and Yankee. This historic comparison, the only constant in the flux of his impressions, persisted for more than a century, and in the course of its development became, to natives as well as to immigrants and foreigners, a constant standard of reference by which American traits were evaluated and the American character assessed. By and large, the comparison seems always to issue in the same valuation: "There are three Christians in a Jew and three Jews in a Yankee." The criteria, however, vary from period to period. At first, the emphasis is on personal and human qualities; later, it is on worldly goods. Moreover, as the Yankee rises in the world, there is a significant change in the appraisal of his qualities; traits which were at first condemned as evidence of a cunning and unscrupulous nature come later to be commended as marks of an essentially progressive spirit.

Typical of this change are two quotations from German observers living some seventy years apart. The first is from an army officer who writes from New York in 1780:

> "The New Englanders," says this correspondent, "have the nickname *Yenkies* since many years. Constantly and in all provinces they were known as merry and—under the mask of sanctity—deceitful folk; their ways became proverbial and, in business, they were trusted with being just as much honest as the Jews."[1]

[1] Moser, Johann Jacob, *Nord-America nach den Friedenschlüssen vom Jahr 1783* (Leipzig 1784) vol. i, p. 751, quoted in H. Schloezer's *Briefwechsel,* pt. ix, p. 384.

The second is from a volume published in 1855:

> "The Yankee especially—that is, the New Englander—has a natural business genius, and can undertake anything. He can begin and make a fortune easier with one idea, than a German with ten. His mottoes are: 'Help yourself' and 'Go ahead.' He early becomes independent, and even in youth learns to push through all possible difficulties. Hence the Jews hardly play any part in America; they find their masters in the Yankees. It must not be thought, however, that these descendants of the old Puritans are made only of shrewd, selfish calculation. It would be the greatest injustice to take the famous Barnum, the prince of Humbug, as the only type of the 'universal Yankee nation.' They are generally liberal, conscientious, temperate, strictly moral, religiously inclined, friends of liberal education, and ardent philanthropists.' "[2]

I

In the earlier literature the prevalent view is that the Jew is no match for the Yankee in versatility, resourcefulness and cunning, and that he is therefore destined to play but a secondary role in the New World. Although, as early as 1804, the author of a Swiss emigration manual is obliged to fall back on the term *Landjude* in order to convey to his countrymen the character and economic function of the oppressive Yankee "land-jobber,"[3] it is the common opinion of most contemporary writers that the Yankee can always outsmart the Jew.

> "The New Englanders," says a work of 1839, "are proud of being smarter than the Jews, whom they do not give a chance for success in their cities. . . . The reason for the great difficulties encountered by Europeans, even by Jews, in their efforts to acquire a fortune in New England, is not so much the better aptitude for business or the cunning of the New Englanders, but their way of doing all kinds of business at the same time, which lowers the price for goods and services by continuous competition and leaves no room for newcomers."[4]

[2] Schaff, Philip, *America* (New York 1855), p. 64.

[3] Winckelblech, Christoph, *Wie's halt ist mit dem Reisen nach Amerika besonders in Kentucky und Genesy. Nach dem Französischen des Herr L. Bridel frey übersetzt* (Basel 1804), p. 91.

[4] Grund, Francis J., *Die Aristokratie in Amerika. Aus dem Tagebuche eines deutschen Edelmannes* (Stuttgart 1939) vol. ii, p. 111.

In the same vein is the following extract from a travelogue published some fourteen years later:

> "We were remarking to a Gentleman who was affording us much pleasant and general information, how few Jews one met in New England; and asking if he could assign any reason, he replied: Oh yes, the reason is, that no Jew on earth is a match for a Yankee."[5]

Similar, too, is the judgment of a German writer in 1870:

> "The Yankees are excellent businessmen. People say that the Jews are clever traders, but in the Yankees they have found their masters."[6]

Indeed, the excessive sharpness of the genuine Yankee as compared with the inhabitants of other American territories is given as an explanation of the fact that Jews stay away from the New England states.

John Bernard, for instance, writing as far back as 1797, draws particular attention to the aversion of the Southern trader to the Yankee peddler:

> "Smarting under this infliction, it can be no wonder that the Virginians indulge in occasional vituperations, insist that the Yankee cheats them in every transaction, and that, however he may vary his commodities from the traditionary wooden nutmegs and red-flannel sausages, swindling is still his talent, his stimulus and local distinction. In proof of this they point to the fact that there are no Jews in New England, the competition being too great for them to exist."[7]

Later, this becomes the general opinion:

> "Theodore Parker has remarked, in one of his sermons," says a writer in 1864, "that New England was one of the few places in the civilized world where there were no Jews. The Yankees are too sharp for the children of Israel. Jews, however, flourish in New York, and still more in the South and West."[8]

The Jewish immigrants themselves assess their economic achieve-

[5] Bunn, Alfred, *Old and New England* (London 1853), vol. i, p. 24.

[6] Bromme, Traugott, *Ratgeber für Auswanderungslustige* (Stuttgart 1846), p. 25.

[7] Bernard, John, *Retrospections of America*, 1797-1811 (New York 1887), p. 45.

[8] Nichols, Thomas L., *Forty Years of American Life* (London 1864), vol. i, p. 389.

ments (up to the middle of the nineteenth century) in a way that seems to confirm this judgment. They observe frequently that the time has been too short for them to get adapted to new conditions or learn the new language, and that many among them come from small towns and villages in Germany, where economic development is slow and not at all equal to the American pace. In other words, conditions are such that they can be no match for the Yankee.

Indeed, at the time when most German-Jewish immigrants had to take to peddling as a means of livelihood, the Yankees were already out of this stage and had begun the industrialization of New England.[9] This situation explains the immigrant's state of mind and the tone of his remarks about Americans. The latter are well characterized by a "Letter from Moses Levi to Levi Moses" contained in a humorous sketch, published in 1840, of life on an inland steamer. A Jewish passenger is made to observe:

> "I mosht afeart America ish no conetry for the Jewish, no more ash Scotland ish vitch hash notink in it at all put pride ant poverty, ant oatmeal and vishkey. Te Yankee all knowish too mush for us, ant ish too mush wide awake, ant sho sharp ash a neetle at making von pargain, vitch give no chansh at all to a poor jew to liff."[10]

Similar utterances, all employing the historic Jew-Yankee comparison, are also reported by other writers. Says Prince Demetrius Augustin Gallitzin, in a biography published in 1861:

> "Once I met . . . a German Jew who had opened a small store in the interior

[9] These reactions, however, belong to a later period. At first, when the Yankee had not yet given up peddling and the German-Jewish immigrant was beginning to resort to it, the two must have been on the same economic level. The Jewish newcomers had much to learn from their more experienced Yankee competitors, particularly in the matter of dealing with rustic customers. Many humorous stories are told about both. We are reminded, in fact, of the Jewish peddler in Germany, whose wit and gay philosophy are described by Johann Peter Hebel in his well-known *Village Tales.* Some of the American stories are couched in almost the same terms! So much, indeed, was the peddler relished for his originality that several writers expressed concern lest the type die out with the coming of railroad and steamship.

[10] *The Letter-bag of the Great Western, or Life in a Steamer* (Philadelphia 1840), p. 143. Published anonymously, this work is now attributed with certainty to Thomas Chandler Haliburton.

of the country, and told him I was wondering why more of his coreligionists do not settle in the country; he was the first Jew I saw outside New York and Philadelphia. 'Gosh,' he said, 'what can a Jew do in America? From one American you can make seven Jews.' "[11]

"I once bought something from a jeweller and optician," relates another author. "He was a Jew, a merry fellow. I asked whether he was doing good business in America, and he replied: 'Well, I am saying what all the others say, you can make two Jews from one American, leaving over one Christian.' "[12]

The same writer, referring to the German Jews, observes that

"Although they have a good social position here, they have only recently started to come in greater numbers. One says the Yankee is too Jewish in trade and religion, even for the Jew himself. Nevertheless, the Yankees are founding societies for converting the Jews."[13]

II

Not unnaturally, the immigrants tended to preserve in the New World many of the anti-Jewish prejudices which they had imported from their homelands. The Germans especially were ready at once to hold the Jews responsible for things they found disagreeable, but which were, in fact, purely American. The Yankees, they declared roundly, had borrowed their business methods from the Jews. This line of argument was particularly prevalent in early anti-emigration literature, where America was commonly represented as a land fit for unscrupulous and adventurous Jews, but not for respectable and ethically minded Germans.

A German anti-emigration pamphlet of 1853, for instance, makes sweeping and sinister use of the Jew-Yankee comparison:

"It is well known that our German compatriots are often badly cheated by their Hebrew 'fellow-citizens.' They are warned all the time, but with very little success. If one of these simple country yokels has been cheated ten

[11] Lemcke, Heinrich T., *Leben und Wirken des Prinzen Demetrius Augustin Gallitzin* (Münster 1861), p. 427.

[12] Löher, Franz, "Am Niagra," in *Deutsche Monatshefte,* vol. v (1855), 458.

[13] id., *Geschichte und Zustände der Deutschen in Amerika* (Cincinnati 1847), p. 441.

times by a Jew, you may be sure that at the first opportunity—despite all warnings—he will let the same son of Abraham take advantage of him again." "You can imagine how the Americans who are known to be 'sharper' than the children of Israel cheat such people."[14]

The same pamphlet also describes Jews and Americans as non-Europeans—an old German map shows the Jews as Africans—and continues with a comparison of Jews and Negroes:

"In reality the 'Africans' are in general better, nobler men and purer Christians than the cold and haggling Jewish-Christian Americans. The superiority of the Americans over the educated African shows only in one respect, as between Jews and Christians in Germany, in business matters. If low trade was 'trumps' in our Fatherland like in America, who knows whether the German Christians would not finally be treated like the Africans in America."[15]

Further, the author reproaches the Jews and Americans for their low standard of commercial ethics:

"Americans like Jews consider themselves the 'chosen people of Jehovah' and therefore believe they can go further in trade and haggling than the rest of humanity. They prefer the Old Testament, because its tendency suits low trade and business better. The Jews likewise consider the Old Testament as the principal basis for their religion. That is why the Jews resemble the Americans so surprisingly in their outward appearance and in their very heart."[16]

Malicious, even offensive, as was their tone, such observations were not inspired by antisemitism, but by a desire to combat emigration. They were directed against leaving one's fatherland, and the emphasis lay on the hopelessness of seeking to better one's position in the New World.

"Merchants and Israelites," says a treatise of 1853, "are known to be less credulous and inexperienced than workmen and peasants. One may say that among five hundred emigrants, one hardly finds fifteen businessmen or

[14] *Über die Auswanderung nach den Vereinigten Staaten von Nordamerika* (Karlsruhe 1853), p. 37.

[15] *ibid.*, p. 41.

[16] *ibid.*, p. 62.

Israelites, the rest are farmers and workmen. A striking fact. Yet, one should think that tradesmen and Israelites should stand a better chance in the 'Land of Liberty,' than in the 'Land of Police and Soldiers' as Germany is often called in lower-class business circles. Businessmen and Israelites know very well that they are better off in Germany than among the brutal American mob and an army of dangerous robbers, crooks, thieves and swindlers. They are clever and experienced and cannot be easily deluded by boasting and hollow phrases."[17]

The motives of the emigrants are represented as misguided, as is also their criticism of Germany, which they want to leave. The German state, runs the argument, is no good to those who want to profit by American "liberty," but persons who are not suited for the New World will find Germany a good place to live in, just because it is not contaminated by this new-fangled ideal:

"For the Jewish Nation, which in so many respects has the same sympathies as the Americans and resembles them most, American Liberty may seem very pleasant; but for the Christians and Christianized Israelites of Germany, American laws and institutions would have most sad and unhappy consequences. Hebrews who wish to see 'American Liberty,' do not know what they are doing."

"Let us thank God that there are not many 'free cities' in Germany, because otherwise all Germany with its good inhabitants, would certainly have been sold and deported. We can be grateful for our many German Governments, else our 'German Brothers from Israel' would have—a long time ago—oppressed, bought and sold us, or offered us on the markets of the world."[18]

"No class of immigrants gets Americanized as easily and quickly as the Jews. No wonder; almost nowhere in Europe could they find a country granting them full citizenship rights like the Union. One should not take it amiss that they deny their European nationality, they certainly do not deny their Oriental one, and in America they find at least again the trading spirit of their people."[19]

This was a comparatively mild statement, evidently written by a lonely German newcomer, who felt like the sole European in a strange

[17] *ibid.*, p. 29.
[18] *ibid.*, p. 13, 37.
[19] *Deutsche Monatshefte,* vol. ii (1853/54), 480.

world. However, as the fight against emigration continued, the tone of such observations became more and more acrimonious.

Emigrant descriptions of America sometimes endeavor to portray the peculiarities of the Yankee without attacking his economic principles and without using the Yankee-Jew comparison. As a rule, however, it is his commercial prowess upon which attention is focussed, and comparison with the Jew then becomes inevitable.

In the first place, the "business manners" of the Yankee are compared with those of the Jew, and criticism is made of the very similar way in which both proceed when selling their wares. Typical is the following from a report on the stores of New York, written in 1819:

> "Many of the shops remain well stocked with an assortment of dry goods in general, and when a customer or stranger goes into one of them with a view of purchasing an article, they uniformly make a practice of asking twice as much as they mean to take. The Yankees think nothing cheap, unless they can get off one half the price at first asked; and it is a common practice among the ladies to go from shop to shop a whole morning, endeavoring to find out who sells the cheapest and, what is pretty certain, they get taken in at the end. The shopkeepers all bear the names of Jews and sharpers in their mode of traffic, and no persons on earth approach nearer to a Jew's manner of dealing, or better deserve the disgraceful appellation."[20]

Jew and Yankee are also compared for their uncanny knowledge of their merchandise and their innate aptitude for trading:

> "Most Jewish immigrants know more about goods than the Americans, perhaps because they used to live among solid businessmen on the other side. However, a competent informant tells me that they cannot attain the ability of the tradesmen born in America." . . .
> "Inclination for business is not a specific property of the Jewish nation, it is a consequence of the Anglo-Jewish way of life, the Anglo-Saxon fosters it almost as much as the Jew."[21]

The prospective emigrant is warned, however, in highly colored descriptions, that business spoils character and that competition is bad

[20] *Clear and Concise Statement of New York* (New York 1819), p. 12.

[21] Gloss, Albert, *Das Leben in den Vereinigten Staaten* (Leipzig 1864), vol. i, p. 471, 503.

for the soul. One author observes that while shopkeepers and merchants may well grow rich and live in affluence, they can never achieve true "culture," because they lack all contact with the higher things in life. He adds that both Jew and Yankee amass their fortunes only at the cost of self-degradation, resorting to falsehood and duplicity and accepting any humiliation for the sake of profit.

> "The American, conceited and proud of being a shopkeeper, appears disgusting and arrogant, and the German Jew, wanting to show off, brags and becomes insolent. Both nationalities show almost the same liking for bad taste in luxury. . . . They surpass each other in bad taste. Harmony in colors, decency in manners, and the fundamental ideas of simplicity in elegance are as unknown to America as to Israel."[22]

> "The American (and in general the Israelitic businessman in Germany) will put up with humiliations, trouble, physical and moral sufferings, if he can only satisfy his egotism and lust for money."[23]

> "It is what we may call: the Jewish system in Christianity."[24]

> "In America, the situation is the same as in Israel. . . . On the whole, both Americans and Jews are disagreeable companions. They know each other's principles only too well and therefore despise, hate and fear each other. When Americans and Jews start discussing 'business,' quarrels and insults are sure to develop. They call each other 'friends,' 'brothers,' 'honest men' or 'crooks,' whatever seems more advantageous at the moment. These people do not know a true and clean friendship, such as reigns among the better classes in Germany, their 'business envy' and jealousy do not allow it."[25]

The European tendency to take the character of Shylock as a stereotype of the Jews is likewise exploited to lend color to the picture of America. One writer characterizes the Yankee by remarking simply that "his greediness is very similar to that of the sons of Abraham";[26] while another reproaches the Americans for imposing harsh conditions when lending money at interest: "No braggart from Gascogne," says he, "can

[22] *Über die Auswanderung etc.*, p. 68.
[23] *ibid.*, p. 52.
[24] *ibid.*, p. 55.
[25] *ibid.*, p. 62.
[26] Trollope, Mrs., *Leben und Sitte in Nordamerika* (Kiel 1835), p. 186.

bluster more, no Jew can practise more usury. Every 'Yankey' is a 'lawyer' in the American sense of the word, a pettifogger."[27]

In one instance, the practices of the American Stock Exchange are compared trenchantly with those of Shylock:

> "Wall Street is the Rialto for merchants, stock jobbers, and note shavers of every class and description. It is the Exchange of New York. The statistical information which one might receive in two months of the various methods of swindling and the different 'ways and means' by which the host of Shylocks who infest it, get rich, would fill a volume close."[28]

The comparison, at first restricted to a particular field of activity, tends later to become generalized, the manners and conventions of Yankee society being regarded as identical, no more no less, with "Shylock's social principles."

> "On the whole, the behavior of the aristocrats in the Northern States towards the working classes corresponds to the sound maxims of Shylock in his conduct toward the Christians. 'I will buy with you,' says the Jew, 'talk with you, walk with you, and so following, but I will not eat with you, drink with you or pray with you.' "[29]

Propaganda of this type seeks especially to demonstrate that with such an inner turpitude of character a man cannot look outwardly decent and dignified. Describing the American, these publications criticize his gestures and bearing, and stress the fact that he often physically resembles a Jew:

> "The movements of the American in social life are affected and formal. . . . We never saw a male or female American who knew how to bow gracefully and give a friendly greeting. . . . Careful observers will notice the same in the manners of the majority of German Israelites."[30]

The physical resemblance of the Yankee to the Jew is sometimes

[27] *Bilder und gesellschaftliches Leben der Nord-Amerikaner . . . Von einer Deutschen* (Reutlingen 1835), p. 44.

[28] Collyer, Robert H., *Light and Shadows of America* (Boston [1838]), p. 14.

[29] Grund, *op. cit.,* vol. i, p. 148.

[30] *Über die Auswanderung etc.,* p. 68.

extended to Anglo-Saxons in general, as in the following description of life in London:

> "My impressions of the Yankees were repeated in London, when looking at small trades-people, several times I took Jews for Englishmen, and Englishmen for Jews. On the provisions-markets, like Tottenham Court Road [or] Leather Lane, on a Saturday night, with their to-do and shouting, people seem more Jewish than in Chatham Street in New York.". . .
> "The Englishman's looks, etc., are more Jewish than those of the American. However, there is still quite some difference. . . ."[31]

Nor is it only in outward bearing that the Yankee is disparagingly likened to the Jew. He is also charged with traits of behavior usually regarded as characteristically Jewish. He is said, for instance, to indulge in the familiar "Jewish" practice of incessantly asking questions:

> "The investigation of truth," says a humorous writer of 1849, "may be performed in three different ways: by asking questions; by making guesses; and by peeping through key-holes. The first method is the most common, and appears to be of great antiquity, though I am unable to say who first invented asking questions. Probably it was one of the Yankee Jews."[32]

Similarly, his spirit is said to become cramped for want of noble thoughts, and evidence of this is found in the aversion to military service which allegedly characterizes both Jews and Yankees:

> "Americans like Israelites have a decided aversion to militarism, such as exists in Germany."[33]

Moreover, he is accused of displaying a baseless and inordinate pride in the mere fact of being an American[34]—a pride which is compared with the "false haughtiness" of the Jew.

[31] Gloss, *op. cit.*, vol. i, p. 547. The same author refers (*ibid.*, p. 485) to the "Jewish-English way of life."

[32] Valentine, W., *A Budget of Wit and Humor* (Philadelphia 1849), p. 139.

[33] *ibid.*, p. 69.

[34] Griesinger, Theodor, *Lebende Bilder aus Amerika* (Stuttgart 1858), p. 223: "No horse-dealer can be more proud of having cheated a Christian, than the Yankee of his quality of being an American."

III

So far we have drawn mainly on foreign anti-emigration literature. But what of the Yankees' and Jews' own estimates of one another? Of the former only a few examples have been preserved in literature, but the following extract, taken from the confessions of a man who calls himself a proud and unchangeable Yankee, may be regarded as typical:

> "I have lived and mixed with people from all parts of the world, but still I like the New England character. When I am traveling and looking for a place to stay over night I feel at home when I strike a Yankee. This talk about free hearted Western men and Southern hospitality is a good deal like Southern chivalry: a humbug. I shall always be a Yankee, and hail from Maine. . . ."[35]

This writer has followed the evolution of life in the West, and his absolute faith in the economic superiority of the American begins to waver. Being a genuine Yankee, isolated in his New England home from contact with other parts of the country, he does not offer any critical examination of the business capacities of the Westerners and Southerners. They rank, he thinks, somewhere after the Chinese, whose trading abilities he seems to appreciate: "These Chinese are the greatest traders in the world. They lay over the genuine Yankee even in buying and selling."[36]

Finally, he compares the Jews' capacity for assimilation with his own:

> "I have been too liberal. There is none of the Yankee shrewdness about me. People never guess that I came from New England. Now, I am going to try to be a Jew from this out. As far as I have noticed, the men who make money here are Jews, mean men and thieves."[37]

The Yankee surely made such a comparison quite often. Other observers, however, describe the cooperation of Yankees and Jews in

[35] White, Katherine A., ed., *A Yankee Trader in the Gold Rush. The Letters of Franklin A. Buck* (Boston 1930), p. 215.

[36] *ibid.*, p. 128.

[37] *ibid.*, p. 214.

times of economic prosperity as easy and without friction, implying in general equal business abilities.

Insofar as the Jewish immigrant's reaction is concerned, in the initial stage of his economic adjustment he had, as observed above (p. 7), a decided feeling of inferiority. Later, however, with the advent of prosperity, his self-confidence increased, amounting at times to a jubilant optimism. Particularly glowing reports came from the West Coast.

> "The Jews," says a representative German writer, "feel very much at home [in America], their genius can emerge much more brilliantly in their lofty contest with the Yankees, much better than in Germany. . . . We know many Jews who have important positions of trust in big business houses owned by Yankees who had no connection with immigrant circles, others who have founded new kinds of factories unknown before, and employ many workers who are satisfied with their employers."[38]

A still more favorable account refers to the situation in California:

> "The goods, from the moment they leave the ships until they get into the customer's hands, pass almost exclusively through Jewish hands. They seem to handle nearly all trade operations, as importers, buyers and storekeepers. Our business streets are tightly filled up with their shops, warehouses and offices. Their position in business is very important and without them trade would stop in our State. . . . The companies handling trade to the interior depend mostly on their assistance, and the shipping-registers and freight-lists swarm with their names."[39]

In times of depression, when weaker concerns fail, the Jewish press mentions with pride that Jewish firms have already reached the level of the solid American firms of long standing, adding that among so many which went bankrupt, there were no Jewish houses and particularly none with German-Jewish proprietors.

[38] *Der israelitische Volkslehrer,* vol. ix (1859), 350-56, quoting an article in Wiesner's publication, *Geist der Weltliteratur.* The article in question was reprinted in *Die Deborah,* vol. v (1859/60), 62.

[39] "Die commercielle Stellung der Juden in California," in *Allgemeine Zeitung des Judentums,* vol. xxi (1857), 27. The article was reproduced from *Voice of Israel,* No. 6.

"Last year," says a typical report of 1855, "a sharp depression reigned in the business world and particularly in the West; many tradesmen became its victims. However, our Jewish business houses stood firm and our merchants kept their reputation of solid, noble-minded and clever men."[40]

IV

Just as in native folklore the progress of America is exemplified by the transformation of the Yankee from a humble, impoverished rustic to the versatile, courageous and resourceful symbol of a rising and expanding nation, so in the European conception of him he changes rapidly into a hero of adventure and a figure of romance. In this development too the time-honored comparison with the Jew plays an important role. The historic community of progress between the Jew and the Yankee in the New World does not pass unnoticed, and a good deal of Jewish cultural coloring is introduced into the popular picture of America. The characteristics of the Yankee are delineated in a manner which suggests the Jew; while Yankee humor, robust and not shy of self-criticism, frequently draws attention to the similarity of outlook which both share. The similarity once noted and admitted, the way is paved for a sense of joint endeavor in a common experiment—a sense which later helps considerably to weld the diverse elements of the republic into a united whole. To be sure, the Yankees sometimes misunderstand their neighbors, Jews included, but such misunderstandings never shake the solid basis of a common way of life. Paramount is the feeling that all are partners in a great new experience.

Yankee sayings and maxims begin to appear as a distinct branch of American folklore, and with them frequent references to the place of the Jew in the Yankee paradise. At first, to be sure, there are suggestions of the Shylock *motif,* but since the relevant allusions are usually made in a tone of humorous self-knowledge, it is probable that they were intended as sly digs at the Yankee himself rather than as attacks on the Jews. Certain it is that in the later period the Jew is generally represented as very much like the Yankee, the old invidious contrast having given way to a recognition of the fact that all men are the same under the skin. The

[40] *Allgemeine Zeitung des Judentums,* vol. xiii (1855), 565.

equality of all human beings, descended from the same primeval parents, is brought out with emphasis:

> "Who were Adam and Eve?
> Yankees, by thunder."[41]

As the new attitude emerges, the Jew-Yankee comparison takes on the character of a simple equation. The most eloquent example of this is afforded, perhaps, by the humorous sketch of a steamboat trip written by a Southern writer in 1852:

> "As the captain passed the money over . . . the lower jaws of the disappointed sharpers fell about a foot, and almost simultaneously [they] exclaimed:
> 'Jewed!'
> 'Yankee'd!'
> 'Bit!'
> The crowd, who were bound to have a good time anyway—and more especially now that the joke was so much richer than was expected—were in a collapsed state; they yelled, cheered and shouted until the cabin fairly shook."[42]

So far as the present writer is aware, there is but one other recorded instance of the word *Yankee* used as a verb, and its synonymity with the expression "to Jew" surely speaks volumes.

Not very different, in point of general characterization, is a description of the New England states given in a German "guide for emigrants" published in 1864:

> "The inhabitants are called *Yankees* in all other parts of the Union. . . . they fraternize closely and are the Jews of the New World, they stand together like one man. . . . They are dominated by insatiable greediness."[43]

In line with this development, the Jew is introduced into Yankee jokes without any suggestion of obloquy or disparagement. As an expert

[41] *Yankee Notions,* vol. iii (1854), 102.
[42] Baldwin, Oliver P., *Southern and South-Western Sketches* (Richmond [1852]), p. 186.
[43] Reidenbach, J. A., *Amerika* (Nördlingen 1870), p. 116.

in monetary matters and stock exchange transactions he is presented simply for what he is, not as a caricature of the ruthless usurer:

> . . . Went out and met Mordecai Ben Jezreen, the Jew broker from Amsterdam. What do you think of Erie? "Oh, it ish goat-great roat, wide gauge—makesh five hundred dousand a month. It will pe par in vone year." Good again, thought I, a Jew never mistakes in money matters. Abraham was the very first man who made a cash bargain. He bought a grave of the sons of Heth, and weighed out the silver for it. His posterity from this very day quit land speculations and went into stocks. Jew knows. "Par in one year," Mordecai says. . . .[44]

Similarly, the diary of a Jewish broker, describing a week in his life, is considered interesting reading matter for the general public:

> "*Sunday.*—No buishness to be done—de Christians all out, making holiday —waited at home for Monshou, he never come. Took a walk in de park, and afterwards directed my steps toward the Battery—pad luck all the day.
> *Monday.*—On' Change till two—man in black coat and white cravat wanted to borrow monish, did not like his looks; in de afternon, made it my buishness to call in Fift Avenue—not at home—pad luck indeed—thought to have touched dere.
> *Tuesday.*—On' Change; berry good luck; met de gentleman wid de white wig; wanted more monish, let him have it, good securitish, like gentlemen wid white wigs. Carried my advertisement to the Herald Office, signed Z. pretty crooked letter dat, always sure to bring in good customers; I may expect calls tonight.
> *Wednesday.*—Met my bery good friend, Mr. Smash, not seen him a bery long time—immediately arrested him for de few dollars he owes me—den went home to prepare for de Sabbath.
> *Thursday.*—Met my son Izaak on Change, wanted me to lend him monish to make up a sum he had promised some young Christian, assured me security was undoubted; but I refused—tink Izaak would get de best of dat bargain; cunning youth is Izaak, quite a credit to his tribe, but he cannot yet come it over his fader.
> *Friday.*—Bery pad in ped all the day long.
> *Saturday.*—Went twice to de Synagogue,—repented of all my shins, felt bery much comforted; must remember to call in de morning on de man in de white wig; nor must I forget to visit de Christian widow and offer her

[44] *ibid.*, p. 379.

some monish, to enable her carry on de buishness. She has written a note to a friend of mine, in which she states her husband has left an excellent property, but that she requires a triffle of ready cash; I will accomodate the poor woman."[45]

Nor is it rare to find typically Jewish jokes related in the confident belief that the Yankee will at once "catch on." The following, for instance, is told as a *Yankee* joke:

"Rabbi Joshua once met a boy who carried something in a covered vessel. 'My boy,' said the Rabbi, 'what have you in your covered vessel?' 'If it was intended for you to know,' replied the boy, 'it would not be covered.' "[46]

The inevitable climax of this tendency is an emphasis on the equality of all men and their common modes of thought. This is brought out expressively in a genial tale which appeared in 1853 in a typical Yankee magazine and which deserves reproduction here on account of its representative character:

Abraham S. is a liberal minded, jovial German Jew, and one of the best I ever knew. He tells an amusing story on his countryman Isaac Finkerhaus. Isaac left Germany in 1844, and wandering westward through the United States, found himself the following year in Santa Fe, New Mexico, then a part of the Mexican Republic. I will now let Abraham speak, and tell his tale in his own words.

"You see when Isaac got here in Santa Fe, times were devilish dull, an' he didn't know to git at to make a living. I knowded he would do anything wath I would tell him to do, 'cause I vas here one year before him, an' know'd de ropes. So one day, says I to Isaac, "Ike, vy de h—ll don't you git to making money? You is bin here a whole munt, an' ain't made de fuss red zent."

"Got knows," says Isaac, "an' you, too, knows t—n vell, I vould make him, should so pe I coot git one leetle start."

"You all knows, boys," continued Ab., "dat Santa Fe is de greatest plaze in de vorld for houseflies. Dare is more of 'em here dan in de whole vorld, an' day is mighty tame, too." So, when Isaac says to me he only vanted a leetle start, I comes out an' lays my plan before him. Says I, "Isaac, you knows dis is Spanish country, don't you?"

[45] *ibid.*, vol. i (1852), 146.
[46] *ibid.*, vol. ii (1853), 226.

"I spegs so," says Isaac, "pecause de people speags Spanish."

"Taint nuttin else," says I, "an ef de country is Spanish country, of course de flies, dey is *Spanish flies.*"

"Now is dey, Abraham?" says Ike.

"Well dey is," says I, "an' you knows dat Spanish flies dey prings four dollars a poun' in Germany. You can catch an' dry four poun' on 'em every day, an' dares twelve dollar made in one day."

"Tank Got," says Isaac, "an' vy you no tell me dat pefore? Me pegin dis day to catch him, an' me vill make de little start mit de Spanish fly."

So Isaac, he goes straight off, mighty trembly, wid his eyes open, he was so full of hope, an' he gits a big black bottle to put his flies in. He began to catch 'em in my store fuss. You would a' died a laughin' to see Isaac wid his bottle in his lef han', stoppered wid de forfinger, a goin' about de room catchin o' flies. He vould eeze his right han' up, half shot, close to a fly, an' all at once, he vould give a sweep around, so, an' sure enough dare vould be de fly catched, an' sometimes more'n a dozen on 'em. Ike worked powerful in my storeroom, an' he sweated a heap; but I vas afeared some t—n fool vould come in an' tell him better, so says I—

"Isaac, you can do mighty vell here, but you can do a heap better, ef you go down to de creek, to de places vere dey kills sheep."

So he goes down dare, an' vorks all day widout eatin' no dinner. Jess before dark he comes back powerful tired, an' sorter low dawn in de mouf. I vas mose dead jess for de vant of about two hours laughin'; but I vouldn't a laughed for a dollar, so I looked solemn, ven I axed Isaac vot luck he had.

"Mine pottle pe no more as haef vull."

"Don't give up, Isaac," says I, "better luck nex' time. Now eat your supper, an' den dry your flies in de skillet."

De flies dat Ike cotched dat day veighed jess tree ounces. He hunted all de nex' day, an' didn't do quite vell. Ven he vas out at vork, I told John Jones, Solomon and Little Tom all about it, an' dey all come moghty near a dyin' a laughin'. De tird day, Little Tom, he muss go an' let all out to everybody.

Ven Issac hearn how everybody vas a laughin' at him, he smell de rat, and know'd how bad he vas took in. He vas de maddest man I ever seed, an' ef now you vant to see a rale mad man, all you has to do is to talk before him about Spanish flies. Dat's de plan some peoples follows wid him, but it vill do jess as vell to go up to a fly, where he can see you, an' make a grab at it—so—makin' b'lieve you vant to catch it."

At this point Abraham is very apt to end his joke, when he tells it on his friend Isaac, since in the sequel the "tables are turned" upon him; but if any one should hint that that is not quite all, he will continue, though a little reluctantly:

"No, dat ain't quite all, I vish to Got it vas. But Isaac swore you see, dat dat trick I played on him he vould make me pay like h—ll; an' sure 'nough he did, aldo I don't like to tink about it. You see, Isaac, he vas in dem times d—n poor, but he soon get vell off, an' vas good pay. One time he vanted a tousand dollar, an' I len' him to Isaac because I know'd he could pay me. Vell, ven he vanted to pay me wid goots in his store at Santa Fe prices, an' dat was den one hundred per cent. Course I vouldn't tink on it. But Isaac played a trick on me to make me take 'em.

One day I heard somebody say, talkin' to somebody else, "Dey tell me Isaac Finkerhaus is certainly about to break!" Ven I heard dat, my bref got sorter short, 'cause I was scared like h—ll about de tousand dollar. So I goes right off to one o' Isaac's best friends, dat know'd his condition, an', says I, pretendin' to be mighty careless,

"Dey say Isaac is gwine to break—I am d—n glad he don't owe me nuthin.' "

"Vell," says Isaac's friend—he vas sot up to it, but I didn't 'spect nuttin'. "Vell," says he, sorter sorrowful, "I don't know how dat is, but I knows dat he owes me tree tousand dollar, an' I can't get the fuss red cent out'n him."

Ven I heard dat, I vas sure Isaac was gone, so, tinkin' I vould be before everybody else, I runs right to Isaac's store, an' takes out my tousand dollar in goots, at one hundred per cent on cost. So soon as de ting vas done, and settled good, Isaac he says to me:

"You is de only man me does owe, Abraham, put me tink him petter to break a leetle to-day, to make you take de goots. So me make five hundred dollar."

I couldn't say nuttin', I vas so mad. Ven I vas goin' away, Isaac, he stop me, an' says he:

"Now, Abraham, you von't *fly* no more, vill you?"[47]

The changed conception of the Yankee and the changed attitude towards the Jew were also reflected in the conventions of the stage. Hitherto, the public had been prepared to accept as true portrayals the burlesque, even grotesque, caricatures drawn by the caprice of dramatists. Now, however, a healthy instinct, born of experience, rebelled against such distortions, and henceforth the figures of Jew and Yankee as pre-

[47] *ibid.*, p. 164 ff.

sented across the footlights had to be true to life. "I believe it is more probable," says Richard Dorson, summing up this development, "that a permanent Yankee folk type existed apart from his dramatic incarnation and was adopted, and not created by the playwrights."[48]

Into the new characterization of the Yankee, Jewish traits inevitably entered. Permanent elements in the merry image of the stage Yankee are his name, always "of homespun timbre" (sometimes "Jacob Jewsharp,"[49] referring to his ability to play that musical instrument) and the scene of his visit to the Big Town, suggestive of the country bumpkin visiting the city.[50]

The feeling that Jews and Yankees are innately akin leads ultimately to a kind of cultural syncretism, the characteristics of both being combined, in popular literature, in a single character. Says a descriptive writer in 1853:

> "In several parts of America there is a curious combination of theatre and museum under one roof; three of which (at New York, Baltimore and Boston) we had an opportunity of attending. So that, in the last of these cities, we were especially invited by the courtesy of Mr. Moses Kimball, proprietor thereof, who expressed a hope, in forwarding us a card of free entree, that we would visit his 'little Yankee theatre.' We availed ourselves of his politeness, and the following is a summary of what passed. We found Mr. Kimball in his office a tall, stalwart, lusty-looking fellow, with a marked countenance, in which it was difficult to determine whether the cautious look of the Jew, or the cunning one of the Yankee, preponderated."[51]

Somewhat later, when the popular conception of the Yankee becomes inextricably associated with notions of "humbug" and "ballyhoo," this cultural syncretism is caricatured by means of comic and bizarre hybridizations. A striking example is the figure of an "Indian Christian Dutch Jew Yankee Actor." There is more in this than mere fun; it is a joke dependent upon observation, and it is not without significance that

[48] "The Yankee on the Stage—A Folk Hero of American Drama," in *New England Quarterly,* vol. xiii (1940), 467-93, especially p. 478.

[49] *ibid.,* p. 478.

[50] Cf. *ibid.,* p. 469.

[51] Bunn, *op. cit.,* vol. ii, p. 109.

the writer who coins it takes pains to affirm that only by the mixture of *all* these national ingredients can "the Yankee Actor" be produced. Indeed, the son of "a Jewish immigrant and an Indian squaw, Mr. Winnerbag, the half-Indian, half-Jew conjurer and comedian," is portrayed as so much of a hybrid that he shows but little appreciation of the Jewish element in his cultural heritage:

> "My father came from there (Jericho) or from Jerusalem, and I'll avoid it. The old Jew cheat to come over to this country, and enter the family of Gray Bear, the fine old Indian. I'll never forgive it, I only wish I could catch him. I'd give him Erebus to eat for a pumpkin squash."[52]

This cultural crossing and blending is described at length in a passage which merits quotation in full:

> "Frame Winnerbag was a son of an Indian squaw and his father was a Dutch Jew, who, turning his jewish nose up at his Gentile progeny, left him to the Christian care of Ephraim Smallpiece, a quaker of New England, who gave the little Indian son of the Dutch Jew the name of Ephraim Winnipeg, which, after the quaker's early death, became corrupted into Frame Winnerbag. It would be difficult to describe the countenance of this man. He had the red man's eye and mouth, and his frame was muscular, while he inherited his father's jewish nose, and was seized or possessed of a pair of red whiskers, which had probably descended to him from his red grandfather, who rejoiced in the soubriquet of Gray Bear. In all other respects he was a Yankee, and when I saw him he was *alive* and *acting*. All these facts put together constituted Mr. Winnerbag, the low comedian, a specimen of an *Indian Christian Dutch Jew Yankee actor.*
>
> It was in the large room of the inn near the railway, at Manyuck, Pennsylvania, that I first met Mr. Winnerbag, who was then in the fire-eating and super-human conjuration line of life, an engagement as an actor having failed him. His bills, which were partly written and partly printed, informed the citizens of Manyuck that "the American Necromancer" would, for two nights only, walk upon bars of hot iron, take an impression in molten lead on his tongue, eat a burning torch like a salad, swallow four and twenty clasp-knives, cut off the head of a live fowl and restore it, and perform the gun delusion. I attended the exhibition and after the performance entered into conversation with the conjurer.

[52] *Uncle Sam's Peculiarities* (London 1844), vol. ii, p. 10.

. . . "My blood is of the red man, stranger; my home is in the woods, which you European robbers—I don't mean you, stranger, but everybody in these States—the European robbers are continually advancing upon. I'm a Wnnipeg *Indine*. Did you ever see one before?"

"No."

"Write to your friends, then, and tell them I scorn to live with the pale faces, but can't help it. I know I am a Winnipeg; I feel it day and night in my limbs and in my state of mind. I know that my grand-father was a chief called Gray Bear, and a better man than General Jackson, by a considerable majority. But those white people out in the Far West have hunted the hunters out of their hunting grounds and you see me here conjuring, like a fool, to a parcel of Manyuck store-keepers (who haven't the heart to come and spend their levies like men) merely because I can't find my own family, and the Philadelphia theatres are quite full, and doing a bad business."

"Then you are an actor by profession."

"Why, I calculate I *can* do a few in that line; at least some people say so, and they never speak a word that isn't true. I shall be at Wemyss's the humbug American theatre, Walnut street, in the fall. A precious *American* theatre, when he is an Englishman and nearly the whole company a parcel of unnatural emigrants, keeping native talent out of employ! But Wemyss is as good an American as any of the pale faces, I guess. The robbers! Where's my home and my family? Where's the present Gray Bear, for the one died? Tell me that, stranger; and tell me if I'm not wronged by these old-countrymen, as they call themselves, who keep come, come, coming over the water, as if there wasn't enough already. They bring out so many actors, too, that a genooin comedian, who can't act all parts, and squeeze himself into the common stage wardrobe, hasn't a chance. Here's a pretty fix. I come here to amoose the Manyuckers with my beautiful delusions, which I paid twenty-five dollars to learn of a blessed cheat of an Italian quack doctor, and so help me, the entire night's amoosements only bring in seventeen levies and some short weights, and I have to pay a dollar and a half for the room."

"You call yourself Winnerbag, I think."

"No, stranger, I don't. I call myself Gray Bear, when I am at home, somewhere between the Blue Mountains and the Pacific Ocean. My father was a Jew cheat, and I don't know *his* name, but I know who my grandfather was, the fine old *Indine,* and that's more than some of these white robbers do. An old New Englander who educated me at Nantucket lower class college, gave me the name of Winnipeg, but he died, and I had to get my living at a theatre, when only *so* high or a little higher. So, one day there was a raffle for a bag of stage properties, and because I won it, they called me Winnerbag ever since. But one name's as good as another, if I can't have my own. Are you a Jackson man?"

"The other ticket entirely."

"Well the, I say d— General Jackson. D'ye think, sir, I'd have such luck as this if he hadn't passed the Treasury Bill? Manyuck here, a large town, and only seventeen levies for the entire series of my popular and beautiful delusions! Scalp 'em, I say. Stranger, I scalp a few now and then—that's a fact."

"It is the blood of the Gray Bears, and was in it before that old Jew blackguard, my father, came to this country and entered into our family. But, d'ye chew, sir?—this is the best lavendish. Here, now; I'll tell you how I fix it. Were you ever behind the scenes, sir?"

. . . It so happened, that in the winter I was at Philadelphia . . . and the Indian Christian Dutch Jew Yankee Actor was in the company. . . ."[53]

V

Between 1830 and 1860, when the attention of emigrant nations was directed to the economic rise of the New World and the success of industrialization, the conception of the Yankee entered a new phase. A magic phrase gained dominance: "Yankee humbug." Like many similar slang expressions, the term *humbug* outran its original connotation. No longer did it mean "malevolent cheating" or retain its primitive suggestion of wilful deceit. Rather did it denote the creation of illusions in order to obtain social and economic success. It became the symbol of American showmanship, of "build-up," the technique of boosting Yankee achievements by surrounding them with an atmosphere of glamor. The "King of Humbug," Barnum himself, exemplified the development by describing himself as "a very good sort of representative Yankee."[54]

Europe agreed to this characterization, but saw in him also the genius of Yankee humbug. Europeans never learned that the same time an appeal was being issued to American patriots to remove "the fashion of the age"—the Age of Humbug.[55] And they would have been surprised

[53] *ibid.*, vol. i, p. 230.
[54] Barnum, P. T., *The Humbugs of the World* (New York 1866), p. iv.
[55] Reese, David Meredith, *Humbugs of New York* (New York 1838), p. 267.

to hear that things which enjoyed a solid reputation among them, like Homeopathy, were actually regarded in America as "foreign humbug."[56]

Jewish immigrants and Jews in the emigrant countries believed that America was essentially the Land of Humbug. In the Jewish folklore and press of America the word is just as frequent as among the American public in general, and the Jews employ it freely to describe conditions in their own congregations and communities. Typical is the following extract from an exchange of correspondence (from New York) concerning the employees of Jewish communities:

> "This year again, immigration from Europe is unusually large. We wish to stress that at present a stream of Jewish teachers, preachers and Rabbis from Germany pours on us. . . . many dishonest and incapable fellows. . . . They are admirably clever in getting hold of and using American humbug. People who had to leave Europe, place the word "Rev." before their names, then add "Rabbi" and shortly afterwards "Dr." In Europe they could scarcely have found a situation as teacher or Chasan in communities with a dozen families. With characteristic impudence, they get themselves paid publicity in the newspapers and appear before the public with sermons clumsily botched together from German books or else copied *verbatim* from them."[57]

The term "Humbug" likewise entered also into the conflict between different trends in Judaism, particularly in communal politics. Organizations and individuals are frequently reproached for humbug, because of their activities and viewpoint. Even the so-called "American *Minhag*" (religious usage) is stigmatized as "humbug and twaddle."[58] Indeed, there are instances of one contending party reproaching the other with not knowing enough about American humbug. Thus, for instance, a Philadelphia controversialist:

> "It is impossible for them to know American humbug and therefore they take the products of humbug for real facts"; there is some truth in this remark but not your correspondent is using humbug, but rather the publish-

[56] *ibid.*, p. 22.
[57] *Allgemeine Zeitung des Judentums,* vol. xxx (1866), 653.
[58] *ibid.*, p. 11.

ers of certain American papers. Humbug makes you laugh, the truth makes you angry. The furious articles in their papers prove it."[59]

There were, of course, also counter-tendencies tending to make it a patriotic deed to do away with humbug:

> "Considering the low degree of culture in some communities," says a report from New York, "one or the other of these Charlatans—through humbug—succeeds to get into a position for some time and to gain a certain reputation. However, even among the uneducated masses there are still enough judicious persons, who soon see through the humbug and are able to separate the chaff from grain."[60]

To be sure, the idea of humbug was in time so much attenuated as to become a subject for amusement rather than of contempt. One ingenious German observer thinks he has discovered that "The Yankee has a merry way of making humbug, like the robber knights of old," whereas the Germans when they try to imitate the Yankees, become "Crooks instead of Humbuggers."[61]

Jewish circles, however, are found reproaching Missionaries with humbug in the sense of outright fraud, as in one case where they declare that a convert advertised as "a learned Rabbi" who had been persuaded to renounce his ancestral faith was really a tailor named Polaski, a deserter from the Russian army in Sevastopol. "Here, like in all other countries," says a press commentary, "people hanker after publicity and nobody is surprised that in the very homeland of humbug they very often dish out clever stories to deceive the public for propaganda purposes."[62]

The concept of humbug disappeared but slowly from the Jewish picture of America. At first the prevalent opinion is that "Although the United States offer very great advantages and so many excellent things have been created and came from there, it is and will be the Fatherland of Humbug."[63]

With the passage of time, however, as America marched on to ever-

[59] *ibid.*, vol. xxix (1865), 655.
[60] *ibid.*, vol. xxxi (1867), 95.
[61] Löher, *Geschichte und Zustände etc.*, p. 412.
[62] *Allgemeine Zeitung des Judentums*, vol. xxxii (1868), 619.
[63] *ibid.*, vol. xlii (1878), 61.

increasing importance in production, humbug became transmogrified into glamor, the "Great Illusion," the ultimate dream of mankind.

VI

During the Civil War, some vestiges of regional limitations still existed; the term *Yankees* had not yet come to designate Americans in general, but was still used by the Southerners as a specific term of opprobrium for the inhabitants of the Northern states. Many a soldier of the Confederate Army wrote verses against the Yankees, such as no European brain could ever have conceived. Accusations of alleged oppression by the Northerners contain a comparison of the Yankee to the Philistines, who did not allow any smith to exercise his trade in the land of Israel:

> "The people of the North seemed to aim at keeping the South in the condition of the Israelites under the iron rule of the Philistines. There was no smith in all the land of Israel; for the Philistines said—lest the Hebrews make them swords and spears."[64]

But this was a mere episode. From the end of the nineteenth century onwards regional limitations disappear, and the Yankee became universalized. The expansion was marked by a parallel development in the folk-conception of him. On the American stage he lost his "local coloring" and was represented as hailing from a cosmopolitan America rather than a rural New England. All Americans came to love the New Englander's character, steeled in the sufferings of the pioneers, and his passion for liberty and peace. At the same time, in Europe, the most popular opera of all times showed the Yankee as the legitimate successor of the Englishman in the role of globe-trotter. "The Yankee is at home in the wide Universe."[65] Faith and the spirit of enterprise were held to be combined in his character. All the world had now come to notice what a volume of fifty years earlier had described as "the indomitable energy of the New Englander in every section of the globe," and to subscribe to the view that one could "place a Yankee on an uninhabited island, with

[64] Manigault, G., *The United States Unmasked* (London 1879), p. 93.
[65] His human value is notably set forth in Claudel's *Annunciation*.

but a bunch of shingles and a jacknife, and he would construct a vessel to convey him home."[66]

VII

The twentieth century New Englander, wishing to save his hereditary Yankee way of life, is faced with a dilemma; he often thinks sadly that the new century in America, levelling all living standards, will relegate him to a museum.

"What is a Yankee?" asks a typical New Hampshire writer, and answers with the last surviving trace of the historic comparison: "The Yankee watches pennies, approves of savings bank accounts, follows the maxims of Poor Richard, and shares with the Scotchman and the Jew the reputation of being 'near,' ready to drive a hard bargain. Almost every New England country village had in the nineteenth century its local 'squire,' who held most of the mortgages of the near-by farms and was known as 'Old Eight Per Cent.' "[67]

[66] *The Yankee Enterprise* (Boston 1855), p. iii.
[67] Fuess, Claude Moore, in *Yankee* (Dublin, New Hampshire), December 1935, p. 14.

THE ROTHSCHILD LEGEND IN AMERICA

THE legend of wealth, which was ascribed to the Jews alone of all immigrant groups, was brought to the New World on the magic carpet of folklore. The European tree which grew leaves of gold was allegedly harvested by the Jew with a sack, and in America, Jack, whose goose had laid a golden egg, was in the end "jewed out by the Jew" of the treasure in the nest. In Cincinnati's enlightened German schools, to be sure, the Jew who gleaned the golden leaves was replaced by a "merchant."[1] The phrase "rich as a Jew" became as familiar in American popular speech and literature as in England, where "the Jew that Shakespeare drew" was the embodiment of wealth.

The heroes of the American "tall tale" reflected aspects of the struggle with the prodigious natural forces of the new continent. Yet these heroes could be actual persons like Davy Crocket and Johnny Appleseed. To exemplify the tricks of the Yankee peddler — the first intimation of a newly evolving world of business — Sam Slick had first to be invented. Since there were no good exemplars of wealth in American literature and folklore, the Jew was useful as a substitute to make concrete the concept of unlimited treasure here. The humorist, to be on safe ground, combined an American historical fact with old-world folklore: "He had been in California and was rich as a Jew."[2]

Still later, when American fortunes had been accumulated, they lacked the respectability which only tradition can bestow. The legion of Rothschild anecdotes — for the most part containing a moral of European business — which are scattered through the early American press indicates that wealth here still required the reflected aura of Europe to win the confidence of the American public. We have a clue here to the process by which the old popular conception of the wealth of the Jews became identified with the personalities of the Rothschilds.

European immigrants made their own contributions to the origin of the Rothschild legend in the New World. In the first place, the Jew as a stereotype was one of the few common conceptions which the different national groups

* For background on the Rothschilds, *cf.* Balla Ignaz, *The Romance of the Rothschilds* (New York 1913); Corti, Egon Caesar, *The Rise of the House of Rothschild* (New York 1927); *Idem, The Reign of the House of Rothschild* (New York 1928); Roth, Cecil, *The Magnificent Rothschilds* (London 1939); and Ehrenberg, Richard, "Entstehung und Bedeutung grosser Vermögen, Das Haus Rothschild," *Deutsche Rundschau*, CVII, pp. 375–92; CVIII, pp. 27–52, 180–207.

[1] Knortz, Karl, *Amerikanische Redensarten und Volksgebraüche* (Leipzig 1907), p. 21.

[2] Shillaber, B. P., *Partingtonian Patchwork* (New York 1873), p. 191.

Reprinted from *Jewish Social Studies,* Volume XIX, 1957

brought with them from Europe. In comparing Jew and Yankee, whom they found on their arrival, the acquisitive instinct of both parties was the crucial point of resemblance. The Rothschilds represented the embodiment of Jewish success in Europe and the rest of the world, even though in America itself, the balance of success in this historic comparison was inclined in favor of the Yankee.[3] Here again the Germans, the largest group in the "old immigration," were familiar with the historic figure of the court Jew who financed their princes and had no difficulty with the concept of a Jewish World Banker, to whom all princes had to come. Former Hessian soldiers knew, moreover, which court Jews were involved in the financial transactions covering the payment of their mercenary wages.[4]

The German-American periodicals, further, revealed a familiarity with Rothschild as a figure of the old country. As the Jew in general was reduced to the common denominator of a human type by all immigrant groups, pump-priming by the Rothschilds — as sketched in European caricature[5] — was likewise their common conception. Nations and empires, even as individuals, had to borrow to carry on and it was the Jew who had the money to give. The reader of the American press developed an intimacy with Rothschild as a financial potentate of which no European statesman could boast, and a condition was reached — at least in the newspaper world — where for once good money drove out the bad and not the reverse.

The American Idea of the European Financial Potentate

At a time when there was as yet no written history of American fortunes, the American public was presented with a well documented business history of the House of Rothschild. Its relations to world affairs and possible social reforms and its connections with historic Jewry were examined.

The Rothschilds are the wonders of modern banking. Sprung from that poetic, that ancient, that mysterious race, from whom we derive all our religion and half of our civilization, we see the descendants of Judah, after a persecution of two thousand years, peering above kings, rising higher than emperors, and holding a whole continent in the hollow of their hands. The Rothschilds govern a Christian world. Not a cabinet moves without their advice. They stretch their hand, with equal ease, from Petersburgh to Vienna, from Vienna to Paris, from Paris to London, from London to Washington. Baron Rothschild, the head of the house, is the true king of Judah, the prince of the captivity, the Messiah so long looked for by this extraordinary people. He holds the keys of peace or war, blessing or cursing. To what will all this lead? Is the holy city to be rebuilt? — the third temple to rear its turrets to heaven? No. The lion of the

[3] Glanz, Rudolf, "Jew and Yankee. A Historic Comparison," Jewish Social Studies, VI (1944), pp. 3–30.

[4] The names, Jud Brüll and Jud Dessauer, among others, appear in the Anspach papers in the Bancroft Archives, New York Public Library.

[5] *Cf.* cartoon "Die Generalpumpe," in Fuchs, Eduard, *Der Jude in der Karikatur* (Munich 1921), p. 120.

tribe of Judah, Baron Rothschild, possesses more real force than David — more wisdom than Solomon. What do they care for the barren seacoast of Palestine? They are the brokers and counsellors of the kings of Europe and of the republican chiefs of America. What more can they desire? We understand that an accomplished and beautiful daughter of this house is married to an American, and intends soon to make New York her permanent residence. The beauty of Judah is not departed, nor is the strength of the house of Israel weakened.[6]

Although an American prospect for the House of Rothschild is here faintly indicated, other descriptions of the financial potentates revolved exclusively around the European scene and in several cases even suggested a sort of social criticism. Thus in a survey of the Rothschilds' European loans, a Tennessee periodical commented:

Can it be possible that the Rothschilds are entitled to such an immense wealth? Were the earth and all its comfort created for the enjoyment of a few? How can they sleep amid their vast possessions, free from the annoying dreams of poverty-tortured humanity![7]

Moral indictments and stern warnings against the Rothschilds' wealth appeared even in the early days of the House:

. . . The former high priests of Mammon have suffered reverses, have been swept of all their wealth, driven to despair, and perished by their own hands, and therefore the man who lives upon the produce of his own industry, may be more happy, and may be more secure than Rothschild, the Jew, with all his wealth and power . . .[8]

In general, references to the Rothschilds simply acknowledged the fact of their wealth, and, occasionally, were humorous:

High Change

Wasn't it Mr. Rothschild, as
Had his partic'lar post
To rub his shoulder 'gainst a king —
Chief of the monied host?

Obsequious courtiers throngin' round
His eye or nod to catch —
The Fate of princes in his shrug,
And battles in his scratch![9]

On his acceptance into good Knickerbocker society, the nouveau riche German Jew was compared with the financial potentate. The Rothschild story, however, remained free of such trivialities; it was rather elevated to a legend by the need to express the essence of capitalism in one great human example, that was, moreover, no individual fortune doomed to extinction,

[6] *Niles Weekly Register*, XLIX (1835–36), p. 40.
[7] "Editor's Table," in *South Western Literary Journal and Monthly Review* (Nashville), I, p. 316.
[8] "Appearance of Rothschild," in *Truth Teller*, V (1829), p. 126.
[9] *The New Orleans Weekly Picayune*, III, no. 44 (1840), p. 4.

but a family undertaking, continuing from generation to generation, and bound up with associations of the ancient race that was so close to the heart of those familiar with the Bible. The transformation of the most prominent European financial story of the 19th century into an American legend at the time that America required a legend of rising capital resulted exclusively from the exigencies of the business ideals of a newly rising American social class. This transformation was accompanied by general observations of the power of Rothschild money in relation to world problems of the time. Practical understanding of the political implications of his wealth was manifested in the following remark: "At this moment, as power is estimated, a Jew is the most powerful man in the world. Rothschild holds in his pocket the peace of the world."[10]

And the citizen could sleep in peace, for as long as Rothschild was not willing to finance war, there would be no war. At any rate this was the assurance given in a ditty with the refrain, "For brother Rothschild gives no cash."[11]

The power of money was approved not only for its effect on the general problem of peace but also on the fate of persecuted Jews of Rumania.

> It is said that the Rothschilds have let it be understood that the Government will find it hard to borrow money hereafter — a report which we hope is true. If the Jewish bankers will teach Christian rulers a few lessons in elementary humanity by cutting off their financial supplies, it will be an application of the "money power" which even the Bryanites might condone.[12]

This recognition of money power as such conferred stature upon the Jew, and an American valuation of Rothschild expressed it in these terms:

> For after all, money is the great power in the world today, more so than ever in any previous age of the world. And so long as money reigns supreme, the Jew will take a leading part in the affairs of the world even if he receive nothing more than a fair field and no favor.[13]

The reverse of this point of view saw only the reflection of Rothschild in assaying the position of Jewry of the time, *e. g.*, the comment of so liberal an organ as *Der deutsche Pionier*:

> . . . the claim to greatness of today's Jewry lies not so much in the scholarship of its great men as in the power of its Rothschilds.[14]

Special situations of American politics evoked practical applications of the stock figure of Rothschild. At the high point of the agitation of the Germans in America against the Roman Catholic Church, a cartoon appeared

[10] "Easy Chair," in *Harper's Magazine*, XVII (1858), p. 268.

[11] *Die Lokomotive* (Philadelphia), I (1851), p. 102.

[12] *The Nation*, LXXI (1900), p. 103.

[13] "The Death of Baron Rothschild," quoted from *New World*, in *Reform Advocate*, XX (1900–01), p. 641.

[14] "The Wandering Jew. A Lecture by Isaac M. Wise," in "Vom Büchertisch,"in *Der deutsc he Pionier*, X (1878), p. 343.

showing Peter's Pence, stuffed in sacks, on its way to Rothschild.[15] At a Populist Party convention, Rothschild, in all seriousness was held accountable for the American economic crisis.[16]

The Transformation

At the starting point, the Jew with the sack, gathering the golden leaves in the forest — at the end, the Jew who moves quite freely in the American leaf forest with all his amassed gold, not to frighten children, but as living proof of the virtue of thrifty capital; the Jew, who was never outwitted even by the Yankee, the Jew as money institution — Rothschild. He is beyond censure, his necessity is beyond doubt, he would have to be invented as an institution if he did not exist, like the equally necessary institution of money. In the whole treasury of Rothschild anecdotes, so eagerly absorbed by the American press, there was no word of censure, no doubt concerning any of his decisions or actions, which could just as well have occurred to any American businessman. The report in Audubon's memoirs, according to which the Prince of Finance did not quite live up to his promised subscription to that famous naturalistic work, must have appeared completely incompatible with the Rothschild of anecdote.[17]

The Rothschild of fiction could not be held accountable for the shortcomings of the factual Rothschild. Ardent Yankee desires created this living wonder as a standard for the stability of capital, circulation of money, investment — all conditions which immature American capitalism had not yet achieved. But it always behaved as though it carried its marshal's baton in its baggage and our humorous poem about Rothschild's financial suzerainty closes with great optimism:

In about - fifty years!
How will some young ones, turned to grey
Look back and mutter "strange!"
Finding themselves the Rothschilds.
Our world frequented "Change"
London, her ocean traffic! pooh —
The rivers of the West
Shall cover with far richer fleets
That very ocean's breast![18]

The historic anecdote in America, told about great men, kings, statesmen, or literary lights, originated with the rise of the new business class. Originally interwoven with countless tales of Yankee tricks and pranks of Yankee

[15] *Puck*, II, no. 50 (1877–78), p. 1.

[16] "Are the Populists Anti-Semitic?," in *Jewish Voice*, XXI, no. 7 (1896), p. 2.

[17] Audubon, Lucy Bakewell, *The Life of John James Audubon . . . By his Widow* (New York 1890), pp. 381–83.

[18] *The New Orleans Weekly Picayune*, III no. 44 (1840), p. 4.

peddlers, it gained its independence with the gradual emergence of new occupational groups, such as the traveling salesman, and the establishment of the general store with its regulated news service. In this development the Rothschild anecdote proved itself invaluable to the animation of the business spirit in the anecdote generally. It was adaptable to all possible circumstances, it had a positive or negative message for all occupational groups, and contained guiding principles of credit for lenders and brorowers. It could also appear in historic guise and be equally instructive to high and low. Its humorous success was most overwhelming, because it parodied the failings of the mighty all too humanly in the light of their weak point — money. Its main concern was the appeal to Rothschild for money on the part of the great of the earth, princes and also other bankers, and how they were judged. And its moral always coincided with the healthy common sense of the American businessman.

The American press transplanted from its English literary models elements of the Rothschild lore that could be adapted to the newly developing American business mores:

> Another maxim, on which he seemed to place great reliance was never to have anything to do with an unlucky place or unlucky man. "I have seen," said he, "many clever men, who had not shoes to their feet. I never act with them: their advice sounds very well but fate is against them: they cannot get on themselves, how can they do good to me?" By the aid of these maxims he has acquired three millions of money.[19]

In the outlook of American business pragmatism the business spirit implicit in Rothschild's instruction to his children was absolutely incontestable:

> I wish them to give mind, and heart, and body and everything to business; that is the way to be happy. It requires a great deal of boldness, and a great deal of caution to make a great fortune; and when you have got it, it requires ten times as much wit to keep it. If I were to listen to all the projects proposed to me I should ruin myself very soon. "Stick to one business, young man," said he to Edward, "stick to your brewery, and you may be the great brewer of London. Be a brewer and a broker and a merchant and a manufacturer, and you will soon be in the Gazette.[20]

Rothschild never became "literature" in America as in Europe, where he was even portrayed on the stage. All stories about him were told from life. Nothing was attributed to him, which would be so impractical as the payment of living flesh, which Shylock made so literary. But just because Shylock's human feelings could not be transferred to Rothschild, some of the latter's business man's character was reflected back on the ill-timed merchant of the old school. Shylock became more understandable to Americans; theatre reporters took great pleasure in noting extracts from the conversation of playgoers in the stalls at countless performances of the Shakespearean drama.

[19] "The Late Mr. Rothschild," in *Spirit of the Times*, XVIII (1848–49), p. 185.
[20] *Ibid.*

Shylocks's business principles were recognized in the statement: "All of us would have done exactly the same thing today;" the pound of flesh, as literary trimming, was not taken seriously any more. Antonio was censured because he was so imprudent as to let his ships sail without insurance.[21]

In the background of the feeling of the spectators lay the clear recognition of the fact that an occupational disaster befell the Jew, because as a capitalist he clung to an outmoded procedure; but modern capitalism à la Rothschild would not permit effective resistance to arise. Only the unsuitable means must be eliminated.

The names "Shylock" and "Rothschild" were never used interchangeably. The contrast in their characters was mirrored in the conflicting functions of their money. "Shylock" represented money drawn out of the life process, while "Rothschild" — whose symbol was pump-priming — represented the infusion of life with the Golden Stream.[22]

Rothschild's Wealth as a Curiosity

At the time when the Rothschild legend was being formed for the great masses of Americans who were fully occupied with the subjugation of nature, wealth was above all a strange show piece. In the Rothschild anecdote, carried by frontier journalism to the furthest cabins of the wilderness, the average American found satisfaction of a spiritual curiosity, which carried him off to distant Europe. Life, magically presented before his eyes as the stage of wealth, brought back the past and let it be seen in the light of new hopes in the new continent. In the enormous quantity of Rothschild anecdotes indiscriminately reproduced in the American press, naked curiosity about wealth was the main interest. It was only after the legend of Rothschild's enviable wealth had firmly established itself that the American press considered its readers sufficiently interested to learn of actual events in the Rothschild family. Authentic biographical data were then served up in small doses.

Occasionally such presentations of Rothschild's wealth encountered some indignation, expressed in the statement, he "holds a mortgage on the city of Jerusalem."[23] The overwhelming reaction was just the opposite, for the legitimacy of wealth as such was accepted in primitive outposts. References to Rothschild's wealth became more and more artful, culminating in the irrational uneconomic:

> Old Baron Rothschild was playing at Marquis d'Alegre's a genuine financier's game — that is to say — for very small stakes. The Marquis was losing. He threw a louis on the table, which

[21] Grund, Francis, J., *Die Aristokratie in Amerika, aus dem Tagebuch eines deutschen Edelmannes*, I (Stuttgart 1839), p. 129.

[22] The German verb, "pumpen" has two meanings: to fill up and to borrow.

[23] "Rothschild," in *Oregon Spectator*, II, no. 14 (1847), p. 3.

rolled on the floor. The Marquis dropped on all fours to look for his money, disturbing everybody and delaying the game. Baron de Rothschild was dealing. "A louis lost," he said, "that is worth looking for," and putting on an expression of deep anxiety, he rolled up a thousand franc note, lighted it at the candle and held it to assist Marquis d'Alegre in the search.[24]

Such fantastic conduct in money matters, occasionally found in the great scenes of American gambling, especially on the frontier, was no doubt influenced by tales of wealthy Europeans.

In the humorous reaction to wealth Rothschild was sometimes depicted as "short" because he forgot to take small change with him.[25] In general, however, money retained its proper value in the scale of conduct.

A Question of Precedence

The story goes:

Baron Rothschild, who knows a thing or two, notwithstanding his enormous wealth, was one day honored by a visit from the Mayor of some neighboring village. At the moment his "honor" was admitted to the presence, the Baron was writing a letter, and without interrupting his employment, told his visitor to take a chair. The village magnate, astounded that a person of his quality should be thus cavalierly disposed of, exclaimed: "M. le Baron, I am the Mayor of . . . .!" "Ah, indeed! then take *two chairs*."[26]

In all these effusions over the wealth of Rothschild, as well as in other aspects of the Rothschild anecdote still to be explored, it is of major importance to note that the individuality of Rothschild, be he Anselm, James or Edward, played no role at all. The individual was considered only as the bearer of the magic name of the house — the banking house. Equally curious was the drama of this wealth, and the domestic tradition — the Jewish tradition — which was ascribed to the Rothschilds and in general depicted as an enhancement of their respectability.

Comparison of the House with American fortunes appeared but seldom and were vague. The statement, "The Rothschilds are eclipsed by a native Californian, Senõr M. G. Vallejo . . ."[27] surely did not convince many readers. An anecdote once appeared, "Rothschild and Astor compared," in which, to be sure, greater wealth was ascribed to Rothschild, but greater ingenuity to John Astor.[28] But the fact that a more voluminous folklore did not arise about that Yankee figure speaks for itself.

Advertisers tried to exploit this comparison:

Stultz the Tailor . . . who is among tailors as Rothschild among bankers . . . . preeminent.[29]

[24] *The Manhattan* (New York), I (1883), p. 158.

[25] *Yankee Notions* (New York), III (1854), p. 63.

[26] *Wilke's Spirit of the Times*, XI (1864–65), p. 149.

[27] *State Gazette* (Austin, Texas), II (1850–51), p. 169.

[28] Devens, Richard Miller, *Cyclopedia of Commerical and Business Anecdotes*, I (New York 1864), p. 151.

[29] *The Cincinnati Miscellany*, II (1845), p. 166.

And most credible was the simple wish, naively expressed, as when a newly disclosed lode in Montana was named just "Rothschild's."[30]

The Respectability of Rothschild's Wealth

The dignity of capital in all its aspects was the most important element that American wealth sought in order firmly to establish its claim on social acceptance. Rothschild exemplified the simplicity of taste to be learned from the noble use of money. In one of the earliest discussions of the House of Rothschild in all its human and business ramifications, that element was brought to the forefront to display even the speculative activity of the capitalist in a kindly light.

Mr. Rothschild's manner of evincing kind feelings toward Solomon Herschel, the Grand Rabbin of Duke's-place, has something in it which is both singular and whimsical: — when any good speculation is afloat, Mr. Rothschild deposits, on his account, a certain sum proportionate to *his own* risk and whatever *percentage* a profit accrues therefrom, is carried by him to the Rabbin to whom he gives a full, true and particular account, even to the utmost fraction. The millionaire, on such occasions, invariably dines with the Levite; and the day is usually passed by the two friends in innocent hilarity and pleasing conversation.[31]

Inherited Rothschild fortunes followed the same simple paths, as seen in the following incident, at the termination of the career of Baron James Rothschild in which reference is made to the still unchanged ways of Jewish tradition at the final earthly rites:

Baron Rothschild inherited a large fortune from his father, who was banker to the Prince of Hesse Cassel. His own fortune was colossal. He left two milliards of francs. Although he was inflexible in business matters, he was capable of acts of generosity. He once lost 11,000,000 francs, but he prevented a famine by the operation. He exchanged Russian paper, which he bought up, for grain, and loading ships with it at every southern port, obliged the speculators to sell theirs at a moderate profit. He also founded hospitals, built a synagogue, and performed many acts of charity among his own people. His family mourned for him in accordance with the touching rites of their religion, sitting upon the floor with rent garments and dishevelled hair and unshorn beards, and meeting twice a day in the room where he lay, to pray. Every poor person who chose to call at the door on the day after his death received a Napoleon and an enormous sum of money was thus distributed.[32]

At magnificent family affairs such as weddings, personal biographical material on the Rothschilds was not lacking. Gossip about the Rothschilds passed avidly from mouth to mouth such as:

Mlle. Hélène de Rothschild's latest escapade in leaving her mother's house because of the baroness' refusal to sanction her marriage with the nephew of a prominent foreign diplomat in the French capital has furnished Parisian society in general and fashionable Jewish circles in particular, with a dainty dish of gossip.[33]

[30] *Montana Post*, I, no. 5 (1864–65), p. 1.

[31] "The Rothschilds," in *Spirit of the Times*, V, no. 13 (1835), p. 12.

[32] *The Overland Monthly* (San Francisco), II (1869), p. 288.

[33] *Town Topics* (New York), XVII, no. 19 (1887), p. 8.

We are likewise informed how the family preserved its decorum in the case of a marriage of one of the Rothschild daughters with a non-Jew:

None of the numerous tribe of Rothschild were present at the wedding to mark their disapprobation of the act, but each sent a costly gift in token of personal affection for the bride and bridegroom . . .[34]

Accounts of weddings especially were set off with descriptions of the valuable gifts. On such occasions the piety and charity of the participants were evident, even in sentimental fashion, for wedding gifts of Jewish orphans were put on display together with the costly trousseau:

Some of the presents were singular. There were three or four prayer books! What satire was this to give the liturgy to an Israelite? Then there were some little objects of worsted work — pin cushions, *mouchoir* holders, watch cases — worth shall we say, fully ten cents apiece, yet placed on an honorable eminence amidst the rain of glittering treasures! These were the humble offerings of the pupils of a Jewish charity school which has often realized how liberal the Rothschilds are; and we love to think that in her own girl's heart, the young Baronesse Alphonse will value these little offerings of gratitude far higher than the costly contributions of the jewellers.[35]

Anecdotal folklore about Rothschild is replete primarily with business-like interpretations of personal situations:

The mother of the Rothschilds lived at Frankfort, and was taken sick at 98 years of age. She said she was certain to live to 100, as nothing belonging to the house of Rothschild must go below *par*. She did, however, for she died at 99½.[36]

Or in the transformation of an emotional quality into a more quantitative one:

When Rothschild was asked whether he would not like to become a temporal King of the Jews in Palestine, "Oh, no," said he, "I would rather be a Jew of the Kings than King of the Jews."[37]

Even with his coreligionists, personal relationships were restricted to purely business dealings:

. . . But these murmurs amount to a tempest in fury in financial society against *Solomon* Baron Rothschild. The *salon* of this prince of Jews is never open to his monied brethren, to penetrate into this paradise of lucre you must prove your escutcheon and all your quarters of nobility most authentically: it is a singular and amusing sight to see the petty pride of the agent de charge, which towers beyond all bearing, amongst the *monde* of July, humbling itself every morning at the threshold of the Jew king of bankers, and the banker Jew of kings, to obtain some commissions for the Stock Exchange — and then come a fête in this palace, and they who have been treated in the morning like clerks, or hop-o-my thumbs, have the door slammed in their faces in the evening.[38]

[34] "Our monthly gossip," in *Lippincott's Magazine*, XXIV (1879), p. 126.
[35] "Rothschild's Wedding," in *Harper's Weekly*, I (1857), p. 253.
[36] *Mariposa Democrat* (Hornitos), IX, no. 10 (1857), p. 1.
[37] *Los Angeles Star*, IX, no. 12 (1859), p. 4.
[38] "Parisian Chit-Chat," in *Spirit of the Times*, XII (1843–44), p. 27.

Sensational reports and detailed stories of business espionage against Rothschild appeared in folklore overtones — one must keep one's distance from men in the same line, for fear of the "evil eye."[39] Almost always in folklore the "evil glance" of the Jew appears more dangerous than that of the non-Jew, even in Jewish folklore and against a fellow Jew.[40] Conversely, the bare fact of propinquity to Rothschild could dispense with rational business behavior:

True, he had never heard the name on Change, but never mind; Rothschild would not have walked arm in arm with him as he did, if he had not been perfectly good . . . upon this affair Mr. Coutts established a credit, which enabled him soon afterwards to establish the Banking-house of Coutts and Co. . . .[41]

Even to represent oneself as a Jew in order to gain entree into the sphere of Rothschild's business operations promised success:

THE QUEEN OF SPAIN A JEWESS

We learn that at a late grand fancy ball at Madrid, the Queen of Spain appeared sumptuously drest and diamonded as a Jewess. Baron Rothschild, had he seen her, would, it is thought, have lent money enough upon her Majesty wherewith to satisfy all the English bond-holders.[42]

On the other hand, the affiliation of the great name in finance with affairs of poetry would cause great excitement and might become the basis for financial speculation — in this case in the book publishing business:

THE ROTHSCHILD POEM

Gold will buy nobility; but millions will neither purchase the nobility of the soul nor the gift of poesy. The higher, therefore, is the gratification which the world must derive from the notice given, in a German periodical, that Cotta . . . is about to publish the "Poems" of the Brother Rothschild. Such a work will create no little sensation in all the boudoirs, as well as the exchanges of the civilized world.[43]

What interest would the general American public show in such personal experience, only too human, gleaned from the biography of the "House"? Compared with the never-ending flow of Jewish Rothschild tales in Europe, it was negligible. Nevertheless, such plain object lessons of life on the continent served to signify what was expected from newly acquired American wealth, if it sought social approval. For in Europe too there were ways for the rich, once they abandoned their aloofness and searched for new social functions, to become useful in many respects, including the exotic. Thus it seems

[39] "Rothschild," *Parker's Journal* (New York), I (1850–51), p. 420.
[40] Lilienthal, Regina, "Ayin hore'," *Yidishe Filologye*, I (Warsaw 1924), pp. 245–71.
[41] *The Pioneer* (San Francisco), IV (July-Dec. 1855), pp. 67–68.
[42] *The Family Companion* (New York), I (1848), p. 116.
[43] *The Constellation* (New York), II (1830–31), p. 135.

particularly paradoxical that in democratic America Shylock turned into a snob, and Rothschild-pretense, on the part of the Rothschild agent in America, August Belmont, was partly responsible for it.

Rothschild's Air

Legendary actions that accented business principles or regard for money are not sufficient, however, to explain the continuation of the Rothschild mythology. The entire status of the "House" in society entered into the legend, *e. g.*, the noble obligations of the rich in promoting the good life, contributing to the creative arts, the acquisition of all kinds of art collections. The "House" personified wealth in a harmonious union of diverse qualities, in contrast to the case of the snob. Rothschild's air was unlike the snobbishness of Shylock and of his agent, the banker Belmont.

A part of the general Rothschilds' legend was their patronage of sport. It had the important function of making betting respectable, when it actually was not, and of implying that what was accepted by Rothschild might well be accepted by the average American. Like the press in general, the sports press presented edifying tales about Rothschild in which sports events were used to emphasize sportmindedness in his storybook character. Rothschild, the sportsman, was even said to have caused the Jews to change their long-standing attitude towards the dog:

> . . . that the Jews of the present day do not consider the dog unclean is certain, for Baron Rothschild keeps a noble pack of staghounds . . .[44]

The real significance of Rothschild's air for American sports lay in the fact that the "Baron" acted as the moral guarantor for horse racing. Society would therefore not boycott it, it would not face bankruptcy or any other difficulty:

> Baron Rothschild on the Turf and Turfmen
>
> . . . His experience was, that the class who is following horseracing as a pursuit was fully as trustworthy as could be found in other walks of life. He had never found any of his racing servants dishonest . . . These are the sentiments of one of the ablest and most sagacious men in Europe — one of the principals of a house whose wealth is so great and whose monetary transactions are so vast that it exerts a powerful influence upon the affairs of nations. We think the testimony of such a man as this, one thoroughly informed upon the subject concerning which he speaks, is a good deal more to the purpose than the prejudiced notions of persons who know nothing about it.[45]

Individual notices concerning Rothschild's stable, such as "Baron Rothschild and King Tom,"[46] seem to be typical of this tendency of the

[44] "The Dog," in *Spirit of the Times*, XVII (1847–48), p. 444.
[45] *Wilke's Spirit of the Times*, XXV (1871), p. 265.
[46] *Ibid.*, XXVI (1872), p. 99.

American sports press. Upon his death an article, "Death of Baron Rothschild," emphasized "his famous racing prediction," the basis for the byword: "Follow the Baron."[47] Loyalty to the Baron was, however, more than just an emotion on the race track; it meant confidence in leadership in more gracious social activities that was readily accorded to the "House."

Shylock — the Snob

August Belmont was both the shadow of the House of Rothschild as well as its distortion. His chief renown rested on his designation as the representative of the House of Rothschild in America. It gave him an almost tragi-comic quality, rarely attributed to the snob. Actually the "representative" was only once completely identified with the "House" in America. It was a disagreeable experience for Belmont, who had long since severed all contacts with Judaism and the historical fate of the Jews, to receive the following letter, which was to remind him of his place in society as understood by the Gentile world:

> Harrisburg, January 1868
>
> . . . We are willing to give you the pound of flesh, but not one drop of Christian blood.
>
> Respectfully,
> W. H. Kemble, State Treasurer.

The indignant answer which he gave as Rothschild's legitimate representative expressed

> regret that the State of Pennsylvania should have for its treasurer a person who could so far disgrace the State . . . to reply to a simple business communication in a manner which must raise the blush of shame on the cheek of every citizen of that great and honored State.
>
> AUGUST BELMONT.[48]

But an inner voice must have told him that his position and origin made him forever vulnerable to the Shylock comparison.

Aside from this solitary incident in financial history, Belmont's case is the classic precedent for the adjustment of the Rothschild legend to the new kind of personality types emerging in American society. By marrying into one of the finest Gentile families, the newcomer, a distant relative of the Rothschilds and a former apprentice in the "House," had skipped society's rule that four or at best three generations make a gentleman. Thereafter, he continued his social climb by skilfully remaining in the shadow of the great men of the European "House." The good reputation of Rothschild's money obtained for him what even a 100 percent integration into Gentile society could not achieve. His German compatriots sang raucously in their clubs that "August Schönberg" should not mix in American politics because of the

[47] *Spirit of the Times*, LXXXVII [New enumeration] (1874), p. 60.

[48] *The Israelite*, XIV, no. 34 (1867–68), pp. 5–6.

"awful" expense,[49] and they drew the three balls of the pawnshop in their songbooks alongside their verses about him.[50]

Meanwhile, a fundamental change occurred in the American attitude towards him, for the American people could not withhold from him their confidence when it was granted by Rothschild. Observers and critics of the period of Belmont's rise emphasize his appointment as Treasurer of the Democratic Party as a turning point and revolution in American public opinion. The Democrats could be entrusted with American financial matters in the same degree as Rothschild entrusted Belmont with his interests. Rothschild's representative had tied his political career to these interests. The practical benefit obtained this way by the Democratic Party cannot be exaggerated. According to a contemporary, he represented "the endorsement of the Democratic promises of good behavior." At the same time he proved to the world that America under all circumstances and under either one of the political parties was a safe area for foreign investments. All these imponderables pertaining to the name of Rothschild made Belmont a king-maker during election campaigns. They were evaluated as follows:

This is to be a summer of Presidentmaking . . . For many years one of the most important factors of this sort of work, on the Democratic side, has been August Belmont. As the representative of the Rothschilds in this country, he has been invaluable to the Democratic party. When the people doubted if the financial and business interest of the Republic would be as safe in Democratic as in Republican hands — . . . Mr. Belmont was proudly paraded as the endorser of the Democratic promises of good behavior. A party which had the support of the Rothschilds might certainly be safely trusted by other capitalists.[51]

The way Belmont put on airs was instinctively recognized as an unsuccessful attempt on his part to imitate Rothschild. Thus he was forever called "Rothschild's representative," even when he did not have to act in that capacity, as at social gatherings. The notion people had of Belmont grew stronger as he rose higher and his snobbishness showed more openly. In matters in which his social success was greatest, as in the recognition he gained as a sportsman, there was quite significantly no room for a Belmont legend. Psychologically speaking, it was impossible for a motto such as "Follow the Baron" to become linked with his name, for his personality was hidden under the snob. It was the latter that people gossiped about, his livery-horses and carriage in luxurious Newport, his place as an *arbiter elegantiarum* at the clubs of which he could boast that his vote meant acceptance or blackballing of any candidate.

Mr. August Belmont is, I am told, extremely disgruntled by the rejection of Mr. Florence at the Union Club. He expresses himself in very free and uncomplimentary terms about it, and

[49] *Arion's Gesangbuch* (New York 1866), p. 130. Text reprinted in Glanz, Rudolf, *Jews in Relation to the Cultural Milieu of the Germans in America Up to the Eighteen Eighties* (New York 1947), p. 53.

[50] *Arion's Gesangbuch*, (New York) 1868, p. 42.

[51] Fiske, Stephen, *Off-hand Portraits of Prominent New Yorkers* (New York 1884), p. 26.

is reported to have said that Mr. Florence can have the entree of clubs abroad that the men who rejected him here would be kicked out of. What with the Loubat matter and the Florence affair Mr. Belmont is likely to have his hands full for the summer.[52]

When Belmont finally made a display of his wealth in the form of art treasures, his portrait was complete: he was considered a plutocrat, indifferent to philanthropic and intellectual currents in the country, to whom Rothschild's financial wisdom would forever remain a secret. There were no anecdotes, no *bon mots* of any kind about Belmont. According to the *New Yorker Handelszeitung* he was nicknamed "King of the Money Changers," owing to his talent for fast arbitrage. His position in the world of racing did not, however, remain unchallenged. Cliques fought each other:

Whenever a member of the Belmont clique rode past, there was no lack of derisive remarks on the part of the Vanderbilt people, and this in turn provoked unprintable answers from those attacked.[53]

Belmont, nevertheless, figured in a vision of Saratoga's future:

Belmont . . . the agent of the Rothschilds was preparing for the grandest race which has ever or will ever take place on this continent.[54]

There was even a public argument concerning his financial transactions, which would have been unthinkable in connection with the "House." The old and completely unfounded accusation against Belmont of having delayed transmittal of Fenian funds and even of having partly embezzled the money in 1865 was used as Republican campaign material against his son, the Democrat Perry Belmont, as late as the Congressional campaign of 1882. The charges were withdrawn after the elections.[55] But at the time of the fight between Belmont and various Irish organizations, his name was linked in people's minds with all sorts of political chicanery. The *Irish American* urged that he be removed from his position with the Democratic National Committee.[56] A similar involvement of the Rothschilds was inconceivable.

Although he had repudiated his Jewish origin and had been accepted among Gentiles as a leader of fashion by reason of his marriage, Belmont's status in society always remained shaky. His partisans were forever constrained to suppress the fact of his Jewish descent. In the contemporary press he was referred to as "a German farmer's boy" or "son of a well-to-do farmer," never as the "son of a rich German Jew." Any suspicion of his Jewish looks was dispelled by describing him as having "the strong features

[52] *Town Topics* (New York), XVII, no. 24 (1887), p. 7.

[53] Frank, Ludwig, "Feuilleton, Silhouetten deutsch-amerikanischer Bankiers," in *Beilage zur New Yorker Handelszeitung*, XXIII (Oct. 27, 1877), p. 2. Messrs. Florence and Loubat were unimportant persons of the Club set.

[54] Landon, Melville de Lancey, *Saratoga in 1901* (New York 1872), p. 8.

[55] Belmont, Perry, *Perry Belmont, An America Democrat* (New York 1949), pp. 299–301.

[56] "The Fall of Belmont; The Fenian Funds," in *The Irish American*, XXI, Sept. 4, 1869, p. 4.

of the real businessman."[57] The *Knickerbocker* magazine once openly acknowledged that it had not been paid for such flattery.

His sycophants tried to explain his social prestige that was based exclusively on his marriage into a well reputed Gentile family by reference to a romantic duel in the South in which he had engaged. There were other Jews, however — German Jews among them — who had fought duels in the South, following the code of honor of that region, and for them there had been no special prestige.

Belmont had entirely separated himself from his Jewish kinsmen in America. They were not only annoyed by his defection, but in keeping with Jewish solidarity, they considered it an abuse of Rothschild's reputation. The greatest insult to American Jewry was that Belmont, time and again, was counted as one of them. His appointment as American minister to the Hague, for example, was publicized as an honor bestowed on American Jews. The Jewish press emphatically rejected this interpretation:

> . . . Mr. Belmont as American minister to the Hague, while comporting himself becomingly in that office, is entitled to the respect of every American citizen. As the head of a house of business, many years established in this city, he has gained the confidence of a large circle. From association, more particularly, as the agent of an Israelite Banking firm, whose reputation and credit is world-current, Mr. Belmont stands reputed as an Israelite; but the fact of his fraternization as such, is more than suspicious. Mr. Belmont married, in the Episcopalian Church, a Christian lady; no doubt, on that occasion, the question of the particular faith in which the prospective offspring were to be raised, was settled satisfactorily to the Bride's father. We have no right — the public has no right to ask one question on the subject. So far, we assert the inviolability of Mr. Belmont's position as a respectable citizen, but when he is to be thrust upon us as a co-religionist, we doubt the value of the accession, question the honor of the association and therefore call for his credentials.[58]

Belmont's art treasures in time became the main foundation for his standing in society. His connoisseurship provided him with a role in a field for which there was no tradition in America. It was easy for Belmont to assume leadership since he had had experiences with art during his European period. He personified "noble Europe" in vulgar America. His mansion at Fifth Avenue and Eighteenth Street held art treasures valued at two million dollars. The mansion became an imitation of the European salon, but there is no evidence that any literary activity developed there.

At critical moments, however, the facade, which people had never quite forgotten, was penetrated, as the following item, combining references to Belmont's hidden traits with false rumor, suggests:

[57] Fiske, *op. cit.*, pp. 26–31; Clews, Henry, *Fifty Years in Wall Street* (New York 1915), pp. 596 ff., 801 ff.

[58] "Nationality of the Jews," in *The Asmonean* (New York), XI (1854–55), p. 140.

THE SALE OF AUGUST BELMONT'S PICTURES

In Fifth Avenue . . . This is the costly dwelling of August Belmont, a wealthy foreigner of Jewish extraction, who long ago came to this country . . .and who now, for business reasons, proposes to quit the country of his adoption and to live the remainder of his days in Europe . . . People would have said, that Mr. Belmont, agent of the Rothschilds, was going back to his European employers to assist them in making money out of the United States debt . . .[59]

The stigma of Jewish descent was again combined with the reproach, so often incurred by the German Jew, that he retired to Europe with his American wealth, which was estimated to be between six and eight million dollars in 1877. The snob had gone out of Shylock — *vide* the sale of his art collection — and only the Jew was left, again raking the golden leaves blown across to Europe from America in the form of America's external debt. Despite the implication that Belmont's move was for the greater glory of the "House," it was said that his relations with the Rothschilds were rather strained, "more than once the tension was such as to make a break appear inevitable.[60]

Legend and Reality

It is difficult to move from legend to reality. Financial news would only have distracted newspaper readers from the fairy tales of wealth they swallowed regularly. On the other hand, there was a certain eagerness for real information.

Some plans of the "House" concerning America had first been noted in the European press, particularly the Jewish papers. In 1837 the chief Jewish paper in Germany reported:

Frankfurt A. M. April 11. The House of Rothschild is planning to enlarge its scope and to carry its activities across the ocean. For this purpose a branch will be established in New York. A young man in charge of this project, Mr. Belmont, left a few days ago to journey to that city via Paris and London.[61]

An agent of Rothschild was mentioned in connection with California's development; Mount Davidson in Nevada was named after him. At that time, the Rothschilds' financial interest in the new continent became a subject of public discussion, and news items such as the following were given space in paper after paper:

The Rothschild. The N. Y. Sun, speaking of the extending investments by Europeans in this country, and the arrival of Baron A. D. Rothschild says, "One of the family, it is rumored, will settle in this country, and aid August Belmont, their New York agent, in extending the

[59] *Golden Age* (New York), II (1872), Nov. 29, p. 9.

[60] "August Belmont," in "Feuilleton," *loc. cit.*, XXIII (Dec. 1877), p. 2.

[61] *Allgemeine Zeitung des Judentums*, I, no. 4 (1837), p. 9.

business of the firm in the United States, Mexico and South America, and eventually to the East Indies and China."[62]

Occasionally the chances of the "House" in America were discussed in one of the news items:

. . . A branch of the house has been established in New York, conducted by Auguste Belmont, a relative of Solomon Rothschild, of Vienna. Republican free trade, however, is not the soil on which the stupendous business of the great loan contractors will best flourish.[63]

The time when America would need large foreign loans to conduct the war between the states was still in the future. Meanwhile the news from Europe continued to refer to the peaceful expansion plans of the "House":

PROJECTS OF THE HOUSE OF ROTHSCHILD

Young Baron Salomon v. Rothschild is at present in New York, and after having stayed for some time at the house of August Belmont, correspondent of the Rothschilds, he plans a trip to the West and South of the United States. It is known that the House of Rothschild has planned for a long time to expand its business interests in America and particularly to establish contacts with the southern parts and California, where there has so far not been any representation of the European bank.[64]

Times were not auspicious for such plans; the Civil War produced a real need for credit to save the Union. A satisfactory answer was never given afterwards to the question about the behavior of the "House" with respect to investment in American loans during the Civil War, particularly how its estimates of the respective chances of North and South were reflected in its speculations. It appeared to the American public that Belmont was the chief source of information and that the attitude of the "House" depended on Belmont's views. Malicious rumors had been spread that Belmont had tipped off the "House" that the South would win, and that the Rothschilds had lost money on this information, which presumably had been recovered after the Union victory by their new speculations in American securities. Belmont's partisans were forced to take notice of this rumor:

It is whispered that only once, in all this time, did he give the Rothschilds wrong advice, and that was when . . . he predicted the success of the Southern Confederacy. We do not vouch for the accuracy of this legend; but, if it be true, and if any losses were incurred by this mistaken advice, the Rothschilds have since more than recouped themselves by their dealings in United States securities, under Mr. Belmont's direction.[65]

Such rumors were particularly stubborn in Irish groups, which later on stirred them up again in a lawsuit against Belmont in connection with the

[62] *The New Orleans Weekly Picayune*, IV (Dec. 11, 1848), p. 525.
[63] "The Rothschilds," in *Spirit of the Times*, XVIII (1848–49), p. 20.
[64] *Wiener Mitteilungen*, VII (1860), p. 7.
[65] Fiske, *op. cit.*, p. 29.
[66] "The Fenian Funds," in *The Irish-American*, XXVIII, Apr. 29, 1876, p. 5.

Fenian funds. On August 8, 1874 the following item appeared in an Irish-American newspaper:

The Rothschilds and the Union. A Card from Mr. August Belmont.

Saratoga Springs, July 31. To the Editor of the Tribune.

Sir — My attention has been called to two articles in your paper, in which you state that the Messrs. Rothschild did not invest in our Government loans during the war, because, they were influenced by my unfavorable opinion.[66]

Belmont disputed this assertion and claimed that he had always recommended investment in government bonds and the "House" had followed his recommendations:

In a conversation with Mr. Sanford, our late Minister to Belgium, some nine years ago, the late Baron Jas. de Rothschild, in Paris, showed him by his books, in my presence, that he was one of the earliest and largest investors in our security during the war . . . It is late in the day for you to try to stir up prejudices against a political opponent . . .[67]

The fact that accusations of this kind in a reputable New York newspaper were copied by another paper left a shadow on Belmont's name, but Rothschild's prestige in America did not suffer at all. During the Civil War the "House" had found other defenders in men who were considered more independent and trustworthy by the American public than Belmont.

Harper's Weekly published the letter of an American diplomat, W. W. Murphy, Consul-General at Frankfort, Germany, by way of correction of an earlier article:

In your paper Harper's Weekly of February 28, you do a great injustice to the eminent firm of Rothschilds here, when you hint that they are like to a certain Rabbi who held opinions that some men were born to be slaves. I know not what the other firms — and there are many of the Rothschilds, all related — in Europe think of slavery, but here the firm of M. A. von Rothschild a. Son are opposed to slavery and in favor of the Union. A *converted Jew*, Erlanger, has taken the rebel loan of £3.000.000 and lives in this city; and Baron Rothschild informed me that all Germany condemned this act of lending money to establish a slaveholding government, and that so great was public opinion against it that Erlanger a. Co. dare not offer it on the Frankfort bourse. I further know that the Jews rejoice to think that none of there sect would be guilty of loaning money for the purpose above named; but it was left, they say, for apostate Jews to do it.[68]

Murphy's statement was also widely reprinted in the Jewish press in Germany.[69] A year later, on September 10, 1864, the question of Rothschild investments again was raised, this time in the *Chicago Tribune*. It was coupled with an attack against Jews, in general:

The question before the country is — Will we have a dishonorable peace, in order to enrich Belmont, the Rothschilds, and the whole tribe of Jews, who have been buying up Confederate bonds, or an honorable peace won by Grant, and Sherman at the cannon's mouth.[70]

[67] *Ibid.*, XXVI, Oct. 8, 1874, p. 5.

[68] *Harper's Weekly*, VII (1863), p. 258.

[69] *Der Israelit* (Mainz), IV (1863), New York, p. 277.

[70] "How Do You Like It?," quoted in *The Israelite*, XI (1864–65), p. 99.

To this the Jewish press had an answer that was short and to the point, based on Murphy's statement:

> The Rothschilds never speculated on Confederate bonds; only one European Jew did, Mr. Erlanger of Frankfort, and he was baptized . . .[71]

All further transactions in American bonds by the "House" were made completely in the open, for the American government published the facts. The historical significance of the "House" in American financial history was summed up in the following editorial in *The Nation*:

> The applications for the new four percent United States bonds have been seven times the amount allocated, and they are at a premium of 7 percent over the advertised price. When you want to borrow money, it is always wise to go to a place where money is. Secretary Sherman understood this when he was in the business of bond-selling some years ago, as the following cablegram, which he published without any sense of shame, testified:
>
> "London, April 12, 1878
>
> "Very pleased we have entered into relations again with American government. Shall do our best to make the business successful.
>
> ROTHSCHILDS."
>
> There ought to be some little pride left in American credit, even in the Senate of the United States. Somebody ought to have the courage to rise in his place and congratulate the people on the fact that foreign investors, both Jews and Gentiles, are tumbling over each other in their eagerness to get our national bonds, and are paying the gold "down on the nail" for them.[72]

Before the end of the century a timely news item about the "House" again caught the attention of a large American public. At the time of the Klondike gold rush, Joaquin Miller sent word from Dawson that an agent of the Rothschilds had offered £1,000,000 for all Alaskan claims, but that he had been turned down.[73]

American Jews and the Rothschild Legend

The adoration bestowed on Rothschild by his fellow Jews had frequently been satirized, among others by Heine. The American press too poked fun at the glorification of anything pertaining to Rothschild:

> LONDON TABLE TALK
>
> In describing the obsequies of the wealthy Israelite, Rothschild, the papers inform us that "an extra number of watchmen, after the interment, will be placed at the grave for a length of time, to prevent the committal of any sacreligious act toward the deceased." We suppose

[71] *Ibid.*

[72] *The Nation*, LX (1895), p. 155.

[73] Harris, A. C., *Alaska and the Klondike Gold Fields* (Philadelphia 1897), p. 535.

this is a hint to "our peoplesh" to keep their fingers off the fingerer of millions. A rumor is current that a large sum is bid for one of his ogles — in the hope that a "Jew's eye" would be worth a fortune.[74]

This kind of persiflage was based on the intimacy of European Jews with the "House." It had grown up under conditions European Jews had experienced; it had not deserted the Jewish community; and it practised charity among the Jewish poor at a time when it was believed that money was the only practical way of solving their problems. American Jews had not enjoyed such immediate contacts with the "House," having had no occasion to request, nor indeed to accept its benefactions. A new Rothschild legend reflecting American conditions developed. Whatever notions people might have associated with the name "Rothschild" did not change in the New World. While the name was widely known — ten Rothschilds aside from thirty-nine Einsteins had emigrated from two South German Jewish congregations alone prior to 1870[75] — the great name remained that of the legend. Although the growing Jewish community in America was quite familiar with the history of the world-wide House of Rothschild, and felt that close family ties united them all, until the end of the "old immigration," the Rothschild legend fascinated American Jews just as it did other average Americans, and the reasons were similar. The legend carried a practical meaning for these men, most of them new immigrants, who usually started their business careers as peddlers and who carried their wealth in their knapsacks as it were. In his secret daydreams the Jewish immigrant saw himself living like Rothschild: entirely secure, dependent on nobody, but valued by everybody; clothed with Rothschild's good deeds, such as he had become rich enough to do himself, and all this in the atmosphere of freedom of a new continent never known to Rothschild in Europe.

Many a Jewish immigrant re-enacted the part of Rothschild when he returned as a rich man to the poor place of his birth. Those who tell about such incidents seem to reflect the same pride in Rothschild as that which had inspired the immigrant ever since he had reached America. If only things went well, each hamlet in Europe, wherever there were Jews, would have its own Rothschild and the larger towns would have a whole stock of them.

Not everything turned into gold in America; even those who established themselves had to struggle hard. Two concepts, however, were mutually exclusive, namely, Rothschild and bankruptcy, or, expressed more elegantly, Rothschild and bad money. To carry on during a crisis meant to emulate Rothschild. American Jews rejoiced publicly after a panic that their firms kept going, that they had not hoisted any white flags of surrender.[76] It would

[74] *Spirit of the Times*, VI (1836–37), p. 259.

[75] Tänzer, Aron, *Die Geschichte der Juden in Jebenhausen und Göppingen* (Leipzig 1927), p. 89.

[76] *Allgemeine Zeitung des Judentums*, XIX (1855), p. 565.

be stated irrefutably that Jews had nothing to do with a given banking failure and that no Jewish firm had been affected by it. Strong exception was taken to an allusion to Rothschild in the report of a bank failure:

San Francisco. — The failure of the banking house of Palmer, Cook a. Co. . . . the bankrupt house was called "the Rothschild of California," against which I protest . . . If all our bankers were Rothschilds or even Jews, the credit of California would be much better now; . . .[77]

The personal pomp of the guilty bankers was not compared with Rothschild's, but rather with the frugality of the American-Jewish businessman who denied himself personal comforts in order to accumulate capital.

Rothschild was openly held up to the Gentile bankers as a model of business prudence. American Jews were said to practice Rothschild's business principles and in that way to escape business losses. To a certain extent the American people must have given credence to such pronouncements. Otherwise it would be inconceivable that a Jewish member of the Missouri legislature could have solemnly proposed after a bank failure that in the future only Jews should serve as bank directors. His people, he stated, knew the banking business — Rothschilds in Europe had proved that —; also, a Jewish banker would walk to his office, not ride in a carriage.[78]

Accordingly, rumors attacking Jewish financiers in America were exploded:

THOSE JEWISH BANKERS

. . . Now that the integrity, enterprise, and substantial standing of our "Jewish bankers" . . . have been demonstrated by their freedom from entanglement in the unbusinesslike and insane speculations that occasioned the crash of last year, and that our government finds it to the national interest to commit its most important financial transactions to the gentlemen whom Mr. Sprague, Mr. Hooper, and Mr. Butler delighted to stigmatize, perhaps we may enjoy an immunity from that miserable, contemptible, vulgar iteration of the assumed religious belief of every man who happens to bear a foreign name.[79]

Immigrants placed a value not only on the financial honor of the "House" but also on its role in English sports:

BARON ROTHSCHILD'S GRAND SUCCESS

. . . at Newmarket and Epsom this spring . . . The success of the Baron caused great enthusiasm among the Israelites of England and of this country. It was affirmed by some that on the night of the wedding between the Marquis of Lorne and the Princess Louise, not a sober Scotchman could be had for love or money in London. That many members of the Baron's faith drank potations pottle deep in New York on the night of the Derby, and again on that of the Oaks,

[77] *The Israelite*, III (1856), p. 78.
[78] "Missouri," in *The Occident*, XVIII (1860–61), p. 307.
[79] *Jewish Messenger*, XXXVI, no. 6 (1874), p. 4.

we know. And reason good! Seldom two such victories befall any man together, and though we hope many more are in store, it may be long before we have so much cause to declare —

"Again the daughters of Judah sing
The lays of happier time,
And strike the harp with the golden string
To the sons of an eastern clime."[80]

Thus American Jews saw themselves reflected in Rothschild's glory as in a mirror: their hopes for success, their quest for recognition in the world of business were Rothschild's success and fame. Rothschild's western representative, Ben Davidson, was accorded due respect by his fellow Jews and others. The "respectable agent of the Rothschilds,"[81] as he was popularly known, was frequently cited for his experience in California.[82] He also distinguished himself as the founder and president of the first Society of Friends of Music in the West. The arrival of a member of the "House" on the Pacific coast was noted in the Jewish press as a special event.[83]

Part of the Rothschild legend in America revolved about plans for the improvement of the condition of the Jews all over the world, in which Rothschild's participation seemed indispensable. As early as 1825 a Gentile religious paper suggested that Rothschild assist in the re-establishment of the Jews in Palestine.[84] Some years after the report that the Rothschilds had purchased Jerusalem was front page news:

Jerusalem. There is a report that the Rothschilds have purchased Jerusalem! We see nothing improbable that in the pecuniary distress of the sultan, he should sell some parts of his dominions to preserve the rest; or that the Rothschilds should purchase the old capital of their nation. They are wealthy beyond the desire, perhaps, even of avarice; and so situated, it is quite reasonable to suppose that they may seek something else to gratify their ambition, that shall produce most important effects. If secured in the possession, and which may be brought about by *money*, they might instantly, as it were, gather a large nation together, soon to become capable of defending itself, and having a wonderful influence over the commerce and condition of the east — rendering Judah again the place of deposite of a large portion of the wealth of the "ancient world." To the sultan the country is of no great value; but, in the hands of the Jews, directed by such men as the Rothschilds, what might it not become, and in a short period of time?[85]

On the part of the Jews Rothschild was fancied as the promoter of American-Jewish colonies; the Jewish press in Germany wrote concerning an earlier colonization project:

[80] *Wilke's Spirit of the Times*, XXVI (1872), p. 99.

[81] "San Francisco," in *The Asmonean* V, Dec. 29, 1851, p. 141.

[82] "Gamblers at San Francisco," in *The Literary World* (New York), IX, July-Dec. 1851, p. 502.

[83] "San Francisco Letter, A Live Baron," *The American Israelite*, XXV, no. 26 (1875), p. 5; "Golden Gate Notes," in *Jewish Voice*, VIII, no. 24 (1890), p. 5.

[84] "Proposed Restoration of the Jews," in *The Western Luminary* (Lexington, Ky.), I (July 1824—July 1825), p. 357.

[85] *Niles Weekly Register*, XXXVII (1829–30), p. 214.

By promoting a Jewish emigrants' colony the Messrs. von *Rothschild* would surely build for themselves the most *handsome* monument among their fellow Jews.[86]

The practical help administered by the Rothschilds to stranded Jewish emigrants in England was noted at an early date in this press:

Spirit of Human Kindness

It is reported in letters from America that during the last great Jewish emigration movement in the Spring a ship was stranded in England with mostly Jewish passengers. A great many of these people found themselves in a very sad situation, from which they were saved, according to the news, by the devotion and warm-hearted sympathy of Mrs. von Rothschild in London. No sooner had she learned of the pitiful condition of her fellow Jews than she offered help and support to them. The refugees cannot find words enough to tell of the humane and noble acts by Mrs. von Rothschild.[87]

Reflection of Rothschild Folklore on the Picture of the American Jew

What impression of the American Jew was formed by American public opinion under the influence of an emerging folklore of capitalism on the new continent?

During the American colonial period wholesale trade was carried on by Sephardic Jews who furnished a substantial part of the funds required to purchase British commodities, the chief American imports. Money shortages prevailed during the first decades of American independence. The role played by the House of Rothschild as the European money-well was the most fabulous fairly tale, and some reflection of this magic was bound tc be cast on the few Jews in the country since their far-flung business transactions brought them ready cash. They lived in some way as if sponsored by Rothschild, and anecdotes about the old-established Jew in American finance, usually called a stockbroker, were characteristically modelled on the Rothschild legend. Wisdom, thrift, a calculating mind, hard bargaining — these were Rothschild's story-book bequests to the American Jews. Whatever seemed worth telling about the American codfish-aristocracy in the East or the pork-aristocracy out West could not compete with the stories about Rothschild. American "gold fever" was an adventure in geography, once the spiritual adventure of making gold had ended. The "golden calf" became a piece of literature just like Shylock. It could not come to life, because the trust in gold and the faith in its power to create human wisdom, such as was the case in the Rothschild legend, had disappeared from America. Neither were conflicts created by gold, for its "curse" was non-existent in America.

[86] "Philadelphia," in *Der Orient*, IV (1844), p. 296.

[87] "Züge der Humanität," in *Die Synagogue* (Würzburg), I (1837), p. 104.

The popular notion that the American Jew was synonymous with Rothschild did not burden him with a "gold curse," but it clung to him with enough persistence to annoy enlightened people. Some Jews even went so far as to disclaim for their race any extraordinary genius in the money making line. On the other hand, Rothschild became the hero of a kind of American "super-folklore" and tall tale:

If Morton were to stand near Lionel Rothschild, he would look like a cracker beside a bridal-cake.[88]

The creation of this "super-folklore" was a contrast to the concept of the "wandering Jew" that heavily burdened people's imagination on the new continent. Himself a kind of comic-book ghost, he was considerably deprecated in America through Rothschild's very existence. Everybody realized that money could purchase a quiet life for the wanderer, and that, on the other hand, it was the search for credit that might lead to a nomad's life. The "eternal Jew," belittled by the Rothschild image, was banished to the literary supplements of the newspapers, where he did not interfere with business.

The Rothschild legend lost its pedagogic value only to the extent that Americans in general began to doubt the value of the monetary yardstick.

American and Jewish Rothschild Folklore

American Jews did not make any substantial contribution to the American Rothschild legend nor did they enrich the international Rothschild folklore — a special creation of the Jewish intellect. There are fundamental differences between the American and the Jewish Rothschild legends. The former deals mostly with the business affairs of the "House," which have no place in the Jewish Rothschild legend. Little biographical information or reference to family spirit appears in the American legend, although there is a certain emphasis on the solidarity of the "House" with the Jewish community. These elements are important in the Jewish folklore since it emerged from Jewish group aspirations. All the human virtues ascribed to Rothschild by the Jewish legend do not exist in the American one, which considers Rothschild another businessman who lives for nothing but his business. It is not strictly "business" to bestow a trousseau on a bride and therefore the American legend has not absorbed the human qualities that are the marks of such charity. The American legend does not include one of the chief characters of the Jewish legend, Rothschild's only creditor, the Jewish beggar. Privileged through the Jewish religious law, he can request payment from Rothschild in just as businesslike a manner as Rothschild duns his debtors.

[88] "Alas, Poor Yorick!," in *Montana Post*, I, no. 50 (1864–65), p. 2.

At a time when the most valuable Jewish Rothschild folklore was still being accumulated, the American legend was deteriorating. The Jewish legend was cultivated by the very groups of Eastern Jews who did so much through their social doctrines to destroy the American Rothschild legend. While there were German socialists in America who could not conceive of world reform without the extinction of the Rothschilds, for the Jewish masses this notion was an intellectual abstraction. Rothschild was far from America but close to the Jewish world.

Although the old Jewish folklore formula: "If only I were Rothschild" has had no importance in the American outlook, the Rothschild image has not entirely disappeared from the Jewish mind. If ever doubt about the wisdom of money can be overcome, meaning will be furnished by the Rothschild character: to serve as a means of Jewish self-identification.

JEWISH SOCIAL CONDITIONS AS SEEN BY THE MUCKRAKERS

The group of American writers of the first decade of the 20th century who were characterized by President Theodore Roosevelt in 1906 as "muckrackers" had one thing in common: they engaged in social criticism of America solely by exposing conditions. Lacking a definite program, they attracted people of various ideologies. The muckrackers were not practical reformers. They certainly were not socialists. All they tried to do was to bring before the American public the inadequacy of the democratic process in coping with the explosive expansion of industrial capitalism in the United States. They succeeded in this task mainly because of the rapid expansion of the popular American magazines. Social criticism was introduced into the columns of these journals and at the same time the price of the most important magazines was reduced from twenty-five to ten cents. Circulation increased tremendously, and since these magazines were read by the entire family this meant also a correspondingly greater increase in the number of readers. It is safe to assume "that the muckrakers touched in one way or another the great majority of American citizens."[1]

Only a small percentage of the readers of the muckraker literature in the popular magazines were workers directly affected by the exploitation of American industry. The vast host of new readers whose interest was aroused by the social criticism of the magazines consisted of individuals who were still economically independent but who nevertheless felt themselves threatened by the process of industrial concentration and who projected their own apprehensions as a threat to the entire country.

[1] Regier, C. C., *The Era of the Muckrakers* (Chapel Hill, N. C. 1932) p. 197. For other literature on the muckrakers see: Faulkner, H. U., *The Quest for Social Justice, 1898-1914* (New York 1931) and Filler, Louis, *Crusaders for American Liberation* (New York 1939).

Reprinted from *Yivo Annual of Jewish Social Science,* Volume IX, 1954.

The opinions of the muckrakers regarding the Jews as found in these popular magazines were on the whole animated by entirely objective considerations. The enormous circulation which they enjoyed made them free from the pressure of advertisers and they did not, therefore, have to cater to the Jewish merchants who advertised in their pages. Nor did the muckrakers ever direct a special appeal to workers. They certainly could not have been concerned with the Jewish workers, who were predominantly recent immigrants and who were, for the most part, incapable as yet of reading an English paper. The Jewish group was conceived by the muckrakers as a completely outside group that still had to be integrated into the total picture of the country. Nor was there any Jewish influence within the muckraker group. All prominent muckrakers were non-Jews. All of them, however, attached special importance to the Jewish group in constructing their image of the future United States. In the words of Louis Filler, "The muckrakers were deeply infatuated with the Jews."[2]

I

The muckrakers displayed little or no interest in the Jewish groups of the "old immigration," those who had come from western Europe and who had by then attained a status of economic independence. Their chief preoccupation was with the compact masses of Jews who were coming from eastern Europe and who were creating new ghettos in the large cities of the United States. The Jewish ghetto became, for these writers, the great social group theme. The Jewish mass man was the classical example of the task at hand—the ghetto as a transformer. A writer in *Colliers Magazine* pointed out that "The Ghetto is perhaps best understood by those who regard it as a transformer of the human current from the Old World into the New—and especially so much of that current as is impelled toward this country by the European oppression of the Jews."[3] European poverty transplanted to America assumed here a completely new aspect because the new immigrant did not understand the factors governing the democratic life of the country. "The people are nearly all of them poor. Most of them are still in the alphabet of free government."[4] Thus the first experience of the immigrant in the new land

[2] *Op. cit.*, p. 118.
[3] "The New York Ghetto," in *Colliers*, Jan. 24, 1903, p. 10.
[4] *Loc. cit.*

was to find that among other unregulated sectors of social life, poverty, too, remained unregulated. What may have been adequate in Europe as poor relief was not even a palliative in America. As the first harbinger of a freedom not yet fully comprehended appeared human dignity, which declined favors that could no longer be of effective help. Thus the character of American, in contrast to European, poverty appeared radically different, and this difference found its classical expression in the ghetto.

> The Ghetto has taught intruding charity to seek other methods of satisfying itself and to send teachers and companions into the Ghetto instead of free soup and free claptrap talk. The pride of the Jew and the ambition of the Jew have vindicated themselves nobly in the face of the temptation which, above all others, must appeal to a Jew most subtly—that of getting substantial things for nothing.[5]

The value of concentration as a protective against the peculiar excrescences of the American political climate was also described by the keen eye of the muckraker.

> The folks of the Ghetto, [he wrote] who scarcely know enough English to understand the predatory demands made upon them by the grafters and the oppressors who always trail the weak, are quite helpless without the support which they get from living together by the thousands. The very thing which in a way keeps them down, their gregariousness, makes it possible for them to keep up the fight for existence.[6]

To the conception of concentration as a protective was added the additional function, namely, to serve as a basis for new creation. Freedom in its American manifestation at first presented a dilemma: the Jewish masses were at first helpless before the exploiting forces in the country until they were able to counter the brutal force of reality with an opposing force—that of the idea. This first rise of the social idea in the recent immigrant and its significance for the destiny of America, the muckraker saw in the first place and above all in the ghetto and he followed with the greatest eagerness the development of this idea among the other immigrants and its influence upon the rest of America. This special interest became a passion with him. "East Canal Street and the Bowery," wrote Hutchins Hapgood, "have interested me more than Broadway and Fifth Avenue."[7] And Ray Stannard Baker later wrote:

[5] *Loc. cit.*
[6] *Loc. cit.*
[7] *The Spirit of the Ghetto* (New York 1909) p. 5.

> No one of the articles I wrote at that time more deeply aroused my interest and sympathy than the one I called "The Rise of the Tailors," which appeared in *McClure's* for December, 1904. It concerned the effort of a number of farsighted and idealistic labor leaders to organize the most poverty-stricken, unrecognized and undefended people in the country—masses of new immigrants who spoke little or no English, who were remorselessly exploited and cheated at every turn. They were the Russian Jews of the slums of New York, and Southern Italians, and Poles and Portuguese and Greeks who were workers in the garment industries.[8]

The same theme appeared in the muckraking fiction of David Graham Phillips. "Marx was a Hebrew—wasn't he? . . . Selma said: Yes, he was a Jew. Both were Jews . . . Marx and Jesus . . . And they were both labor leaders—labor agitators."[9] It was natural that the most famous of all muckrakers, Lincoln Steffens, came to see in all Jewish problems an incentive to activity. The articles that Steffens wrote on the East Side may well serve as an introduction to all later study of American social problems. These reports made him the teacher of an entire generation. Moreover, his personal contact with Jewish people in America, as he himself indicates, formed one of the most important moments in his biography.[10]

II

In the depth of their hearts the new social critics accepted the dynamic industrial development of America as a positive fact. They were merely ashamed of the fact that it created such distasteful human conditions. They felt the need of a sort of spiritual chivalry, at least toward the most obvious victims of the industrial Moloch, and the first object of this sentiment were the various minority ethnic groups among the new immigrants. Each one of these groups was studied sympathetically in terms of evaluation of its characteristics and of its potentialities in the development of the country. The compact Jewish group from eastern Europe however, challenged greater attention, than any other. Their conditions of life were unfamiliar to the Anglo-Saxon writer and were not covered by anything in his previous experiences with the European cultural world. Sec-

[8] *American Chronicle. The Autobiography of Ray Stannard Baker* [David Grayson] (New York 1945) p. 181.

[9] Phillips, David Graham, *The Conflict* (New York 1911) p. 62.

[10] See *The Autobiography of Lincoln Steffens* (New York 1931) and *The Letters of Lincoln Steffens* (New York 1938).

ondly, the Jews were the one group that was forced to migrate because of active persecution. The two decades of American newspaper reporting on the persecution of the Russian Jews served as a direct introduction to the subsequent critical evaluation of their adjustment in their new homeland. There is a direct line from the newspapers and magazines of the pre-muckraking era, with their penetrating reports on the Russian Jews, to the subsequent popular magazines of the muckrakers and their detailed and masterly studies of Jewish immigrant life.

Lincoln Steffens first came into prominence as a journalist with his articles on the East Side Jews in the New York *Evening Post.* As early as 1895 we find in this newspaper a description by him of the New York ghetto that may be considered the basis for all his subsequent observations. Steffens wrote as follows:

> It is estimated that between 111,000 and 112,000 Jews live in that part of New York west of the Bowery, bounded by East Houston Street, Ludlow Street and East Broadway. Of the number nearly half are children, and not more than 15,000 of the adults can speak English or even a foreign language fairly intelligible to other people. They come from Russia, Poland and Hungary, and the jargon most of them use is based upon Hebrew, and is made up of several languages and dialects and resembling no distinct European vernacular. Having been in this country but a short time, some of them only two or three years, very few more than twelve or fourteen, they have preserved their distinctive customs and practices almost inviolate, and are as orthodox and foreign to-day as when they first landed from the emigrant ships that brought them to these shores. By reason of their speech they are cut off from communication with the new world about them, their environments are Jewish, their acquaintances are Jews; if they buy and sell, their business associates and customers alike are of their own race. They recognize and understand no law but that dictated by their rabbis.[11]

Eight years later Steffens once again underscored the immobile and ethnocentric character of the Jewish ghetto population and even justified the expansion of the New York ghetto that had taken place.

> New York's ghetto people [wrote Steffens] are censured for not going into less thickly settled parts of the city. It is pointed out that they pay rent in Hester Street and Clinton Street and Norfolk Street and Chrystie Street which is far greater than the rent they would have to pay in much more comfortable parts of the city,

11 "Customs in the Jewish Quarter," in the *Evening Post,* April 11, 1895, p. 2.

> where they would be less crowded, where their children would have more room for recreation and where the air would be purer and the opportunity for earning money greater. But we might as well censure a blind kitten for not going out on its own initiative into the busy world.[12]

On January 1, 1895, the *Evening Post* published a report of the Hebrew Charities. Among the 7,508 applicants for aid, 1,486 came from Austria, 650 from Germany and 4,984 from Russia. *The Evening Post* added that the number of Jews in New York City exceeded 300,000.[13] These figures clearly show the complete predominance of eastern European Jewry, particularly Russian Jewry, and they are in accord with all other figures of that decade that are available. To this special group and its dramatic fate the popular newspapers turned their attention quite early. Departure of Russian Jews from their homes, their arrival in American ports, descriptions aboard the ship were frequent features of the newspapers and magazines. "More Jews to Leave Russia,"[14] meant the coming arrival of new immigrants, or "Jewish Exiles to be Returned,"[15] explained the prohibition of the landing of Siberian exiles in San Francisco. Such were the typical headlines of the period. At the very beginning of muckraking we encounter in the magazines illustrated reports, with scenes of Jewish immigrants aboard ship.[16]

Interest also turned at an early stage from the facts of eastern European Jewish emigration to its causes. Russia's treatment of the Jews was reported and discussed at length. "Treatment of the Jews in Siberia"[17] may be cited as a characteristic headline for a news story which linked all possible manifestations of Jewish persecution. Comprehensive studies of the treatment of Russian Jews were found in the last decade of the 19th century in those publications that later became representative of muckraking.[18] Simultaneously, concrete suggestions for aid to Russian Jews were discussed.[19]

An isolated voice against such aid appeared in a publication that later became a leader in muckraking—*The Arena.*

[12] *Collier's,* Jan. 24, 1903, p. 10.

[13] "Hebrew Charities," in the *Evening Post,* Jan. 20, 1895, p. 8.

[14] *Evening Post,* Nov. 21, 1893.

[15] *Evening Post,* Sept. 2, 1893, p. 1.

[16] "The Promised Land," in *McClure's Magazine,* vol. xx (1902-1903) 66-74.

[17] *Evening Post,* Nov. 11, 1893, p. 18.

[18] Hubert, Jr. T. G., "Russia's Treatment of Jewish Subjects," in *The Forum,* vol. xi (1891) 103-14.

[19] de Hirsch, M., "Refuge for Russian Jews," in *The Forum,* vol. xi (1891) 627-33.

> The very dregs of foreign immigration [wrote Eva Valesh] always settle in New York, and the recent importation of the Baron Hirsch Jews can hardly be viewed in the light of philanthropy by this country. Their passage here is paid. They are taught the tailoring art in trade schools at twenty dollars per head. On leaving the trade school the sweat shop is the avenue of employment offered them. It is probably a cheap and expeditious method of disposing of this class, so far as Europe is concerned, but it is an additional burden to this country in a quarter where conditions were already well-nigh hopeless. Every industrial evil typical of the tenement quarter is aggravated by this new class of immigration.[20]

Such unfriendly voices, however, were exceptional.

Public sympathy was predominantly on the side of the Russian Jews and behind the efforts of world Jewry to rescue them by emigration. The few opponents of Jewish immigration among the muckrakers expressed their convictions much later, at a time when their social criticism was a thing of the past. An examination of the periodicals of the period provides the unmistakable impression that public discussion of the persecution of Jews in Russia came to the fore in those very publications that pioneered in American social criticism.[21] Their articles in these publications dealt with the Russian Jew as a human being, his circumstances, his striving for personal liberation from handicaps and his self-education and consequent success in the world. Simultaneously, there was elaborate exposition of the Americanization problems of the Jewish immigrant group as a whole.[22] These trends also coincided with fictional treatment of ghetto life in English by the first Russian-Jewish writers who had outgrown the milieu.[23] It is no mere coincidence that Abraham

[20] "The Tenement House Problem in New York," in *The Arena,* vol. vii (1892-93) 580-86.

[21] *Cf.* Yarras, Victor, "The Jewish Question in Russia," in *The Arena,* vol. iii (1890-91) 118-121; "Russia and the Jews," *ibid.,* vol. xxx (1903) 123 ff.; Weber, John B., "The Kishineff Massacre and Its Bearing upon the Question of Immigration into the United States," in *Collier's Weekly,* vol. xxxi (1903) 8; "The Massacres of Jews in Russia," *ibid., v*ol. xxxvi (1905-1906) 12-13; "The Massacres of Jews at Kishineff," in *The Outlook,* vol. lxxiv (1903) 203, 262, 298; "Jewish Persecutions in Russia," *ibid.,* vol. lxxv (1903) 381; "Persecution of Jews at Kishenev," vol. lxxvi (1904) 2; "The Result of the Kishinev Trial," p. 2.

[22] *Cf.* Poole, Ernest (as Told to Him by a Zemstvo Official in Southern Russia), "A Jewish Girl's Struggle to Rise in Russia," in *The Outlook* (1906) 125-31; "The Story of Manuel Levine," *ibid.* (1907) 413-19; Scott, Leroy, "A Daughter of the Russian Revolution," in *Everybody's Magazine,* vol. xvii (1907) 407 ff.; "Story of an Ambitious Russian Jew," in *American Magazine,* vol. lxvii (1908-1909) 236 ff.; "The Story of a Russian Jew," in *The Outlook* (1905) 376-78.

[23] Davis, Phillip, "Making Americans of Russian Jews," in *The Outlook,* (1905) 631-37.

Cahan's *The Rise of David Levinsky* first appeared in a muckraking magazine.[24]

The economic success of the Russian Jews in the United States suggested to some the thought that it was the function of the Russian Jew in America to maintain economic connections between the two countries by the establishment and advancement of Russian industries and by furthering trade relations between Russia and the United States.[25] At the same time these organs also directed their attention to the general and Jewish trends that animated the social organism of the new arrivals. One finds discussion of the relation to the general spirit of America as well as of the hotly contested problem: Zionism vs. Socialism?[26]

One aspect of the immigrant problem that had assumed a dominant place in the political discussion of the times was that of the immigrant vote. Was this vote a group vote, in the sense that certain immigrant groups as a whole were led by "national" politicians for special reward into the fold of the one or the other party? This became a vital question for both opponents and advocates of free immigration. It was even more crucial from the point of view of each of the national groups. Of all the objections raised against the "new immigration" the only one that was effective was the one grounded on the danger of the "foreign vote." Thus the *Evening Post* wrote:

> What is most remarkable in the discussion is the fact that little or no attention has been given to the undoubted, notorious, undeniable harm they do the country as additions to the voting population. This has been ignored in a most curious way by the champions of restriction although there is hardly a day in which it does not jump into our faces . . . The degradation of our city government is largely due to the readiness of the natives to let the immigrants sack the cities in return for their support in the Federal area . . .[27]

For a while the same danger threatened the Jewish immigrant group. The rise of politicians who pretended to be able to deliver or to influence the "Hebrew vote" was readily noted in the press.

24 *McClure's Magazine,* vol. xl (1912-13) 92 ff.; vol. xli (1913) 73 ff.

25 Ford, Alexander Hume, "The Russo-American Jew," in *Pearson's Magazine,* vol. x (1903) 233-39; "America's Debt to the Russian Jew," in *Collier's Weekly,* vol. xxxi (1903) 10.

26 Baker, Edward M., "Judaism and the American Spirit," in *The Arena,* vol. xxxii (1904) 166 ff.; Beaumont, Saul, 'Zionism or Socialism: Which Will Solve the Jewish Question?" in *The Arena,* vol. xxxix (1908) 54-58.

27 "The Harm of Immigration," in the *Evening Post,* Jan. 14, 1893, p. 6.

> Most of the Hebrews who hold office in this city are men who are known as "professional Hebrews." They make their living by being Hebrews and making a pretence that they have great influence with their race.[28]

The following is an example of the treatment accorded to one such politician of the time:

> Harburger represents the east-side Hebrews of the lowest class, who followed the fortunes of Tammany until they saw better chances of plunder in the camp of the enemy. He has made his living out of public office nearly all his life, and he has obtained office on the strength of his supposed control of Hebrew votes. He is practically unknown to the prominent Hebrews of the city.[29]

In this political struggle the attempt was made to draw a line between the uptown and East Side Jews.

> The better class of Hebrews of this city are not proud of the men of their race who hold important offices. Some of them say that these men represent only the lowest Hebrew element and should not be regarded as representative Hebrews . . . It is a popular belief that these men are representative Hebrews, and that the race has been honored or "recognized" by placing them in public office. The fact is that Hebrews above the Baxter Street standard are ashamed of the men who have been put forward as their representatives, and would very much prefer no recognition at all to the kind they have received.[30]

Time rendered its clear decision. No "Hebrew vote" was established and consequently no one could boast of delivering it to a party. Moreover, the Jewish immigrant group demonstrated its political independence in a series of significant elections to a degree that pointed the way for the other immigrant groups. By the time the muckraking era arrived this development was already completed. Anxiety and doubt as to the political maturity of the Jewish immigrant had been overcome and the evaluation of this fact was undertaken in a comprehensive manner in the popular magazines of the muckrakers. Burton J. Hendrick commented as follows on this fact:

> Politically, the Jew's individualism is his saving grace. It prevents him from organizing in a mass. There is no such thing as the "Jewish vote" as there is an "Irish vote," and still, to a considerable extent, a "German vote." The Hebrews of New York are not controlled as a

[28] "Hebrew Office-Holders," in the *Evening Post,* March 4, 1895, p. 9.
[29] *Loc. cit.*
[30] *Loc. cit.*

> unit by political leaders. They vote for one party at one election for another at the succeeding. Better than any other element, even the native stock, do they meet the two supreme tests of citizenship; they actually go to the polls, and when once there, vote independently.[31]

After a painstaking analysis of the results of the election on the East Side, the writer continued:

> Politically, therefore, it cannot be said that the Jews are a problem. In partisan politics their influence is decreased because of this very independence. Their leaders are unable to deliver their votes and thus are unable to demand much patronage. Of the thirty-five district leaders of Tammany Hall, in spite of the preponderance of the Jewish population, only one is a Jew. In all the East-Side districts except one, the Irish still control the party machinery.[32]

The difference in recreational and drinking habits between the new Jewish immigrants and the other immigrant groups also had important repercussions on the political situation. "The advent of Israel on the lower East Side of the metropolis," wrote James Creelman, "resulted in the closing of hundreds of bar-rooms."[33]

Or as a New York saloonkeeper put it in his memoirs:

> There were scarcely any Jews. Both Tye, the sales-agent, and Drugan, the later owner of the saloon, had dwelt on this last fact, saying that Jews are no drinkers and therefore n.g. for our trade.[34]

The saloon as a decisive factor in elections completely lost its function in Jewish neighborhoods or in sections in which Jews infiltrated. Gradually it became clear that it was impossible to master the new situation with the old means and personal influences.

> But beginning with the 80's the great Jewish and Italian immigration, which has overwhelmed the two earlier races, began to pour into the city. These people, especially the acute and intelligent Jews, could not be handled by the old time brutal, saloon-keeping Irish politician . . .[35]

The two ethnic groups of the "old immigration," the Germans

31 Hendrick, Burton J., "The Great Jewish Invasion," in *McClure's Magazine,* vol. xxvii (1906-1907) 306-21.
32 *Loc. cit.*
33 "Israel Unbound," in *Pearson's Magazine,* vol. xvii (1907) p. 123-39; 239-60.
34 "The Experience and Observations of a New York Saloon Keeper as Told by Himself," in *McClure's Magazine,* vol. xxxii (1908-1909) 308 ff.
35 Turner, George Kibbe, "Tammany's Control of New York," in *McClure's Magazine,* vol. xxxiii (1909) 119 ff.

and the Irish, had actually used the saloons as centers of political machines. Political cartoons of the time frequently depicted their struggle as a fight between the German beer barrel and the Irish whiskey bottle. Things changed with the coming of the new Jewish immigrants. The serious attitude of the Jewish immigrant group toward the workaday problems made hopeless any attempt to regulate their political behavior from the saloon. Similarly the employment of gangsters against the Jewish population on the part of the local political machines was a total failure.

> These gangs were used, at first, fully as much for the intimidation of the Jewish voters as for "repeating." The Jew makes the most alert and most intelligent citizen of all the great immigrant races that have populated New York. He was a city dweller before the hairy Anglo-Saxon came up out of the woods, and every fall the East Side resolves itself into one great clamorous political debating society. In spite of all the efforts of the organized Jewish criminals in this district, it repeatedly gave a slight Republican plurality.[36]

In the final analysis, the influence of the Jewish population was felt, according to the critics, in their independence rather than in their closed vote.

> Not that the Jews of New York necessarily vote together, for they are recognized as a singularly independent and reform-seeking element in politics and it is this very independence which gives a growing importance to their voice in the civic affairs of the metropolis.[37]

Thus the writings of the muckrakers surveyed the salient features of a period in the development of American Jewry that was drawing to an end. By this time American Jewry consisted mostly of members of the "new immigration." The basis for this unfolding of new political powers in the American Jewish population was its integration in the economic life of the country, which was predicated upon the economic necessities and the abilities of the new immigrants, and led to a continual conquest of new economic positions. This process was seen by the muckrakers in all its acuteness and they appreciated its significance for the country as a whole. The problems of economic

[36] *Ibid.*, p. 121.

[37] Creelman, James, "Israel Unbound," in *Pearson's Magazine*, vol. xii (1907) 124.

and social adjustment of the new Jewish immigrants was thus brought to the forefront of American public opinion by the social criticism of the muckrakers.

III

The leading characteristic of the new social criticism of the muckrakers was its dispassionate description of social conditions. This was true of their *belles-lettres* as well as of their journalistic reporting. Their keen and observant eyes laid bare the living conditions of the Jews in the ghettos of New York and Chicago. They paid special attention to the tragic precocity of the life of Jewish children and the weight of heavy responsibilities which they often carried. This can be seen in the following masterly description by Lincoln Steffens.

> The children acquiring English quickly, with the adaptability of tender years, often assume the responsibilities that would rightfully belong to their elders. One girl of eleven habitually signs the checks and does all the writing necessary in transactions with certain charitable bureaus that help her mother, and during her mother's illness undertook the cooking, washing, and general superintendence of five younger children, one of whom was an infant. When the baby had croup she doctored him herself, and on another occasion kept a paid position for her mother, proving an admirable substitute until she could be relieved. This small maid is well up on the customs of her race, being able to give a fairly clear definition of the habit of wearing wigs . . . prevalent among east-side women, and answering questions in regard to other religious regulations with intelligent promptness.
>
> Another little girl is the real, although her mother is the ostensible, janitress of a big tenement-house, the child conducting all the interviews with the Board of Health officials, the streetcleaners and other authorities, and personally conducting interviews regarding the renting of rooms, collecting, etc. She undertakes to make her baylodgers behave well and to enforce proper attention to the contracted area dignified by the term of "yard," generally coming off victor in the pitched battles in which she has to engage.[38]

All the earnestness of life seized the observer who had to evaluate what he had seen on the East Side and register his impressions. Ray Stannard Baker wrote:

> I can never forget my first visits to these workshops, the crowded homes in slum tenements, the swarming, half-fed children—and

[38] "Customs in the Jewish Quarter," in the *Evening Post*, April 11, 1896, p. 2. See also Darrow, Clarence, "Little Louis Epstine," in *The Pilgrim* (Dec. 1903) and Adams, S. H. *Blinky: A Story of the East Side* (New York 1897).

> the sweat, the noise, the obscene poverty. It took hold powerfully upon my sympathy and my imagination. I wanted to write an entire book on what I found; I wanted it filled with pictures, both photographs and the finest available drawings, of what I had seen. But there was no room—and no time—although the magazine did give me generous space and used many good pictures.[39]

Descriptions by muckrakers of tenement houses and sweat shop conditions were frequent and numerous.[40] But it was not the crushing poverty nor the hard struggle for existence that impelled the intransigeant observers of new things in American life to the ghetto, but a higher evidence of an entirely different kind, which reflected the things perceived in a transcendental transfiguration. America saw here for the first time an idealism arising from the struggle for existence of the poor masses and a practical solidarity of all in the striving for a better life built, in turn, upon a better organization of man's labor.

> What thrilled me most of all [wrote Baker] was the extraordinary idealism and patience with which these poor men and women came to their own help. They had to suffer everything, not only the loss of their jobs, but literally hunger and cold, in forming any organization at all. They kept at it for years, they struck again and again and when they were discharged and left homeless, other workers re-formed their lines and finally succeeded in organizing and re-creating the entire industry. The reform had come finally, as all great reforms must come, from within, from the men themselves. . . .
>
> It seemed to me at times that this was the most remarkable exemplification of a true American and democratic approach to the solution of problems I had ever known. It seemed also an exemplification of the magic of the American system in lifting men into new freedom, new independence, and a new attitude toward life. All of these things I put into my article.[41]

It is difficult to conceive that the "rise of the tailors" could have stirred the hopes of the most powerful group of American writers, and even more, that their strikes could have become a herald of the future America and thereby could have risen to symbolic significance and become at times the only reality in which the socialist element among the intellectuals sought solace. And yet these strikes were quite

[39] *Op. cit.*, p. 181.

[40] McKenna, M. J., *Our Brethren of the Tenements and the Ghetto* (New York 1899); Markham, Edwin, "The Sweat-Shop Inferno," in *The Cosmopolitan*, vol. xlii (1906-1907) 327.

[41] *Op. cit.*, p. 181.

different, something new, as can be seen in the contemporaneous analysis of Lincoln Steffens. The identification of the eastern European Jewish immigration with one major industry made it possible for all labor conflicts in that industry to appear in bolder outline.

> For years [wrote Baker] the fortunes of the East Side have risen and fallen with the garment-making industry. It is the typical trade of the tenements. No other industry in New York City, or in New York State, employs so many workers. Thousands of shops there are in the crowded districts below Fourteenth Street, and they produce over half the ready-made clothing used in the United States; a vast industry, supporting hundreds of thousands of souls, yet almost unknown to the outside world.[42]

And the union was the sole stay of the Jewish tailor. "He would hardly know that he was in free America were it not for the union."[43]

A decade before the flowering of the muckrakers the labor struggles of the Jewish tailors had been brought to the attention of the American public. Lincoln Steffens had reported on the tailors' strikes on the East Side of 1895-97.[44]

The era of the muckrakers saw also some of the worst defeats suffered by the striking Jewish tailors. Nevertheless it remained the opinion of the critics of the period that the successes of the workers achieved through the union could no longer be cancelled for they had become part of the public interests of American life. The belief in the solidarity of the Jewish workers, ready to bring the highest sacrifice for their principles, remained unshaken.

> These Jewish idealists, indeed, were prepared to risk everything —the high wages, the short hours, the excellent shop conditions they had secured after years of struggle—in order to maintain the principle they felt to be at stake.[45]

R. S. Baker told about the contributions made by the better paid workers for the benefit of their struggling brothers:

> What other class of men would contribute from fifteen to twenty percent of their wages to any cause whatsoever—and take the chances at that of being deprived of work entirely—with the dreadful alternative of the East Side staring them in the face? What

[42] Baker, Ray Stannard, "The Rise of the Tailors," in *McClure's Magazine,* vol. xxiv (1904-1905) 126-39.

[43] *Ibid.,* p. 129.

[44] *Evening Post,* August 10 and 12, 1895; July 11 and 22, 1896; May 17, 1897.

[45] "The Rise of the Tailors," in *McClure's Magazine,* vol. xxiv, p. 134.

> religion would draw so much from its followers? No one can understand the meaning or the vitality of trade-unionism, or appreciate the depth to which its roots have struck into our soil, until he has seen a strike like this.[46]

Baker also described the change of feelings that came over the Jewish worker when he became an entrepreneur and noted the middle class traits of his private life.

> And as a class these Jewish Garment-Workers are saving, frugal, progressive, eager to educate their children: tomorrow not a few of them will become employers and live in up-town houses, themselves troubled and probably bitter over the attitude of the union men whom they employ.[47]

Going beyond the fate of the Jewish immigrants, there now came into existence literary evaluations of American Jewry in all branches of economy, education and science.[48] Even Jewish agricultural colonization attempts were noted.[49] The special adaptability of the Jewish country merchant was stressed. In the South, for instance, his treatment of the Negro turned the scale in his favor. "If the Jew has a department store in a Southern City, he succeeds partly because he is so flexible in falling in with the peculiarities of blacks and whites alike. To say Miss or Mrs. to the colored purchaser is to get her trade."[50]

In the discussion of their positive contributions to American economic life the fact was stressed that in many economic sectors one Jewish group confronted another, *e.g.,* entrepreneurs against workers. "They came with qualities and traditions so diverse that their competition among themselves (as between German and Russian Jews) is as relentless as it is against any other class of the community."[51]

A major theme of the muckraker's description was the monster of American capitalism. Included among the portraits of the outstanding captains of finance and industry which they drew were now

[46] *Ibid.,* p. 134.

[47] *Ibid.,* p. 132.

[48] See for example Herbert N. Casson's "The Jew in America," in *Munsey's Magazine,* vol. xxxiv (1905-1906) 381-95.

[49] Pincus, Joseph W., "A Significant Experiment with the Jews in Agriculture," in *The Independent,* vol. lv (1903) 2337-43.

[50] Brooks, John Graham, *As Others See Us* (New York 1908) p. 42 and p. 41.

[51] *Loc. cit.*

a number of Jews.[52] For the sake of comparison, the house of Rothschild was also included.[53]

The searching look of the muckrakers perceived the contrasts within the capitalist system that had nothing to do with capitalist interests but derived from the traditional position of the Jews. Thus Lincoln Steffens, in a study of the political power of American capital, wrote:

> None of the Jewish banking houses is "in it." Some financial critics include Kuhn, Loeb & Co., as Ryan did, and they show Jacob Schiff and other Jewish names in great directorates, but the Jews and the big insiders confirm my conclusion, and explain it. The Christians (so to speak) say the omission of the Jews is deliberate and personal; that Morgan has a race or religious prejudice against the Jews. The Jews themselves set aside this explanation in a very Christian spirit. One of the leaders among them attributed it to "an unfortunate experience Mr. Morgan had with a certain Jewish house" and the rest put it to "accident." Whatever the true explanation is, the "independence" of the Jewish interest is important. It is one more proof of the unintelligent innocence of the wickedness of the "money monster." No man who intended to put himself at the head of a perfect monopoly of money power would lock out the Jews.[54]

The results of this treatment of the Jewish capitalists were thus envisioned:

> They are powerful financially, both here and abroad; and they are good fighters. Slow to enter into a quarrel; once in they make it a war; they join hands all around the earth and, since they have sense, which other, younger peoples seem not yet to have developed, of their children's children unto the third and fourth generation, a financial war with the Jews might mean a divided Money Tower for generations to come.[55]

Another attempted explanation went back directly to the time when the German Jew entered the trade in securities and the interest groups of foreign capital marshalled their allies in the United States.

[52] "Captains of Industry (Charles Frohman, Joseph Pulitzer)," in *The Cosmopolitan*, vol. xxxiii (1902); "Captains of Industry (August Belmont, Jacob Schiff)," *ibid.*, vol. xxxiv (1902-1903); "Captains of Industry (Meyer Guggenheim and His Seven Sons)," vol. xxxv (1903); Lyle, Jr., Eugene P. "Founding the House of Guggenheim. The Guggenheims and the Smelter Trust," in *Hampton's Magazine*, vol. xxiv (1910) 256-67; 411-22.

[53] Phillips, David Graham, "The Empire of Rothschild," in *The Cosmopolitan*, vol. xxxviii (1904-1905) 501-15.

[54] "It. An Exposition of the Sovereign Political Power of Organized Business," in *Everybody's Magazine*, vol. xxiii (1910) 458.

[55] *Ibid.*

> The Yankee against the Jew
>
> The start of the Government's billion and a half refunding operation in 1871 marked one of the most interesting and important periods in the financial history of the country. For the first time in America, that great instrument of modern finance, the underwriting syndicate of security merchants (or private bankers), was to come into use; and, for the first time was to come that cleavage in American financial interests which has existed essentially ever since. On either side of the transaction were ranged the greatest traders of the Western world, the Yankee and the Jew.
>
> The alignment was perfectly natural. The two parties represented, as they do to-day, the two great bodies of foreign capital invested here: the New Englanders the English; the Jews the German. Jay Cooke, the leading candidate for the refunding work, most naturally allied himself with the German Jews, who had come into business relations with him in their sale of Government bonds abroad. Drexel—early a friend of Cooke's, but since Cooke's overshadowing success a jealous rival—was his chief competitor. Side by side with Drexel fought the New Englanders—the old-time dry-goods dealers, the Morgans and the Mortons.[56]

Thus, after having brought the role of the Jewish worker to the attention of the American public, the muckrakers directed their descriptive analysis to the Jewish capitalist. In their extensive descriptions of general Jewish life they also included accounts of other phases of Jewish economic activity, such as petty trade, peddling and handicraft, woven into the general picture of the Jewish immigrant group.

IV

The visitor to the closed Jewish residential district was struck first by its surprising and absolutely novel character.

> Striking east from Broadway and crossing the dividing line of the Bowery, in the neighborhood of Grand Street, the average New Yorker comes upon a country of whose habits he probably knows less and with whose inhabitants he certainly has much less in common, than if he had crossed the Atlantic and found himself in Picadilly or Pall Mall.[57]

This difference in kind found its classical expression in the young reporter Lincoln Steffens, who scrutinized all its details and oriented

[56] Moody, John and Turner, George Kibbe, "The Masters of Capital in America. Morgan: The Great Trustee," in *McClure's Magazine,* vol. xxxvi (1910-1911) 3-24.

[57] Hoffman, Katherine, "In the New York Ghetto," in *Munsey's Magazine,* vol. xxiii (1900) 608-10.

toward it his studies and personal habits. In his autobiography he tells us a few things about his reporting workshop, about the *mezuza* on the door of his East Side office, his fasting on Yom Kippur, his visits to synagogues, strike scenes and the conflict between the old and young generation. In his newspaper stories all this was presented in the simplest lines, as can be seen from the following example:

> Most of the older Jews, the kind who habitually wear long, black beards, a long black coat, shiny and shabby, buttoned across the breast, and a Russian felt hat, have calm, rather reverent faces, but the excitement of bargaining rouses them to unwonted animation, and they lose for the time their thoughtful, philosophical demeanor.[58]

Traditional religious practice helped to create the local character of the East Side, in the workaday as well as in the transformation that this part of the city underwent on holidays. On grey workdays one predominantly saw only petty trading.

> Peddlers are plentiful in the Jewish quarter; peddlers of candles, three in a bunch, to be used in religious rites, of artificial flowers, imitation peacock feathers and dyed grasses, peddlers of second-hand frocks and coats, of cooked and uncooked food, of combs, celluloid collar-buttons, and perfumery; but the most picturesque peddler of them all is he who sells packages of dirt, of genuine mother earth from Jerusalem, . . . Sales are managed on Oriental principles. There is always plenty of chaffering; the seller praises his goods, the buyer undervalues them. At length, after both parties have exhausted argument . . . a sale will be made.[59]

Business assumed an entirely different aspect in the pre-holiday season, when the need for all kinds of permanent goods came to the fore.

> This is the season also of the Hebrew book trade, for thousands of orthodox people who are forgetful of their prayer-books during the year and let them get lost, now find themselves in need of new ones. Then many of those who can afford it will want to appear in the synagogue in a new praying-shawl. The book-dealers, as a rule, sell these things and palm-branches and citrons as well as all sorts of religious publications. Nor are the clothier, the hatter, the shoe-dealer, and the jeweller left out of consideration, for who that is

[58] "Customs in the Jewish Quarter," in the *Evening Post,* April 11, 1896, p. 2.

[59] *Ibid.*

> not out of work will fail to invest in a new suit, or a hat, or a pair of shoes, or a watch and chain for the greatest of holidays? . . Take it all in all, it is a money-making season as well as a money-spending one, at once the most solemn and the most cheerful part of the Jewish year.[60]

Old and new tendencies met in the preparation for the festival and yet conflict was avoided. Each one went his way.

> And many of the irreligious ones relax their atheism on those days as on Yom Kippur, . . . "It is safe and does no harm," said a non-believer who scorned the ignorance of the orthodox and laughed as he told what his people do.
> . . . All day to-day the East Side was busy preparing for the days of Rosh Hoshana. There was cleaning of clothes and o homes and the bathing-places were full. Hester Street and Essex and all the other market places were in commotion, the women and old men being out making purchases of fish at four cents a pound and rare fruits like pears and pineapples, or best of all, persimmons.
> . . "Don't you go to the concerts or theatres?" "Oh, I do," said a tailor, "I'm going to a ball uptown, but the others don't. They keep it holy." ". . . And where are you going to-morrow morning?" "Oh, most of our club are going bicycling out to— . . ."[61]

The preparations in the synagogue crowned all these activities. The entire organizational structure of the Jewish population was manifest above all in the manner in which such houses of prayer came into existence. The keen eye of the reporter discerned the essential.

> Few orthodox congregations are large enough to afford a separate building for a house of worship. Most of them are small societies made up of fellow-townsmen and bearing the name of their native place. Almost every town within the pale of Jewish settlements in Russia, Austria, or Rumania is represented here by a synagogue. Accordingly, the average congregation must be content with a room and bed-room on the top floor of some overcrowded tenement-house, the smaller room usually being set aside for the female worshippers, who follow the chasan through the portieres. Most of these struggling societies sublet their rooms for weekdays to melamdim . . . who teach their scholars in the afternoon, when they come from the public schools. As a rule, a synagogue is also a kind of club-house, the more devout of the members coming to spend their leisure moments there, reading Psalms, swapping news of the old home, or exchanging notes upon the adopted country. In addition to the permanent

[60] "When the Shofar Blows," in the *Evening Post,* Sept. 25, 1897, p. 2.
[61] "The Jewish New Year," in the *Evening Post,* Sept. 7, 1896, p. 5.

congregation, of which there are several hundred in the Jewish quarter, at least as many temporary ones spring into existence for the great holidays. To accommodate these, every dancing hall and assembly-room, and many a sweat-shop is transformed into a synagogue, and every tailor or teacher of Hebrew who lays any claim to musical gift enters the list in competition for the place of cantor or chorister. The two large Jewish theatres of this city, the Windsor and the Thalia, are announced as houses of worship for the coming festivals, with some of the leading Jewish actors for chasans.[62]

The reporter was also well acquainted with the financial basis of the synagogue.

> The net proceeds from the sale of seats are in many instances the main source of the congregation's income. Hence, the hiring of a good cantor is generally viewed in the light of an investment. . . . Some celebrities are paid for the four principal services of the Days of Awe as much as $1,000, but such virtuosos apart, $200 would be a fair average of the cantor's fee, although the humbler congregations cannot afford to pay more than $50 for the season. . . .
>
> The wealthier synagogues engage their chasans by contract on a snug monthly salary, and often import them from some large city in Russia or Galicia; so that the Hebrew communities of those countries are said to have been drained of their best religious singers by their brethren of the New York Ghetto, who are by far the highest bidders in the world's cantor market.[63]

The transformation of the community of worshippers back to workaday existence appeared to the reporter as an incomprehensible metamorphosis:

> To look at this whispering, gesticulating, nodding, ecstatic crowd, it was almost hard to imagine them in any other role than holding communion with their Maker or studying His sacred laws. But Minha over, each at once assumed a work-a-day air, and as they kissed the Mezuzoh parchment on the door-post in haste to get out into the noisy street, there was again before the observer a cluster of tailors, peddlers, store-keepers, each with the seal of wordly care on his face.[64]

The chief concern of all thoughtful critics of the period was Americanization—the education of the young as well as the adults among the immigrants to a proper understanding of American ideals. In respect to the Jewish immigrant, Americanization coincided with

[62] *Evening Post,* Sept. 25, 1897, p. 2.
[63] *Ibid.*
[64] "The Poor in Israel," in the *Evening Post,* Oct., 1897, p. 10.

the fact that a specific Jewish educational system had been transplanted from the Old into the New World, that Jewish parents discharged the duty of training their children through the establishment of schools with regard for the traditional values and that simultaneously they realized the importance of general education for the future of their children in the New World. Both, school scenes and general attitude to knowledge and education, Jewish as well as secular, formed the subject of description by the muckrakers in fiction and in reporting in the popular magazines.

Here is Lincoln Steffens' report on the East Side:

> These humbler Jews have certain distinct characteristics. They are born musicians, natural gamblers, abstemious, and earnest admirers of education and the benefits education confers. Among the ignorant of other nationalities the man of higher origin is oftimes regarded with distrust, but this is not so among the Jews; they are proud of their leaders being educated, and no matter how ignorant they may be themselves, though it is affirmed that the poorest among them can read and write in their native language, they crave education for their children, and strive to give them advantages.[65]

Thus the general atmosphere of the ghetto was set for youth organizations and their educational program and their lively activities.

> There are a number of boys' clubs in the district, in which the members take great interest, and try to improve themselves, taking part in literary debates and the discussion of current events in national and municipal affairs. Altogether it is plain that with the intelligence and activity displayed by the growing children of the race the Ghetto of New York must lose some of its Oriental characteristics in the next quarter of a century, but it will take a great deal of leaven to leaven such a compact mass.[66]

The same opinion was also expressed about the children of the group that attempted to settle on farms. A reporter on the Chesterfield Settlement, in Connecticut, had the following to say:

> This modern spirit is seen everywhere. It was a strange sight to me to see a group of typical little Jews gathered in the Chesterfield school house listening open-eyed to lessons from a Yankee schoolteacher from the next village, a girl who said that nothing could be more encouraging than the quickness with which these children learn. In six months after coming from Russia they talk English as

[65] *Evening Post,* April 11, 1896, p. 2.

[66] *Loc. cit.*

> well as if they had been born here. On my way back to New London I saw the Chesterfield base-ball club, composed of Russian lads, at work with all the enthusiasm of our native born experts.[67]

The same we hear from Woodbine:

> The Russian children are remarkably quick in learning English and compare favorably with American scholars of the same age. Fifteen of the older boys form a fire brigade, proud in the possession of uniforms and a chemical engine upon wheels. In the evenings all the year round there are classes for adults, the average attendance this last spring have been forty.[68]

There are also other stories of the life of Jewish young people. Lincoln Steffens attempted to give us the story of a Jewish girl who strayed from the straight path.[69] In the general fiction of America the story of the rising Jewish hero was as a rule accompanied by a description of his apprenticeship years.[70]

General education in the direction of cultivating the taste was attempted in the ghetto by means of art exhibitions. The results varied, as Steffens wittily described:

> It is grievous to report that notwithstanding a very appreciable improvement in apprehension over last year, the interest of the beholders centers more in the names of the owners than in those of the artists or even in the pictures. The name of Mr. Straus or Mr. Bloomingdale or Mr. Schiff is worth for their conjuring to such names as Gerome, Schreyer, or Inness. The pecuniary end of the whole business they also seek for with extreme diligence. "Are not the pictures to be sold?" inquired an aged Jew of one of the custodians, of his own race. Explanation was most difficult; but when the old man finally understood, he piously and unexpectedly exclaimed in jargon which may be translated: "Oh, that is grand! It will keep many away from vice."[71]

In the study of Jewish character and of individuals steeped in Jewish values, the muckrakers penetrated at last into the actual spiritual life of the Jewish group, its spiritual movements and its relation to the position that Israel occupies among the nations. They saw the problem of antisemitism in the light of the social contact between

67 "Russian Jews as Farmers," in the *Evening Post,* Sept. 5, 1894, p. 5.

68 "Russian Jews as Farmers," in the *Evening Post,* Sept. 6, 1894.

69 "Schloma, the Daughter of Schmuhl," in *The Chapbook* (Chicago) vol. v (1896) 128-32.

70 Cahan, Abraham, *The Rise of David Levinsky.*

71 "Paintings on the East Side," in the *Evening Post,* May 9, 1896, p. 12.

Jews and non-Jews in America as well as in the echo of the Dreyfus affair. Finally Zionism was also discussed.

Antisemitism in the various European countries had been discussed by the American press as far back as the end of the 19th century. A characteristic explanation of the time was that "it is safe to say that the spread of antisemitic feeling is a product, more or less direct, of the socialistic feeling which is now in the air in every country and seeking expression by all sorts of channels."[72] For local consumption, however, antisemitism was something altogether different. Its specific American function of excluding the Jew from social life was achieved in full precisely at a time when the economic rise had created an upper stratum of Jews. Cases of rejection of Jewish candidates for membership in various clubs became frequent, which enabled the daily press to establish fearlessly the existence of social antisemitism.

> The "Christian Place," or the Jew-free club, is a prejudice which in the main keeps Jews and Christians socially apart in nearly every city in the country, which excludes Jews more or less from all the leading summer hotels, and would probably prevent Mr. Seligman's entrance to any other non-Jewish club in New York. In fact, there is no social phenomenon of the day more familiar to all New Yorkers, and particularly to the philosophers of journalism, than this prejudice . . . as notoriously as the sun at noonday, and is of long standing. . . .[73]

In instances of the private social sphere the right of the club to exclude Jews was generally conceded. General prejudice, however, was fought strenuously by the popular magazines of the muckrakers. The attack on a funeral procession in the New York ghetto in 1902 was considered of general importance by the muckrakers and they recorded the reaction of the Jewish population to the incident.

> For their indiscriminate use of the nightstick the police have been criticized severely by the Jewish newspapers, and their readers have held mass meetings of protest against what they are prone to regard as an anti-Semitic demonstration to which the officers of the law lent their aid.
>
> On the Mayor's order, an inquiry into the whole matter has been started, and a vigilance committee of the Jews is at work.[74]

72 "The Jews in Europe," in the *Evening Post*, Jan. 4, 1893.

73 "Club Candidates," in the *Evening Post*, April 17, 1893.

74 "A Riot in the Ghetto," in *Collier's Weekly*, vol. xxix (1902) 23.

The general study of the moving spiritual forces in America led to the perception of distant associations between historical Judaism and the foundations of American culture.[75] The critical appraisal of religious conditions in America was an important subject of the muckraker. A study of parallel conditions in the Jewish community was made by R. S. Baker.[76] Gradually the development led to an understanding of the inner conditions of the Jewish people throughout the world. Zionism in its early stages had not aroused as much attention in America as an Europe. Yet precisely among the observers of the Jews of the ghetto there were such who properly recognized its moral impact for the Jews.

> Zionism represents, to me, all that is good in the Jewish ideals, and I have never found that a Jew who has no sympathy with Zionism has the moral qualities that entitle him to respect. Next to the Law, Zionism seems necessary for the life of Judaism.[77]

The magazines of the muckrakers opened their columns to the Zionist leaders,[78] and a number of articles appeared about the land of the future: Palestine.[79]

All in all, the end of the muckraking period left American Jewry with a solid diagnosis of its most important aspects by competent outsiders. The muckrakers contributed to the understanding of Jewish life in America no less than to the elucidation of other social conditions.

[75] Seward, Theodore F., "The Unity of Christianity and Judaism," in *The Arena*, vol. xxvii (1902) 351-66; Baker, Edward M., "Judaism and the American Spirit," *ibid.*, vol. xxvii (1904) 166 ff.

[76] "The Spiritual Unrest. The Disintegration of the Jews," in *American Magazine*, vol. lxvii (1909) 590-603.

[77] McKenna, M. J., *Our Brethren of the Tenements and the Ghetto*, p. 12.

[78] Nordau, Max, "The Zionist Movement," in *The Independent*, vol. lii (1900) 2191-92; Gaster, M., "The Truth about Zionism," in *The Forum*, vol. xxix (1900) 230-39.

[79] Meyer, Martin A., "The Jewish Colonies in Palestine," in *The Independent*, vol. liv (1902) 2347-53.

Department of Religious Studies
Moore Reading Room
University of Kansas